BOISGUILBERT

ECONOMIST
OF THE REIGN OF LOUIS XIV

BOISGUILBERT

ECONOMIST
OF THE REIGN OF LOUIS XIV

HAZEL VAN DYKE ROBERTS

SUBMITTED IN PARTIAL FULFILLMENT OF THE REQUIREMENTS FOR THE DEGREE OF DOCTOR OF PHILOSOPHY, IN THE FACULTY OF POLITICAL SCIENCE, COLUMBIA UNIVERSITY.

NEW YORK: MORNINGSIDE HEIGHTS
COLUMBIA UNIVERSITY PRESS
MCMXXXV

Published 1935

Printed in the United States of America

**TO
THE MEMORY
OF
MY FATHER**

PREFACE

THE writings of Boisguilbert should have a peculiar interest for all students of the social sciences. For the political scientist there is an intimate view of the working of a political system. In a world in which it has become fashionable to decry the ineptitude of democracy, it is not amiss to see set forth the indifference to the general welfare and the corruption of absolutism and the depths to which it can sink. At the same time, principles of government are enunciated which are yet to be put into practice.

The sociologist may find a contemporary record of much of the life and poverty of the masses, a life in which the amenities of the community were disrupted by suspicion and hatred toward one's neighbors. He may find an ideal of voluntary submission of the individual to the group, not for the purpose of subordinating the individual to the State, but to prevent the oppression of any class.

The historian who "has not read these pages scintillating with irony, this eloquent accusation where passion is placed in the service of justice and reason, knows only imperfectly the France of the seventeenth century. If history is more than the recital of battles, or the biography of princes and their ministers, or even than a picture of letters and of arts; if it wishes to see brought to life the people whose annals it retraces, and is not content with some brilliant personalities, it is indeed in Boisguilbert, as in a perfect mirror, that the image of that unhappy society must be sought. None has thrown more light on this sad past; none has better depicted, in order to flay it, in order to enlighten and to save his fellow citizens, the wretched financial system of the fatherland of the Corneilles and of the Racines, of the Pascals and of the Bossuets, that world of which it has been said with a great felicity of expression that heaven seemed to produce great men only to have bad institutions patiently accepted."

For the economist he is an example of one who saw the significance of the details of the business of everyday life, little of which escaped his keen observation; who set forth these details with meticulous care, yet who was never lost in them; who reasoned so clearly with respect to them that they were marshaled to form a perfect whole. This whole is the magnificent conception of economic interdependence, which the world has not yet fully grasped. But there is not only the idea of economic interdependence: intimate relationship is also shown to exist between the political and the economic life of a people. "However important are the qualities of the climate and the soil of a country . . . in determining its wealth . . . the skill or the errors of those who govern contribute not less to it than does nature." Boisguilbert "merits truly, as a thinker, to be called the Christopher Columbus of the economic world." "In his writings are found posited the expression of the fundamental principles of the science." Indeed it may be said that the economist who has not at least a bowing acquaintance with Boisguilbert lacks a knowledge of the richest single source of his own field of thought, and the statesman who does not know him is ignorant of one who set forth some of the profoundest ideas of practical government and the noblest ideals of statesmanship.

It is not without reason that, from Mirabeau on, the few who have known Boisguilbert's writings well have been characterized by enthusiasm for him; for "a citizen whose simplicity caused him to be neglected in a dazzling age, and to whom posterity must render the homage merited." When Félix Cadet refers to him as "my hero" it is understandable, as is the fact that I. E. Horn's study, *L'Économie politique avant les physiocrates,* is so largely devoted to him.

His writings still richly reward one for the time spent upon them. With the developing concern for price parities and the circulation of income his thought takes on a renewed interest. There is, in truth, a curious similarity between much that is being said and written about present-day economic difficulties and what he wrote so long ago. Leaving out of consideration his language, and taking into account the economic development of his time, it is obvious that his ideas are fundamentally modern. It is this which leads me to an appreciative exposition of his writings rather than to a critical analysis of them. The latter would lead to a history of static and dynamic theory and statistical development. Indeed Boisguilbert lends himself to interpretation rather than to negative criticism. He goes the long way around at times, but, as Horn says, if he departs from the right track, he nevertheless arrives at the correct place. Again, he covers so much ground that it would appear little short of ungracious to criticize him for omissions, viewed in the light of developments in economic thought over a period of more than two centuries. Fully to be appreciated he must be considered in relation to his time, and to his purpose, which was not to write a formal exposition of economic theory, but to awaken a politically, economically, and socially decadent people.

Especial emphasis has been placed upon Boisguilbert's own descriptions of trade restraints and their effects, because the student of economics who is not familiar with these restraints and their effects in seventeenth-century France has but the vaguest idea as to the origin of the theory of *laissez faire*. Properly to be appreciated it must be seen, not as of spontaneous origin, but as the expression of a protest against impossible restrictions and conditions.

In spite of efforts to eliminate repetitions, many are unavoidable. This is due to Boisguilbert's own informal development of theory, which is interjected, as it were, in what was intended only to be an explanation of the current economic problems, and due to the fact that he saw them all as interrelated. Thus it is impossible, for instance, to separate his theories of trade and of money without some overlapping, as is the case with value, rent, and laissez faire, while they are all tied up with his theories of taxation and fiscal administration.

Because of the nature of the context, translations have been made as literal as is possible in reasonably clear English. Where any especially free translation has been resorted to the French has been given. The only liberty which has been taken which is not shown in the text is the breaking up of Boisguilbert's interminable and involved sentences wherever this has seemed desirable and possible. Perhaps I should add that I have quoted freely because Boisguilbert's own writings are not accessible to many readers.

Acknowledgment is gratefully made to Professor Wesley C. Mitchell for his painstaking reading of the manuscript and his suggestions, and to Professor H. Parker Willis and Professor Emeritus Edwin R. A. Seligman for their criticisms and encouragement. Professor Seligman, especially, was under no obligation to perform what may well have been an onerous task. It would have been difficult, however, not to seek his advice on a historical work dealing so largely with public finance. I have developed the material, however, in my own way, and in so far as any part of the study is controversial I absolve them of any responsibility for the views set forth.

Finally, I should be remiss if I failed to mention the fortitude of my family and of my friends, who have patiently endured Boisguilbert's idiosyncrasies while I have been striving to understand them.

New York H. V. R.
April 1, 1935

CONTENTS

BOISGUILBERT

ECONOMIST
OF THE REIGN OF LOUIS XIV

INTRODUCTION: ECONOMIC CONDITIONS UNDER LOUIS XIV

Scattered over the country certain wild animals, males and females, dark, livid and all sunburned, are seen bent over the ground which they work and which they turn with an invincible persistency. They have articulate voices, and when they stand upright they disclose human faces, and in truth they are men. At night they retire into dens where they live on black bread, water and roots. They spare other men the pain of sowing, of cultivating and of reaping in order to live, and thus deserve not to lack this bread which they have sown.

LA BRUYÈRE

WHO does not know La Bruyère's vivid description of men reduced to an animal-like existence? On their bent shoulders rested the burden of an ambitious monarch, and the weight of an aristocracy which had forgotten that privilege entails responsibility. The wretchedness of the cultivators of the soil, of *les misérables,*[1] was accepted as in the nature of things. Suppose they had only bread to eat. Why should they expect more? Yet there arose to champion them a man who was to give the world strangely new ideas: that the consumption of the masses is as important in a national economy as their production; that no nation can endure if it rests upon human misery; that no one class can be permanently prosperous unless other groups thrive. This man was Pierre le Pesant de Boisguilbert, an all-but-forgotten Norman magistrate, who in one of the darkest periods in French history felt himself called to save his native land almost as certainly as had Joan of Arc three centuries before. Constituting himself adviser to the ministry of finance, he vainly gave counsel which had it been followed would have gone far toward saving France a century of fiscal disorder and the terrors of the Revolution. In his efforts to awaken as stupid and selfish a governing class as the modern world has known he was not quite

[1] *Les misérables* were those "having only their arms for their subsistence," the propertyless.—*Factum de la France,* Paris, 1843, p. 322.

alone. He was assisted by two of the great figures of the age. Fénelon appealed to human sentiment to have conditions changed; Vauban, to justice. Boisguilbert relied upon justice and reason. In doing so he gave modern capitalistic economics its form, but his was no philosophy of *sauve qui peut*.

France was in the midst of the War of the League of Augsburg when Boisguilbert published *Le Détail de la France* in 1695. The finances of the government were in serious condition. The current expenditures, exclusive of interest, exceeded 116 million *livres*. The revenue from taxation was 119 millions. But of the latter sum 50 millions were absorbed by interest due on sums obtained by means of *affaires extraordinaires* [2] and *rentes sur l'Hôtel-de-Ville*.[3] There was accordingly an annual deficit of almost 50 millions.[4] Thereafter, under the amazing ineptitude of the controllers general of finance,[5] Pontchartrain and Chamillart, and the increased expenditures incident to war, the condition of the finances grew steadily worse. When *Factum de la France* was published in 1707, the War of the League of Augsburg was over, but the country was involved in the War of the Spanish Succession. In February 1708, Desmaretz, "the most skilful, modest and incorruptible financier of this epoch," succeeded Chamillart. On account of the condition of the finances he took over their control only out of devotion to the king. Small wonder

[2] Certain methods used to obtain extraordinary revenue. See below, p. 122. This term will not be translated because there is no English equivalent for the exact thought.

[3] *Rentes sur l'Hôtel-de-Ville de Paris* constituted a large part of the funded debt of France. They (but not borrowing as such) were first used by Francis I. Unsecured by any specific revenue, their name was derived from the fact that it was the custom for an entire issue to be purchased by the provost and municipal magistrates, who resold them, or were otherwise interested in them.—Daire note, *Factum de la France*, p. 295. All references to Boisguilbert's writings, unless otherwise specified, are to *Économistes financiers du 18e siècle*, E. Daire, editor, Paris, 1843.

[4] *Ibid.*, "Notice historique sur Boisguillebert," pp. 165–166.

[5] The *contrôle général des finances* was "an institution the functions of which varied greatly. Before Louis XIV, the controller general was an official subordinated to the superintendent of finances. Louis XIV, in 1661, suppressed the superintendency and ascribed its functions to the controller general, who became a veritable minister of finances. The successors of Colbert retained these functions. The controller general joined in his hands the powers of our ministers of the interior, of commerce, of industry and of public works."—A. Talbot, *Les Théories de Boisguilbert*, Paris, 1903, p. 4, note 1.

he did not wish to assume the burden that was being thrust upon him! There was short-time paper outstanding amounting to 482,844,611 livres; the current expenditures for the year 1708 amounted to 202,788,354 livres. Yet the revenue for the year had been so consumed in advance that only 20,388,338 livres remained free to meet these demands on the treasury. One can understand that he "felt all the weight of such a commission." But the king also "understood perfectly the state of his finances," and he assured Desmaretz "that he did not demand the impossible."

With Europe coalesced against France, extraordinary revenues had to be obtained. There was no choice, Desmaretz thought, as to the means to raise them. He resorted to the methods used by his predecessors, "although the success of them was very doubtful." New *rentes* on the Hôtel-de-Ville were issued; new *traités* [6] were made. Paper money continued to be issued and "created a great disorder in commerce" so that it was necessary to try to eliminate it. The embarrassment of the government could not be made public; nevertheless concealment was impossible because the "discredited papers due to the public" made the condition obvious.

Desmaretz thus summed up the results of his seven years' administration of the finances: from January 1, 1708, to December 31, 1714, the total expenditures amounted to 1,533,201,176 livres, or an average expenditure of 219,023,027 livres. For the same period the ordinary revenue plus the capitation and an income tax of one-tenth (the latter established in 1710) produced on the average, "after deduction made for ordinary charges," only 75,000,000 livres. There was therefore an average annual deficit of 144,023,027 livres, or a total of 1,008,161,189 livres for which funds had to be obtained. But during the same period, by all the extraordinary methods resorted to it had only been possible to raise 691,660,338 livres, leaving an actual deficit of 316,540,813 livres to be covered at the end of 1714.[7]

[6] See below, p. 119.

[7] Desmaretz, *Mémoire sur l'administration des finances,* Paris, 1715, pp. 4–8, 12–14, 47–49. (The slight discrepancies in the figures are those of the report itself.) Such was the condition inherited by the regent which induced him later

The financial requirements of the government had never been greater. Why were the ordinary revenues falling at a time when every effort was being made to increase them? Why had it become impossible to provide the extraordinary funds required?

The answer is to be found in the economic condition of the country. The countryside was desolate; industry was unbelievably depressed; the people on the land were reduced to a diet of "black bread, water and roots"; the inhabitants of cities and towns were hungry. Boisguilbert described the conditions in *Le Détail de la France.* Reading this one feels that his account must surely be an exaggeration; but that he understated rather than exaggerated is shown by other contemporary records.

Horn, in his study of Boisguilbert, devoted a chapter to a description of *la misère* from sources of the day which cannot be regarded as "suspect." [8] Fénelon, for instance, addressed an anonymous remonstrance to the king which does not lack frankness:

> Your people whom you should love as your children and who until now have been devoted to you, die of hunger. The cultivation of the land is almost abandoned; the cities and the country are depopulated; all the trades languish and no longer nourish the workmen. All commerce is destroyed. . . . Instead of drawing money from these poor people it is necessary to give them alms and to feed them. All France is no more than a great almshouse desolated and without provisions. . . . You are importuned by the crowds of people who demand and who murmur.

Fénelon, as tutor to the duke of Burgundy, heir presumptive to the throne, was responsible for inducing Louis XIV to obtain from each intendant a complete summary of conditions in his generality, for the instruction of his royal charge. The memoir to the intendants in 1697 bears the imprint, in the information requested with regard to the administration of the *tailles, aides,* and *duanes,*[9] of having been inspired by Boisguilbert's description

to lend an ear to the proposals of John Law to relieve the government of its embarrassment. The system of Louis XIV, it may be added, was one which bred deficits. Expenditures were made by the king in consultation with his Secretaries of State without being planned with the controller general. The latter was simply charged to obtain the funds required.—*Ibid.*, p. 51.

[8] J. E. Horn, *L'Économie politique avant les Physiocrates,* Paris, 1867, chap. i.

[9] Property taxes, excises, and customs duties.

of abuses set forth in *Le Détail de la France* two years before.[10]

The intendants who made the reports cannot be suspected of being interested in showing conditions worse than they were. They were among the chief beneficiaries of the system. Likewise Boulainvilliers, who compiled the reports, was "a product of his time, and especially of his class." His concern was for the state into which the old nobility had fallen rather than for the people as such. But he declared that the reports of the intendants showed either "lack of application, or incapacity, or an interested reticence." [11] At that, a more dismal picture of economic decay could scarcely be drawn.

In the generality of Orléans commerce was so reduced, and the number of taxes so multiplied, that there were fewer merchants (6,182) than officials (7,747).[12] In the generality of Rouen, one of the richest generalities in the kingdom, with a population of 700,000 persons, there were not fifty thousand who ate all the bread they wished, and who did not sleep on straw. The population of the city of Rouen had decreased from eighty thousand to less than sixty thousand.[13] In the generality of Alençon half the houses were falling to pieces. "Poverty spreads everywhere a sadness and a ferocity which is surprising." [14]

In Lille there were more than four thousand merchants or masters, some of whom had employed as many as twelve hundred workers, with a total output forty years before of five hundred thousand pieces of goods. *La misère* had practically killed the industry. The *sagetteurs* and the *bourgeteurs* were the two principal manufacturers of serges. The "jealousy existing between these two bodies formerly produced a very profitable emulation,

[10] Comte Henri de Boulainvilliers, *État de la France* [London, 1727–1728] 2d ed., London, 1737, Vol. I, pp. 10–21. All references are to the second edition.

[11] *Ibid.*, "Préface de l'auteur," Vol. I, p. 43. "Interested reticence" is a free translation of *prévention*, but it is obviously the sense in which Boulainvilliers intended to use it. It is thus expressed by Horn, while in Lavisse (*Histoire de France*, Vol. VIII [1], p. 214) it is stated that in comparing these memoirs of the intendants with their letters to the controller general "there are found obvious differences, even contradictions. One is astonished at the silence which many of them maintain on capital facts. . . . One suspects alterations, or, at least, mitigations of the truth."

[12] *État de la France*, Vol. II, pp. 321–322.

[13] *Ibid.*, Vol. IV, pp. 6, 9, 32.

[14] *Ibid.*, Vol. IV, p. 106.

but it has degenerated into hate and envy which ruins both." The population of Lille had increased, "but in a manner which brought no profit." [15]

In Auvergne the pay of the lace workers, which had formerly been sixty or seventy thousand livres, was reduced to thirty thousand livres. Auvergne had also produced very fine paper "for all Europe." This industry was likewise reduced one-half.[16] In Touraine twenty thousand workers in silk, eight thousand looms, seven hundred mills for the preparation of the silk, and forty thousand spinners which had been in existence in the days of Richelieu had been reduced to one thousand looms, seventy mills, and a total employment of perhaps four thousand. The number of looms making ribbons had been reduced from three thousand to sixty.[17] Almost everywhere the story was the same: houses falling to pieces for lack of repair; lack of ability to buy food even at the low prices prevailing; decreasing population; high infant mortality. Practically the only exception to this sad state was the metal industry which was making war supplies, and that portion of the textile industry producing coarse cloth for uniforms. Even the war, however, seems to have been of dubious importance as a stimulant to these industries. Officers as well as troops were exceedingly underequipped. The difficulty the government experienced in paying for supplies did not create an eagerness to provide them.

Hear what Vauban, who knew the country as a whole perhaps better than any person in France, has to say:

As a result of all the researches which I have been able to make in the many years that I have applied myself thereto, I have indeed vigorously asserted that recently almost the tenth part of the people is reduced to beggary, and actually beg. Of the nine other parts, there are five which are not in a condition to give alms to the former, because they themselves are reduced almost to that unhappy state. Of the four other parts which remain, three are very uncomfortable and embarrassed with debts and suits. In the tenth where I place all the persons of the sword, robe, ecclesiastics, laity, high nobility, distinguished nobility, those in military and civil service, the larger

[15] *Ibid.*, Vol. III, p. 483.
[16] *Ibid.*, Vol. V, pp. 168–169.
[17] *Ibid.*, Vol. IV, p. 377.

(*bon*) merchants, the *bourgeois* living on *rentes* and the most well-to-do, one cannot count over a hundred thousand families, and I do not believe I am untruthful when I say that there are not ten thousand of them, little or great, who are completely comfortable. . . .[18]

Boisguilbert, writing before Fénelon, the intendants, or Vauban, maintained that the national income had decreased to one-half that of 1661.[19] Let one count the loss of income of a house, of a farm, of a village, he said, and from this can be deduced what the loss is for the kingdom. In the election[20] of Mantes, for instance, the loss is two million four hundred thousand livres "by count made through a correct and certain calculation verified on the estates." This, he added, does not include industry, which produces four times as much as the land; accordingly for a single election there has been a loss of at least ten millions. Of this canton, where the vineyards were being destroyed to escape the ruinous taxes levied upon their product, he exclaimed: "Let one not lose sight of the vines of Mantes, because they are truly the measure of which it is necessary to make use in order to evaluate the disasters of the entire kingdom." [21]

Time after time Boisguilbert returned to the condition in Mantes. Did he quote it so often because it represented the worst condition, or because its losses had been most carefully calculated? Both, perhaps. But there are other indices of the diminution of the national income. The loss of one-half of the income of France, he asserted, is also shown by the registers, leases, and contracts, as well as by the evidence of men. Everywhere "the disorders are inescapably apparent." In "the canton of Bourbon alone one hundred and fifty domains or farms [are] abandoned to the crows and to the owls." Half the kingdom is useless to the prince and to the people, and he feared the contradiction neither of God nor of man as to what he said relative to its state. Again, he would be subjected to bodily punishment if he were exaggerating the evils which he combated. The kingdom is witness to it. "The cadaver we have under our eyes on

18 Sébastien Le Prestre de Vauban, *Dime royale*, Daire edition, Paris, 1843, Preface, pp. 34–35.
19 *Le Détail de la France*, Pt. I, chap. iii.
20 Subdivision of a generality.
21 *Factum*, pp. 273, 290.

account of the desolation of lands and commerce, purges this pronouncement of all suspicion of calumny." [22]

As a result of the state of the kingdom, a few individuals lived in the most extreme magnificence and abundance, but the greater part were in the most abject poverty.[23]

[22] *Ibid.*, pp. 273, 290, 327, 340, 347. *Le Détail*, p. 218. Letter to Desmaretz, Sept. 16, 1708.

[23] *Le Détail*, p. 177.

I

THE TIME PRODUCES THE MAN

The hope of the public felicity is perhaps the sole real good, or rather the sole consolation which exists on earth for the upright man. Is he not too happy to have in the fatherland a friend, with whose happiness he may occupy himself, and whom he may have no fear of surviving? But, it may be added, who has charged him with the public cause? Nature, when she gave him sympathy and courage.
CONDORCET.

IN THE middle of the seventeenth century there was growing up in Rouen an intelligent and inquiring son of a prosperous Norman family. His was no ordinary environment. Son of a lawyer, a local councillor of the king, cousin to one of the great poets of France, and through him, indirectly connected with her great military hero, Vauban; to this family background there must be added bustling Rouen, the busiest commercial center of France, and finally Normandy itself. Normandy! With what pride and love this son was later to refer to the province as the "Greece of France." Normandy, mother of so many illustrious sons; Normandy, with her ancient charter; Normandy, the garden spot of France so lovingly cultivated. Out of this superior and composite environment came one who was to "open to the human mind a new career."

Pierre le Pesant de Boisguilbert[1] was born in Rouen on February 17, 1646. His life was just to span the reign to which he would devote all his efforts. Service to the king was the family

[1] Boisguilbert himself except in two or three instances spelled his name Boisguillebert. This is obviously an older form, and may have been preferred as a result of his interest in languages and love of history. His father and brother used the shorter form. As both sons were seigneurs de Boisguilbert, "Boisguillebert" may also have been a method of differentiation resorted to by the one. Boisguilbert is the common spelling of the locality from which the family derived its name (also spelled Bosc-Guillebert, it is located between Rouen and Fourges), and is also used by Boisguilbert's descendants. Arthur de Boislisle and Félix Cadet, the foremost authorities on the life of Boisguilbert, used the shorter form, which is also followed by the present writer.

tradition. His father and grandfather had been respectively local councillor and secretary to the king. The family was ennobled in 1620 by Louis XIII. Boisguilbert thus belonged to that hybrid class, the nobility of the robe. Its roots and traditions, and something of its virtues, were those of the *bourgeoisie*. Lifted above the latter socially, in its growing importance, in its manner of life, this magisterial class was taking on some of the characteristics of the old nobility. Essentially it was to remain a distinct, bureaucratic class, a fourth estate, indeed, in point of number.

In his study of social and economic problems it was perhaps this division of class interest, combined with his judicial training and experience and his inherent spirit of justice, which gave Boisguilbert his ability to see the relation of all the parts, rather than the parts alone. Superficially he was *bourgeois* in sympathy. He regarded himself as the spokesman of the people, the cultivators, the business men. But essentially he rose above class or distinction. His concern was the common good of the whole. To see a prosperous France, rooted in prosperous individuals and classes; to have each individual and class see his or its part in the national economy, such was his fundamental interest.[2]

Boisguilbert's early education was with the Jesuits at Rouen. He was then sent with his brother to Paris to complete his studies. There he was a student at Port-Royal,[3] and in the family

[2] Prior to the early part of the 1860's when Arthur de Boislisle discovered the letters of Boisguilbert to the controllers general, nothing was known of his life except what is given by the Duke of Saint-Simon, who knew and respected him. This correspondence is found in Volumes II and III of the *Correspondance des contrôleurs généraux des finances*. In 1865 *L'Académie des sciences morales et politiques* made Boisguilbert the subject of a competition for the following year. Two works were crowned at the annual public session on July 14, 1866: I. E. Horn's *L'Économie politique avant les Physiocrates*, and Félix Cadet's *Pierre de Boisguilbert, précurseur des économistes, sa vie—ses travaux—son influence*. Boislisle's *Mémoire sur Boisguilbert* received only honorable mention because it did not deal with the theories. The latter was never published as a whole, but its contents were utilized in "La Proscription du projet de dime royale et la mort de Vauban," in *Comte rendu de l'acad. des sc. mor. et pol.*, (Paris, 1875), and in the *Mémoires de Saint-Simon*, Paris, 1879–1928, Vol. XIV, appendix xii.

[3] Cadet infers this from the short preface to Boisguilbert's translation of Herodien's *Histoire romaine*, in which reference is made to "'Monsieur d'Andilly'" and "'those famous *Anonymes* so famous throughout France'" to whom is due "'whatever education I have had among them in my youth.'"—Cadet, p. 6.

tradition completed his education at the *École de droit,* obtaining the title of *avocat.*[4]

Boisguilbert may have owed much of his religious toleration and courage to an intimate association with Jansenists at Port-Royal, and Jesuits and Calvinists at Rouen as well as to his own spirit of independence and of justice. It is impossible to determine his religious affiliations from his writings. It is only obvious that he was a deeply religious individual who looked upon creeds with an objectiveness unusual in a day of creedal strife. Cadet especially speaks of his courage in referring to "the new religion" in view of the fact that the government had ordered it to be called "the so-called reformed religion." [5]

Through his father, Nicholas le Pesant, who was a nephew of Martha le Pesant Corneille, mother of Pierre and Thomas

[4] Horn, p. 48. Boisguilbert may have been speaking from experience gained in his own student days when he later said that the three years spent at the law school were largely wasted. The students, he declared, were debauched by bad associates, and learned only to spend. Furthermore, there appeared to have been connivance in obtaining their degrees, which permitted these young boys to return home and act as magistrates. In suggesting reforms for the French lower judicial system, he declared that these graduates who returned to become magistrates were unqualified for their work. The universities taught only Roman and canon law, he remarked. In practice, however, common law, he said, was followed in many of the provinces, which rendered the young bachelors of civil or canon law unfit to carry on judicial functions. He suggested, in view of this, and of the idling away of time on the part of students, that the three years of university study be changed to three months, and that thereafter they spend three or four years as subordinates in a royal court. (*Projet du rétablissement de tous les premiers juges de France.* Memoir with letter of August 21, 1709.) Back of this proposal much is indicated both as to the state of the French judiciary, rapidly becoming a major problem at the time, and as to Boisguilbert's ideas. He was writing at a time when the nobility of the robe was being ruined by affaires extraordinaires. The bench was being deserted until there were not sufficient judges to sit on cases. The judges were giving up their offices rather than be ruined by the taxes upon them, and the families from which the magistracy was normally replenished could no longer afford to educate their sons at the universities. The courts were also losing their dignity because of the youth and inexperience of the judges.

The inference is that Boisguilbert, with his alert mind and power of concentration, thought that by hard work the students could learn in three months what they actually obtained in three years. The sounder proposal, as far as legal training was concerned, would have been to suggest that common law be taught in the universities. But in the actual proposal is to be found a fundamental principle underlying Boisguilbert's thinking, namely, the necessity of combining theory and practice.

[5] Cadet, pp. 9–11, quoting Depping, *Correspondance administrative,* Vol. IV, p. xxviii.

Corneille, Boisguilbert was related to two great poets of his time. Pierre Corneille, forty years older than Boisguilbert, was at the height of his career and a great figure in the literary life of France when Boisguilbert was an impressionable youth. The decision to forsake the family tradition of the law for a literary career may be attributed to the influence of the dramatic poet on the boy's thinking. The classical and historical themes of the Corneille dramas could well have interested the student in history and in the study of Greek and Latin. He translated *Dion Cassius de Nicée, abrégé par Xiphilin,* and Herodien's *Histoire romaine,* which seem to have been sorry failures. He had, as Cadet says, the proper ideal for a translator: that, as Boisguilbert explained in his preface, one must not only make known " 'the thoughts of an author in translating, but that it is necessary to render beauty for beauty.' " But it is humorous to think of the realistic economist of a few years later attempting to satisfy a literary public enamored of elegance, of propriety, and affectation. If the good Abbé Mongault, whom Cadet quotes as later objecting to such statements as " 'the emperor had to go *décharger son ventre,*' " thought Boisguilbert too literal minded, he must indeed have shocked the delicate sensibilities of *les précieuses* who were his literary contemporaries.

Boisguilbert, during this early period devoted to literature, also wrote a now-forgotten life of *Marie Stuart, reine d'Écosse,* which went through two editions in 1674 and 1675. The author's preface is worth quoting, because it shows that the habits of thought so characteristic of Boisguilbert in his economic writings a quarter of a century later were formed at an early date.

The Reader is not to be impos'd upon, as if I design'd to entertain him with a Romance, when I give this Book the Title of an Historical Novel; for I assure him, That my View in writing it, was not only to tell the truth in the general, but even not to deviate from it in any one Circumstance of my History, which alas! Too many are ignorant of; since one Party with Father Caussin extol Her for a Saint, and a Martyr; and the other, by giving a blind and implicit Faith to Buchanan's wicked and unjust Calumnies, represent Her in the odious shape and Character of a Prostitute or worse; but begging their Pardon, I may with Truth affirm, That both have err'd, tho' in a very different Manner; the one out of an Excess of Charity; and the other, from an inexhaustible Source of Malice: However a Probability of Truth is not wanting in what either advance; since on the one hand, Her Subjects cloaked their Rebellion under a Pretence of Zeal for maintaining the Protestant Religion; and She on the other, had always the Misfortune to be caught in all the Snares, which her Enemies laid against her Honor: Having only the inward Consolation, That the Ills, which befel Herself or her Subjects, were not owing to her own Inclinations or Commands, which is fully justified in the following History, which I have copied from fifteen or sixteen different Authors. And if I appeal to Camden oftener than to any other, it is, because being a Subject of Queen Elizabeth, whatever he advanced in Favor of Queen Mary, ought without any Scruple, to be accepted as undeniable Truth.[6]

Having attempted two literary forms and failed, Boisguilbert gave up any further attempt at a purely literary career. It is possible that his turning to a new field was due to a developing interest in current affairs which he later spoke of as having arisen during this period,[7] as well as to his difficulty in obtaining a livelihood with his pen.

Although he was the elder son, Boisguilbert was for some reason disinherited by his father. It has been suggested that this was due to his decision to turn from the family tradition of the law. This, however, does not seem to be plausible in view of the fact that Boisguilbert was launched upon a successful legal career

[6] This excerpt, which shows Boisguilbert's sentence structure and punctuation, is quoted from *The Life of Mary Stewart, Queen of Scotland and France,* "Written Originally in French, and Now Done into English. With Notes illustrating and confirming the most material Passages of this History, collected from Contemporary and other Authors of the Greatest Character and Reputation." By James Freebairn, Edinburgh, 1725. With difficulty one finds that the work was written by one Sieur de Boisguilbert. The translation was published through private subscription, the list of subscribers including the most illustrious names in Scotland. The first paragraph of the "historical novel" may also be quoted: "The life of Mary Stewart, Queen of *Scotland* and of *France,* has something so extraordinary in its Conduct, and so fatal in its End, that without swerving from the Truth, the plain Narrative of it will appear no less surprising, than the Fictions of any modern Romance." It is interesting to compare the opinion expressed in the preface and in this paragraph with an opinion expressed in 1932: "Mary . . . is 'the great romantic subject,' the most maligned woman who ever lived and the most overpraised."—"Mary Stuart, Woman and Queen," review of *The Scottish Queen,* by Herbert Gorman. *New York Times Book Review,* Sunday, November 20, 1932.

[7] Letter of May 5, 1702. All letters from 1700 to 1708 are in *Correspondance des contrôleurs généraux des finances,* Vol. II, append. xii.

long before the death of his father. The latter bought for the younger son, Nicholas, an office as councillor in the *parlement*[8] in Normandy, and this son inherited the family estate. It is more probable that an important factor in the disinheritance of the elder son was a matter of personal conflict between father and son. Boisguilbert later was to show a peculiar inability to get along with people. If the father were of an equally domineering type, conflict would have been inevitable. Furthermore, if the father were a conservative, as is not improbable, the radicalism of this son must have been a source of extreme concern, whereas the younger son appears to have conformed easily and to have accepted the general view without too much questioning. There is indication that this disinheritance affected Boisguilbert deeply. Twice in his letters to Chamillart, the controller general, he spoke of being indebted for his fortune "after heaven, solely to myself."[9] There could be more than the mere pride of a self-made man in the remark, especially in its repetition. The restless energy, the subordination of every other interest to success in any undertaking, may well have sprung from a conscious or un-

[8] See note, pp. 20–21. Because the pre-Revolutionary French provincial *parlements,* or courts, were different in meaning from the English *parliament,* the French term will be retained

[9] Letters of Oct. 27, 1703 and Dec. 28, 1704. The father's epitaph doubtless was written by the elder son, the literary member of the family. It shows that there was either a remarkable similarity between the characteristics of father and son, or that the latter idealized the character of the father by endowing him in death with the substantial qualities which the son possessed to so singular a degree. The epitaph itself is not without interest:

"Here lies Messire Nicholas Lepesant, during his lifetime chevalier, seigneur, and patron of Boisguilbert, councillor of the king in his councils and master of his chamber of accounts in Normandy. His solid piety, his exact justice and his ardent charity attracted to him the esteem of all who knew him. He spent the last twenty years of his life in visiting the poor, in consoling and assisting them. He was so touched during the last year of the universal poverty caused by the extreme scarcity of grain that it has not been doubted that the sorrow which he experienced as a result of it shortened his days. He has founded in perpetuity a hundred livres of incomes to be spent for grain to be distributed every year to the poor. He died April 19, 1694. Pray God for the repose of his soul. Noble dame de Bonissant, his wife, has erected this epitaph and has rendered this duty to the memory of a husband, the sorrow of whose loss will endure until death. She lived until April 9, 1700, and returned her soul to her creator on holy Wednesday, and rests here." This inscription, says Cadet, is on a stone on the exterior tower of the château of Boisguilbert, having been saved at the time of the demolition of the church Sainte-Croix-Saint-Ouen, Rouen.—Cadet, pp. 4–6.

conscious rivalry with a brother who had supplanted him. Family conflict may thus have been a drive back of his striving to make a fortune and to rise in the legal profession until he had achieved for himself a position similar to the one which his brother had obtained so easily.

On September 26, 1677, Boisguilbert was married to Suzanne le Paige de Pinterville, daughter of the former procurer general of the Court of Aides in Normandy.[10] By her he had two daughters and three sons. Thus it is the tenderness and experience of a father which is indicated in his pages where is shown so much solicitude for the children of the poor, and so much knowledge and observation of the ills of under-nourished children, whose maladies, he said, are so likely to be fatal.[11]

On January 12, 1678, shortly after his marriage, Boisguilbert became Vicomte de Montivilliers, in Normandy, holding the position until 1689.[12] During these years he also engaged with success in agriculture and in commerce. He amassed what appears to have been a comfortable fortune for that time. It enabled him, in 1689, to buy two judicial offices in Rouen. As the wealthiest magistrate of his class in the generality, he was able to live for six years without drawing his salary; he was able to pay more than one hundred and sixty thousand livres of taxes on his offices between 1689 and 1709, and he spoke of having had twenty thousand livres on deposit in 1694 with the Sieurs le Couteux. His death record refers to him as "Seigneur of Boisguilbert, Pinterville, Maupertuy, and other places."

The intendant of Rouen, reporting on the generality in 1697, stated that because of their impoverishment, the old nobility could no longer maintain their former standards of living, and that the magnificence formerly associated with them had become instead a characteristic of the new nobility of the robe. From this, and from his position among the Norman magistrates, one may infer that Boisguilbert maintained his family in a certain elegance, and

10 The two families were either friends or relatives. Her mother, Suzanne du Four, was Boisguilbert's god-mother.—Horn, notes, pp. 48, 50.

11 Boislisle states that the family possesses a portrait of Boisguilbert and his wife, attributed to Largillière, which was exhibited at the Trocadéro exposition in 1877.

12 See note, pp. 20–21, for the duties of the position.

even such splendor as he would consider to be in keeping with his position; but from his strictures on those who consume their capital, one may likewise assume that he never lived beyond his means.

This fortune made by his own efforts must have had a definite effect upon Boisguilbert's character and his conduct. It must have added to his feeling of confidence and superiority, and to the independence of spirit which was so characteristic of him. It was his financial independence, as well as his ability and his judicial position which placed him on an intimate footing with the great merchant, Thomas le Gendre, with the greatest bankers in France, the Sieurs le Couteux, and which gave him the benefit of their wide financial experience.

Although from external sources so little is known of his life, Boisguilbert has left a clear imprint of himself in his writings. Cultured and well-to-do, he was according to every indication a fairly extensive traveler for his day.[13] His intimate references to conditions in different parts of France, his close observation of the living habits of the English workers as contrasted with those of France, his description of the Rhone at Lake Geneva, seem to show more than second-hand information. With Paris and its officials his letters indicate almost as much familiarity as with Rouen itself. With his *entrée* to the Corneille household in Paris, familiarity with the theater one would expect him to have had, and his frequent use of the actor in illustrations causes no surprise; nor do his comparisons of France to a stage where a drama is being enacted. He indicates also a familiarity with chamber music when, in a figure of speech, he refers to the dominating importance of the one "who beats the measure and assigns to each his part." It is a scholar who refers approvingly to the efforts of Francis I to reëstablish letters in the kingdom by giving pensions to "attract people versed in all the sciences," and to his purchase of manuscripts "of the works of the best and rarest authors," with which France, on account of "the ignorance of the preceding

[13] Saint-Simon, contrasting Boisguilbert's life with the activity which had characterized Vauban's, refers to the former as *le sédentaire à Rouen*. (*Mémoires*, Vol. XIV, p. 330.) In comparison with the military activity of Vauban the characterization might have been applicable. But Boisguilbert appears to have led far from a sedentary existence, student though he was.

centuries, had been very badly provided." It is legal training and judicial experience which underlie the methods which approximate those of the modern research worker in the insistence on obtaining the facts which is noticeable in his writings. But it is the training of Port-Royal, renowned for its emphasis upon mathematics and philosophy, which is indicated in Boisguilbert's logical reasoning and his grasp of underlying principles.

In a day when the practice of agriculture in France was scorned by the elevated classes, Boisguilbert had the courage to engage in it, to master its details, and to become its great defender. Without emphasis on agriculture, the classicism of the French life of the period is shown as a thin veneer. Boisguilbert, a true classicist in spirit, modeled his life after that of a gentleman of Greece or Rome, who combined knowledge of practical agriculture with studious and rich leisure and devotion to the State. Or, it may be said, it was a return to the habits of a Montaigne, who passed from the activity of his garden to the seclusion of his study to meditate and to write, or of a Sully, who would reluctantly give up his farming and horse breeding for affairs of State.

Aside from the fact that he built up his fortune during the period, nothing is known of his life between 1678 when he became Vicomte de Montivilliers and 1689 when he came to Rouen. Did his position and the management of his property absorb all the extraordinary energy of the man who "never liked to lose his time"? Was Boisguilbert, who had first elected writing as a profession, inactive with his pen between 1676, the date of his last translation, and 1695, the date of the publication of *Le Détail de la France?* Was he referring only to the latter when he said in 1702 that his zeal and his anxiety for more than thirty years had enabled him to foresee, as he had publicly written, that the way France was governed would cause her to perish if it were not changed? [14] Was the inveterate letter writer silent during these years, or was he carrying on a correspondence with a broad acquaintanceship? Was he writing any of the numerous anonymous pamphlets attacking conditions and purporting to have been published in Brussels, Amsterdam, or Cologne? This cannot be determined without

[14] Letter of May 5, 1702.

a careful examination of the field with reference to content and style. There was nothing written at that time, certainly, that Boisguilbert cared to, or dared to, acknowledge and to include in his collected writings.[15]

In 1689 Boisguilbert bought the two magisterial offices of president and lieutenant general in the bailiwick and presidial seat of Rouen. His letter of investiture was issued on November 9, 1690.[16] Letters patent for the position were issued March 16, 1691. Boisguilbert, as Horn said, expecting to obtain only such a position as his younger brother possessed, as councillor in the parlement, fell unexpectedly into the two offices named, which were "more conformable than that of Vicomte de Montivilliers to the traditions of the family, and to the need of activity which tormented him." [17] Referring specifically to one of the offices purchased by

[15] There is a similarity in the economic ideas of certain of the writings and those of Boisguilbert which cannot be wholly ignored. *Soupirs de la France esclave,* for instance, obviously was not written by Boisguilbert. The style is completely different; there is a virulence which, strongly expressed as are Boisguilbert's writings, he never displays; many of the ideas are at variance with his; it attacks governmental expenditures, which Boisguilbert never does, and the gabelle, which he does not treat. Yet there are passages which could come from *Le Détail, Factum,* or *Traité du mérite,* and in which idioms characteristic of Boisguilbert are to be found, as well as the same attack upon Colbert and the dating of the difficulties of France from 1660. *Soupirs de la France* is attributed to Michel Vasson. Vasson, judging from the content of this work, appears to have been Jansenist or Calvinist. He was born in the adjoining generality of Orléans. He was born in the same year as Boisguilbert. They had a common interest in history. If they attended Port-Royal together they would have known each other. If they knew each other, they obviously continued the friendship in after years.

[16] The first paragraph of this investiture is as follows: "Louis, etc., to all those who shall see these presents, greetings. We have chosen and named our dear and well-beloved M. Pierre Lepesant de Boisguilbert, heretofore our councillor Vicomte de Montivilliers, to fill one of the offices of councillor in our court of parlement in Normandy, to which we had caused to be expedited our letters of dispensation because the Sieur de Boisguilbert, his brother, is councillor in the said parlement. But as the offices of our councillor president and lieutenant in the bailiwick and presidial seat of Rouen are vacant, through the voluntary resignation which the Sieur de Brevedent has placed in our hands, We have believed that a better choice could not be made than the person of the said Sieur de Boisguilbert, in the hope that he will fulfill our expectations, having the qualities required to perform its function[s] to the assuagement and satisfaction of our subjects." The complete letter is given by Horn, Appendix, pp. 363–365.

[17] In order to give some notion of the local administrative and judicial organization of Rouen, the generality of Rouen and the province of Normandy, in which Boisguilbert had a part, the following summary from the report of the intendant

Boisguilbert, the intendant said that the office "of lieutenant general has . . . become very considerable through the diverse functions which have been given to it; such, among others, as the inspection of police and the presidency of the *corps-de-ville*." [18]

Boisguilbert's enormous energy had indeed not been fully absorbed by his office of vicomte and the pursuit of his own fortune between 1678 and 1689. He had studied the economic and social conditions of France, and his reputation as an economist was established by the time he came to Rouen. His mind, which could encompass so much, had already led him to arrive at definite ideas

---

of Rouen is furnished: The *corps-de-ville* (corresponding roughly to our municipal councils) of Rouen had, since the fourteenth century, been "composed of six magistrates *(echevins)* having at their head a bailiff (*bailly*) or his lieutenant general. This form . . . existed until 1695, there having been a creation then through all the kingdom of perpetual mayors in the cities." The Norman parlement (comparable to our court of appeals) consisted of a president and councillors (one of whom was Boisguilbert's brother Nicholas). It had jurisdiction over all Normandy, which was divided into four bailiwicks (*bailliages*). At the head of each bailiwick was a lieutenant general, who had jurisdiction over nobles and ecclesiastics, and had some inspection of trades until this function was taken away from the office with the creation of lieutenants of police in the provinces in 1699. Each bailiwick was divided into four *vicomtés,* each presided over by a *vicomte,* who had jurisdiction over the *roturiers,* or non-nobles and non-privileged. The *vicomtés* in turn were divided into *sergenteries.* In 1649 the office of bailiff of Rouen was "joined to the government." Thereafter the lieutenant general presided over the *corps-de-ville.* Consequently, this was one of the functions of Boisguilbert.—*État de la France,* Vol. II, pp. 8–9, 20–21.

[18] Horn, referring to the fact that Boisguilbert's appointment as lieutenant general failed to give general satisfaction, said it was because the duties of the office were not well defined as a result of the manner in which the office had gradually grown in importance. "When toward the end of the thirteenth century Roman law commenced to be substituted more and more for local and common law, the bailiffs and seneschals, for the greater part almost illiterate, found it impossible to exercise their functions. An ordinance of Charles VI (May 27, 1413) . . . permitted them to have lieutenants." This privilege was abused. In 1493 the number of lieutenants either a bailiff or seneschal could have was limited to two: "a lieutenant *général* (or principal) and a lieutenant *particulier,* replacing the other in case of impeachment. An ordinance of Louis XII (March 1498), decreed that judicial offices must henceforth be confided only to doctors and *licenciés,* and forbidding the bailiff and seneschal to exercise judicial duties unless they be graduated, forced them to abandon entirely their most important functions . . . to their lieutenants." At the same time the king took over the right to name the lieutenants, and the lieutenancy was thus transformed into an "office which was bought and became a veritable property." "Its value increases when, to put an end to the differences, an ordinance of Charles IX (January 1560) declared that in the future all the bailiffs and seneschals shall be of the short robe, that is to say, that the administration of justice shall belong wholly and exclusively to the lieutenants" (pp. 54–55).

as to the cause of the disorder in the kingdom and to formulate proposals for reform. In 1691 he could speak of his "system." As early as 1689 he had at least roughly drafted the text of *Le Détail de la France*. Scarcely was he settled in his new offices before he sought and obtained an interview with the controller general, Pontchartrain.[19] The audience cannot be said to have started auspiciously. The Duke of Saint-Simon gives us the picture. The brusque provincial was evidently not at all awed by the pomp and ceremony. When he had approached Pontchartrain, "he demanded of him that he listen with patience, and immediately said to him that at first he would think him crazy, that next he would see that he merited attention, and that in the end he would abide content with his system." But Pontchartrain, disagreeable at the best, was impatient as a result of the certain solutions to which he had listened. He "began to laugh, answered curtly that he would be satisfied with the first, and turned his back." [20]

So ended the conversation that Boisguilbert hoped would mark the beginning of the salvation of France. Most men would have been discouraged by the rebuff. But Boisguilbert seems never to have doubted that the key to the economic regeneration of France lay in the adoption of his system of reforms. No one else in the kingdom could do what he promised to do; [21] no one else so combined theoretical knowledge and practical experience. If others were reluctant to hear, or could not understand how this regeneration could be brought about, he must try that much more to make himself heard and understood.

Rebuffed by Pontchartrain, Boisguilbert continued to plan, to write, and to undertake the conversion of those around him to his ideas. In a land almost destroyed by those who put their own interest above the general welfare, he had "no other object than to render service to the king, to the public," and to the ministers themselves. After waiting four years for the adoption of financial measures which would introduce an element of hopefulness into

[19] The exact date is probably uncertain. Saint-Simon, writing in 1707, places it in 1691. It was before the publication of *Le Détail*, in which reference is made to it (p. 257).

[20] Saint-Simon, *Mémoires*, Vol. XIV, pp. 326–327.

[21] *Factum*, pp. 341–342.

the situation, he proceeded in 1695, after the distressing famine years of 1693–94, to publish *Le Détail de la France.* This work was without practical results, as Boisguilbert said later, because "there was still, as it were, oil in the lamp."

With little hope of accomplishment under Pontchartrain, during the period between 1695 and 1700 Boisguilbert's mind was turning more and more to theoretical speculation about conditions in France. In this time he seems to have thought out, if he did not actually write, *Traité des grains.* He was also in close touch with the intendant of Rouen, De la Bourdonnaye, and with him was evolving a plan for an important experiment. This plan was to try his administrative reforms in a limited area. He was confident that the results would serve as a model for all France. Hope for carrying out such an experiment was ended with the transfer of De la Bourdonnaye to Bordeaux.

In the meanwhile, there was a new creation of offices, among them that of lieutenant general of police. The functions of the magistracy of police were essentially the maintenance of law and order, economic justice, health and sanitation, and public morality, including the censorship of the press. These functions were largely derived from those of the office of lieutenant general which Boisguilbert already owned, the value of which was consequently reduced. He therefore bought this newly created office for one hundred thousand livres, which was in reality the re-purchase of, or a tax upon, his existing one.

So far as it had to do with commerce and industry this was a position for which Boisguilbert was especially qualified; but so far as it demanded restrictions it ran counter to his ideas. It was a position in which a person of his independent spirit, his knowledge and views, was certain to run into difficulties. They were not long in coming. Cadet takes up at length his troubles with Pontchartrain [22] over the question " 'of ignorance, or of irregularity in the permissions to print' " which Boisguilbert gave. The office, it seems, had no authority over publications passing the length of a *livret,* or over those dedicated to the king. Pontchartrain threatened to take the jurisdiction away from the "subaltern

[22] Who in 1699 became chancellor.

magistrate" who was inclined to exceed his authority and the spirit of censorship prevailing. Nevertheless, Rouen continued to be the center of forbidden publications in spite of complaints that " 'all sorts of forbidden books' " were published there " 'with more license than in any other place in the kingdom' "; that in that " 'city a great commerce was made, with license, in all sorts of bad books.' " The office of censor was indeed no position for the father of laissez faire. Boisguilbert knew too well on his own account the irksomeness of restraints on the freedom of the press, and was far too liberal in his views to be able to conform in this respect and to satisfy authority and conservatism. In his position as censor of the press at Rouen, Boisguilbert displayed a liberalism, as Cadet says, comparable to that great liberal of a later generation, Malesherbes.[23]

Even more interesting were his difficulties with the local authorities over the question of control of prices and of weights and measures. It is hard to decide who must have suffered most from the inevitable conflicts arising: the specialized Boisguilbert in contention with a group attempting to act upon matters about which, from his standpoint, they knew nothing, or this group over-ridden by a man impatient and domineering as a result both of temperament and of his superior knowledge. The differences of opinion began soon after his appointment to the new office of lieutenant general of police. On January 16, 1700, De Beuvron, lieutenant general of Normandy, wrote to the controller general that he had just met M. de Boisguilbert, with the members of the city council of Rouen, and that the former was determined to "have all that which appertains to him by the edict creating his office. I am burdened with asking your orders and explanations on all the difficulties and disputes which can arise, and in order that things may be done peaceably . . . [I would have you] make him understand that the less he can demand in the way of affairs and regulations, and the less he importunes you, the better this would be for him. I should indeed also be glad to please him, because he has asked it of me, and has shown me all sorts of

[23] Cadet, pp. 39–44.

courtesies in his advancement; but I do not know if his too great vivacity and his impetuous disposition do not make him have pretensions which are not always sound. . . . It would be desirable for him, as for many others, if he should wish to follow somewhat the counsel and advice of his brother the councillor." [24]

The argument had to do with the price of bread, in which Boisguilbert, the economist, was holding out against the hit-or-miss policy of the council. Incidentally, it was an argument in which Boisguilbert's theory of proportional prices was involved. One can imagine him giving involved, but heated, disquisitions on his theory while a bored and indifferent city council and the provincial parlement wondered what it was all about, and what it had to do with the price of bread which must be kept as low as possible.

The sequel to the complaint against him appears in two of Boisguilbert's letters to the controller general. In one, dated the 14th and 15th of June, 1700, he wrote that he had disagreed with the commissioners of parlement because it "would be necessary to increase and not to decrease [the price of bread], as you will see by the paper and by the estimates which I give myself the honor to send to you. The late M. Pellot had an authentic attempt made to find what bread should be worth in relation to the price of wheat. He found that when the *mine* [i.e., 6 bushels], a measure of Rouen which is a little more than half the *setier* of Paris, is worth six livres, brown bread (*pain bis*), which governs the other, must be sold at fourteen *deniers* [denier=1/12 a sou] a pound, and similarly in increasing or diminishing. In the six months that I have been in charge wheat has never been less, namely, from ten livres, ten sous the mine, and now it passes eleven livres; nevertheless, I have left bread at the price of eighteen deniers the pound, which is more than four deniers below what it ought to be according to the order established in 1683. The result is that I am tormented by the bakers to raise their price according to these papers and reasons, to which it seems to me there is no answer. All I can do is to lighten the penalty when the violation is only moderate. This seems to me less injurious

[24] *Correspondance des contrôleurs généraux*, Vol. II, No. 72, p. 22

than the increase which is a kind of alarm which never fails to cause wheat to go up in the markets afterward." [25]

On second thought Boisguilbert evidently decided that it might be well to play safe in the matter of winking somewhat at the law with regard to weights and measures as a means to give what he considered to be economic justice. Two weeks later, on July 2, he wrote that he would be obliged to close his eyes to the lack of weight, which causes "less rumor than the increase in price, which is a kind of alarm in the country at the beginning of the harvest. As there are some persons in this country who have care to inform you of all my conduct, I beg you to remember this when they will write you that I permit the bakers to make the bread too light." [26]

So it appears that Boisguilbert compromised with the commissioners by not changing the price of bread, but that he achieved his determination to be fair to the bakers in another manner. His persistence in this matter becomes clear when it is understood that his entire theory is built around the principle of a price to the producer which will cover all expenses and give a fair profit. So important was this to him in the maintenance of social well-being, that any means taken to bring it about would be justified.

This incident gives some insight into the character and disposition of the man. The few brush strokes which describe his peculiar temperament are vivid ones. Saint-Simon, for instance, says that *son esprit vif avoit du singulier,* while de Beuvron refers to *son trop vivacité et humeur bouillante.* These observations, combined with the content of his writings, the terrible persistence of his letters, his conflicts with his professional associates at Rouen, and his determination to see his ideas dominate, make it possible to reconstruct the personality of the man. We see the enthusiast, with an infinite compassion for the economically helpless and oppressed, with a profound contempt for human stupidity, with a relentless hatred for those who sought their own advancement

[25] *Ibid.,* Vol. II, No. 145, p. 41. To understand the full significance of the last remark it is necessary to know the content of *Traité des grains,* in which Boisguilbert explains the factors causing the price of grain to rise or fall at times out of all relation to the changes in the actual quantity of grain. The price of wheat in 1700 was just beginning to drop after the preceding shortage from 1696 to 1699, and continued to fall until the great famine of 1709.

[26] *Ibid.,* Vol. II, No. 157, p. 45.

and welfare without troubling themselves about the general interest, applying himself in a fiery impatience to securing economic justice and fiscal reform. In this effort he displayed the same fanatical zeal which Calvin and Knox had shown a century earlier in the field of religion. Boislisle says of him, that,

> whether it was a question of administrative affairs or of judiciary powers, even of simple debates on precedence, he displayed everywhere the same feverish activity, the same mad ardor, the same need of innovation and, above all, of domination, as did that other precursor, Jean Bodin, who, sent to Rouen to reorganize the forests, was characterized by the provincial Estates as a "great disturber and transgressor of the laws and customs of the country and of the Norgeneral, with the magistrates of the secondary jurisdiction, Boisguilthe parlement, with the city council, with the gilds (*corps d'arts et métiers*), as with the intendant, with the governor or his lieutenant man charter," and even as "the principal enemy of France." With bert did not cease to raise conflicts, to sustain contests, struggles, where appeared always a character disturbing, restless, unsociable.[27]

Such is the picture drawn from Norman records through the decade prior to 1700. His contempt for authority and position was obviously as unusual as it was maddening to those who experienced it. The old Marquis de Beuvron, one of the most influential of the old Norman nobility, father of the lieutenant general of Normandy who complained of Boisguilbert a few years later,[28] as early as 1692 indignantly wrote to Pontchartrain:

> The lieutenant general of this bailiwick is regarded by all those who know him as the most ungovernable and incompatible man in the world, with many other defects that I do not speak of, and although I regard him as a man who is not wise, and although I scorn the greater part of his discourse, nevertheless it is very disagreeable, in spite of all I can do, to see myself exposed to this, and to have to endure, in the presence of all the nobility of a country, all the excesses, raving, and lack of respect shown me by the said lieutenant general.[29]

Boisguilbert was not unaware that he differed from other men. In truth he prided himself upon the fact. It was both a certain *naïveté* and a consciousness of his own powers which led him to exclaim in reply to a criticism of him made to Chamillart: "I

[27] Saint-Simon, *Mémoires*, Vol. XIV, append. xii, p. 581.
[28] See above, pp. 24–25. [29] *Op. cit.*, pp. 581–582.

glory in having a singular character, without which I should not have unusual ideas." [30]

How can one account for Boisguilbert's temperamental difficulties? Were they due to an innate contrariness and desire to dominate, or were they the result of the conditions under which he lived? The latter seems a much more plausible view to take. As an individual he possessed warm human sympathy and understanding, but intellectually he lived alone. From the standpoint of his economic ideas he belonged to a much later date. Everywhere he was faced with opposition on account of his liberalism. His offices required him to enforce laws in which he disbelieved. Mentally, therefore, he lived wholly in an atmosphere of constraint and restriction. The same had been true of Bodin, to a lesser degree, more than a century before. Such a condition must necessarily have affected their relations with others. Boisguilbert saw France being ruined by adherence to restraints and privileges; to change this became almost a religion with him. It was difficult for him to compromise with his ideas and ideals in which he had a sublime faith. He also believed implicitly that the people had only to learn wherein their true interest lay in order to demand a change. It was because he felt that he was the "author" of a great discovery in the same class with Copernicus, Galileo, and Columbus that he was willing to undergo martyrdom and a life of conflict in order to see his ideas prevail. It was this, rather than dominance for its own sake, which seems to have determined his behavior. His mission, he felt, was to save France, and "the safety of States is like that of souls, in which that which is called importunity and impudence in the one becomes an obligation in the other." [31]

It was this feeling of an obligation to devote himself to the welfare of France which gave him the courage to say to Chamillart, the controller general, the charming, well-meaning, but weak favorite of Louis XIV, that he looked upon and listened to as oracles those who dared propose methods contrary to common sense.[32] To complaints made and to petitions presented to Paris and Versailles for his removal from office he was immune, if not because there was sympathy with his ideas, certainly because of

[30] Letter of July 18, 1703.
[31] Letter of June 25, 1705. [32] Letter of Feb. 22, 1705.

fear of them. He was a fearless critic of the government who must at least be kept encouraged and conciliated to keep him from publishing.

Boisguilbert himself did not appear to mind criticism. He wrote to Chamillart, in response to attacks made upon him, that

Wisdom does not consist in a well-composed exterior, smooth speech, and a brilliant performance in all that appears externally.[33] If under this cover passions reign, especially physical ones, a gross ignorance, and a lack of success in all affairs of importance, it follows from all points: *pulchra facies, sed non cerebrum habet*. I wish indeed to be judged on this level. By the grace of God, in all my life, there has been no youthful behavior (*action de jeunesse*), being indebted, after heaven, for my fortune, only to myself.[34]

There was a touch of the Jansenist doctrine of election rather than braggadocio in his statement when he told Chamillart that he had a kind of virtue which was to succeed in all his endeavors.[35] There was in him a feeling of being destined to succeed. It was this which led him to persist in his efforts to influence others. It was this which made him impossible to his associates. But that it was the domination of principles rather than personal domination as such which he sought in the end, is amusingly illustrated by one of his letters to the controller general. A dispute had arisen between the first president of the Norman parlement and Boisguilbert, lieutenant general of police, as to who had the right to give permission to transport grain from Rouen to Paris by boat. This authority, which Boisguilbert had exercised heretofore, was being questioned. He begged the controller general not to decide in favor of the first president without giving him a hearing. In conclusion he added: "I believe that, to put everybody in accord, this transport should be free, without permission from anyone, and that no more clearance is necessary to have grains go from Rouen than from d'Andely and Vernon, from where it is carried daily to Paris without any formality." [36]

Although officially only a "subaltern magistrate" as Pontchartrain had disdainfully called him, and although occasionally chastised by Chamillart for his presumption, Boisguilbert for many

[33] This appears to be a thumb-nail sketch of his own lack of social graces.
[34] Letter of Dec. 28, 1704.
[35] Letter of Nov. 20, 1704. [36] Letter of Dec. 14, 1705.

years occupied a position which was not to be ignored. Due to his various offices in one of the most important bailiwicks in France, his writings, his financial independence, his intimacy with the intendants, his relations with the controllers general, his acquaintance with other high government officials, and his contacts with men of large affairs, his importance in the generality was probably second only to that of the intendant himself, and certainly was greater than that of any other magistrate of his class in France.

Local problems, and the struggles which accompanied them, were, nevertheless, mere incidents in Boisguilbert's life. His chief interest was a more ambitious one than that of conflicts with the Rouen city council and the Norman parlement. His aim was nothing less than the economic rehabilitation of all France. The dawn of the new century found him full of hope that at last he would be able to achieve this through his reforms. No one else in France was so familiar with the administration of the finances and with the economic and social conditions of the people at the same time; no one else saw so clearly that the two were different aspects of the same problem; no one else had resolved these problems into their elements; no one else rightly saw where the difficulty lay and what was necessary to bring about a change. And now Pontchartrain, who would not listen to him, was gone from his control over the finances. Chamillart, Boisguilbert's friend of years' standing, had succeeded him as controller general in 1699, and Boisguilbert would have his ear.[87]

[87] Chamillart had been intendant of Rouen from 1689 to 1690. He had been familiar and sympathetic with Boisguilbert's plans and ideas at that time, and may have been instrumental in gaining Boisguilbert's interview with Pontchartrain.

II

SCHOOLMASTER TO THE CONTROLLER GENERAL

The government of a State is something so difficult, and at the same time so delicate, that it . . . is necessary . . . to sacrifice everything to it.

LEGALLY entitled councillor to the king, Boisguilbert took seriously the position (of which one of the functions was to keep the central authorities informed on conditions in the provinces),[1] and constituted himself something of an economic adviser to Chamillart. Led on by the fact that conditions were steadily growing worse, he began a series of letters to the new controller general which constitute a unique chapter in history. It was, in truth, a bombardment, to use one of his own terms, which in content ran from the condition of the harvest, including the heading of wheat, the quantity of straw, and the probable price of grain, to suggestions as to how the finances of France should be reorganized. As to conditions, he expressed the hope that Chamillart would approve his continuing to keep him informed in "detail as to what goes on in the country. As affairs there are in a perpetual movement, there is always something new that a minister must know, without which it is impossible for him to succeed." [2] In order to show the effect of the existing system, and to make clear the necessity for the reforms in the finances and their administration which he desired to see introduced, he discussed money, prices, consumption, trade, economic solidarity, with a view to educating the ministers in practical affairs without a knowledge of which, he declared, a country is subject to all the errors of bad government. In essence he made an effort to train

[1] An edict of Feb. 4, 1567 of Charles IX required among other things that the provincial officials, including bailiffs and seneschals, should inform the king of the state of the crops.—Horn, p. 140.
[2] Letter of Oct. 3, 1700.

in economic principles those who determined the nation's fiscal and economic policies, and to acquaint them with the problems arising through the contravention of these principles.

Boisguilbert thought that especially those in positions of authority must know about the difficulties under which the masses lived and tried to better their condition. Who could forget his minute description of the rise of *un misérable* to affluence in the country, where "an egg worth three deniers produces a pullet; this pullet, a fat hen, which is sold for thirty or forty sols; these thirty or forty sols [buy] two suckling pigs; these two pigs, easily milk-fattened at little expense, bring sixty livres; these sixty livres, a horse, with which one equips a tiny farm (*demi-labourage*), or one peddles small wares, which can produce great wealth. Although this detail taken according to the letter produces something rather ridiculous, it is at the same time absolutely true, and rich farmers and merchants are seen daily who began by carrying for a long time all their property and warehouses on their backs." But if ministers must understand the everyday life of the people they must equally understand how easy it is for a bad financial system to ruin them either on their way to comfort and ease, or after this has been attained.[3]

It is largely through these revealing letters that more is known of this extraordinary individual than the mere fact that he was a Norman magistrate who wrote on the economic problems of his time and incidentally outlined modern economic theory. It is in them that his life and his activity are disclosed.[4]

Boisguilbert ordinarily dictated to a secretary, which must account for much of his diffuseness and many of his errors. But the letters to the controllers general, although exceedingly long in many cases, were painfully written by hand. In a letter to Desmaretz he apologized for not using his secretary, and for the

[3] Memoir attached by Boislisle to letter of July 18, 1703.

[4] We are indebted for these letters to Nicholas Desmaretz, nephew of Colbert, who, as director of finances from 1703 to 1708, was so largely responsible for organizing and keeping the archives, and to Arthur de Boislisle for uncovering and deciphering them. Because of their relative inaccessibility, and because their informal style adds to the other difficulties of reading Boisguilbert, and because they so disclose the spirit of the man as well as his ideas, it has seemed desirable to let him speak through them as far as possible. In only a few cases have entire letters been quoted.

difficulty the former would have in reading his handwriting, which was none too legible. This, he said, was a favor accorded to him by the controller general on account of the nature of the content of the letters which must not be seen by others. Thus the letters constituted an arduous task for Boisguilbert, and for the ministry because of the difficult problem of deciphering and trying to absorb their content. That they were carefully read and studied is indicated by their condition. Parts are underlined; penciled marginal notes appear, Boislisle states, and at times they are even copied in full. They seem seldom to have been answered, but this did not deter their author from continuing to write assiduously, assuming that his ideas were at least being considered.

Boisguilbert opened his campaign to convert the new minister to his ideas with a lengthy memoir. It deals with the relation of land and commerce and endeavors to make clear that it is not to the advantage of the rich and privileged to throw the burden of taxes upon the poor. The introduction is especially interesting as showing so much of his economic philosophy:

The general interest of all men, as well as a whole kingdom, although today [it is] the least understood of all, is their common maintenance. It is impossible for all individuals not to be very happy when the public enjoys a complete felicity. It is on this principle that formerly when the Romans invested a citizen with a magistracy, he was placed in office simply with these few words: *See that the public suffers no loss.* Thus it is a great mistake not only tranquilly to see the destruction of one's fellow man, but even to form from his ruin a stepping stone to try to make one's own fortune. This is done regularly in France in two ways: either by [his] actual destruction, which does not lack examples, or by failure to aid him to support a weight which is more than his share, and which inevitably cripples him. In its consequences, this injustice costs all those who would take advantage of their position in order to practice it with impunity, four times as much, as is seen at every instant in almost all the sections of the kingdom.

The first interest of the rich and the owners of land is that the country be cultivated, and as a consequence inhabited, not only for the management of lands and commerce, but also for the consumption of that which grows. Without this the ownership is useless and cultivation at a loss. This is generally known, but as every individual believes he is charged only with his personal interest, not only does he give no attention to it in practice, but he even pursues a conduct wholly opposed to it on occasion, and works all the time to destroy consumption and to depopulate the kingdom, which is a necessary consequence of it. [This is done] in the false notion that the small number of privileged is of no consequence and not at all perceptible in relation to all the body of the State. On the contrary, however, experience daily makes it clear that, as there is nothing more contagious than disorder, the change that the body of the State, which forms the property and the wealth of everyone, receives from it, throws back a portion of loss by this iniquity, which exceeds three or four times that which these privileged persons thought to earn by their injustice.

It is well known, that when enemies are ready to enter the kingdom, and to burn and to pillage the frontiers, the most remote regions which will perhaps never experience disaster, must nevertheless contribute equally with the most exposed to repulse the common adversary. [This rests] upon the reasonable opinion that if the evil is not stopped at its beginning, it will soon sweep over the kingdom. It is the same situation and the same interest in the taxes due to the prince. It is unfortunate that the ordinary revenues, which are their domains,[5] cannot suffice for the expenses as formerly, either on account of the alienation of those properties, or of the unexpected coming of new functions (*affaires*). But as that is a necessary evil it is unnecessary to increase the evil, as is done daily, in ruining the poor, or rather the consumption of all the kingdom, by the unjust apportionment [of taxes]. It will be made clear by a setting forth of the facts, that on the contrary the more taxes the powerful pay, and the more they exempt the feeble from them, the richer [the former] will be. By this they will gain four to one in a moment, and the King likewise.[6]

In Paris Vauban was seeking to have his reforms adopted.[7] The relation between Boisguilbert and Vauban was an unusual one. There was no blood relationship, for, although Vauban later,

[5] It is scarcely necessary to add that Boisguilbert was speaking here in terms of the past. Gradually, in addition to the domains, the taille, the gabelle, the aides, and the duanes had become ordinary sources of revenue. It should perhaps be mentioned that the domains included not only the crown lands, but also any rights and dues, such as tolls, belonging to the king as seigneur of his properties, and the more recent rights pertaining to the crown, as postal fees, and the *contrôle*, such as marriage, etc.

[6] In editing the correspondence Boislisle was uncertain about the position of this memoir of which the introduction was quoted. He finally, and I think incorrectly, placed it with the letter of July 18, 1703.

[7] His proposal for a *dîme royale* appears to have been given serious study at this time by the authorities.

in a letter to the controller general, referred to Boisguilbert as "my nephew," their relationship was simply one of intimacy assumed on account of the connection of each with the Corneille family. In their last years, however, their interests and their writings were in many respects so parallel that it is difficult completely to separate them. In some ways the relation between these two reminds one of that between Ricardo and Malthus a century later, although it was less intimate. They were in agreement as to the facts with regard to France, but they heartily disagreed as to the means to be taken to save her.

If Boisguilbert appears to be the less generous of the two intellectual combatants it is because he lacked the gentleness of spirit which so characterized the old general. Boisguilbert had not been polished by the amenities of court life, but had struggled in the arena of practical affairs. He was a hot-headed reformer with his feet planted firmly on a practical knowledge of agriculture and commerce, and he had no doubt as to the correctness of his own views. Much as he respected Vauban and his intentions, Boisguilbert would not passively see the existing evils replaced by an unworkable system, as he regarded the proposal for the *dime royale*. Vauban had borrowed much of the theory of *Le Détail*, and, according to Boislisle, Boisguilbert in early conversations had provided Vauban with statistics. But Boisguilbert regarded the latter's proposal to eliminate the existing forms of taxes and to replace them with a single tax of a tenth of the product in kind as utterly impracticable. It was obviously Vauban whom Boisguilbert had in mind when he referred, from time to time, to "bearers of astonishing novelties," to theorists who were without practical experience.[8]

Boisguilbert went into the matter at length for Chamillart's benefit. He had learned at Paris, the former stated, that Vauban had read to the king his project for a dime royale to remedy the disorders of the *taille*.[9]

This [he says] was written for the most part by a priest of Tournay

[8] Boislisle says it was jealousy which caused Boisguilbert to attack Vauban's proposal. It seems rather than jealousy to have been something of the attitude taken by the modern economist on the feasibility of the single tax.

[9] See below, chap. vi.

exiled to Rouen. I have believed myself obliged to advise you as to what passed between them and me. This was to the effect that their project is ridiculous in the proposition and impossible in the execution. And not being content with that I have sent them a little treatise which I wrote the following day, drawn from knowledge of commerce in the country, of which they have not the least understanding, although [this is] absolutely necessary in order to reason upon such a matter.

He enclosed a copy of this detailed criticism of the dime, in which he set forth twenty "insurmountable objections" to remedying the disorders of the taille by a dime royale modeled after the ecclesiastical one. Any one of these disadvantages, he declared, would be sufficient to ruin the project.[10]

Boisguilbert had already sent memoirs on money and the causes of the recurring famines in France. The capitation and the taille next engaged his attention. He sent two memoirs on the former. In a letter with them there is a slight glimpse of the investigator who would learn at first hand.

I instruct myself at all times more and more. Yesterday, having gone into the country toward Neuf-Bourg . . . by chance I questioned a farmer of a neighboring parish, as I always do. He told me that the farmer of M. de Vieuxpont, had, on 2,500 livres of rent, paid 15 livres of taille, and that this must not surprise me, considering that it was about the same everywhere with respect to the farmers of the influential. So much for the taille. As for the capitation, I find the same abuse, as you will see, my Lord, by the memoir of the laity, and eight days later you will have that of the ecclesiastics, which will surprise you more than all the rest.[11]

Boisguilbert, student of history and of early French law, contrasted the practices and tendencies of the past with those of the France of his day. In part he obviously used this as a method to disarm criticism and the objection that his principles were radical and untried. But in truth he seems never to have doubted that greater justice and liberality had characterized France in times gone by. He begged Chamillart to attach himself to the principles of the past. Do so, he asserted, and the State will never lack revenue. The first of these principles, and the "corner-stone, is always to increase privileges (*les droits*) and never to diminish

[10] Letter and memoir of June 13, 1700.
[11] Letter of Dec. 31, 1701.

them when it is a question of a tariff (*un droit*), as there are many of them [i.e., duties] which will bring about twenty times more wrong to the people than the king will receive profit." He proceeded to show that cutting the export duties in half would not reduce the return to the king, but that "the king's tax-farmers are concerned not to let this fact be known." [12] He continued:

The only reasonable objection that has been raised against me, is that it is dangerous to propose diminutions at one point in order to replace them at another, because people are accustomed to the one and do not wish to hear the other referred to.[13] Having had the honor to know you personally for a dozen years, I am convinced, as are the people, of your intelligence and of your pure intentions. It is this which will keep me from being stopped by these preconceived opinions, and I shall bring you . . . my plan, which will be difficult only because it will be necessary for you to make use of *barbarians,* to use the language of Rome at the time of her decadence, which gave no other name to the inhabitants of the provinces, even those of Greece. Thus Normandy, which is called the Greece of France,[14] must not hope to be better treated. Everyone is in consternation at the aspect of the storm which threatens, and I—I have not a moment of fear, not believing that a State is in an evil situation when, in order to go out with glory from a perilous action, it is only necessary to exact five thousand livres from a benefice of fifty thousand livres of rent, which has cost nothing, and one thousand livres of capitation from one who enjoys more than twenty-five thousand livres, above all when this is replaced from another source, as I maintain you can do.[15]

Boisguilbert now began to prepare Chamillart for the coming interview, to save time, no doubt, but also, as he was to do later, to work out a basis of agreement on fundamentals, so that they might proceed to the more immediate problems of ways and means.

Approve [he says] if you please, that, from now until three weeks hence when I hope to have the honor of greeting you, I continue to indicate to you some maxims fundamental to the restoring and the safety of France, to which it is wholly essential to give attention. The

[12] See below, pp. 129–130.

[13] This argument was later used by Bâville. See below, p. 70.

[14] This expression was not without significance, as can be seen, for instance, by turning through Voltaire's catalog of French writers in the *Siècle de Louis XIV*. Pierre and Thomas Corneille, Fontenelle, Mézerai, Saint-Évremond, Saint-Pierre—these names merely head a lengthier roll.

[15] Letter of Feb. 4, 1702. The last statement is a reference to the increase of income which Boisguilbert thought would be experienced by everyone with the returning prosperity he foresaw as resulting from a reform of the fiscal system.

first is that the State has never had so great a need of extraordinary aid, and never was so little in a position to procure it. [This is] due to the fact that the people are found in the position of a man who gives up his property with money in his pocket which he does not surrender at all because [to do so] will not discharge him, and he does not wish to live destitute. The second is that all the persons who compose the Council of the King do not understand by experience that the time is very disastrous. The administration of the finances not resting on their shoulders, they are far from understanding a good which they believe will injure them, such as the freedom of the highways and the just division of the taxes. It is not necessary to raise the dead [16] to prove the truth of your project so that [the Council] may [not] discredit it. Their interest is an abnormal one. It [derives from] the fact that the beginning of all reorganization being the discovery of mistakes, and even of something more, of the preceding ministries, those who still rule through them, or their representatives, find themselves scheming, by the most violent cause which can exist, to contradict everyone, and to take direct parts. There is only one means, as I have given myself the honor to advise you numberless times, which is first to render them suspect (*récusable*) by informing the King of facts so certain and at the same time so frightful, that they make him a perpetual shield for their fine reasons that would easily be turned into ridicule if they came from the lips of a [private] individual.

The third maxim, my Lord, and [one] which will make your design succeed, is to place the pistol against the stomach of the present conjuncture, while stating that, without violent constraint, and observing an exact justice, as in all other States in the world, you are ready to furnish the necessary money, and if someone wishes to charge himself to do more, while submitting to a penalty in case of non-success, you will be disposed to follow his route. And the fourth, finally, which is the principal one, is to furnish honest wages to those who will serve the King in his finances, and not to permit anyone to profit an iota through indirect ways, [a practice] which is the source of all the trouble, and which has come to such a high point that it is senseless to approach persons of influence by any other route.

Now certainly this was speaking to the king's minister in a manner daring in its frankness. Boisguilbert himself thought so, for without retracting any of his statements, he proceeded in the remainder of the letter very diplomatically to guard against eventualities.

[16] This expression is always a reference to Colbert.

MM. the ministers have made it a principle to listen coldly to all the advice that could be given, cull out that which might be useful, and then to regard the author as a traitor or as a courtier whom one wished to see perish after his usefulness has ended. This conduct is neither that of a Christian nor of an honest pagan, and causes a minister always to move in darkness. That one who gave advice to the late M. Colbert on the *contrôle des exploits,* which is almost the only fiscal edict that can be said to have been advantageous to the people, had the Bastille for his recompense when he wished to demand [the reform] a little too quickly. And this was due to the fact that, until you [came], all the persons in [official] positions have had an interest much greater or more obvious than that of the success of their ministry, namely, the conservation of their position. They must have thought that they risked it if the public came to know that not all that which was perfect sprang from them alone, as I have given myself the honor to advise you many times. Nevertheless, the government of a State is something so difficult, and at the same time so delicate, that it has need of all, and it is not immune to such personal conduct. It is necessary, on the contrary, to sacrifice everything to it. It is this which has caused all the great princes, and [those] who governed best, often to be chided, as it were, by their ministers when [the former] knew them [to be] wise from experience and benevolence. There are outstanding examples in the reign of Henry IV with respect to the duke of Sully. This prince dared not make an expenditure of ten thousand livres for fear his minister would reproach him with the fact that there was nothing with which to pay his debts. I take the courage to give you this fact to show you that any master is badly served who wishes to hear only applause. You are far removed from this.[17]

Following this letter, and in further preparation for the interview, Boisguilbert sent a long list of *Maxims or Incontestable Principles to Reëstablish or Sustain France in the Present Conjuncture,* which hinge on the principle that it is essential "to have agriculture and commerce as the sole aim, as [they are] the only source of revenue, payment, or contribution of money." It must be understood once for all time that to fail to grow "the products that one neglects to make grow, because of the just fear of the possibility of being ruined thereby," and to fail to sell those which are grown, "as regularly happens on account of violent causes which can easily be stopped in a moment, is as if one gaily threw

[17] Letter of Feb. 8, 1702.

the money equivalent into a whirlpool. There is no difference between goods which one can sell when one wishes, and ready money." But to accomplish such ready convertibility of goods into money, it is necessary to regard the freedom of the highways as the source of all sorts of commerce, and consequently of wealth. "A sea filled with pirates is impassable; but the land in France is more covered with obstacles on its roads than all the most decried seas in the world." Finally he declares that it is essential

to employ superior individuals who understand the ways of the deprived life, regardless of birth and employment, in assuming as incontestable that the benefit of mind and merit will never be at the disposal (*nomination*) of names and of wealth. Few or no popes have been canonized since it has been necessary to choose from the cardinals, and again to exclude all those who are not Italians, or attached to any crown, that is to say, [to choose] from a dozen men. Canonize no one who may not have accomplished some miracle, at least in his profession, whatever that may be.[18]

The interview took place, but Boisguilbert was coolly received as a result of his temerity. He sulked in his tent for awhile thereafter, but not for long. In May he took up the battle once more:

At the last audience which you had the kindness to give me I thought that my presence gave you no pleasure at all, and that, as a result, my plan would be to show my regard for you by my silence in every respect on general affairs. Nevertheless, things have come to such a point of desolation that I dare say to you, my Lord, that if you wait a moment to have recourse to just taxes, [such] as exist in all the [other] kingdoms in the world, and not to confiscations by creation [of offices], the ordinary revenues will fail, that is to say, the taille and capitation will suffer a diminution, and the farmers general [of the aides and duanes] will demand rebates because of the failure of consumption.

The just contribution by powerful persons to taxes is so essential to the maintenance of a State, that in England, where it cannot be said that the great nobles lack pride, they pay taxes as a matter of course, and in France, where they are wholly submissive to the prince other-

[18] Boislisle was uncertain about the position of these *Maxims*, which he placed with the letter of Oct. 27, 1703. He thought they might belong with the letter of July 18, 1703. It seems to the present writer that they belong after the letter of Feb. 8, 1702, especially as in it Boisguilbert says he will continue to send maxims before his interview. They bear no relation to the other two letters and do to this one.

wise, they do not at all think it is acting contrary to this submission to refuse to pay that which is due him very legitimately according to the most ancient laws.[19] You will make thereupon, my Lord, such reflections as will please you. But I submit myself as guarantee to procure for you in fifteen days the fifty million livres that you lack, in which all the risk of failure is that the king will not receive the entire sum, because at the same time I shall form for the people double, nay triple, that which they will pay. There is where I end; my zeal or my anxiety for more than thirty years [has enabled me] to foresee, and [I have] written publicly that the manner in which France is governed will cause her to perish if it is not stopped. I speak only as do all the merchants and cultivators.[20]

Chamillart punished Boisguilbert through his purse, as he was seemingly to do regularly when the latter became too daring and gave displeasure. In October Boisguilbert wrote:

In 1689, when the generality of Rouen had the honor to have you as intendant, the King demanded the sum of forty thousand livres for new wages [21] from the court of this city. Difficulty was encountered in the apportionment, and you took the trouble to make it yourself, after having heard all the interested parties many times. It was found so just that the same rule has been used in all the taxes which have since been levied. But I am quite surprised to see that, in approximately the same sum which is demanded just now, the apportionment is all made, and I have a half more than I had in 1689, and all the other officials are eased considerably with the exception of Sieur Chevalier . . . who also has an increase. As this, my Lord, may be an important precedent for the future, not to be able to count on any certain rule on like occasion, and as my office has diminished two-thirds [in value] since 1689, and [has been] separated from the mayoralty, and from the lieutenancy of police, which forms a separate employment, I have convinced M. d'Herbigny that I should give my-

[19] Boisguilbert particularly quoted from the ordinance of Charles VII, in the year 1445: " 'We wish equality to be guarded among our subjects in the charges and burdens that they have to bear, without one carrying or being forced to carry the burdens and charges of another under the shelter (*ombre*) of privilege and of clericality or otherwise, and we wish the instructions and royal ordinances to be guarded according to their form and tenor.' "—*Le Détail*, p. 221.

[20] Letter of May 5, 1702.

[21] This was a euphemistic term for one of the multitudinous taxes levied upon the same thing. De Souligné, a French *émigré*, lifting rather bodily from *Le Détail de la France* and publishing as *The Desolation of France Demonstrated* (London, 1697, p. 18), said that the king was always demanding sums from the offices under the names of taxes, loans, increase of wages, additions, new rights, prerogatives to the office, etc.

self the honor to write to you, as he also promised me to do, to beseech you to send him the facts with regard to this matter, in order that you may be informed more clearly concerning it.[22]

For once Chamillart, deigning to reply, sent a scathing answer to Boisguilbert:

The detail of this affair of the increase of wages passes through the hands of M. d'Armenonville. He has wished to follow, apparently, the memoirs that you have given him in having a new apportionment made in the increase of wages in the bailiwick of Rouen, in which he has increased you considerably because it was known that you were more able to pay than the others. Remember, on this occasion, since you beg for it, that all your project hinges on the plan of making the burdens proportionate to the property of those who pay, and that not all men know how to be just.[23]

No more unjust answer could have been made. Boisguilbert, as he was later to remind Chamillart, had always prided himself on his contributions to the government, and he was desirous of aiding France in her need. This was another matter. It was a tax upon a particular piece of property, in which certainly as to the sum due, one of the fundamental principles for which he stood, was being abrogated. He was finding that there were other ways to punish presumptuous advisers to the king's ministers who urge haste than to send them to the Bastille.

For six months Boisguilbert was silent; but he was not idle. In this period he wrote *Factum de la France*. His unquenchable spirit of optimism came again to the fore. After all it was not a personal conflict between him and Chamillart which mattered. It was the existence of France which was at stake. It was Boisguilbert's first principle of conduct that personal interest must give way to the general interest. This principle he rigidly applied to himself. France needed him. His differences with others were in the realm of ideas, and the conflict resulting did not carry over beyond that realm.

In July 1703 he wrote again. The letter is noteworthy because in it he described *Factum de la France,* and first proposed to provide additional revenue of eighty million livres which was to

22 Letter of Oct. 23, 1702.

23 This answer was noted, as were all answers, on the margin of the letter to which it is a reply.

continue thereafter to form the underlying theme of his letters.

Although the least degree of prudence would make me close my mouth forever on general affairs,[24] nevertheless, in view of the fact that the evil I have always foreseen increases daily, as well as the number of the enemies of the King, whereas the means to resist them diminishes visibly, I have not been able to prevent myself, after six months, from composing a letter which I have the honor to address to you. In this I offer [to provide] a sum of eighty million livres a year beyond the ordinary revenue, even [with] the capitation in the state that it is. This includes fifty million livres of extraordinary [revenue, a sum] that it seems to me you showed me there is required, ten million livres [for payment of *rentes*] that I believe the King or the State has contracted in increase of debts, and twenty million livres for a fleet which is necessary not only in order to procure an advantageous peace, but even in relation to the utility of the people. The blockaded sea costs France more than one hundred million livres a year, as much on account of the diminution [in price] that this brings to the merchandise which must go out, as from the increase [in price] which that entering receives. Nevertheless, although [the proposal of an additional] imposition of eighty million livres on the people may make me appear unduly credulous, I can say, on the contrary, that having submitted my manuscript work to an infinite number of rich and perspicacious persons, although they might easily conclude that I was placing their capitation four or five times as high, yet they heaped benedictions upon me, because I immediately established four times as much in [the value of] their property.

I say *immediately,* my Lord, and for twenty pages I overwhelm those who would wish to attack this truth, in giving back to them with usury the ridicule with which they pretend to clothe me. I have all the people on my side, who demand as a sole favor that capital [25] be not at all attacked, on the faith of which all commerce depends, and that capital sums (*sommes immobilières*) shall not be demanded from it. They destroy all kinds of consumption because the people find it impossible to furnish them except by stopping all expenditures. This destroys the value of provisions, and makes it impossible for any farmer to pay his master, which creates the height of poverty, as is proved today. Please take the trouble, my Lord, to inform yourself of

[24] Reference to the additional tax burden he had received, and which he obviously regarded as having been imposed to punish him.

[25] *Les immeubles.* This term is at times used by Boisguilbert in the sense of capital investment and *les meubles* as income. Here the reference is to resale of offices which, destroying the value of the old ones and creating new exempts, placed additional burdens on the remaining payers of the taille. Offices, according to Boisguilbert, were by legal fiction classed as real property. See also note, p. 122.

[the price] at which young coneys have been sold this summer in Paris. You will find that those of Gaillon, which are always the most expensive, have been at less than five livres on the average, and the others at three livres, that is to say, indeed, less than it costs to raise and transport them. Those of the farmer of M. the archbishop are worth fifteen hundred livres, yet he cannot pay a sol on his rent, while the King does not receive the hundredth part of the loss that the cause of this disorder brings to the State. This is only a barometer, and it is the same with all other products. Nevertheless, to bring this to an end, it is necessary only to give peace to immovables, which will take only a half-hour, just as, at the siege of La Rochelle, bread, which was worth one hundred sols the pound in the city, was placed at one sol at the end of an hour when the gates were opened. If Cardinal Richelieu had said that he could not allow this city to capitulate and eliminate famine as a result, because the King then had a war on in Italy or Germany, would it not have been said that instead of being a great man he had lost his sense? Everywhere today this same idea is held, and even more. It is thought that there is no other resource to draw France from the most momentous conjuncture that she has ever experienced, than the same methods which have ruined her in time of peace. She has been able heretofore to make mistakes with impunity on account of her great power, and that indeed as a result of Providence who has wished it as a brake, in order to conserve a kind of equilibrium, which is the support of States.[26] But at present France has too much of nothing, or rather she has need of everything, and the defects of the past will become useful to her, because the profiting from her losses will be a kind of storehouse for the necessities of today. For I maintain that only two hours are required, as at the siege of La Rochelle, because it is only necessary to cease a simple act of violence done to nature, and not to create anything or to form [anything] new. I beg you very humbly, my Lord, to accord me three hours of your very precious time to bring you my work myself. This time will be longer than the preceding [interview], but very brief in relation to the design. I will wager for my temerity, my police office, for which I paid thirty thousand écus, having reimbursed the vicomte for a part, and you can create a new one if you do not think that you have never spent time better in your life. The most difficult thing is to persuade [you] that a subject concerning whom you have been given all sorts of pictures, can be the author of such a great work. But I glory in having a singular character, without which I should not have unusual ideas.[27]

[26] A reference, evidently, to the principle of balance of power enunciated at the treaty of Westphalia a half century before.

[27] Letter of July 18, 1703.

Chamillart did not accord the three hours interview desired. He was, however, sufficiently interested to reply:

I shall believe three hours and three months well employed to labor at such a work as the one which you propose to me. But I apprehend indeed, from the knowledge that I have acquired of affairs over a long period, that there is very much more chimera in your project than reality. If you wish to send [the manuscript] to me, I promise you to read it, and if I find anything the least practical therein I assure you that I shall profit from it.

In October 27 of the same year Boisguilbert wrote again. An interview had been arranged for the following week. From it he expected much. He has importuned Chamillart with his letters for fifteen years, he says, because he thought that under his ministry France's problems could be solved; it was impossible for them to be solved under the others.[28] De Vaubourg, who had been intendant at Rouen for fourteen months, he declares, after daily intercourse does not accuse him of theorizing as does Desmaretz.[29] Boisguilbert quotes De Vaubourg as having said openly that Colbert would have called upon him for advice because of his knowledge of agriculture and commerce. He refers to the fact that he is exposed to all that can be said against the most degraded of men,

but you will permit me to say to you that, leaving out of account that which is common to me along with many greater men than I, my life has passed for fifty-seven years without any reproach or youthful behavior, and a perpetuity is attached to my duties and to my fortune for which I am indebted, after God, wholly to myself alone. This vindicates me as far as those who judge without envy, passion, or prejudice [are concerned]. Besides that, my printed works will be a great help to me as well as to you, my Lord. The people will pay [taxes] voluntarily when they see that you serve them openly and above board, and not with bombs from which *ils sauvent qu'il peut.*

Again he lays down principles in preparation for his audience, the first of which, as the basis for the others, is the recognition of the past ruin of France. He wishes to arrive with this agreed upon.[30]

Boisguilbert, who had been so proud of his self-made fortune,

[28] Reference to Le Peletier, who succeeded Colbert, and was controller general from 1683 to 1689, and to Pontchartrain, who held the position from 1689 to 1699.
[29] Desmaretz and De Vaubourg were brothers, and nephews of Colbert.
[30] Letter of Oct. 27, 1703.

was beginning to suffer greatly from the pressure of *affaires extraordinaires*. In January of the following year he was moved to speak of it:

> I do not at all have the effrontery to speak to you of a personal affair in which I am asked for more than thirty thousand livres, with the suppression at the same time of the thing taxed. If I had not paid one hundred thousand livres and more since your ministry,[31] perhaps I could pay them. It is only the impossibility which can prevent me from obeying as I have done all my life. I was the sole judge in Normandy in 1693 who sacrificed neither his person nor his property in the demand for new wages. If you would indeed wish to have the goodness to give me some delay in view of the one hundred thousand livres, which make my case unusual, perhaps I would be in a position to satisfy.

He was led to hope to be given more time to make this payment from the fact that Chamillart had just received his proposals with some degree of favor. He quotes from the letter of the latter: "You have done me the honor to indicate in your last [letter] that you would exert all your powers close to the King for the success of my enterprise. . . . I await this success with the utmost impatience." The only favor he asks in turn is that he be allowed to administer the reforms in some region which he would make "a model for all the kingdom."

> My eighty million livres are neither visionary nor problematical, as it is neither visionary nor problematical that all grain and liquors are sold at present by their possessors only at the loss of all it has cost to produce them. Since this causes the ruin of all the vocations which depend for their existence upon them, you ought not to be astonished that everyone is poverty-stricken, and the poor more than the rich. When grains are at a still lower price [the poor] will not be able to procure them from the moment that the rich, not being paid, can give them nothing to earn. Here, my Lord, are elementals of government which one cannot doubt.

Boisguilbert was eager to publish. He delicately felt out Chamillart on the subject: "My last writings, if they were public, as they are not through pure respect to you, would cover with shame the objections of the lack of specie, which is not a raw material (*denrée primitive*) in France, as one assumes, and as they

[31] That is, in five years.

are in Peru." [82] This was one subject, however, upon which Chamillart was adamant, as Boisguilbert was to learn.

As early as March 14, 1700, Boisguilbert wrote that he had sent a memoir on money.

> You will remember . . . that at the beginning of your ministry I assured you that you would double the revenue of the King, as well as that of the people, within four years from that time. But as this cannot be done on the basis of the existing principles it has been necessary to establish the errors of the past. I think I have more than done this with regard to lands and commerce. And as money plays a great rôle in this, although to this time no one has given attention to it, I thought that you would approve my sending you [a memoir] which I owe to the study I have given to [this rôle played by money]. [It is good] unless I am mistaken, which I have never been thus far, thanks be to God, in anything which I have undertaken.[83]

He turned to the subject again, and in July 1704 wrote a remarkable series of eight letters. The first one is devoted largely to money. It apparently impressed Desmaretz, through whose hands all his letters seem to have passed before reaching Chamillart. On its envelope he noted: "Observe the underlined places. July 7, 1704. Examine with M. Ch[amillart]." The second deals with money and credit.[84] The third summarizes the first two letters, and undertakes further to show that there is no shortage of money in the country. In this he also announced that three other letters dealing with the sale of goods would follow.

These letters were the result of the fact that to bring specie in from other countries, in itself, had no place in his reforms. Chamillart and Desmaretz, on the other hand, thought it was a pure chimera to pretend to raise eighty million livres of additional revenue without an import of specie. Boisguilbert wrote in an effort to convince them that they were in error. Essentially his doctrine was: Take care of trade and money will take care of itself.

On July 9 he wrote,

> The next-to-the-last letter that I have had the honor to write to you, should have made you understand that to make a country rich it is not a question of there being much silver, but that it should march and

[82] Letter of Jan. 6, 1704.
[83] This memoir referred to is missing.
[84] For a portion of the first letter and all the second, see below, pp. 211ff., 215ff.

circulate always, and of what this celerity consists, and what causes it. My last one has shown you that when this speed of movement of silver does not suffice for the number of masters it is obliged to serve, it produces an infinity of children, whom it clothes with all its authority. These are bills of exchange, or paper money (*argent en papier*), that is to say, inexhaustible matter provided there be enough workmen to coin it. These [workmen] are the merchants or courtiers of consumption.

His proposal to increase the income of the king and of the people, he states, is possible through the aid of the increased circulation of money in the country and the credit instruments which would arise with increased consumption, but he will also show that there is no actual shortage of specie in France. On the contrary, he maintains that there is almost double that which existed in "1660 and the year or two following," when "the country was unquestionably as rich again"; when "estates rented and sold at double, and offices at quadruple what they are at today."

There are other proofs of this decreased wealth:

The bureaus of consumption, or signs of prosperity, such as taverns and tennis courts, suffer the same fate. In Paris alone, although the place the least affected (*flétri*) on account of carrying booty there from the provinces, there were one hundred and sixty tennis courts in 1660, rented for more than the sixty which remain, and which are reduced daily. At Rouen, from twenty-five [they have been reduced] to three only. And it is the same throughout the province. Caen alone has one, although all the closed places had them formerly. . . . As for taverns, I believe that ten thousand have been destroyed in Normandy alone. Nevertheless, with all that, my Lord, I maintain that in the conjuncture of depression where we are, there exists almost double the silver that was found in those years of wealth and abundance.

Here is, if you [please], the proof in writing, and whatever interest those who surround you may have not to agree to these most certain truths, it is at least necessary for them to keep quiet on the following: In 1642 only two hundred million livres were found in the reform [of the currency], and in 1694, there were more than five thousand and forty million livres, leaving out of account the proportion of silver vessels which had more than quadrupled. But, my Lord, this growth or increase did not at all come suddenly, but by gradation, year by year, in proportion as the metal arrives in Europe from the countries where it is born, in which the production (*fabrication*) is approximately always the same, as well as the quota that France takes in the custody of ships and galleons. For this reason in 1660 the kingdom could scarcely have acquired more than one hundred million livres of increase, in order to allow it to be five hundred and forty million livres thirty-four years afterwards in 1694.

Since that time, those who reason very badly, or rather who, being the cause of all the disorder, accuse heaven rather than themselves for bringing about the depression, pretend that quantities have passed into foreign countries, voluntarily for the payment of armies, and secretly by indirect interest. This is perhaps true to some extent; but it is necessary to agree that it has come in since that time, especially after the union of France with Spain, whereby the first has had more than her share in the increase in the past years. Moreover, the silver taken into Italy [for the army], is not absolutely lost, and you very sagely permitted trade in the grains of Languedoc with [the Italians], which brings back a part of the silver.

The armies of France and Spain procure the greater part of their needs at Milan, where it is known that the Swiss make great commerce, almost all merchants, who come to buy in France, especially at Lyons. Thus I maintain, that all considered, there is as much silver as in 1694, and the more or less has nothing to do with my proposition, for, finally, should I agree with all my contradictors, they would not ask me to decrease the amount by two hundred and forty million livres. This would be an exaggeration which would not establish their case, since it is far from being the same as in 1660. I am not at all a dreamer, my Lord, in what I have advanced as practicable in two hours because of the possibility of sale of goods. I maintain that there is a sufficient amount [of silver] to form both four hundred million livres for the people and eighty million livres for the King.

Boisguilbert struggled against the prevailing ideas with respect to money, stating that "silver is indubitably only a letter of reciprocal exchange for the delivery of goods. Whether letters of this nature be written on paper of large or small volume, whether there be few or many words, does not matter. The only essential is the quantity of money that one gives on order to pay. One lives on goods and not on silver, which is worth only as much as one can procure one's needs with it."

Following this letter he sent a beautiful one which is essentially a transition from the three which had preceded to those coming immediately after.

As you assuredly understand me clearly, I shall not explain myself further, but shall pass, if you please, to the remedy. This depends on the principle that it is not money in itself which makes men or countries rich and happy. It is purchasing power, or the amount of it which is possessed, [which] places one in a state to procure the needs of life. I shall mention [in passing] that the silver cooking utensils which are found in Mexico do not prevent her from being worse off than in places where they are made of iron. It is, then, not silver, my Lord, but commodities and provisions which are the end and the object of prosperity. That is not all. However liberal nature may be in a country, men are necessary to make [products] grow and to consume [them]. Without this the owners of the best lands are no better off than if they possessed sands, since in the final analysis, every country and every kingdom is a pasture which is worth only as much as there are animals to graze it, and animals which are not muzzled. When this [muzzling] happens, as it has in France today, both [pasture and animals] perish, and the master as a consequence. It is this divorce, my Lord, or this separation of beasts and pasture, which forms *la misère* of France. There is silver, you must not doubt it; there are goods, and men to consume them. But the latter are muzzled, so that both the pasture and the beasts perish, and silver, which is only the servant of commerce, remains useless. This happens as soon as it reposes a moment for lack of a master to enjoy it. More than five or six million reasonable creatures who drink only water as an ordinary rule, and at least half of the hogsheads of liquor which are lost, whether [actually] produced or from lack of production, not to speak of other products, present the same picture of pasture with muzzled animals.

He extols the importance of domestic over foreign trade which was the object of so much greater solicitude:

[It has been] thought to compensate for the ruin of domestic commerce by attention to foreign trade, which has never been and never will be more than the hundredth part of the former. . . . You know, my Lord, with what pains, and with what expense the companies of Guinea, Madagascar, and the Indies have been established, and you are not ignorant, furthermore, of their little success. Had they been as advantageous as they have been failures they would never have compensated for the tenth part of the losses which these so-called heroes [85] caused within [the country]. It is not at all necessary today, in order to remedy the disorder, to cross the seas and go seek (*mendier*) foreigners. Thus the allegation of the war without becomes absolutely vain and frivolous. It is a question only of giving peace within the State, where a frightful war goes on, first between the King and his people, between whom a continual commerce is necessary. In order to bring this about it is necessary to establish certainty by the

[85] Colbert and those responsible for the policy.

observation of laws of the strictest justice, whose contravention has always prevented [certainty] between whatever sort of subjects or regions this may be. It is necessary to use it from region to region, from year to year, and from product to product, all of which must be in a perpetual traffic, in order to aid each other reciprocally as is required. Thus, being in a continual balance with regard to that of which they have too much and that of which they have too little, instead of two extremities, which are always naturally very defective, there will be formed a very perfect whole. It is this alone which can make a State very happy, whereas the contrary can only make it very wretched, as the kingdom is today. It is known from experience, that it is found in this sorrowful situation, not from lack of men, goods and money, but because these three things, very perfect in their union, and in their accord, and perishing in their separation, far from aiding one another by a continual concord for the common good, are found in a perpetual war, and work day and night only for their mutual destruction. It is this reconciliation, my Lord, which is the problem, and it is this commerce which must be reëstablished.

To end this homily, Boisguilbert gives one of his homely but effective illustrations:

In order to finish this letter, my Lord, I have the audacity to say to you that Messieurs, your predecessors, believed that authority could take the place of everything, and that the laws of nature, of equity, and of reason were made only for those who are not absolute. They did not dream that it is only of God of whom one may wisely believe: *ipse dixit, et factu sunt*. They did as that one who foolishly stated that oats were not necessary to make a horse go; that [the urge] was supplied by whip and spur. They can [be used] for the first journey; the second one kills the animal and places the master on foot. Messieurs, your predecessors, had a rule of whip and spur; but you will remain on the road if you give oats, which is much more conformable to your inclinations. It is on this [basis] that I offer you my services, which will be the subject of my succeeding letters, that is to say, the reëstablishment of bread and wine by unmuzzling and freeing the mouths of beasts. After that do not doubt that these [products] will march, and silver [also] as a consequence. It recognizes no other orders than that of consumption, in which these two products hold so great a place.[86]

On July 20 Boisguilbert wrote a long letter welding together the factors of commerce, consumption, and money.

[86] Letter of July 1704, no day of the month given, but belonging between those of July 9 and 15.

A greater error [he says] can scarcely be seen than that which rules over the greater part of men with respect to money. They almost all look upon it as a product born every moment in the bowels of the earth, as in Spain, which perishes through usage, as it does in that country; whereas in France it is necessary to consider it as a continual child of consumption which is born and dies at all hours of the day, without, nevertheless, ever being born or dying except by fiction. It has these two destinies with relation both to every individual who receives it and to all who give it up; but in so far as money itself is concerned, it subsists always in a like quantity with slight diminution plus that replaced from new colonies as [the new metal] comes to us annually from the country of its natural origin. It is easy to see by this reasoning that as it is the effect of consumption, it is likewise the object of it, and that it plays these two parts at the same time with respect to those who carry on trade by means of it. It dies with the [buyer] and is born with the [seller] as soon as both have profited in a market or trade. But as soon as they can no longer agree or concur, the silver and the products of each dwell at their sides, not without violence to both. Thus the interest, both of the possessors of silver and of products, is that there be much consumption, which can never be unless there is very much commerce. In this way the well-being of all classes, whatever they may be, depends on the bringing by everyone of the value of his vocation to the highest point possible, in the certainty that all subjects are so many parts of a clock which coördinate in the common movement of the machine, the derangement of one sufficing to stop [the clock] entirely. Nevertheless . . . everyone thinks only to profit at the expense of his neighbor, without ever considering that [the latter's] destruction will soon bring about his own. This [in effect is to] declare a strong war on silver, [so that] instead of a free course, it can almost never make a step that is not hindered, being in motion only so long as there are buyers as well as sellers of all the sorts of merchandise which are at stake. From the moment that one [factor], namely, the buyer, is missing, the other multiplies more than is necessary, the product remains [motionless] and [likewise] silver as a consequence. It is this which forms the depression.

"Galimatias!" So noted Desmaretz on this letter. As schoolmaster to the ministers of France Boisguilbert had not been very successful. But he expressed hope in this very letter: "I believe, my Lord, that I have made you understand why, although this reëstablishment [of commerce] would be so easy, it has not been done. It is for the same reason that, if you were not in power (far from hoping for it), I would not write a line to propose it, never having liked to lose my time." Unfortunately, he still had much to learn about Chamillart.

The last of these July letters, a singularly revealing one, was written two days later. Here is shown the many-sided character of the man; the dynamic personality which calmed itself by composing Latin verses; the Norman, devoted to commerce and the promotion of his fortune, engaged in what he regarded as the anomalous position of adviser to the king's ministers; a d'Artagnan challenging all comers, not with the sword, but with the pen.

There is no one with whom I refuse entering into combat, but [I accept] on condition that [the contest] will be by writing, and that each pleader may continue only for three lines at the most. There is no need of longer discourse when it is a question only of fact, and of yes and no. Let no other expressions than these two terms be received, which, although excluded from the country to which I belong, have not ceased to form all my jurisprudence. In my picture in Latin verse, which I made in an outburst of fever which did not permit me to read, write, dictate, and question, the sole employments of my life, my spirit, which had received a surcharge of warmth, commanded me as a beginning:

Quamvis Neustraicis ad lucem venerim in oris,
Nulla venoenatae traxi contagia terrae.

In truth, my Lord, you understand well that [the mixing in] the inquietude of public affairs, not being the means to adjust (*accomoder*) his own, would not seem to be the proper rôle for a Norman. Nevertheless I am [taking part in these affairs,] and, although my imagination does me a favor, and does not conceal any of the disagreeable circumstances which follow this conduct, I can say assuredly that I have never repented it, since you are not made like the others, and since you know more than any of the Messieurs, your predecessors, considering that one does not vex you in wishing to apprise you on matters of fact, [an occupation which] it can be seen that one never finishes.

Finally, my Lord, to continue to sacrifice the rôle of a Norman, I shall not dissimulate at all that there is no middle ground for you to take in surveying this scorn of commerce concerning which I have dared supplicate you for a month.[87]

No response appears to have been made to these letters. Boisguilbert waited a month. On August 22 he wrote to Vauban. His attention to the public interest, which had been the principal occu-

[87] Letter of July 22, 1704.

pation of his life, had given him the honor to know Vauban personally for eight or nine years. That is, he had known him since the publication of *Le Détail de la France*, which had influenced Vauban so greatly.[38] Now, he says, the progress of the public disorders has served as "the sharpest goad" to make him employ himself with more "exactitude." Thus "whatever applause the public may have given to my first work, that work is nothing, according to experts, in comparison to that which I have done since." He states what he can do for the king and the people. But the opposition of the court, which is associated with all the partisans,[39] he declares, prevents the ministers from bringing about reforms. Finally he asks two hours of Vauban's time for a secret interview such as took place eight years before.

Whether this previous interview was the only one which Vauban and Boisguilbert had had, or whether it was simply an interview which had occurred under unusual circumstances, is not clear. That they had been in touch with one another with respect to Vauban's dime since that time is clearly indicated in Boisguilbert's letter to Chamillart on June 13, 1700, in which the impression given is that of a face-to-face discussion.[40]

Vauban immediately wrote to Chamillart:

I have found, Monsieur, on arriving here, a letter from M. de Boisguilbert, lieutenant general of Rouen, which I have believed it necessary to send to you because he promises mountains and marvels if only he is heard. As this has to do with your ministry of finance, I have thought it necessary to give you notice of it immediately. I know well that he is little awakened from the standpoint of intelligence; but that does not prevent him from being capable of giving (*d'ouvrir*) good counsel. That is why I believe you would not be wrong to have him come to Étang[41] when you are there. Sometimes the worst fools give the very best counsel to the wisest. Have the goodness in time and place to remember the request that I have made for my nephew.

It is impossible to take the remark concerning Boisguilbert's

[38] The book had so impressed Vauban, says Saint-Simon, that he had wished to meet its author. Boislisle states that they had met in 1694.

[39] See below, p. 120. [40] See above, pp. 35–36.

[41] Chamillart's country place.

intelligence seriously without casting serious reflections upon Vauban's own intelligence. Vauban himself had felt the impact of Boisguilbert's penetrating criticism, and other contemporaries, including the Duke of Saint-Simon, appreciated the capacity of the man, who, through his influence upon the Physiocrats and upon Adam Smith, was to have so great a part in shaping the course of economic theory. It is more reasonable to think that Vauban understood the mentality of the controller general, whose limitations were beginning to be well understood by 1704,[42] and that the reflection is in reality upon him rather than upon Boisguilbert. It is also possible that Vauban was thinking of Boisguilbert's peculiar temperament. Looking upon him as a relative, he may have felt free to play upon his idiosyncrasies in order to flatter Chamillart provided it brought the interview which Boisguilbert so greatly desired and which Vauban was generous enough to assist in bringing about.

Another month went by, and on September 21 Boisguilbert again wrote to Chamillart. It is a letter of one who feels full of confidence in his own achievements. All the authors of great discoveries had not so much to show as I, he boasts. No one said ten years ago that *Le Détail de la France* was the work of a crazy person, he declares.[43] He wants Chamillart to adopt all his views, but to change nothing without "planning with the people by means of the preceding publication of measures that are going to be taken." Again he comes back to money. The "importance" of money "is not at all subject to ordinary laws," he declares. He has written a treatise, he states, which is only preliminary to another treatise. In this he shows that the scarcer silver is in France, the more there is of it.[44] He begs for a half-hour of Chamillart's time in order to read to him this short pamphlet on money.

[42] See Cadet, pp. 69–70, for the estimates of Mme de Maintenon and Saint-Simon.

[43] This statement leads one to think that Boisguilbert had heard of Vauban's remark.

[44] This refers to the writing of *Causes de la rareté de l'argent* as preliminary to *Dissertation sur la nature des richesses, de l'argent et des tributs.* This is verified by the order of the memoirs in his first complete edition, in which their order follows the order in which they are mentioned in the letters as they are composed.

This request for an interview elicited a disagreeable response from Chamillart:

Retract two things in your system, both equally false; after that I will listen to you as much as you wish. But as my mind is not as subtle as yours, I am obliged to tell you that we shall never agree as long as your reasoning does not approach to a greater extent certain truths which all men are capable of understanding. The two things that I hold false are: first, that the scarcer money is in France, the more of it there is. A quack of this sort will push his reasoning to that point; but he will be refuted (*confondu*) by a physician more skilled and more substantial than he. . . ." [The second point concerns the financiers.] They are protected only as much as is necessary. They can easily be dispensed with when something better is available, and it is that which reacts against you and your reasoning: to attack me at a point so weak, and which has never made any impression on me. I wish indeed to give you two hours, eight days from tomorrow at Fontainebleau.

Boisguilbert strongly resented being regarded as a visionary and as a theorist, an attitude toward him which was his handicap in dealing both with Chamillart and Desmaretz. Having thanked Chamillart for inviting him to come to his residence on the following Thursday, he insists that they should first reach an agreement as to what the specific marks are which differentiate practice from speculation.

Here, if you please, is what they are, and have the goodness to remember them, in order that this may be agreed upon when I shall have the honor to arrive in your presence. Without this it will only result that I shall demand pardon for my temerity, and take leave of you. Speculation then, my Lord, consists in working on projects formed in the head, which have never yet appeared, and the like of which has never been seen. Practice, on the contrary, only imitates and conforms itself to that which is already established and followed with success and applause by the greatest number. Speculation promises and works miracles from what it invents, but without any guarantee on its part, knowing the uncertainty of sciences, and consequently of theory; practice, on the contrary, sees to it that its subjects gain their life on its success when they have once attained the usage of their art, and it is a market place without fear. Speculation cannot reduce its dreams to writings, that there is not raised immediately an infinity of contradictors who combat the new doctrine on paper. It is that which brings about the two hundred sects or heresies in the

Christian religion, which mutually condemn one another. When practice writes, there is no opposition, and all the books which have been written on the arts are still without reply. On this picture, my Lord, judge, if you please, the process as much by the past as by the present. Let the defenders of the first seek as much as they please. I am sure that they will find no example for that which has been practiced since 1660. As for myself, I maintain that I propose nothing except what is and has always been in use in all the nations of the world, even in France until the innovation noted.[45]

Boisguilbert could thus be exceedingly modest at times. Nevertheless, he seems sincerely to have believed that his two great demands, free roads and just taxes, had been the common heritage of mankind until evil days had fallen upon France.

The interview was highly successful. Boisguilbert was elated. He wrote to Chamillart to thank him for having received him so courteously, and expressed his certainty of Chamillart's success if the latter's views are well executed.[46] After years of disappointment, Boisguilbert began to feel that he would see the fruition of his dream of a France regenerated. But in his exultation and his eagerness he had overstepped the bounds Chamillart had set for him. He told the latter that he was sending a summary of his work on grains. "It is printed to render the reading less fatiguing, having permission for two leaves without privilege." He has withdrawn, he says, the few copies to send them to Chamillart himself, to Desmaretz, and also to M. d'Armenonville.[47] Boisguilbert had long wanted to publish his work on grains, which had been written for the public quite as much as for the ministers. This opportunity was an entering wedge for him to obtain permission to do so.

Without waiting for a reply he wrote again that in the following month he would send a summary of a work which he thought should be published. It shows, he states, that there is a "solidarity of interest in the same merchandise which causes the good or evil which one part experiences to be communicated immediately to all goods, as a human body." This doctrine, he says, must be

[45] Letter of Nov. 1, 1704.
[46] Boisguilbert always generously or diplomatically spoke of any concession he obtained from Chamillart as the latter's views.
[47] Letter of Nov. 14, 1704.

made public to make all France see that it is to the interest of the entire country that the conditions in the provinces of the aides, duanes, and arbitrary taille be corrected.[48]

Filled with hope for the success of his reforms, Boisguilbert grew bold. He had been asking for years for an election to be confided to him. Now he asked that he be given a generality. He would make it a model for the whole country, he said, on Chamillart's account, and not on his own. "I do not seek individual glory. I shall be only too well recompensed for the service that I should have the honor to render to you and to the public, in the part that I should take in a general reëstablishment." "I am filled with all the defects in the world, my Lord, but I possess a sort of merit which is to succeed in all my enterprises, sacrificing everything, religion almost, for the execution of that which I have once undertaken."

He offers to take the generality at his own risk and peril. For thirty years, he says, he has prepared himself by the practice of all the details, and the knowledge of all the regions in the kingdom. His mind would be very stupid if he did not have some advantages over those whom the *première sortie* from Paris places in possession of the government of the provinces. The ruin of his own family would mean less to him than the pleasure he would derive from having contributed to the reëstablishment of the public.[49]

This letter marked the apex of Boisguilbert's hopes. His faith and his effervescent spirit caused him to forget that Chamillart could punish him cruelly whenever he became too presumptuous. He had scarcely mailed this letter when he received a reply to his preceding one, reprimanding him severely for printing the treatise on grain. The content can only be determined by Boisguilbert's reply. He does not think, he says, that writing is made public by being printed, when no copies of it are to be found, or that by doing so he exposes Chamillart to evil consequences on the part of the people, in making him imitate Sully who had declared war on

[48] This reference is to *Dissertation sur la nature des richesses.*
[49] Letter of Nov. 20, 1704.

the enemies of the exportation of grain. He does not think that these two faults merit what he calls the greatest of punishments, namely, Chamillart's indignation. The reprimand on his two faults has justice and foundation provided Chamillart thinks he has worked for thirty years, and has importuned him for fifteen out of pure imagination, and if there is little evidence that he can contribute without violence and without difficulty to finding the sums required.

It is certain, he continues, that similar crimes have little relation to the penalty he is drawing, and that it would be advantageous to convert it into a simple reprimand. Religion does not permit one to believe that a man, "whatever his age" can ever pass for an "incorrigible." When he says that all the money that the king needs can be provided in fifteen days without government borrowing, or without desolation, he has not expressed merely his own individual views.

> [I am] simply more sincere or more imprudent than other men. The very great opinion that I have of your integrity made me think that I alone did justice to it, and that the silence of others was criminal. [I was] far from finding myself alone culpable, as I find [myself to be] from a sad experience. The cruelest [thing] is that I see myself deprived of my sole resource, namely, the hope of ending the evils in which my situation gives me a part proportionate to the movement I have taken to stop them.

He finishes by saying sadly, and with an air of finality, that

> My last work will be on money. I shall take the courage to send it to you in manuscript in a month, while respecting, nevertheless, my ban, since you have condemned me to it. It is a work which would be much applauded if it were made public, since I prove that people reason on this metal a little more grossly than is done on vines. I would only have to abandon the manuscript to chance; as there is nothing except respect for persons of position, the publishers would seize it immediately, as they did my first book. But I shall console myself easily for the deprivation of this pleasure, if, being addressed to you alone, it can obtain for me pardon for my crimes. These can make you change with respect to me, but cannot diminish the attachment, the individual esteem, the great opinion of your understanding and your integrity, as well as the very profound respect with which

you have permitted me to say for fifteen years, my Lord, your very humble and very obedient servant,

Boisguilbert [50]

This profoundly moving letter written by one who had devoted his life to France, and who was being punished like a child, must have made Chamillart feel that he had been unduly harsh. He answered immediately and more at length than usual. He is even more desirous than is Boisguilbert to see the latter's plans for revenue succeed, he tells him.

Nothing prevents you from continuing, except your itching desire to publish. But, since unhappily not all that which you propose is as good as you are persuaded it is, there are indeed people who would read your works without understanding them. As you have condemned many [books] which perhaps have not merited it, if you wish to abstain from seeking the plaudits of the public until it is the King's pleasure to give a final consent to it, you will find no one who interests himself more than I in the success of your enterprise.[51]

Boisguilbert's devotion to Chamillart was deep. The contact with him through these letters, moreover, always encouraged him to think that he might be able to aid France as he knew no one else could. Had this link with the central authorities been broken, Boisguilbert would have been filled with despair. Chamillart's letter raised him from the depths of discouragement to a renewed hope.

If his reply, as well as his preceding letter, is humble it is because he lived in a disciplined age. But along with the humility of his answer there is an undercurrent of sharpness and courage which is unmistakable. He refers Chamillart to his preceding letter as answering his demand that he give up the desire to publish. Whatever the self-love which reigns among those who write, he continues, he will sacrifice the applause he could expect from the public on the publication of his works. "If I had not already been of this mind, the praise that the examiners have given me on all the book, of which this leaf is only an abstract,[52] would have made

[50] Letter of Nov. 25, 1704.

[51] This letter, according to Boisguilbert's reply of Dec. 2, was written on Nov. 29, 1704.

[52] This indicates that the work printed in 1704 was *Mémoire sur les bleds*, and not *Traité des grains*, as is commonly assumed.

me succumb to the temptation, by not concealing the manuscript very carefully." Boisguilbert quotes Chamillart as saying that he speaks "evil of those who do not merit it." His reply is that he names no person; he makes "war only on errors, not believing any more than did you when you came to Normandy in 1685, as it seems to me, with the other commissioners of the Council, that the purpose of your trip was to make a panegyric on the methods established since 1660. At least the circular letters carried nothing approaching it, any more than the owners of vineyards in the election of Mantes, with the fall going to fifteen parts in sixteen . . . are very much disposed to wish that the civic crown be accorded to the authors of such conditions."

If his own expressions are strong, he asserts, they are "much less vigorous than those found in many books published with privilege, notably the memoirs of M. de Sully, Mézeray, and even Saint-Évremond. All my doctrine has never and will never contain more than a word, namely: Give to the people and they will give to you." [53]

But the "itching desire to publish" as Chamillart had called it, was still chafing Boisguilbert. The persistence which had always urged him on would not now allow him to give up hope of winning Chamillart's consent. He seemed to feel that it was Desmaretz, director of finances, and close to Chamillart, who was especially influencing the latter. He thus proceeded to write him a long letter setting forth conditions in France, including the changes in the price level, which grain had not shared since 1660, because of the restriction on its export. He warns Desmaretz that things have come to such a state that continuation of existing methods will be fatal. "Judge, sir, if a monarchy can hold for a long time with such methods, especially when attacked by all Europe. . . ." Finally he begs him to intervene to have Chamillart let him publish his treatise on grains.[54]

Again he turns to Chamillart, who has obviously reprimanded him for pressing for too hurried action:

I dare say to you that if my letters require haste, the condition of

[53] Letter of Dec. 2, 1704.

[54] Letter to Desmaretz, Dec. 20, 1704.

France does not require less. Although there may be no one in the kingdom who personally suffers more than myself, I look for my well-being only from a general cause. Attention to oneself, and privilege, to which everyone has confined himself with impunity for forty years, without troubling himself about the public interest, sacrificing it, even, almost always to his own profit, is solely what is causing France to perish. M. Desmaretz has done me the honor to write to me that although you were convinced, and he also, of the maxims on grain, nevertheless, as it is not the sentiment of many persons in power this caused very much difficulty.

But Boisguilbert hoped to convert public opinion to his view that the excessively low price of grain harmed both rich and poor. It was this which was back of his desire to publish his treatise on grain. He felt it to be supremely vital to France. He therefore broached the subject again:

It is because I have seen that it was not agreeable to you that my works be made public, that I have not abandoned the manuscripts to chance. If I had let them out of my sight, they would never have missed being published without any effort on my part, so that no case (*incident*) could have been drawn up against me any more than [against] M. de Cambray [55] for his *Télémaque,* as well as others. I never lose the respect due to persons in power, either in writing or in my discourse, so I have nothing to fear on that score. . . . If my *Traité des blés* had been published, public opinion would have caused eyes to be opened on a restriction so harmful. . . . When M. d'Argenson,[56] [while I was] on my last trip to Paris, wished to remark to me that the great cheapness of grain, whatever it was, was the sole preserver of public felicity, especially at Paris, I asked him if he conceived that the farmers could cultivate at a loss, and give nothing to their landlords. His frank response to me was that this pretension was ridiculous. But on the discussion as to the expense necessary, and as to the price of grain required to cover it, I found him very short, not knowing the first word about it. But he did not at all wish to depart from his principle that it was absolutely essential that grains be cheap.[57]

Boisguilbert then tells Chamillart to send for three retail dealers in Paris, a chandler, a grocer, and a draper, and make them show

[55] Fénelon, who was archbishop of Cambrai.

[56] Prefect of police at Paris.

[57] There appears to have been something Socratic in Boisguilbert's method of questioning which probably did not add to his popularity with his social and official superiors.

their records of five years ago when wheat was worth eighteen livres the setier. "You will see that they sold six times more than they do at present." [58]

Boisguilbert had hoped to be allowed to try his experiment in a generality. He now refers to the fact that Chamillart has promised to confide a "canton" to him. Although the use of this term was rather broad, it is obvious that Boisguilbert understood that Chamillart would limit him to an election. He does not scorn it however. "I wish for this more than to live," he says, "for [its effect on] the reëstablishment of France." He only hopes it will not be in a village. With the hope of obtaining it he will henceforth seek only Chamillart's plaudits, "although all my fellow writers (*mes semblables*) may always succumb to this temptation [to publish], which is keener even than the passion for wealth." But the public must support the change in the grain policy which was fundamental to his reforms. To him, therefore, there was no inconsistency in his statement that he would seek praise only from Chamillart and in his immediately begging him in the same letter for permission to publish.

As it is a question of the interests of the public, it is held sovereign in this question (*en cette partie*); that which it will accept or refuse is a certain guarantee of success. Permit me to publish my works and you will see the praise they will bring me from the greatest number who can understand. Those who live on the destruction of others I renounce trying to persuade.[59]

Chamillart presumably rebuked Boisguilbert severely again. The latter is bewildered as to the cause. He asks pardon for whatever may have produced displeasure. Then, after telling Chamillart that he "looks upon and listens to as oracles those who dare to propose methods contrary to common sense," he proceeds to ask for a half-hour's time.[60] Chamillart's sarcastic response is that one must have lost his mind to believe that, in spite of the thirty years Boisguilbert had devoted to the study of conditions in France, one man could know more than all the rest put together.

[58] Letter of Dec. 23, 1704.
[59] Letter of Dec. 28, 1704.
[60] Letter of Feb. 22, 1705.

Again a long silence, which for Boisguilbert meant but one thing. He was in disfavor and disgrace. In June he again pleaded for an interview. He renews the same prayer, he says, in spite of personal circumstances which should cause him to pay court to Chamillart by a perpetual silence on such matters.[61] But the safety of the State does not permit him to remain quiet. His principles have been reduced to two sheets of paper, but he must give the key orally. He asks for the last audience of his life. His death, he declares, will show that he will hold his word, as he does not believe he could survive his complete ruin and that of his family, "which is inevitable if the course of things continues."

Indirectly this letter tells much about the former interviews. Chamillart's custom, it seems, was to have Boisguilbert approach him as he came out from his meals at noon or evening. The latter requested a morning interview, "because people have little or no intelligence at other times." One suspects that he did not doubt his own alertness of mind whatever the hour might be. But obviously, however, he had subjected his method of procedure during the audiences to severe scrutiny. He would change it. Now he told Chamillart he would "convince" him not "by reasoning, nor by discourse, which only greatly embitters minds [when carried on] between equals, and verifies nothing when the subjects are of very different positions, as in the present case, because respect prevents [one] from disputing and even from answering." He would, on the contrary, use only "proof, demonstration, and experience as certain and infallible as . . . that two and one make three." [62]

Chamillart answered to say that if Boisguilbert wished to renew relations with him, he would have to show him that the increase in the king's revenue would come from foreign countries, in part at least. He knew France, he said, almost as well as Boisguilbert, and the latter would have difficulty in persuading him that eighty million livres beyond what is already being paid could be drawn from the people. Clearly Chamillart had been right the preceding year when he said that there were many who would not understand

[61] There was a new levy of ten thousand livres on Boisguilbert and all the judges in Normandy, which he declared could not be paid individually or as a body.

[62] Letter of June 25, 1705.

Boisguilbert's writing. He had not understood them, and he had had the benefit of private instruction. Nevertheless he granted the interview.

Following their discussion Boisguilbert wrote a very short, but ominous note: "I do not know what the consequences are of the last audience which you did me the honor to give me. But I am indeed assured that you will presently have no choice between acting as do other nations in the world, which is solely all I propose in commenting on your first views, or counting on an extremity that one almost dares not envisage. It is by [setting forth these alternatives] that you will close the mouths of contradictors." [63] This stern warning obtained immediate results. Chamillart's notation says that they will "consult together at the first opportunity."

There now began another period of confidence that a new day would come to the distressed land. From Chamillart, Boisguilbert apparently extracted a promise that if he could obtain the coöperation of De Bouville,[64] intendant of the adjoining generality of Orléans, and of D'Armenonville, a director of finances, whose home was the château of Rambouillet close by, they could use the election of Chartres for an experiment with a view to introducing the reforms generally. At the same time some concession with regard to the exportation of grain was obtained.

Late in August he wrote from Bizy, De Bouville's château, where he had met and converted De Bouville to his principles. As to grain, the "simple rumor of your permission to export wheat has raised it from seven [*livres per setier*] to eight. Judge, if you please, of the rest, when it will please you to cultivate this plant." [65]

Boisguilbert soon wrote to Chamillart again to warn him of the opposition any attempt at reform would encounter. The "court sees only *partis*," [66] he said, "and Paris only usurers," that is, the financiers, therefore you "will assuredly encounter enemies" in any reform it is desired to bring about.[67] The warning was timely.

After their first meeting Boisguilbert and De Bouville continued to hold conferences and to correspond. In the middle of Septem-

[63] Letter of July 4, 1705.
[64] Brother-in-law of Desmaretz. [65] Letter of Aug. 27, 1705.
[66] See below, pp. 119–120. [67] Letter of Sept. 10, 1705.

ber Boisguilbert had an appointment with De Bouville and D'Armenonville at the latter's home at Rambouillet. Boisguilbert as always was relying upon getting the coöperation of the people by creating a demand for his reforms. From Rambouillet he was immediately to follow De Bouville to Chartres and to Orléans, to work there, and to put the people in the same frame of mind as those in Normandy, "which is to pay the king the racquet in order to keep from being forced by the bat." From the few conferences he has held, he is certain, he declares, that they will regard Chamillart's views "not as bombs, from which *sauve qui peut,* but as anchors, which insure the vessels against the storms and tempests which [otherwise would] completely submerge them." [68]

Before the meeting at Rambouillet, De Bouville also wrote to Chamillart:

I have examined very carefully the memoirs of M. de Boisguilbert, of which I have made an abstract. After having heard him on all the objections I made, I have found his reasoning very sound, and nothing is more desirable than to execute his project, changing some points to which he agrees. But, in order to replace the funds that the King draws from affaires extraordinaires, the principle of his propositions, and without which his system falls, the capitation must be doubled. It is necessary to know if you agree to this. Without doubt it will at first make persons weep who will not understand the good that this will produce as a result, and who will consider only the present evil, which is to pay double what they are paying. But the officers and others more subject to pay their part of affaires extraordinaires apparently will receive this increase with joy. Assuming, sir, that you wish indeed to double the capitation, I believe that there will be no difficulty in the other things upon which he and I are in agreement. I shall have the honor to carry all the memoirs to you at Fontainebleau whenever you order me to do so. The said Sieur de Boisguilbert has told me that he will go to Rambouillet to confer with M. d'Armenonville, in accordance with the permission that you have given him. As for myself, I depart tomorrow, all inconvenienced as I still am, to commence the apportionment of the tailles, in which there will be much more work than in the years past, on account of the declaration of the King suppressing privileges. I shall pass by Rambouillet with the said Sieur de Boisguilbert if he passes here.[69]

[68] Letters of Sept. 14 and 17, 1705.
[69] De Bouville to Chamillart, Sept. 22, 1705.

Boisguilbert was eager to act immediately. But De Bouville and D'Armenonville, sympathetic though they were to the plans, as officials dared not move so fast. They knew the system which bound France. De Bouville wrote Chamillart from Rambouillet:

I came here last evening with M. de Boisguilbert, who arrived at my home an hour after I had the honor to write to you. We smoked a good part of the evening in the study of M. d'Armenonville, whom the said Sieur de Boisguilbert instructed in his project, and the conversation went on for three hours again this morning. . . . We three are found in approximate agreement, which is that it is necessary to increase the capitation and absolutely end affaires extraordinaires. And as M. de Boisguilbert claims that you had told him to come into the generality of Orléans to make a canvass of his project, and to induce the people to demand the execution of it, we have believed, M. d'Armenonville and I, that this trip was premature, and that it would be necessary before that for you to be very explicit, because, if this project were to be rejected, the extraordinary recoveries might suffer a great retarding on account of the prejudice against affaires extraordinaires which the trip of the said Sieur de Boisguilbert would have roused in the people. Thus we have thought that it would be more proper for me to obtain two or three officials of the election of Chartres, and the receivers of the tailles, with whom, and [with] the said Sieur de Boisguilbert, I shall work on the formation of the rolls of the said election. After that, I shall have the honor to give you an account of what we have accomplished. M. d'Armenonville, who leaves Saturday to go to Fontainebleau, will have the honor to inform you more at length of all our conversation.[70]

Boisguilbert also wrote to Chamillart from Rambouillet, a letter full of confidence as to the result of the project. Not again would he have the opportunity to do so.

[70] De Bouville to Chamillart, Sept. 24, 1705.

III
DEFEAT

The élite of every generation suffers for humanity.
AMIEL

RUMORS of the strange happenings at Chartres were being bruited around. Boisguilbert's ideas were known. There were deep forebodings. The forces of reaction began to gather.

A warning of the opposition that might be expected is shown in a letter from Le Camus, first president of the Court of Aides in Paris, to Chamillart:

Sir, I am informed that M. de Bouville works at Chartres to set up the rolls of the tailles to make a trial of a new form of imposition. This project is going to strike at all the regulations and to establish novelties, whose consequences can be detrimental both to the public and to jurisdictions which have been established for so many centuries on this matter. [Therefore] I beg you, sir, before acting upon your resolution to issue a decree, to do me the favor of acquainting me with this project on which M. de Bouville is working, in order [that I may] make such observations on it as are believed most useful, and not to make any changes in the ancient usages without understanding perfectly their utility, the appearances of which are often deceiving.

This letter was from the head of the highest court in France having jurisdiction in fiscal questions. It was not to be ignored. Chamillart answered as follows:

It would be desirable to change the form of the impositions. The absolute power that the collectors have to regulate the total for each individual according to their passions or their interest,[1] creates an unspeakable disorder. The matter of the tailles is quite known to me, as I studied it to the bottom in the little time I was intendant of the province of Normandy. Nothing will be done lightly, and if anything is done it will certainly be for the public good.[2]

[1] See below, pp. 112–113.

[2] The letter of Le Camus is dated merely September, 1705. Chamillart's drafts of replies are never dated.

Chamillart was beginning to weaken before opposition. When Boisguilbert wrote asking that he be received immediately at Fontainebleau, he was told that he could see Chamillart after the latter returned to Paris. Two days later the request was renewed.[3] Chamillart replied: "We have not less knowledge, or less good intentions than you. Believe that if some utility can be drawn from the work that you have done, and from the different conferences that I have had with you, and with M. de Bouville, in the last place, nothing to that end will be neglected."

On July 4 Boisguilbert had given Chamillart two alternatives: to adopt reforms which he regarded as embodying the principles of all civilized nations, or to face "an extremity that one almost dares not envisage." On October 17 he wrote again apparently with this earlier letter in mind. He has heard, he says, through MM. d'Armenonville and De Bouville that Chamillart has not made up his mind, although he has persuaded these most illustrious and enlightened persons, as well as M. de Chamlay,[4] to his views. He cannot understand, he states, on what ground Chamillart should be leaning to the alternative, "that is to say, the maintenance of the present situation, which seems to me to be no other thing than an impossibility to recover the needs of the State in a conjuncture where it is altogether a question of a complete revolution."[5]

Chamillart answers to say that "no one is more in agreement" than he with Boisguilbert's "general principles."

If we had need only of reasoning on paper, I would give you an authentic acceptance, which would confirm to posterity that no one has carried further than you his zeal for the welfare of the State.

[3] Letters of Oct. 7 and 9, 1705.

[4] Louis-Jules Bolé, Marquis de Chamlay, friend of Boileau, Racine, La Bruyère, and Saint-Simon, a representative of the Louvois, as contrasted with the Colbert group in the government, had, soon after Chamillart became controller general, been placed in general charge of contacts with Boisguilbert. In addition to writing to Chamillart, the latter seems, as is indicated by occasional references, to have carried on a regular correspondence with De Chamlay. De Chamlay was especially busy with Boisguilbert at the time of the Chartres episode. In a letter to Desmaretz on September 16, 1708, Boisguilbert says that three years before De Chamlay had worked on his memoirs for three months without stopping.

[5] Letter of Oct. 17, 1705.

But as it is necessary to realize promptly eighty million livres a year beyond that which is now raised on the subjects of the King, you must not be surprised if our operations cannot be as quick as your ideas. It is not a question of an alternative. . . . Be persuaded that I have drawn all the advantage [which I can] from the work you have done.

The most powerful and perhaps the ablest intendant in France at this time was Bâville in the province of Languedoc. In his letters to the controller general, and in his report as intendant in the memoirs for the Duke of Burgundy, there is glimpsed a coldness, a cruelty, something almost sinister, that is reminiscent of provincial rule in antiquity. In the heretic- and sedition-ridden region of the Cevennes he obtained results. His influence was to be reckoned with. It was in large measure his proposal for a capitation which had been adopted in 1695. It was this capitation, based upon vocations and classes, pressing as cruelly upon the poor as the taille, which it was proposed to reform. His advice had been sought on the advisability of supplanting this offspring of his brain with Boisguilbert's proposal for a tax of a tenth of all incomes.

Bâville wrote at length to Chamillart:

After having carefully examined the proposition to abolish the capitation and to have the tenth of the revenues of individuals paid, it appears to me that it would be very dangerous to make use of this expedient, and that there could not be much certainty of any success from it. It is dangerous because people are accustomed to the capitation, and will not for a long time [become accustomed] to this tenth, which will be very difficult to establish. Whole years will be necessary to overcome the difficulties. Prompt and easy aid is required, and I think that there will be an extreme repugnance for declaring one's property and for revealing family secrets.[6]

[This tax] is the last of the extremities, and so contrary to the spirit (*génie*) of the nation, that nothing more insupportable could happen to it. Thus declarations can be expected which are not at all true. How can merchants, men of affairs, usurers, be expected to declare what money they have? If it is necessary to make an inquisition of that in order to condemn them fourfold, this will be of an infinite slowness; and to wish to presume that what is possessed will be declared truly and in good faith is to presume that men will be

[6] Boisguilbert anticipated and answered this objection in *Factum*, p. 337.

just and reasonable where it is against their own interest. This must not be expected of most men. But without dwelling at length on the great inconveniences which are found in this proposition and which appear at first sight, it is necessary to consider it only with relation to property and to persons. As to property, it is in land or in money. If it is in land, the cost of production takes half the product; the taille takes almost a third in the sections of the real taille;[7] from the remainder it is necessary to pay extraordinary taxes, the capitation, and to support the family. An infinite number of persons are in this position (*espèce*). How can they be required to pay beyond what they are paying? That is impossible. It is indeed necessary to be careful and not to reason in this affair on the idea of Paris, where property is mixed, and where the richest people in the kingdom live. They would be able to pay a tenth of their incomes without inconveniencing themselves very much; but in the provinces, where the greater part of the inhabitants live from their land, it is not the same, and the burden is so great that it cannot receive any further increase. In this category (*espèce*) are all the nobility who are not of the first order.

As to those whose property is in obligations and in bills, who are the richest [persons] in the kingdom, and from whom more aid might be expected, I think I can say that true declarations never will be made. Each one explaining in his own way the burdens on his property, the needs of his family, and the nature of his debts, he will deceive even himself in order to give declarations which will produce nothing. I have run through the different groups, and I find that, outside of financiers, merchants and usurers, the rest already pay the tenth, or approximately so, by means of the capitation, and the gain would not be worth the trouble of making this great change. Furthermore, there is the danger, in leaving off one of these perceptions in order to establish another, that both will be lost. This can be understood by an estimation of all the faculties of individuals who are sufficiently known in the provinces. It is found, on examining this in detail, that the officers of justice, gentlemen, bourgeois, pay already, generally speaking, the tenth. What is the use to make so great a change, and to cause a displeasure so sharp to families as that of being obliged to reveal their resources, without drawing an obvious utility from it? [Such a tax] would be good in a country which pays neither taille nor capitation.

Not seeing, therefore, either the possibility of a prompt aid, or a utility, and [foreseeing] much inconvenience, it seems to me not fitting to expose everyone to the movements which might result from the establishment, in the present conjuncture, [of a tax] so contrary

[7] See below, p. 110, including note.

to the inclination and to the taste of everyone, and [one] which will chiefly produce all the chagrin and all the displeasure that can be foreseen. We have all the trouble in the world to raise the taille and the capitation; it is necessary often to employ troops for this purpose in this province. How can it be hoped easily to make this new levy which would be still more disagreeable? On what, it is necessary to ask, would one levy the capitation of artisans, domestics, peasants, and the greater part of the dealers who have no fixed incomes, and whose property consists in merchandise? And this loss would perhaps be greater than the profit that will be drawn from the tenth of the incomes of those who have them.

Here was apparently a commendable concern for those oppressed with the weight of the taille and the capitation; the very group whose burden Boisguilbert hoped to lighten. They could not indeed stand additional burdens, but they were carrying almost all of the taille, and far more than their share of the capitation. Bâville's anxiety, it is feared, was for the lesser nobility of whom he speaks, who were legally exempt from the real taille in Languedoc, and in the other *pays d'états,* and who paid little or no taille in the *pays d'élections.*[8] It was they who would be embarrassed by declaring their property and revealing "family secrets." Some of the points made are very sound, especially, for instance, that in regard to the difficulty of getting correct declarations of intangibles. But the spirit of the criticism is simply to let well enough alone, at a time when neither financially nor socially could such an attitude be justified.

Bâville, however, did not fail to make a positive suggestion to replace that which he had attempted to tear down.

But, it will be said, if this expedient is not good, where can better ones be found? It is true that almost all the affaires extraordinaires are exhausted, having been made and remade so many times.[9] All the industry and all the application of the subordinates cannot make them succeed, because the sources are so dried up that finally it has come to the point where only expenses can be found. This ruins individuals, and produces very little for the King; and if one does not suffer from these expenses, which are often turned into vexations on the part of *traitants,* none of the *affaires* [of the latter] advance.

Nevertheless it is not less true that, ordinary revenues and the capi-

[8] See below, note, p. 110.

[9] That is, the same offices sold and resold so many times.

tation not sufficing to sustain the burdens of the State, it is necessary to find some extraordinary aid proportional to the present needs. It cannot be denied that it is necessary to seek it where money is, because all the *affaires* which have not this object produce only trouble and nothing effective.

Greater knowledge than mine is necessary to find these means. There is one of them which has great inconveniences, as all of them will have that are invented for such a purpose, but at least it will not be so discommodious, or so disagreeable, as that of a tenth of incomes. The rich will be made to pay it, and they will not have the displeasure of disclosing the secret of their property. *Rentes* can be established in the *denier douze, quatorze, or quinze* [10] as would be found fitting, namely, in Languedoc on the *don gratuit* [11] . . . and in the other provinces on the gabelles or on the taille.[12] These declarations would state that [the loan] would be divided by dioceses and by municipalities, to be acquired by the inhabitants as follows: to those who subscribe voluntarily, at the denier douze, and by those who will be appointed by the municipalities, at the denier quinze.[13] If there is need of thirty million livres, it will be necessary to establish one hundred thousand livres of it in Languedoc every year for three years, or fifty thousand livres if it is desired to reduce it to fifteen million livres, because Languedoc has not produced the twentieth [of the revenue] of the kingdom since the conquests of the King.[14] In this way one can have fifteen million livres every year for three years.[15]

Thus did Bâville propose that the fundamental and far-reaching reforms of Boisguilbert, which would have gone far toward reconstructing a decadent social order, be set aside in favor of a loan forced by a bankrupt government from a bankrupt people. One kind of *affaires* was to be supplanted by a new form.

10 Eight and one-third percent, 7 percent and 6⅔ percent.

11 "*Dons gratuits*" were originally voluntary contributions made primarily by the clergy and nobles to take care of shortages in the revenue or for extraordinary needs. Under Louis XIV they retained their euphemistic name, doubtless to save the face of the payers, but in fact they were compelled by the king, and were also exacted of municipalities. Those of the pays d'états were included in the ordinary revenue.

12 These revenues, incidentally, especially the latter, had been anticipated in large part for several years in advance.

13 The decline in the government's credit during the decade preceding is shown by comparing this proposal with *Le Détail*, p. 240, where the inference is that the *denier dix-huit* (about 5½ percent) is a high rate for the government to pay.

14 Putting down heresy and sedition.

15 Bâville to Chamillart, Oct. 11, 1705. *Correspondance des contrôleurs généraux*, Vol. II, pp. 277–278.

Boisguilbert was now threatened with financial ruin. He had been the target for affaires extraordinaires for two reasons. As the wealthiest magistrate of his class in the community he represented the easiest source for the tax farmers to gain their funds. On the other hand he himself seemed to think that Chamillart used this means to punish him whenever he had given displeasure. He had devoted himself to the interests of France when he was building up his own fortune and later when he was enjoying it. Now he was pleading his own cause as well as that of France.

In replying to Chamillart's last note he takes up his own case:

I learn with extreme displeasure that the work of all my life and the singular attachment that I have had for your person for sixteen years has produced no other effect than to draw your indignation upon me. I have been spoiled by the public, which has led me to think, that, in offering you eighty million livres of increase on its behalf in order to be exempted from exigencies impossible in the execution, although ruinous [even] in the simple demand, I pleaded its true interests. If for some time I have pleaded this cause before you with over-forwardness, you will please pardon these convulsive movements of a nature which has ceased to be directed by reason, seeing itself at the point of complete dissolution. It is my inevitable ruin that I have wished to conjure with that of the people. I restrict myself just now to myself, and ask you very humbly grace and pardon for the past on account of my intentions, which have always been very sincere. That is all God exacts. I beg you to leave me enough of your protection to be one of the last exposed to impossible demands, [such] as I experience just now to a very high degree, since you have understood with M. de Bouville, that their cessation [i.e., affaires] has consequences which surpass my knowledge.[16]

Chamillart's reply was a final repudiation of Boisguilbert's time and effort and thought expended for France.

I have worked with M. de Bouville on a project which the imagination, the ardor of your mind, and the zeal that you have for the public good, have made you believe possible of execution. If it were only necessary to give you praise, no one would merit it more than you. . . . But, to sustain the expense of the war, instead of having eighty million livres on paper, it is absolutely necessary to realize them. M. de Bouville, himself, more capable than any intendant of making use of it, agrees with me [that] to devote himself wholly to it, [and] to

[16] Letter of Nov. 5, 1705.

work with knowledge to divide the burden equally, requires an infinite time; that many of the intendants are not sufficiently sedulous, or sufficiently instructed to do it; that this object applies only to two-thirds of the kingdom, because the pays d'états, which compose at least the third, must be separated from it; that this work, by its extent, demands at least two or three years to be brought to perfection, and that, having been achieved, it would not produce the third of what you have led me to expect with so much certainty. This induces me to spare the people in the future with regard to affaires extraordinaires, and to draw through borrowing a part of the aid of which His Majesty has need. Officials will be spared. I agree that it is late, and that they are almost ruined; nevertheless, there are at least half of them who would prefer to see creations, combining of offices, and of rights, than to see the capitation carried higher. Believe that I fear the ruin of the people as much as you do. We think the same on the rest, but your views are not so extended as mine, because you are not charged with the weight.

Bâville's objection had been conclusive. His proposal had been adopted. This marks a tragic point in French history. France had produced the man who could well have saved her a century of much wretchedness and the terrors of the Revolution; a man whose ideas would have produced a bloodless revolution in her affairs. Her great misfortune was to have had a weak and wavering minister, lacking the courage for definitive action at a time when decision and strength were required. The French people had lost a battle fought for them by a champion, and as one of her earlier historians had said, "a lost battle has a long tail." The old régime was perpetuated for a while when it rejected the opportunity to reconstruct itself. But in the autumn of 1705 it rendered itself vulnerable to the eventual destructive lashing of the tail of defeated justice and reason. This lashing would come in the name of liberty, fraternity, and equality, but the underlying principle would be the same.

To Boisguilbert the decision to temporize with an expedient where bold and revolutionary reforms were necessary, was sheer madness. He hastened to reply:

Permit me, please, to show you that the use of the King's credit to relieve the needs of the State, which you tell me you prefer to that which I have taken the courage to propose to you for a long time on the side of the people, appears to me [to be] a great mistake. This is not only my view, but that of every person who has the least understanding of the state of affairs. Borrowing is a step which must be absolutely voluntary on the part of the lender, and it will not last long, assuredly, when this rule is not adhered to. On the contrary, it makes money tighten up more completely than before. But how, my Lord, can you count on a free will to procure this effect of considerable loans, since *force majeure* has succeeded in bringing them to an end in more than ten thousand places, where innumerable individuals allowed themselves to be sold, or imprisoned rather than to lend to the King? This is due to inability [to lend] for the greater part, but the others [refuse to lend] because they see that the King will never pay his debts, not even the current ones, having declared that his debts are not his at all, but those of the State? Thus, if I dare to say so, you prefer an impossible means, as everyone knows, to ways presented by the people themselves, who alone have the right to decide it, since they have to pay. I advance this with certainty.[17]

Chamillart's answer is an attempt to justify his course of action as controller general:

If your eighty million livres were as certain as you think, do you believe that I would seek another means to relieve the King? It is a great misfortune that you regard as a reality, from which one can draw immediate help, a thing, which, through a long period of time, would produce [but] a small part of the eighty million livres that you wish freely to give to His Majesty with the consent of the people. The experiment that M. de Bouville has made in the election of Chartres can make you understand sufficiently, and him also, what the King would be able to draw the first year from the fruit of your labor and of your continual reflection for sixteen years.[18] I can assure you that, although I may not have written so much as you during this time, I have scarcely thought less on the means of sustaining the State, and to do it in a manner that would conserve a part of the property of individuals, and without disorganizing their affairs, as is done by affaires extraordinaires, which have been resorted to since I have become controller general, only on account of the pressing

[17] Letter of Nov. 16, 1705.

[18] In a letter of September 16, 1708, to Desmaretz, who was then controller general, Boisguilbert says that the work with De Bouville in Orléans fell through because De Harlay, first president of the parlement of Paris used his influence near the king to prevent exportation necessary to raise the price of wheat to a level which would permit all the estates to be cultivated without loss. "As, my Lord, it is, of all points *conditione sine qua non,* it was necessary to abandon everything."

need for money. Unhappily your guarantee is not sufficiently great for the object which you embrace. I am so greatly burdened by it, and you only to a small extent, that you permit yourself to be deceived without running great risk. I am more informed than you; my intentions are not less good than yours. Actually give me eighty million livres and we will be in accord tomorrow. If I thought I could find in two years what you offer in two hours, I should not seek other aid. I do not pretend to reject your work. I shall use it as well as I can, but I shall not abandon other means until the former be wholly assured.

Boisguilbert responded to this letter with as much irony as Chamillart had directed toward him. The inference is that although the intentions of the controller general might be good, the methods used belied it. He refers to the aides: To "put many bureaus, many tax farmers to the number sometimes of six or seven, [to collect taxes] on the same liquor, and in the same place, is openly to declare that it is tax farmers that one wishes, and not the revenue of the King, for which one alone would suffice." The same wine, he says, which in Anjou and Orléans sells for one sol a container, sells at Caen and in lower Normandy for thirty sols. He proposes to put an end to such differences. When he talks about results in two hours, he refers to the restoration of trade, which, he declares, alone makes it possible to pay taxes.[19]

Thoroughly annoyed by this gad-fly which would not leave him alone, Chamillart tells Boisguilbert that he wishes him to cease his letters.

I believe that you reason very soundly, and that, if you were in my place, you would find the King eighty million livres in two hours time, since you are persuaded of it. That which gives me more reason to be convinced of it is the vivacity of your mind, and its facility to write to me all the time. But as I am not so alert, and as I do not move so quickly, and as much more time is necessary for me than for you, although the matter be of the utmost importance, I could scarcely find that which would be necessary for me. I pray you to resume at another time when I can have leisure to listen to these propositions.

On January 14, 1706, Boisguilbert again sent a frantic appeal

[19] Letter of Nov. 26, 1705.

both for himself and for France. He wrote that he had bought for one hundred and fifty thousand livres all the offices which had been created anew on his old ones, permitting neither constraints nor levies to be made against him such as his fellow judges had permitted. This he had done from sympathy with the general condition of France.

[But now,] without departing from the rule that I have imposed upon myself for fifteen years, not to abuse the honor of my relations with you for personal affairs, I take the courage to talk to you about them. You will understand, if you please, my Lord, that I did not wish to believe what I was told: that to buy anything from tax farmers is to contract one's ruin, because they take care to make a catalogue of those from whom they easily obtain money. [This they do] in order to return to see them sooner when they must sell the same merchandise [i.e., office] again under another name. Thus it has happened numberless times, as unhappily I prove today. Having, then, had this imprudence to a high degree, I suffer the result of it to a proportionate extent, that is to say, to a complete ruin, since my one hundred and fifty thousand livres of goods [i.e., offices] are destroyed by the creation of similar things, accompanied by a tripling of the taxes, which ruins the raising of them on the first. . . . And to console myself for the loss of a property so dearly and so recently bought for the second time, since I have only acquired wages [20] in the denier thirty-three on that which I had already, I am asked for fifty-eight thousand livres.

This, he says, will ruin him. He cannot pay the least part of it.

Behold my portrait, or rather that of all France: to be ruined without the King gaining thereby. . . .

You can regard me as crazy, my Lord, as much as you please, as well as all those who mention me to you. But after having remarked to you that the notableness (*singularité*) of my views, which gives me this name in common with the authors of all new discoveries, redounds to my greatness (*me tourne à gloire*), I am ready in three hours work, provided it be with the consent of the people, which depends only upon the publication of my works, [to furnish the funds required by the King, and to bring prosperity to the people.] I speak with certainty, since those with whom I have conferred on the project have consented to it with enthusiasm for me. And as it is by a general interest, the agreement of thought among a hundred

[20] That is, taxes. See above, note, p. 41.

persons [is an indication of what would] hold equally [true] for all the others.

Turning to England, whose people and institutions he so admired, he says, that there, where the harmony of commerce is not destroyed, "it is not at all *sauve qui peut* and enrich oneself who can by the stripping of one's neighbor, as [has been the case] in France with impunity for forty years." He begs Chamillart to open his eyes to the condition of the kingdom, and if he thinks it can be drawn out of its existing conjuncture by the continuation of like methods, he is alone in thinking so, "not having seen anyone, not even in the King's Council, who was persuaded of it." To eliminate affaires extraordinaires and to apportion taxes equally, he declares, will recreate five hundred million livres of income in France, "that is to say, of consumption of goods." "Nevertheless this grace will never be accepted by those who surround you, considering that it will be their complete dismissal that you will give them."

Again he reverts to his own affairs:

I beg you in the name of God, my Lord, not to put my wife and my children on the street along with my movables, on account of the impossibility of my paying fifty-eight thousand livres on effects that another band of tax farmers will take from me at the same moment. This is a custom introduced only during the past fifteen years—to take his property away from a man, and then to tax for the maintenance of a thing that he no longer possesses, as I prove today to a frightful degree. I do not think that this should be my fate under your ministry, or that the attachment and the respect that I have had for you since I have had the honor to know you should end in [my] having to supplicate you not to reduce me to the last degree of poverty.

Did Chamillart deliberately punish Boisguilbert by setting traitants upon him when he had given displeasure? This cannot be known with certainty. Boisguilbert's letters have indicated that he himself thought so. It appears not always to have been by chance alone that the demands came so regularly when he was in disfavor with the controller general.

Boisguilbert wrote Chamillart a second letter in January. It is significant because in it he appears to have given up hope of obtaining any of his reforms. It represents a new point of departure.

You know that in the relation that you have permitted me to have with you for the general reëstablishment, I have never mixed my personal affairs, although [they were] most exposed to, and even crushed by, the storms of the time. I have believed that my quota of a public good would suffice to make me happy. Now that this resource is taken from me, allow me to demand of you the same grace that God accords to all the faithful, namely, freedom to address him daily for their individual needs. The extraordinary sums that I have paid, which have no counterpart approaching it in any official in the kingdom, have served only as a means (*semence*) to draw on myself the exigence of like sums. M. d'Armenonville has done me the honor to write me that it was not at all the intention of the King or you to exact from anyone the impossible. Have the goodness yourself to regulate, on the exposition of the facts, what is within my power, and for this purpose to accord me permission to greet you at Étang, when I shall go to Paris for this purpose in eight days. If at the same time you wish to listen to a proposition of the inferior judges for two million livres which they will give you without constraint, and even with pleasure, I shall have the honor to inform you of it. The fracas will assuredly be less great than that of the marriage of the two bodies of Rouen just contracted, which resembles very much those which are made for official reasons, that is to say, in spite of the parties, [a union] which scarcely produces happy *ménages*. You will find traitants immediately, without any guarantee on the part of the King, for what I shall have the honor to propose to you. As these things are more in harmony with the methods of the time than the attentions which have occupied my whole life, I hope they will not be an obstacle to the permission that I beg you to accord me to salute you at Étang.[21]

The indefatigable Boisguilbert could not break the habit of so many years, or easily submit to defeat. In March he again wrote. In June he sought another audience:

M. de Chamlay writes me that you have informed him that the great burden of affairs with which you are surrounded causes you to put off the audience that you would indeed have wished to accord me, and for which I have been ten days in Paris. On this I shall take the courage to say to you that I ask you only a half-hour to refuse or accept [my offer] to construct the draft of an edict, which, without risking, troubling, or disconcerting anything, will carry the capi-

[21] Letter of Jan. 15, 1706.

tation to more than one hundred million livres a year with the consent of the people. Rouen is ready to pay an increase of four hundred thousand livres, which is more than the tax on one hundred million livres. Judge, if you please, if you have any occupation of greater importance, of which the honor of the success will be attributed to you, and not to me, who will claim only that of having worked on your views when you first appeared in Normandy. Accord me please this last audience.[22]

He was given an appointment for Saturday at three o'clock.

This audience, like all the earlier ones, was fruitless. Boisguilbert's tireless efforts of a lifetime, to reconstruct the economic life of France, had been to no avail against the fear of some to change, and the entrenched self-interest of others. It was an admission of defeat at their hands which caused him to lash forth in what is perhaps the most powerful and ironical attack in the annals of history and economics, *Supplément au Détail de la France*, and finally to resolve to take the case of France to the people by publishing his writings, which he had been forbidden to do. Boisguilbert had long been sustained by his belief that the oppressed people would listen to reason if the facts and his proposals were presented to them; they would support him by demanding the reforms in such certain tones that it would be impossible to deny them. In January or February, 1707, he brought out a complete edition of his works in two small volumes under the general title *Le Détail de la France.*

This publication by Boisguilbert was accompanied almost simultaneously by Vauban's *Dime royale*. The content of the *Dime royale* had been known to the court for years. Vauban himself had read it to the king. Chamillart was thoroughly familiar with the works of Boisguilbert. Under ordinary conditions the books might have been proscribed and the authors merely have suffered reprimands. But these were dark days at court. The War of the Spanish Succession was going sadly against France, and nerves frayed by this and by internal difficulties were in no state to temporize. Boisguilbert especially might have escaped by being looked upon as an eccentric who would have to be endured. The controller general and his aids

[22] Letter of June 17, 1706.

had scarcely been able to understand what he was saying, so they could depend upon the people understanding him no better. There was thus an element of safety from the demoralizing influence of his ideas. But in the preceding three years, in a state of frenzy over conditions, he had overwhelmed the controller general with more than a letter a month demanding an end to the existing abuses and the establishment of the reforms which he suggested. He had goaded beyond endurance the weak Chamillart, torn between the interests of France and the interests of bureaucracy and the established order.

It was not a time of freedom of expression. Both men knew their times, and knew the risk they were taking in writing frankly and freely. Boisguilbert interjects this revealing statement when he begins an attack upon the methods of tax collection: "The rigorous pursuit and the investigations which have been made on many occasions, not to speak of public opinion, purge this pronouncement of all suspicion of slander or of sedition." Again he speaks of the thankless job of giving advice to the king's ministers, "who listen coldly, cull out what can be used, and then regard the author as a traitor, or as a courtier whom one wishes to see perish after his usefulness has ended." He had always attempted to avoid the suspicion of sedition; nevertheless, as Boislisle says, he had proceeded with "an imperturbable valiancy, a heroic indifference for his own person." As for Vauban, who had spent his life in the service of France and of his King, who had encircled France with impregnable fortresses against the enemy without, he would build his last one with his pen against the enemy within. But the odds were against the two patriots; the opposing force, too strong.

Vauban's action, considering his position, could not be overlooked. On February 14, 1707, and again of March 19, the *Dime royale* was proscribed[23] and its author dismissed from court. The old warrior, one of the great heroes of France, could not survive the blow of having his patriotic act regarded as a

[23] The first proscription was ineffective because it failed to state where the book had been published as the law required. In the second decree the book was declared to have been published at Paris, although in reality it appears to have been published at Rouen.

criminal offense. Learning of the proscription on the evening of March 24, he became ill, and within a week, on March 30, 1707, he died, after having placed a copy of the *Dime* in the hands of his confessor to determine if he had anything on his conscience.

On March 14, 1707, exactly one month after the first proscription of the *Dime,* the blow fell upon Boisguilbert. He was sentenced to exile for six months. Here was tragedy. Here was the defeat of two noble souls.

Three days after the sentence Boisguilbert wrote to Chamillart:

I ask your pardon very humbly if 112,000 livres of taxation paid by me since your ministry, [and] a like sum now demanded of me, have not made me lose my reason in disobeying your orders, in the hope that the public would join its prayers to mine to obtain from you methods [concerning] which, with your approval, I had the honor to write to you so long. I have received an order to go to Brive-la-Gaillarde. I am persuaded, my Lord, that my punishment would be less great than my crime, if my situation were like that of other men; but for me to leave Rouen is to reduce a wife and my large number of children to beggary, now that I receive nothing from [my] estates, and have no other means to subsist than the daily emoluments of my office. I have begun by causing to be suppressed, everywhere I have been able to find them, the copies of all I have made, and by burning all my manuscripts in very great number. If, after the example of God, my Lord, you wish indeed to use mercy toward me, you will know by the consequences that my repentance is true, the voluntary penitence of the author being more effective on these occasions than any punishment one can cause him.[24] I beg you, my Lord, not to punish my wife and my children for a crime which I alone have committed, and that your character, all filled with good, accord me forgiveness. My silence in the future will show you my gratitude.

The plea was without effect. The affront of the terrible irony and ridicule of the *Supplément au Détail le la France* was too great to be forgiven. Boisguilbert departed for Brive wishing to leave his sons in charge of his offices. This was not permitted. As was to be expected, not even in exile was this indomitable man, who had "never liked to lose his time," idle. The economist rising above the disturbed husband and father, he proceeded, we

[24] This is perhaps a reference to the striking gesture of Fénelon in his pulpit after the publication of the *Maximes des saintes.*

are told by Saint-Simon, to study *la misère* in the new locale, in the region which a fellow spirit, Turgot, later attempted to govern as "a model for all the kingdom"; where a half-century later Turgot, in effect, carried out the earlier cherished dream of Boisguilbert.

In April Boisguilbert wrote a letter to Chamillart which is both humorous and pathetic in its persistency. Nothing could better illustrate the characteristics of the man: his lack of personal animosity, his frankness, his tenacity, the dominance of a single idea—to save France. In it he promises,

> not to speak or write in any manner whatsoever of the government, except for your consideration alone, when you will have given me permission to do so, hoping that, after the example of God, who immediately forgets the past when he pardons sinners, you will wish to accord me the grace to greet you when I shall return to Paris. I have burned all my manuscripts in very great number, with the exception of a copy of the *Memoirs* of M. de Sully in eight volumes annotated by me, with guides to the number of a hundred only attached to the pages. By this means, without leafing through, or even opening the books, you will see in half an hour all the policy by which a cavalier of thirty-five years of age, without study, in three months reëstablished the whole kingdom, very much more desolated by a double war, civil and foreign, than it is today. This was not without arousing all the Council and all the Court to arms, to the point that they wished to have him assassinated, of which he was warned by the King himself. The first principle of his regulation is the free exportation of grain, without taxes, without permission, and without passport, King Henry explaining in a letter written by his own hand that all is lost when anything else is resorted to. This point costs today, with the abandonment of half the land, four times more than the war. I have been told that you understand this point very well, but that the King is prejudiced to the contrary. Perhaps if His Majesty saw the sentiments of his ancestor, he would prefer them to those of M. the first president [of the parlement] of Paris [De Harlay] and of M. d'Argenson [prefect of police of Paris], especially as they are contrary to yours and to those of the public.[25]

Here was indeed a man who, as has been said, knew neither "bitterness nor discouragement."

How many times had Chamillart had the example of Sully

[25] Letter of April 11, 1707.

held up before him! His fury on receiving the letter is indicated by the reply which he noted in his own handwriting:

Since you still address yourself to me after having given to the public all your extravagances, the sole good counsel that I might be able to give to you is to burn your remarks on the memoirs of M. de Sully, and to try to imagine for once in your life that one should know enough to apply examples as models only when things are somewhat in the same proportion, and that a kingdom is rich enough to sustain the expenses that Kings wish to make it bear. If you understand well what I wish to say to you, and which is not difficult to understand, you will occupy yourself in the future with rendering justice, and you will renounce the government of the State.

In June, Boisguilbert's brother, councillor in the parlement of Rouen, wrote to Chamillart. This letter gives some explanation of Boisguilbert's own unsuccessful effort to have the sentence remitted:

My sister-in-law, in the despair of the unhappy state to which the interdiction of my brother has reduced her and her family, has resolved to leave, with her children, to throw herself at your feet, and she has begged me to accompany her, my Lord. I have not dared completely to refuse her, my Lord, because she is a lady of merit and of virtue, who suffers for a fault in which she has had no part. I have only asked her to approve my having the honor to write to you again. I flatter myself that you will have the goodness to honor me with a word of response through compassion.[26]

Chamillart's reply to the unhappy family gives some indication of the essential measure of the man.

If she should appear with you in this country to demand grace of the King in the manner she has resolved, I shall not be able to keep myself from representing to His Majesty that the family, far from recognizing his goodness in moderating his interdiction to six months, which is a penalty little proportioned to what M. de Boisguilbert merits, thinks it is authorized to complain: that His Majesty does not at all suffer when the government and those who have the honor to be in the ministry are attacked. I shall add indeed, that the sole means to procure some diminution of the six months time to the Sieur de Boisguilbert is to make clear by his repentance and the sorrow of his family that he merits it.[27]

[26] Letter of Nicolas de Boisguilbert to Chamillart on June 27, 1707.

[27] Talbot says, apropos the proscription of the *Dime royale* and of *Factum*, that "it should not be necessary to see in the pursuits carried out against the

If there were many at court who insisted upon the punishment of this presumptuous magistrate, it is also true that Boisguilbert had powerful friends among the more liberal element who exerted themselves in his behalf. According to Saint-Simon, through his efforts and those of De la Vrillière, one of the Secretaries of State, the forwarding of the order of exile was delayed as long as possible, and the sentence reduced from six months to two. He seems to have been absent for a longer period than this, but as is shown by records bearing his signature, he was back at his judicial duties by July 23.

Boislisle contrasts the nobility with which Vauban received the news of the proscription of the *Dime* with the lack of dignity, the humility, shown by Boisguilbert when notified of his condemnation to exile. To be fair it seems necessary to compare the condition and the earlier experiences of the two men. Vauban had heretofore known only applause. Financially he had not suffered, at least not by specific attack. He was a man of seventy-three years of age whose family was settled.

In the case of Boisguilbert there was a totally different situation. He had a certain family position to uphold, yet he was financially ruined. He had married comparatively late and his children were as yet unsettled. As the head of a young family he could not in this instance afford to indulge in dignity and pride. Thirteen years younger than Vauban, he was furthermore accustomed to attack, to persecution, to threat of punishment. He had learned through long experience to extricate himself from dif-

---

Dime and the *Factum* proof that the government of Louis XIV condemned the ideas professed by Vauban and Boisguilbert. . . . The sentences of February and of March, 1707, were motivated by the sole fact of the publication of the two works in spite of the prohibition by the government. [He notes:] That is to say that the exile inflicted upon Boisguilbert struck the lieutenant of police charged with censoring the press rather than the too impatient reformer. But the projects of their authors were not absolutely rejected. It is indeed thus that Boisguilbert understood it and he did not lose hope." (*Les Théories de Boisguilbert*, p. 18.) There is an element of truth in this. The ministry of Louis XIV clearly was willing to listen, privately, to proposals for reform, and even to severe criticisms of government policies. But the awakening of public opinion was feared. The government must be permitted to adopt any reforms it saw fit to adopt, but they must not be forced by a people which was regarded as having no function but to pay what was exacted. Nevertheless Boisguilbert shows that it was not the censor, but the "too impatient reformer" whom he saw as always threatened with punishment.

ficulties with the central authorities by the simulation, at least, of an attitude of obedience and humility. There were, in truth, rather effective methods of dealing with those who would do otherwise. In a day of marked social striations, humility on the part of a social and official inferior was required for dealing successfully with his superiors. Boisguilbert had developed a degree of suppleness from the almost endless necessity to placate both the chancellor and the controller general. Neither by temperament nor by experience was he one to die of disgrace. From the standpoint of an egotist, certain of the greatness of his ideas, comparing himself with Copernicus and Galileo, there is every reason to believe that he would have enjoyed, would have felt honored by, the rôle of martyr. But the practical man within him had not the slightest desire to end his days in the Bastille, as it were. He could be far more useful to France elsewhere. Dedicated to the service of his country and his fellow men, he could not accomplish his purpose except by putting pride and dignity aside. Martyrdom might ultimately accomplish results; he sought immediate ones. Only by placating Chamillart was there the slightest hope of winning adherence to his reforms. There was nothing which he would not subordinate to this end.

There is a difference of opinion as to the exact work which was proscribed. The idea that it was *Factum de la France* rests upon the fact that the proscription itself refers to *Moyens très-faciles de faire recevoir au roi quatre-vingts millions*, etc., which is the subtitle of *Factum*. Cadet thus assumes that the proscription was of a 1705 or 1706 edition of *Factum*,[28] which he thinks included *Supplément*. This he says was wrongly called *Supplément au Détail de la France* by Daire in his modern edition. Boislisle feels certain that it was *Supplément* which was pro-

[28] The actual existence of such an edition is unknown. Saint-Simon, to be sure, refers to "a very short booklet" as the source of the trouble. But Saint-Simon is not always absolutely accurate, and he rather indicates the proscription of *Supplément*. The tradition as to the existence of an early edition of *Factum* rests upon old catalogs. (Boislisle note, *Mémoires de Saint-Simon*, Vol. XIV, p. 594.) I find, however, no indication of such an edition in the letters, and regard it as improbable that Boisguilbert published anything in 1705 or 1706. It is clear, though, that the works circulated in manuscript form, and it is possible that catalog references are to manuscript forms only. If anything was printed, it would have been only an abstract of the complete work.

scribed, but he is unable to account for the proscription referring to *Moyens très-faciles,* etc.[29] Cadet thinks that after his return from exile Boisguilbert proceeded to edit and publish his complete works, and in this manner he accounts for the existence of the 1707 edition. This view, as well as that of the proscription of *Factum* itself, seems untenable. Cadet apparently never examined the two editions of 1707 carefully. The 1707 edition of *Le Détail de la France* contains all of Boisguilbert's writings, including *Supplément au Détail de la France.* Thus Daire, and not Cadet, is correct as to its title.[30] Furthermore, it is extremely unlikely that Boisguilbert, chastened as he was, would immediately republish a work which had just been proscribed and for which he had been severely punished.

It seems more probable that finally despairing of obtaining any fundamental changes directly through Chamillart, immediately after his last audience in June or July, 1706, he prepared all his works, including *Supplément,* for a complete edition. They were brought out in two small volumes entitled *Le Détail de la France.* The complete title reads: *Le Détail de la France sous le règne présent; augmenté en cette nouvelle édition de plusiers mémoires et traités sur la même matière.*[31] The second volume still has *Le Détail de la France* on the title-page; but the caption title reads *Factum de la France, ou Moyens très-faciles,* etc. Included in this volume are *Factum, Mémoire sur les blés, Causes de la rareté de l'argent, Dissertation sur la nature des richesses,* and *Supplément au Détail de la France.* Chamillart or his assistants had read all except the last, and Boisguilbert had asserted that he never said anything disrespectful of those in power. Certainly it was this second volume which brought trouble upon Boisguilbert's head. It was Volume II, subtitled *Moyens très-faciles,* etc., which was proscribed, and it was *Supplément* alone which caused the

[29] Saint-Simon, *Mémoires,* Vol. XIV, append. xii, pp. 593–596.

[30] It should be added, however, that Daire was wrong in publishing it as a supplement to Boisguilbert's first work published in 1695 as *Le Détail de la France.* It was rather a supplement to the complete works, published as an enlarged *Détail,* as it were.

[31] Aside from the unity of the subject matter, a second reason for giving the complete works this title would be to reduce the possibility of proscription by covering the works, as it were, by the new edition of the old title, which had safely undergone many editions until 1701.

king to "suffer" through the attack upon his ministers and which actually fell under the ban. That it was not an edition of *Factum* published in 1706 in conjunction with *Supplément* which was proscribed seems further evidenced by Chamillart's letter to Boisguilbert in which he spoke of the latter having given "all his extravagances" to the public.[32] Moreover, in the second edition in 1707, brought out under the title *Testament politique de M. de Vauban,* the *Supplément,* the memoir which had given offense, was omitted.

Chamillart did not long continue to be controller general after Boisguilbert's return from exile. In January, 1708, he was succeeded by Desmaretz, nephew and protégé of Colbert, who had been a director of finances and Chamillart's chief assistant since 1703. Like Chamillart he attempted nothing new, although he disapproved of, and expected little from, the existing methods.[33] Lethargy and hopelessness seem to have seized even the better element of those in power. Desmaretz himself in his report to the regent apparently has given the real explanation for the resigned indifference, which is apparent. The controller general, he says, has no control over expenditures, nor is he accountable for them "since the regulation of September 5, 1661, by which the late King suppressed the Commissioner of Superintendents of the Finances permanently. The late King carried on all the functions himself, and no payment was made except by virtue of the

[32] See above, p. 85.

[33] See above, p. 5. Desmaretz had not acted more or less as intermediary between Chamillart and Boisguilbert, and had not been in touch with the latter without being influenced by his ideas. He says, for instance, in his *Memoir on the administration of the finances* (p. 8), which could more properly be called an apology: "I knew that the order and economy of a good administration alone was capable of giving specie its first circulation and of reviving confidence." So too, Lavisse quotes from a letter written by Desmaretz in 1712 to Mesnager, who was on a special mission to England: "I avow to you that I do not believe any consequences harmful to the commerce of France are to be feared from giving all nations a reciprocal equality. My opinion is that the more facility one gives to foreigners to bring their merchandise and the productions of their country to us, the more the sale of ours is facilitated. Uniformity and liberty given to commerce always produce wealth in the country where they are established." (Lavisse, *Histoire de France,* Vol. VIII[1], p. 218.) Here are Boisguilbert's ideas. The persistency and the sincerity of his teachings had brought results where he had thought there was only enmity to them.

ordinances and estates that he signed; the controller general has simply been the executor of the orders of His Majesty."[84] With this loss of responsibility, there had also vanished, after Colbert, wholehearted interest in vital reforms. The power of the monarch had been built up at the expense of the rights of the people by a succession of powerful ministers. This power achieved, it was slowly to undermine the vitality of that which it had sought to strengthen.

Boisguilbert's disappointing experience with Chamillart, from whom he had expected so much, had clearly left him broken and disheartened. There had been a crowning disillusionment. He had thought that the publication of his writings would stir all France. The continued indifference of the people, whose "advocate" he had so long regarded himself to be, could only have filled him with a final sense of defeat.[85] His interest was now centering more and more around the future of his family and his own financial difficulties. It was as if, hopeless concerning France, he would place his own house in order.

Boisguilbert was in touch with Desmaretz, and in two or three of his letters a spark of the old spirit can be discerned. De Vaubourg, the brother of Desmaretz, who as intendant of Rouen had been Boisguilbert's friend, was now in Paris. Boisguilbert corresponded with him. In contrast with the frequently harsh and arrogant treatment Boisguilbert had received from Chamillart, whom he had regarded as a friend, and for whom he had

[84] Desmaretz, *Mémoire sur l'administration des finances*, p. 4.

[85] Saint-Simon speaks of the acclaim which greeted Boisguilbert on his return from exile. Boislisle doubts that the people of Rouen, "who before that had scarcely appreciated their magistrate, or his character, or his economic works," gave him such a reception. But, he says, "There is no question but that *Factum de la France* benefited from the proscription and had a success without parallel in the history of prohibited books. At least seven editions appeared before the end of the year 1707, of which three bore the title *Testament politique de M. de Vauban*. . . ." Boisguilbert's "sole concession to the ministers was to suppress the seditious pages of *Supplément*. . . ." ("Le Projet de dime royale et la mort de Vauban," *Comte rendu de l'acad. des sc. mor. et pol.*, 1875, Deuxième semestre, pp. 535–536.) Cadet, who listed the editions, does not speak of seven editions in 1707, but only of two. That such wide reading failed to effect an organization of the people to demand the reforms was probably due to two reasons: first, the content was not clearly understood; secondly, there was the hope of change under a new reign which must come before long.

shown in truth the love of a brother, there is something essentially noble in the consideration he received from Desmaretz and De Vaubourg. Boisguilbert had long regarded, and had publicly proclaimed Colbert as the cause of the troubles of France. He had attacked him with especial severity in *Factum*. Yet these nephews of Colbert treated the aging patriot with respect and even with tenderness. They acceded to his personal requests. He had been ruined by taxes under the Chamillart régime; but Desmaretz had intervened at the beginning of his ministry and ordered that only half his "wages" and none of his property be taken.[36] In May, 1710, Boisguilbert wrote to De Vaubourg about his taxes, setting forth what he could pay. There is something touching about De Vaubourg's reply. Whatever the request, he wished to grant it. Having said that he would have Desmaretz write to the intendant at Rouen to take care of certain items enumerated by Boisguilbert, he says: "See if I have indeed understood your intentions, because after meditating long over your letter, I still doubt my having been able to understand them. In case I am not right, change by short postscript either on the margin of my letter or on a copy."

After Boisguilbert's return from exile, there was published the second edition of his works with the proscribed *Supplément* omitted. *Testament politique de M. de Vauban,* it was called. Horn thinks it was published without Boisguilbert's consent. A careful comparison of the two editions of 1707 shows this to have been impossible. In the latter edition there is corrected for instance, an important typographical omission in the earlier edition.[37] Furthermore, although *Supplément* is omitted, it includes a very brief work, *Sentence du Châtelet de Paris qui fixe le prix du pain,* which is not in the other. The comment on the judicial decision fixing the price of bread is by Boisguilbert himself. This is shown unmistakably by the style and the ideas.

Cadet says that Boisguilbert made use of "an innocent ruse to give authority to his words." This would seem to be the true explanation of the *Testament politique*. But there may have been

[36] Boisguilbert's letter of March (no day recorded), 1710.

[37] "Laisse faire" is omitted in the phrase *pourvu qu'on la laisse faire* where first used in his famous paragraph in *Factum*, chapter iv.

something further. Boisguilbert was a man of deep sentiment, loyalties and attachments. He and Vauban had differed over the means to be taken, but they had fought for the same end: to save France from greed, self-interest, and incompetence. He had never regarded Vauban as the real author of the proposal for a dime royale. He thought the proposal unworthy of the marshal whose special knowledge lay in another field. It was as if he would share his own life's work as a monument worthy of the aims of the other. A single memorial it would be for the two who had labored and suffered for the same cause: the cause of the people of France. The name of the great general would give a wider circulation to the ideas which would eventually bring about what Boisguilbert had hoped to accomplish quickly. The latter had declared that his works must some time be published so that posterity would know that he had spared no effort in its behalf. Vauban also had worked for posterity; but he was dead and the *Dime* was proscribed. Dead, they would continue to work for France as they had worked while living. If Boisguilbert's proposals differed from Vauban's own, still Vauban, while living, had helped the former to gain a hearing for his ideas. "Never a man more gentle, more agreeable, more obliging." He was "perhaps the most upright and the most virtuous man of his century." Thus has Vauban been characterized. He would have approved any aid he might continue to give to Boisguilbert; he would have appreciated the tribute of having his name joined to a work he had admired so greatly. If the economic thought thus attributed to Vauban surpassed that in his own *Dime,* nevertheless he had shared the loftiness of the underlying ideals.

Again in 1712 Boisguilbert brought out two editions: *Le Détail de la France, par Bois-Guilbert,* and *Testament politique de M. de Vauban.* Publishing these two editions was Boisguilbert's last effort. It followed what must have been a bitter disappointment, namely, a distortion of one of his reforms by Desmaretz. In 1710 the latter put into effect Boisguilbert's tax of a tenth on incomes, not as a part of a general reform, and, as was intended, as a means to lighten the burden on the people, but as a grievous addition to the taxes already crushing them. This was the only part of his ideas and of his life's work Boisguilbert was ever to see effected.

In spite of having achieved nothing for France during his lifetime, Boisguilbert died, one suspects, a profoundly disappointed, but not an embittered man. He had failed in his two great objectives. His personal ambition clearly had been to rise, through sheer intelligence and merit, to an intendancy. His fundamental ambition had been to reform the fiscal system of France and to bring to her a prosperity commensurate with her natural wealth and the industry of her people. He accomplished neither. But he knew his worth. He was one of the great discoverers. Their recognition, he realized, had come late, but it had come. He had suffered ridicule; he had been persecuted; he had been looked upon as mad. But such, he knew, had been the common fate of pioneers in the field of thought. He died believing that his great ideas were for the future. Free roads; just taxes; prosperity for all the people—they were nature's plan. They would come. His ideas indeed belonged to the future.

France, who delights to honor her worthy sons, has singularly ignored this great patriot and thinker. Yet from the standpoint of his aims, his indirect influence on her political history, and his proper place in the history of the social and economic thought of a world, this pioneer would not have been unworthy of a place in the nation's Pantheon. Rouen has honored him with a portrait in her library near that of the great Corneille.[38] Appropriately enough she has also given a quay his name. But that honor greater than meaningless statues and streets, a memory that lives on, France has largely refused him. He is there, in her books and in her histories, derided by some and unsung by others who used his ideas. Voltaire meticulously listed all the writers of the age of Louis XIV, among them many long since forgotten and unworthy of being recalled. He had read Bois-

[38] Durand speaks of the "handsome, regular, frank and loyal features of the portrait of Boisguilbert" in the vestibule of the library of Rouen. His "thin, firm lips surmounted by a fine mustache, his determined, willful, and melancholy expression, indicate however, at the same time the thinker and the man of action."—Durand, *Essai sur les théories monétaires de Pierre de Boisguilbert,* Poitiers, 1922, p. 96.

guilbert's writings; yet he refused the author of *Le Détail de la France,* one of the few men of the age who made a permanent contribution to a new field of thought, a place on his roll of honor. He imputed the authorship of *Dime royale* to Boisguilbert, yet it is hard to understand how the literary tyro could have made such an error. Such of the economic ideas as he could grasp, and the principles of liberty, justice, and reason he seized upon as his own, but he spat on the author. "One Boisguilbert," he disdainfully referred to him. Daire states that in eight references to Boisguilbert which Voltaire made only once did he speak favorably of him. He spoke of him only "to commit a grave bibliographical error and to outrage the memory of this upright man, whom his hate-filled pen still pursues, in many other places in his works, with an inconceivable animosity."

Boisguilbert retained his judicial offices until the last. On August 8, 1714, he relinquished them. His eldest son succeeded him as president and lieutenant general of civil law in the bailiwick of Rouen; the second, M. de Maupertuy, had been the alternative lieutenant general of police for two years. Two months later, on October 10, 1714, he died. Although the third child of his parents' marriage, he survived his father only twenty years, and his mother, fourteen. His easy-going brother Nicholas, one year younger, lived until 1737. Pierre, restless, rebellious, indefatigable, wore himself out for France, only to be forgotten by her.

> On Thursday, October 11, 1714, the body of the late messire Pierre Lepesant, during his lifetime chevalier seigneur of Boisguillebert, Pinterville, Maupertuy and other places, councillor of the king in his councils, lieutenant general civil and of police in the city, bailiwick and vicomté of Rouen and president of the presidial seat of the said place, husband of dame Susanne Le Paige, living in the rue Malpalu, aged sixty-nine years, died on the tenth, having received all the holy sacraments, was inhumed in our church, in the presence of messire Gabriel Lepesant, chevalier seigneur de Pinterville, councillor of the king in his councils, lieutenant general of civil law of the city, bailiwick and vicomté of Rouen, and president of the seat of the said

> place, and of messire Jean-Pierre Lepesant, chevalier seigneur de Maupertuy, councillor of the king, alternative lieutenant general of police in the said city. (Great tolling of bells.) [39]

So passed the first modern economist. So passed a great figure, destined by nature to play a stellar rôle on history's stage; compelled by circumstance to take a minor part.

[39] The death record of Boisguilbert from the register of the parish of Saint-Maclou, Rouen.—Horn, note, p. 68.

IV

WRITINGS AND STYLE

Action is not taken against an author on the form of a work, the foundation of which cannot be attacked.

LE DÉTAIL DE LA FRANCE! The "title, it is true, is not very clear," said Dupont de Nemours a half century after the death of Boisguilbert. Not quite clear indeed! If it is understood only to imply an exact account of conditions in France why did Boisguilbert not call it an *État de la France,* as was usual with such detailed accounts? Presumably Boisguilbert's contemporaries were confused also as to the meaning. If so, it explains why the author translated *le détail* from the old French in the second edition, which bore the title, *France Ruined under the Reign of Louis XIV. "The Ruin of France."* Such is the title exactly stated. Boisguilbert, student of languages, in *le détail* had utilized a word with a double meaning, either one of which would accurately describe the content of the work he had written.

So with *Factum de la France.* A memoir? A statement of the facts with regard to France? Nothing so innocuous. It is an accuser who speaks. *Factum*—a legal brief. The case of France against those who ruin her is called. It is a plaintiff at the bar of justice. Does this title explain the use of the subtitle, *"Moyens très-faciles de faire recevoir au Roy quatre vingts millions,"* in the proscription? Did the government refuse publicly to acknowledge that a brief had been drawn up against it?

Boisguilbert's principal economic works are four in number: *Le Détail de la France, Factum de la France, Traité des grains,* and *Dissertation sur la nature des richesses, de l'argent et des tributs.*[1] In addition to his letters and memoirs to the controllers general, which form an important part of his writings, there are

[1] These, with *Supplément au Détail de la France,* are included in E. Daire's *Économistes financiers du 18e siècle.* Paris, 1843.

four minor works: *Traité du mérite et des lumières de ceux que l'on appelle gens habiles dans la finance ou grands financiers,*[2] *Mémoire abrégé sur les blés* (essentially a summary, of *Traité des grains*), *Causes de la rareté de l'argent,* and *Supplément au Détail de la France.* To these there should be added a very brief statistical study on the *Sentence du Châtelet de Paris qui fixe le prix du pain, 6 mai, 1649.*[3]

Le Détail de la France, first published in 1695, went through at least nine editions between that date and 1712.[4] Forbidden to publish anything else, the other writings appeared only in the complete editions of 1707 and 1712.

Because of the restrictions on publishing, there was no relation between the dates of the writing of the various works and their publication. *Le Détail,* for instance, is definitely dated as being written in 1689 by reference to "the vessels of silver reduced to money these days past," which refers to an edict of 1689 requiring all silver in any form exceeding one ounce in weight to be carried to the mint to be reduced to coin.[5] In a request to publish on November 14, 1704, *Traité des grains* is referred to so casually as his work on grain as to indicate that it had not recently been written. With the exception of his *Traité du mérite,* it is the only memoir the date of the writing of which cannot be definitely fixed. It is highly probable, however, that it was written around 1700, and certainly before *Factum.* That it was written before the latter is evidenced by the fact that in the edition of his complete works it follows *Traité du mérite,* and precedes *Factum,* and by the fact that all the other memoirs follow the order of the announcement of their being completed. *Causes de la rareté de l'argent* is announced in letters of July 1, July 22, and September 21, 1704, and *Dissertation sur la nature des richesses* in letters of November 20 and 25 of the same year.

Though each is complete in itself, yet so unified was the aim

[2] Reproduced in the appendix of I. E. Horn's *L'Économie politique avant les physiocrates.*

[3] For the complete titles of the various writings, see Bibliography.

[4] These editions are listed by Felix Cadet in the *Bibliographie raisonnée* of his *Pierre de Boisguilbert, précurseur des Économistes.*

[5] *Le Détail,* p. 213.

of all of Boisguilbert's writings that they constitute a single whole. It was not by chance alone that when he came to bring out an edition embodying them all he called it *Le Détail de la France.* In many respects, the later writings are essentially developments of the earlier work.

At no point was an exposition of economic theory an end in itself. Boisguilbert wrote to enlighten ministers and the public on what underlay the economic problems of the day. He took the problems up separately in order to emphasize them, to increase their force, to bring them individually into prominence. Thus he deals with taxation and the administration of the public finances; again with the condition of agriculture; now with money; but finally they are brought together and shown as interrelated parts of one general problem, the decline of the economic life of France. All lead to an emphasis upon the meaning of wealth, upon consumption, to the importance of exchange of goods as making consumption possible, to the necessity for freedom to carry on exchange uninterruptedly, to liberty, to laissez faire. In all this, he used "theory to explain facts, and facts to explain theory."

Le Détail de la France summarizes the conditions existing in France at the end of the reign of Louis XIV. It shows the errors, the defects, the abuses of the fiscal administration of the country, and their effects. It emphasizes the intimate connection between public and private finance. It proposes such fiscal and administrative reforms as would permit the economic life of the country to prosper and the government to have adequate revenue. The book is excellently organized. The first part deals with the diminution of the national income; the second, with the causes of this diminution; the third, with proposals for its reëstablishment.

Factum de la France is a restatement after ten years of the argument in *Le Détail de la France.* It was made necessary by the failure of the latter to achieve any results toward reform, and by the fact that conditions had grown steadily worse after 1700. Paradoxically *Factum* is at the same time more violent and more moderate in tone than *Le Détail.* It is savage in its reply to those who opposed reform; it is violent in its demand that the passive acceptance of the situation on the part of the ministry cease, and in its demand for changes in the system that had prostrated the economic life of the nation; it is calm and moderate in its attempt to conciliate those who stood to lose by a change in the system; it is simple in the reforms demanded. Boisguilbert and his friends regarded *Factum* as superior to *Le Détail,* as he indicated in his letters to Chamillart and to Vauban. It is on *Factum* that Mirabeau left notes. A century later Horn declared that in *Factum* Boisguilbert is more the economist than in *Le Détail.*

Traité du mérite is an exposition of the necessity for, and the advantages of, a simple tax system, and an attack upon the *gens habiles* who had introduced and maintained a complex system to further their own ends.

Traité des grains is a description and analysis of the agricultural conditions of the country. It is an attack upon the Colbertian system which subordinated agriculture to industry. The futility and the danger of having grains (or raw materials) produced at a loss is the dominating note. It was particularly addressed to the people, and had for its immediate purpose to explain the cause of the famines which were recurring so frequently. It is a noteworthy sociological study, and deserves to be known as the first significant analysis of value.

In *Causes de la rareté de l'argent* Boisguilbert replied to those who declared that the troubles in France were due to the lack of specie. In it the paradox is posed that the less money there is, the more there is. It deals with the phenomenon of hoarding and the significance of velocity of circulation. Here also is to be found Boisguilbert's most ambitious analysis of money as a means or as an intermediary in the exchange of goods for goods.

Dissertation sur la nature des richesses, de l'argent et des tributs is Boisguilbert's final and unifying work; it is at the same time the most purely abstract and theoretical. In the emphasis upon the significance of the labor supply, upon the division of labor and exchange; in the definition of wealth, the emphasis upon consumption, the rôle given to money; in the assumption of self-interest, divine providence and harmony of interest, and finally in the concept of laissez faire, it may be regarded as the prototype of *The Wealth of Nations.*

Supplément au Détail de la France is the stern and despairing effort of a man who had dedicated his life to save France. Powerful, almost brutal in its directness, it sums up the woes of the country and demands that the people be permitted to pay the king the revenue required in ways that would be possible without destroying them. It is the most dramatic summary in the field of economic literature. No one who has read it can ever forget the recurring *Faut-il attendre la paix?* Michelet says of it that the men of 1789 produced nothing so eloquent.

In reading Boisguilbert, the words of Talleyrand, that "language was given to man in order to disguise his thoughts," take on more force than that of a mere witticism. Not that Boisguilbert was purposely obscure. On the contrary he was intent on being understood. The difficulty is that of an involved style, unexpected metaphors, a figurative use of terms and manner of speaking, to say nothing of the terms which, in the course of the past two centuries, have taken on new meanings while tending to slough off the old. Speaking of *Factum,* Boislisle declares that "a certain eloquence bursts through inextricable mazes of an obscure phraseology, boresome repetitions, vulgar ways of speaking, and in spite of errors of style, of barbarisms of language and syntax; defects so discouraging that a specialist alone can read the works of the Rouen magistrate for the need of the cause, even with the arrangements and ameliorations of the modern edition. Moreover, it is necessary to say that *Factum,* like *Le Détail,* probably had scarcely any readers in France, and assuredly no successful ones." [6] But in spite of the difficulties, having drawn back the many veils which obscure the thought,

[6] *Mémoires de Saint-Simon,* Vol. XIV, append. xii, p. 594. When in *Factum* Boisguilbert states that *Le Détail* "had no success, and that not the least attention was paid to it," he refers to lack of reforms resulting, and not to lack of readers. Boislisle's statement that neither book was read is belied by the number of editions of *Le Détail* and by his own statement as to *Factum.* (See above, note, p. 90.) A view quite at variance with Boislisle's is given by Rivière. (See below, p. 167.) That the essence of the thought was understood by a select group, at least, is indicated by a survey of 18th century French thought.

delight in what is found amply repays the effort to uncover it. Boisguilbert's writings are precious relics which may well be objects of veneration on the part of economists.

"But there is more," "that is not all," every few pages these phrases are met, or else it is explained that it is necessary "to make a digression." Nevertheless, the "mazes" through which one must find one's way are not accidental. Boisguilbert himself explains them in a half-apologetic manner. "It is necessary," he says, "not to examine things in general, [a process] which is always subject to confusion, but to enter into the particular." "It is necessary to enter into detail." He tries to make clear "in particular as well as in general" why delay in instituting reforms is unnecessary. He "enters into detail in order to clarify the thinking of prejudiced persons in regard to the necessity for the free exportation of grain." Again a knowledge of the detail of all the kingdom, of its classes and conditions, is essential to a minister. Without this he cannot succeed, and Boisguilbert himself is providing the necessary knowledge.[7] Such are the reasons for the "mazes" of which Boislisle complains. They result from the working of a legally trained mind which would determine the facts in the case; an inductive approach to social phenomena, on the basis of which his principles were deduced. They result from a particular type of mentality, which possessed the most astonishing powers of observation, which nothing seemed to escape, and for which everything possessed significance; a mind which could reduce the details to a pattern and weld them into a whole through the power of analysis and deduction. Boisguilbert attributed to others his own capacities and interests. But in his attempt to promote clarity of thought on a subject, he confused those who were bored with carefully limiting phrases, who were less willing to enter into interminable detail, and who would have preferred to have the subject treated "in general."

Although with few exceptions Boisguilbert wrote in the third person, there is an intimacy sensed that is almost conversational in its effect. This is perhaps the result of an informality of expression which adds to the charm and to the difficulty of read-

[7] *Le Détail*, pp. 204, 229, 250–251. *Factum*, p. 320. *Traité des grains*, p. 373.

ing him. His diffuseness and repetitions are also obviously due in part to his custom of dictating. But like his endless details, his "tiresome repetitions" must not be regarded as solely the result of chance. They were deliberately made to draw attention to, and to emphasize, the points made. *Encore une fois*. How often the expression is encountered. "One will not repeat what has been too much detailed." This idea "will be reiterated on almost every page of this work, for fear it will be forgotten." To understand and to endure these repetitions it is necessary to understand Boisguilbert's purpose and his times. He was trying to convert a nation to ideas and policies which he felt to be vital to the very existence of the State; he was opening up a new field of thought which no one thoroughly understood except himself. In the new lessons which must be learned he had to be drillmaster as well as teacher.

Cadet complains of the diffuseness, the negligence, the errors, the obscurity, the repetitions. These defects he regards as due to Boisguilbert's haste in writing in the midst of his duties, and under the threat of persecution, and to the fact that his alert and penetrating mind was not given to the discipline of good writing. It would not have been surprising in a writer of the sixteenth century and early in the seventeenth century, he says, but it is so in the days of Fénelon, Racine, and La Bruyère.[8] But here Cadet is lacking in a certain understanding. He forgets Boisguilbert the judge and historian and thinks only of Boisguilbert the economist. He forgets that through his reading Boisguilbert was living more in the past than in the present; that in this respect he belongs to the sixteenth century as well as to the turn of the next century. It is only by turning to the edicts in the midst of which he lived that one can understand, for instance, his frequent use of such constructions as *ont fait et font, a passé et passe,* and *tant produites qu'à produire,* which complicate his pages. All told, in the combined rôle of judge, historian, and economist he is holding an inquiry, as it were, on the economic condition

[8] Cadet, pp. 104–112. Nevertheless even so great a writer as La Bruyère did not always write perfectly when he wrote hastily. See his letters to the Prince of Condé, of whose grandson, the Duke of Bourbon, La Bruyère was the tutor.—La Bruyère, *Oeuvres,* Paris, 1865, Vol. II, pp. 477–517.

of France, and "it cannot be said in this species of criminal process, that the accusation may not have fulfilled its first obligation, which is to prove, by the presentation of the *corpus delicti*, that the crime has been committed." [9]

Boisguilbert's real shortcomings are of a kind which require the utmost attention on the part of one who would know his exact thought. There is his habit of carefully qualifying a statement once and repeating it elsewhere without the qualification. For instance: "silver converted into money cannot furnish any of the needs of life." Elsewhere he speaks of silver as being of no use in itself. Then thinking in relative or comparative terms, such as, "the degree of excess or moderation of debts is determined, not by their particular amount, but by the resources of those who pay," he expresses himself absolutely—*ce qui ne va à rien*. Such defects are responsible for many of the exaggerations for which he is criticized.

There are other obstructions to an easy understanding of the thought. There are contractions such as, *les fonds* for "the value of the land," or "the income from the land," for example; there are allusions, such as, to free the roads "is the raising of the siege of La Rochelle"; there is irony in such phrases as *la perfection* and *le beau ménage*, for instance, which must not be read literally. Moreover, economic terminology was as yet undeveloped, and Boisguilbert groped to express an idea without the economy of expression that a recognized terminology makes possible. Therefore it is evident that if Boisguilbert is read it must be for his ideas in spite of the manner in which they are expressed.

Boisguilbert was aware that he was regarded as presenting difficulties to his readers. He seemed to think, however, that the fault was not so much in his work, but in his critics, that they were underlings. *Le Détail*, he says, has been called obscure by its critics. They have declared that it cannot be understood. But he avers, "one may not take action against an author on the form of a work, the foundation of which cannot be attacked." "St. Augustine and Lactance have been shown by time to have

[9] *Traité des grains*, p. 387.

been wrong, rather than the one who announced the antipodes."

If the defects of his style may not be overlooked, Cadet, for instance, does not fail to consider its "sparkling beauties." He speaks especially of the conviction carried to the reader. Boisguilbert writes not as a publicist by profession, but as a patriot who loves France passionately, and who sighs to see her ruined by ignorance. His eloquence comes from the heart, and in it there are its great qualities, warmth, movement, energy, irony, familiarity, elevation, and picturesqueness. Again, he can be remarkably concise and powerfully deduce his ideas, and his refutations are models of their kind. Then there is the alert and vivid imagination which furnishes him with the happy means of gripping the reader, while his homely figures of speech, with their truth, simplicity, and appropriateness, now gay, now gentle, now sad, soften the coarseness.[10]

The figures which recur most frequently in Boisguilbert's writings are particularly appropriate to the thought and to the theory. For example, the use of the alembic or distillator, to illustrate the sacrifice of great quantities of goods to obtain so little revenue for the sovereign; and of the balance or scale as representative of the equilibrium desired in economic life and the ease with which this equilibrium may be disturbed. Then, there is the clock which suggests the necessary coördination required among all the interdependent parts of a complex economic structure; and finally, there is the flowing stream which illustrates the smoothness in the functioning of economic life which he thought should characterize it.

To sum up, it may be said that Boisguilbert is as full of surprises in his method of expression as in his thought. In spite of all his obscurities, one reads him with a smile. Where else can one find such a characterization of mob action as in the following, where the staccato style so suits the thought:

En un mot, le peuple est assurément comme un troupeau de moutons que l'on voudrait faire entrer par une très-petite porte, et très-embarrassée; il n'y a qu'à en prendre un ou deux par les oreilles, et les tirer par force, aussitôt tous les autres s'y poussent avec la même

[10] Cadet, pp. 112–119.

violence dont il avait fallu user pour y conduire les deux premiers. Et quand il y aurait une très-grande porte tout contre, exposée à leur vue, qui, les conduisant au même lieu, leur donnerait un passage bien plus aisé, il ne serait pas possible à force de coups de leur faire prendre ce parti, mais ils continueraient de s'étouffer les uns les autres pour suivre les premiers. Voilà le portrait du peuple, et sa conduite dans ses démarches tumultueuses, surtout à l'égard des blés.[11]

And where else may one find the prosaic topic of taxation dealt with so exquisitely; the cadences flowing with the slowness and the dignity of the stream which has reached the end of its course:

Il faut que les tributs coulent aux mains du prince comme les rivières coulent dans la mer, c'est-à-dire tranquillement, ce qui ne manquera jamais d'arriver, lorsqu'ils seront proportionnés au pouvoir des contribuables, tant sur les choses que sur les personnes: la dérogeance qu'on a apportée à cette règle est seule cause de tout le désordre. Un monarque en doit user envers ses peuples comme Dieu déclare qu'il fera envers les chrétiens; savoir, qu'il demandera beaucoup à qui aura beaucoup, et peu à qui aura peu. Et sur le même style, un père de l'Église atteste que, de quelque grand prix que soit le paradis, Dieu ne le vend aux fidèles, quelque misérables qu'ils soient, que le prix qu'ils le peuvent acheter: voilà l'unique niveau des tributs.[12]

What economist has treated laissez faire so poetically as Boisguilbert in the paragraphs beginning: "Les blés sortent de la terre par le travail de l'homme et les influences du ciel, de la même manière que les eaux coulent des sources; ils ne tarissent jamais tant que le cours est libre." [13]

In a word . . . if Boisguilbert is not a good writer in the full acceptance of this term, he has . . . written beautiful pages, worthy of being read and reread as historical pictures and as economic analyses. . . . They bring to life this penetrating genius who did not allow himself to be dazzled by the superficial brilliancy of the miraculous reign; who seized upon the evils of the people, marked their cause with a sure hand, and indicated their remedy; who, finally, opened to the human mind the new path of social philosophy.

[11] *Factum*, p. 326. [12] *Ibid.*, pp. 333–334.
[13] *Traité des grains*, p. 387. It is difficult not to think that this beautiful passage showing the effect of man-made *digues et chaussées* was the inspiration for Adam Smith's passage with its figure of a dam in *The Wealth of Nations*, Cannan ed., London, 1925, Bk. IV, pp. 13–14.

V

THE TAILLE

France is treated like an enemy country that one would never see again.

WHAT had brought about such a condition in France that Boisguilbert would devote himself with a religious intensity to save her? What had ravaged the richest nation in Europe like an enemy's horde?

Modern historians enumerate among the causes of the economic conditions at the close of the reign of Louis XIV, the wars of this ambitious monarch, his extravagances, and the revocation of the Edict of Nantes. Louis XIV carried on three important wars during his own reign beginning in 1661. The first of these, the war with Holland, lasting from 1672 to 1678, "had not been a severe strain" on the nation's resources.[1] The more destructive wars did not begin until 1689. In the interval there was comparative peace for eleven years. Yet in this period the records indicate that the country was profoundly distressed. In 1687 a commission had been appointed to determine the causes.

Few rulers have spent with a more reckless extravagance than Louis XIV. Nevertheless, even his expenditures have been grossly exaggerated. Perkins, for instance, relates that the cost of Versailles, his greatest extravagance, has been estimated at from 500,000,000 livres to 4,600,000,000 livres. But Perkins states that the building accounts more recently discovered show that the palace, the accessories, the decorations, and the works of art cost 116,000,000 livres,[2] or approximately the amount of the ordinary revenues for one year.

As to the effect of the revocation of the Edict of Nantes,

[1] James Breck Perkins, *France under the Regency, with a Review of the Administration of Louis XIV*, Boston and New York, 1892, p. 112.
[2] *Ibid.*, pp. 139–141.

Boisguilbert indicates that the flight from the land had started earlier. This is confirmed by Esmonin, who shows that the desertion had begun as early as 1673, or at the very beginning of the war with Holland.[3] That the revocation of the edict was not a primary factor in the decline of the economic life of the country is again the view of Perkins: "The amount of material injury which it did to France has . . . been greatly exaggerated. Historians write as if that country was in a highly prosperous condition before the revocation, and by the result of that act alone was reduced to poverty and distress. . . . This is far from being correct." [4]

Certainly these three factors contributed to the decline which had reached such abysmal proportions before the end of the reign. But the deep-seated causes must be sought elsewhere, in factors which would necessarily have impoverished the people had the country known only peace, had the king been ever so penurious, and had the Protestants been left to pursue their lives unmolested. It was the hemming in of the economic life of the people by a vicious fiscal and economic system which Boisguilbert regarded as the fundamental factor destroying France. Such is the view of the Lavisse *Histoire de France,* according to which the wars and the revocation of the Edict of Nantes are classified as accidental or contributory causes, and the economic and fiscal systems as the profound and constant causes of the decline in economic activity.[5]

It was the *means* used to raise the ordinary and extraordinary revenue which was the *first* and *principal* cause of the destruction of the wealth of France, Boisguilbert declared. The venal administration of the finances was a canker gnawing at the vital parts of France; a gangrene, attacking, as he said with a double meaning, "her noble parts." This "sacrifice . . . of the general welfare to individual interest is the principal and perhaps the unique cause of the ruin of France. . . . There is the key to the diminution or the loss of the wealth of France." [6]

A contemporary explanation of the depression was the ex-

[3] See below, note, p. 117. [4] *Op. cit.,* pp. 199–201.
[5] *Histoire de France,* Paris, 1900–1911, Vol. VIII[1], pp. 202–214.
[6] *Le Détail,* p. 236. *Factum,* p. 301.

istence of the war. Boisguilbert reminded his readers that war years had usually been prosperous years, placing "everything in movement." [7] He considered other explanations:

Although the cause of the decrease of the wealth of France must be a thing as certain as the decrease itself; nevertheless, although everyone be in agreement with respect to the one, it is far from being the case with the other. The high commissioners sent throughout the kingdom to find means to reëstablish that which was defective, were a certain indication that people were not persuaded that all was perfect. And as this endeavor has been without result, one wishes to believe that it has not been easy to agree upon the cause of the evil, and as a consequence upon the remedy. Some pretended to say that there was no more commerce; but that was to set forth the disorder itself as the cause of the disorder. Others advanced [the opinion] that there was no more money; but we have just seen in the changing of the specie how much they were mistaken.[8] And the others, finally, alleged the increase in the revenues of the king, not to speak of the taxes, which would have taken away all hope of change, [it] being difficult to diminish a thing the causes of which demand the augmentation and never the diminution. The slight foundation for such reasoning has been made sufficiently clear in the first part of these memoirs. That is why we will speak of them no more, in order to pass on to the true cause of these disorders.[9]

Thus Boisguilbert rejected the explanations offered, and turned to his own analysis.

The wealth of France had so greatly decreased, Boisguilbert declared, because of the decrease of consumption.[10] Goods are worthless unless they are consumed. Therefore to discover the cause of the ruin of France, it was necessary only to discover the

[7] *Traité des grains,* p. 365.
[8] Reference to the edict of 1693, in which the marc of silver was changed from 29 livres, 6 sous, 11 deniers, to 32 livres, 6 sous.—Daire note, *Le Détail,* p. 180.
[9] *Le Détail,* pp. 179–180.
[10] Perkins confirms this lack of demand as the cause of the difficulties: "The commercial policy of Colbert was continued after his death, but we find no signs of increasing prosperity. French industries, which have been thought to owe their first great development to his influence, continued to diminish instead of increase for more than thirty years after he died. . . . The trouble with the French manufactures was . . . a lack of demand. The exports to other countries were greatly diminished. The farmers were too poor to be large consumers. A barefooted peasant, clothed in rags and living on chestnuts and black bread, had no money with which to purchase either the luxuries or the comforts of life."—*France under the Regency,* pp. 113–114.

cause of the ruin of consumption. This had ceased, he stated, first, because it was "forbidden." People dared not consume on account of the uncertainty of the taille, which was absolutely arbitrary. Secondly, consumption was "impossible" because of the aides, which had destroyed the wine trade; because of the provincial duanes which so adversely affected domestic trade, and because of the export tax which had destroyed the value of grain. Such was Boisguilbert's summary of the principal causes of the existing conditions.

Vauban gives a contemporary corroboration of this analysis as to the effect of the taille, aides, and duanes:

> The wandering life that I have led during the past forty years and more, having given me the opportunity to see and to visit many times and in many ways the most of the provinces in the kingdom, sometimes alone with my servants, and sometimes in company with some engineers, I have often had opportunity to observe and to reflect upon the good and the bad points of the country; to examine the state and condition of it and that of the people, whose poverty, having often excited my compassion, has given me occasion to search for its cause. This having been done with very much care, I have found that it corresponds perfectly with that which the author of *Le Détail de la France* has written. He has developed and brought to light without mincing matters (*fort naturellement*) the abuses and evil customs which are practiced in the collection of the tailles, the aides, and the provincial duanes. One wishes he had done as much for affaires extraordinaires, the capitation, and the prodigious number of exempts existing at the present moment in the kingdom, which create scarcely less evil than the other three, which he has so well described for us.[11]

Vauban's criticism of the omission is scarcely justified. The capitation, for instance, was established only in the year *Le Détail* was published; yet in the first edition there is a pointed criticism of the inequality of the tax.[12] It had, Boisguilbert thought, one of the characteristics of a good tax, but its defects are not spared in *Factum*. Likewise, while specific chapters are not devoted to affaires extraordinaires or to the exempts, nevertheless, what is said could scarcely have been made stronger, and they form the subject of innumerable letters to the controller general.

[11] *Dime royale*, Preface, pp. 31–34.
[12] *Le Détail*, 1695 ed., p. 255.

The mere listing of these causes means little. It is essential to understand their operation in order to see how a fiscal system, badly conceived, woefully administered, and having degenerated through corruption, fraud, and self-interest, could take so important a part in prostrating the economic life of a great nation.

There were two forms of the taille [13] in France in 1700: the *taille réelle* and the *taille personnelle*. The former tax was sufficiently imperfect to be condemned, but it is the personal taille which has the unenviable reputation of having been the cruelest tax in history. It was this arbitrary tax in the pays d'élections that Boisguilbert condemned.[14] Hereafter the term "taille" refers to the personal taille and not to the real taille.

[13] From *tailler,* meaning to prune, to cut out, to clip off.

[14] The *taille* was originally a feudal impost levied by the feudal lord on his men. It was at first levied by the king in his own domain in his character of feudal lord, and extended later to his other subjects. Originally called an *aide, fouage,* or *subside,* it was the first of the direct taxes levied. At first an extraordinary source of revenue, it gradually became ordinary around 1439. It could not, nor could any tax, be levied outside the king's own domain unless those whom it was proposed to tax consented to the imposition. Out of this requirement grew the provincial assemblies. (Esmonin, *La taille en Normandie au temps de Colbert, 1661–1683,* Paris, 1913, pp. 1–2.) The taille, says Daire, corresponded to the modern *impôts fonciers et personnels et mobiliers.* The *real taille* was a tax on the presumable income from land, and was the form found in the *pays d'états,* that is, the provinces constituting from a fourth to a third of the kingdom, each of which had its own elective assembly, which voted the taxes imposed by the king. (Britanny, Provence, Dauphiné, Burgundy, Franche-Comté, Artois and Flanders, especially.) The assessment of the taille, therefore, may be said to have been determined by the local tax-payers. The lands of the nobles and of the Church were legally exempted from the payment of the real taille. The *pays d'élections,* constituting the remainder of the kingdom, had no provincial assemblies. In these provinces the apportionment of the taille among the elections and parishes was made by the intendant, that is to say, by central authority. (It should be stated that for purposes of fiscal administration the provinces were divided into generalities, with an intendant at the head of each one; the generalities, into elections governed by a tribunal, the members of which were called *élus,* and legally entitled councillors of the king; the elections in turn were subdivided into parishes.) Theoretically the intendant was supposed to be aided in this task by the élus of the elections. In practice the sharing of the function seems to have had no meaning. The *personal taille* of the pays d'élections was a much more complicated tax than the real taille of the pays d'états. In its simplest terms it was a tax upon the presumable income of the taillable persons, but it consisted essentially of two taxes: 1. The tax on real estate, which in turn was divided into two parts: (a) *La taille d'exploitation,* that is, on land under cultivation and on buildings such as mills, foundries, workshops, etc., used for productive purposes. Theoretically such property of nobles and of the Church was subject to this tax. In practice all the rich and powerful

The evils of the taille were threefold. First, it was uncertain both for parishes and for individuals. Secondly, it was unjust because it was not in proportion to the ability of the *taillables* to pay. Finally, the method of collection was objectionable. Everyone in the parish took turns as collector, and each collector in turn was ruined. Of all the *corvées* in France the collection of the taille was the most onerous. There was "no one, even the most wretchedly poor, who would not sell his shirt to obtain exemption from this servitude." [15]

The Imposition

The total amount of the taille to be raised in any one year was determined by the needs of the central government for that year. This total settled, it was divided among the generalities by the commissioners of the king's council, and the amount for each generality was forwarded to the intendant. In the generality the intendant proceeded to apportion the total among the elections and the parishes. After the parish total was received, on a Sunday afternoon after church, the individuals of the parish elected the parish *élus*, or collectors,[16] whose duties were to assess individuals and to collect the tax.

The arbitrary character of the tax was due to the power of the intendant over the apportionment of the total among the elections and the parishes. It led inevitably to an abuse of the power. No sooner was the amount for the generality received than the influential individuals began to pay "court to the intendant to secure favorable treatment for their parishes in the apportionment

---

secured almost complete exemption from the tax on such property. (b) *La taille d'occupation*, that is, on dwellings and related buildings. From this portion of the tax the property of nobles and of the Church was legally exempted. 2. The second part of the tax had as its base the presumable faculty of the taillables. Theoretically, again, the nobles and the Church paid this. But in practice, both, as well as the wealthiest members of the third estate, secured exemption. "In sum, then, the taille was a land tax which touched only the poorest proprietors of the kingdom, and a *taxe mobilière* which bore exclusively upon the least rich classes of society." (Daire note, *Dime royale*, p. 32.) The free cities, Paris, Rouen, and others, having originally commuted the tax, paid no taille.

[15] *Le Détail*, pp. 162, 220. *Factum*, pp. 282–284, 320, 322.

[16] The number of collectors varied according to the size of the parish, but in no case exceeded seven. No individual was supposed to serve more than once every four years.

of the taille." As a result it was not at all unusual to see a small parish pay twice the amount of a large one. There was a double incentive for a parish lord to use every effort to obtain the lowest assessment possible for his parish. Not only was the amount to be collected reduced by this means, but the lord's own farmers were favored in the local assessment according as he himself had succeeded in procuring good treatment for the parish from the intendant. Having relieved his farmers of the taille, the rents on his lands were raised accordingly. The gain, therefore, went to the lord and not to the farmers. Consequently, it was "not unusual to see in the same parish farms of three thousand or four thousand *écus* of rent contribute only ten or twelve écus of taille, while one of three hundred or four hundred écus of rent [would] pay one hundred écus." "Some of the well-meaning intendants would stop the exemptions of the farmers of the nobles and others, but they dare not. It would cause jealousy, and as the great lords are among the exempt, it would be necessary to begin with them as examples, which cannot be done. Thus they abandon all attempt at reform." [17]

The action of the intendants in favoring parishes in the apportionment of the taille "authorizes in some manner a like conduct in the assessment of individuals within the parish." These abuses Boisguilbert describes vividly. It must be remem-

[17] Cadet (pp. 171–173) quotes Turgot (*Observations sur un projet d'édit*) as saying that in spite of the arbitrary power of the intendants over the apportionment of the taille, they would not abuse the power because of the desire not to dishonor themselves publicly. But Cadet says that Turgot judged others by his own high standards, and he proceeds to show that Boisguilbert was right in his attack upon the abuse of their power. Cadet quotes in particular a letter from Colbert (Depping, *Cor. adm.*, Vol. III, pp. 33–34) to the intendants on August 26, 1663, ordering them "in the name of the king to make the apportionment of the taille 'without having regard to the suggestions of anyone.'" But how could Colbert expect results from such an order when he himself proceeded to undermine it as is shown by the following letter of September 25, 1663, one month after the above order: "'M. le comte de Saint-Aignan told me that the inhabitants of Loches were very wretched, and it would be well to relieve them both with respect to the taille and the tax on salt. And as he is one of my particular friends, I shall be obliged to you if you will aid me in making his recommendation effective.'" (*Ibid.*, p. 50.) To be sure Colbert adds that "in these things equity and justice must always prevail over all other considerations." But there had been a hint from the powerful Colbert that no intendant would disregard whatever the "equity and justice" of the case might be.

bered that the collectors, who also assessed, were elected in turn annually. So when new collectors were elected for the ensuing year, they began by avenging themselves on those whom they regarded as having injured them under similar circumstances "down to the third generation." Next they favored their relatives and friends, rich and poor. But their greatest interest was to relieve their own poverty. The taille was assessed by the plural vote of the collectors. As a consequence their votes were sold, and failing to agree on the assessments, they sometimes sat around in taverns where the meetings took place for three months before agreement was reached, increasing their own expenses and delaying the collection. In the meanwhile the receivers of the taille, who advanced the first quarter of the tax to the treasury, and upon which they were paid interest, would begin to push the collectors for the repayment of this advance. Finally, the farmers of the lords of the parish, of the gentlemen of influence, of judges, down to attorneys and sergeants, were "considered," that is, assessed a smaller sum than was justified by the value of their property. The result was that the weight of the taille fell on the small cultivators, farm laborers, artisans, and merchants.[18]

The Collection

It would be difficult to find a more humorously tragic picture than Boisguilbert's description of the collection of the taille.

As this collection is the most disagreeable *corvée* imaginable, the collectors, whatever their number, wish to collect it only in a body, and march through the streets conjointly. So in places where there are seven [collectors], seven persons are seen, [and] instead of relieving one another, [all] tramp continually through the streets. And as [only] a small part of the taille is collected in any one year, the

[18] *Le Détail,* Pt. II, chaps. iii–v. *Factum,* chap. v. Cadet, pp. 161–181. Horn, pp. 224–236. Esmonin, chap. iii; chap. vi, pp. 353–377. Adam Smith says, apropos the assessment of the personal taille, that "These circumstances are judged of, in the one case, by officers of the election; in the other by those of the parish; and both the one and the other are, more or less, under the direction and influence of the intendant. Not only ignorance and misinformation, but friendship, partly animosity, and private resentment, are said frequently to mislead such assessors."—*Wealth of Nations,* Bk. V, p. 339. All references to *The Wealth of Nations* are to the Cannan edition, London, 1925.

collectors of the present year march, or rather pillage, on one side, while those of the preceding year do likewise on the other. And when there is some *étape* or *ustensile*[19] to collect, as new collectors are required, they form a new brigade on the model of the others. These taken as a whole, not to speak of the collection of the salt [tax] which is done in the same manner in many places, compose a species of army, which, during a whole year, loses its time in beating the pavement, almost without receiving anything except a thousand insults and a thousand imprecations. And this is due to the fact, that, after the assessment, the interest of the taxable individuals, who count on no protection,[20] is to conceal all kinds of show of comfort by a complete cessation of commerce and consumption.[21] Likewise on account of the collection they have another reason, which is to pay sou by sou, after a thousand constraints and a thousand levies (*exécutions*). [They pay this way] either to avenge themselves on the collectors for having imposed too large a sum, retarding by that [means] the turning in of receipts and making [the collectors] undergo the actions of process servers (*courses d'huissiers*), or to prevent those of the following year from assessing a like sum on account of the difficulty of [obtaining] payments. So after having walked a whole week [the collectors] often obtain only maledictions. On the other hand, they are crippled with expenses by the receivers

[19] Special war taxes.

[20] That is, who are not farmers of the influential.

[21] Those who have read the *Confessions* of Jean Jacques Rousseau may remember his description of the effect of the taille and the aides. Wandering through the country "weary, fainting with hunger and thirst," he entered a peasant's hut. "I entreated the countryman to give me some dinner, offering to pay for it. He presented me with some skimmed milk and coarse barley bread, saying it was all he had. . . . Presently after . . . he plainly saw I was an honest, good-natured young man, and did not come to betray him . . . he opened a little trap-door by the side of his kitchen, went down, and returned a moment after with a good brown loaf of pure wheat, the remains of a good but rather highly flavored ham, and a bottle of wine, the sight of which rejoiced my heart more than all the rest. . . . When I again offered to pay, his inquietude and fear returned. . . . I could not imagine the motive of his fear. At length he pronounced tremblingly those terrible words, 'commissioners' and 'cellar rats,' which he explained by giving me to understand that he concealed his wine because of the excise and his bread on account of the tax imposed upon it; adding that he should be an undone man if it were suspected he was not almost perishing with want. What he said to me on this subject made an impression on my mind that can never be effaced, sowing seeds of that inextinguishable hatred which has since grown up in my heart against the vexations these unhappy people suffer, and against their oppressors. This man, though in easy circumstances, dared not eat the bread gained by the sweat of his brow, and could only escape ruin by exhibiting an outward appearance of misery!"—*The Confessions of Jean Jacques Rousseau*, London, 1901, Vol. I, pp. 244–245.

of the tailles, who have erected these constraints to profit from their offices. And if it happens that some parishes, with the aid of loans which they obtain, pay on the day named without having undergone actions, they are certain to have an increase the following year, because in the apportionment of the taille [among the parishes] the receivers are completely the masters under the pretext that they are the guarantors of the collection. As a result, it is necessary for the collectors to be on their feet every day throughout the year; and many who have money concealed make them come a hundred times to their houses in order to receive the payment of their taille. And as we are endeavoring to show that the collection costs the people more than the taille returns to the king, in view of the manner in which things are done, the details [such as those] of which we have just spoken will be continued.

When, after the insults and the imprecations, through which the taillables have gotten rid of a part of their bile and anger, it is necessary finally to come to the payment, this is how things are done: the collectors dare not push the taillables too much, for fear of suffering a like treatment in their turn. As a result, although they have the power to levy on movables and to carry them away in default of payment, it is necessary, nevertheless, before making use of these extremities, for the collectors themselves to have suffered forced constraints on the part of their receivers, that is to say, many actions by process servers and sergeants. When the latter have first arrived, it is necessary to regale them in taverns in order to prevail upon them to make only a simple action and not a levy on the property, and it is necessary to make gifts of money in addition to that which is due for their action, of which they have only the least part. All this, however, is only at the beginning, for in the end, there are only levies.

Beasts are then led from the parish in general, without inquiring if the persons to whom they belong have paid their taille completely or not, which is a matter of unconcern. Money must then be given to the process server to keep him from leading the animals very far away, and to prevent him from selling them without delay. But when the year is about to end, it is no longer a question of actions or of levies, but of imprisonments. Again money must be given to the process servers, so that instead of taking the collectors to prisons, which are often far off, they will place them under arrest in a neighboring inn, where they live at the expense of their fellow collectors.[22]

[22] The collectors were personally liable and *solidaire* for any portion of the tax placed on the parish which they were unable to collect for each quarter as due. Meanwhile the receivers of the taille only imprisoned one or two of the collectors as representative of them all while the others proceeded with

But if the jailor claims them, or has gained the good graces of the receiver by his *savoir faire,* it is necessary to lead them to prison. . . . Moreover, every time the collectors turn over funds, it is necessary not to forget a present of produce for M. the receiver, however much it may cost; otherwise, whatever evil one suffers would be still worse. Finally, considering the manner in which the taille is apportioned, is assessed, and is paid, and since vengeance for the overcharge that one feels to have been imposed on him is perpetuated from father to son, it is necessary to agree that [the taille] is equally the ruin of property, of bodies, and of souls.[23]

As Boisguilbert says elsewhere, "if the demons had held council to consider the means to damn and to destroy all the people of the kingdom, they would have been able to devise nothing better to achieve such an end."[24] The sociological results were not less disastrous than the economic effects. Community life was disrupted by bitterness, hatred, and suspicion.

Such were what Boisguilbert called the "sinister effects of the arbitrary taille." There were secondary effects which he felt to be not less deplorable. The first of these was the dispossession of the small owner who could no longer afford to own land. This land was bought up at excessively low prices, usually by the lord of the parish.

[But] little properties which are no longer being bought or owned by taillable individuals, are given or leased for nothing on occasion, for lack of a buyer. This is a loss to the body of the State which is communicated imperceptibly to the great estates, which around Paris as elsewhere are sold for only half of what they formerly brought. From this there follows the ruin of a great number of people, because mortgages contracted on the former prices, as well as shares (*partages*) and other things, which are easily paid when lands are at their original value, can no longer be paid on account of the decrease. [Thus] it is necessary to come to foreclosures, in which, [because of] the decrease [in price], the expenses of justice and of

---

the collection. Finally if the amount due was not paid by the specified time, the personal property of all the collectors was seized. This proving insufficient, the collectors named six taillables of the parish, from a list of twelve of the nonexempts which was submitted by the receivers. This group was solidaire for the remainder of the tax, and their personal property likewise was seized in default of payment. The solidarity for the taille arose from the fact that it was considered a debt of the parish, and not of the individuals therein.—Esmonin, pp. 487, 495–496.

[23] *Le Détail,* pp. 186–187. [24] *Factum,* p. 274.

waste taking everything, the debtors and creditors are equally ruined.

There is another pernicious effect: the owner of a little estate treats it carefully and makes improvements on it, either in planting or in fertilizing the land. But when this same land becomes part of a great estate, it ceases to be half as valuable, and [is worth] nothing at all so far as the taille is concerned.[25]

And finally, the third and last effect of this uncertainty of the tax is that it is necessary to avoid all show of wealth because of the reasons treated heretofore. And as the soul of agriculture and cultivation is the fertilization of the land, as no one does this without animals, one would hardly dare have the necessary number of them even when one could, for fear of paying double because of the envy of neighbors. Thus it is common to see in parishes where there were formerly one thousand or twelve hundred sheep only a quarter of the number now.[26]

There was only one way to escape the destructive effect of the taille if one were "unprotected." This was to flee from the land and villages either to the free cities which had no taille, or to the cities and towns in which the taille had been placed *en tarif*, or to migrate to another land. The desertion of taillable places had become so great that attempts were made to prohibit it.[27] The taille being a debt of the parishes and not of the individuals as such, many of the towns and cities wished to escape the evil

[25] "It seldom happens . . . that a great proprietor is a great improver. . . . There still remain in both parts of the united kingdom some great estates which have continued without interruption in the hands of the same family since the times of feudal anarchy. Compare the present condition of these estates with the possessions of the small proprietors in their neighborhood, and you will require no other argument to convince you how unfavorable such extensive property is to improvement."—*Wealth of Nations*, Bk. III, pp. 362–363.

[26] *Le Détail*, pp. 189–190. Adam Smith discusses this point: "In the countries where the personal taille takes place, the farmer is commonly assessed in proportion to the stock which he appears to employ in cultivation. He is, upon this account, frequently afraid to have a good team of horses or oxen, but endeavours to cultivate with the meanest and most wretched instruments of husbandry that he can. Such is his distrust in the justice of his assessors, that he counterfeits poverty, and wishes to appear scarce able to pay any thing for fear of having to pay too much. . . . The public, the farmer, the landlord, all suffer more or less by this degraded cultivation. That the personal taille tends, in many different ways, to discourage cultivation, and consequently to dry up the principal source of wealth of every great country, I have already had occasion to observe."—*Wealth of Nations*, Bk. V, pp. 340–341.

[27] The flight of the inhabitants from the most highly taxed parishes and those especially burdened with the quartering of troops had begun as early as 1673, says Esmonin (pp. 523–524).

effects of the tax by paying annually a fixed amount in a lump sum, reimbursing themselves as they saw fit, usually by a tax on the products consumed within the place. This was termed placing the taille en tarif. It was seldom permitted even when the onerous conditions imposed could be met. It doubled the amount paid, says Boisguilbert, but the places in which this was done immediately began to prosper.

The taille was not farmed, and was not, Boisguilbert states, the source of large fortunes as were the aides and duanes. Nevertheless, the receivers were interested in seeing the continuation of the system. They not only received their salaries, but a remission of nine deniers per livre for advancing the taille to the king, as well as gifts from the collectors in return for leniency in making the collection.[28]

[28] *Le Détail,* Pt. II, chaps. vi–viii and p. 196. Esmonin, chap. vii. Cadet, pp. 181–188.

VI
AFFAIRES EXTRAORDINAIRES
THE AIDES AND DUANES

There is no difference between goods which can be sold when one wishes, and ready money.

OF THE principal sources of ordinary revenue under the old régime in France, the taille, as has been said, was the only one which passed directly from the people into the treasury. The aides and duanes, on the contrary, passed through the hands of intermediaries. So too did affaires extraordinaires. Before taking up these taxes which played so disastrous a part in the lives of the people, it is well to take a glimpse at these intermediaries.

Les traites were originally tariff duties exacted on goods entering or leaving the kingdom and certain provinces within the country. "The duties were as numerous as those of the aides. Altogether they were confused to the point that it was almost impossible to distinguish between them." The terms *le parti* and *le traité* originally applied to the agreements entered into between the government and the farmers of the aides and duanes. By the end of the seventeenth century they connoted any financial operation depending on the advance of funds on the creation of indirect taxes or of offices, that is, contracts giving the purchasers of the contract the right to tax goods or sell offices in return for the consideration involved.

Theoretically at least, the contracts were let to the highest bidder. In practice, as the influential members of the nobility and the ministers themselves became interested in this certain source of great wealth, it became, on the contrary, a matter of interest on the part of those having control of the letting of the bid to have the latter as low as possible. As in any other business, the principle of buying low and selling high was involved. In other words, it became a matter of self-interest on the part of many individuals ostensibly serving the State, to see that as little as possible was paid for the right to levy a tax, and that as much as possible was collected.[1]

The individuals purchasing the right to collect the taxes were known as *traitants* (tax farmers) and *partisans* (contractors). Where the amount involved was too large for the means of single individuals, *partis* (societies), were formed and shares sold.[2]

The traitants and partisans were the "indirect interests," *le cortège funeste,* which Boisguilbert refers to as destroying France. Although the disorders caused by indirect interests are clearly apparent, he says, and although the king, not to speak of the people, has a very great interest to bring them to an end, "no one to this moment has been sufficiently daring to declare war upon them, or rather upon their maneuvers."

In the midst of universal wretchedness, traitants and partisans were building huge fortunes "by fishing in troubled waters," and by considering their own interests rather than the general interest, which to Boisguilbert was the supreme crime. "It was formerly a crime to be a party to, or to receive gratuities from, *gens d'affaires*" (i.e., traitants), he declares, "and thirty years ago a learned theologian published the statement that to be a partisan is to risk damnation. Things have changed since then. Today persons of the highest piety have no scruple about taking part in this trade, but even avow it publicly."[3] It was this small

[1] One of Colbert's reforms was, not the fundamental one of eliminating the ancient custom of farming the taxes, but actually the letting of farms on the most advantageous terms possible.

[2] Perkins, in his history of the regency, wrongly attributes this custom to the influence of John Law. Speaking of the Paris brothers, contractors, he says that, "In imitation of the Company of the West [i.e., the Mississippi Company], an association was formed to which the contract was assigned, and shares to the amount of 100,000,000 livres were issued." (*France under the Regency,* p. 455.) The custom, as a matter of fact, was a much older one. Thus, in the days of Henry III, the "great *parti* of the salt which exploited almost all the *gabelles* of France was a *société par actions,* in which Mme de Joyeuse, sister of the queen, was interested to the extent of 150,000 écus; the duke de Joyeuse, 160,000; D'O, superintendent of finances, 65,000; the chancellor de Cheverny, 70,000 . . . M. Amyot, [a secretary of State] 16,000." —Lavisse, *Histoire de France,* Vol. VI[1], p. 236.

[3] *Factum,* p. 287. So sure a way to financial success were such undertakings

group of three hundred individuals, says Boisguilbert, which blocked the reforms so ardently desired by fifteen million people, whose spokesman he considered himself to be.[4]

The irony of calling traitants the "farmers of the king" did not escape Boisguilbert. The duty and the function of a man who holds an estate is to make the land as valuable as possible, he declares, but these farmers have thought they could not serve the king better than by destroying everything, and by ravaging the country worse than the armies of enemies. As for partisans, they never attach themselves to anything except, like fire, to destroy it.[5]

Affaires Extraordinaires

The multiplication of traitants and partisans and the methods

that the king authorized certain members of the court, including the relatives of Mme de Maintenon, to repair their fortunes by taking a part with the traitants.—Cadet, pp. 78–79, 95.

[4] *Le Détail*, p. 218. Boisguilbert attributed the disorder in the French finances and the rise in importance of traitants to the influence of Catherine de Medici. She "liked to spend more than the ordinary revenues produced," and had recourse to "strange means" to raise extraordinary funds. These strange means were the farming of new taxes and of offices to her followers, the Italians, *les habiles financiers*, who found a simple tax system, and left one so complicated it was beyond the comprehension of the average individual. The same spending and financial disorder, he says, continued under Henry III. Henry IV and Sully were great heroes to Boisguilbert, because Henry submitted himself to Sully's "happy ignorance" rather than to "the clever financiers," and together they succeeded in bringing order into the finances. But it was to be another Medici who was to undo all that Henry and Sully had accomplished. Under the regency of Marie de Medici, widow of Henry IV, even the ministry, Boisguilbert declares, became corrupt. After 1660, he states, in spite of the personal integrity of Colbert, the number of traitants grew still larger. (*Factum*, pp. 299–309.) For evaluation of Boisguilbert as a historian, see note, p. 146.

[5] *Le Détail*, pp. 207, 218. *Factum*, pp. 287, 313, 346. Lavisse, Vol. VI[1], pp. 235–236; Vol. VII[1], p. 201. Adam Smith, commenting on tax farmers, says: "The farmers of the public revenue never find the laws too severe, which punish any attempt to evade the payment of the tax. They have no bowels for the contributors, who are not their subjects, and whose universal bankruptcy, if it should happen the day after their farm is expired, would not much affect their interest. . . . Even a bad sovereign feels more compassion for his people than can ever be expected from the farmers of his revenue. He knows that the permanent grandeur of his family depends upon the prosperity of his people, and he will never knowingly ruin that prosperity for the sake of the momentary interest of his own. It is otherwise with the farmers of his revenue, whose grandeur may frequently be the effect of the ruin, and not of the prosperity of his people."—*Wealth of Nations*, Bk. V, p. 387. See below, p. 306.

employed by them to raise the indirect taxes, caused the yield from the aides and duanes to decrease when the demand was for more revenue. The ingenuity of the government was brought into play to find new sources of revenue which the situation required. None was more ruinous in its consequences than affaires extraordinaires.

Affaires extraordinaires may be defined as the methods used to raise extraordinary revenue in which the intermediary of traitants was resorted to. For instance, *traités des affaires extraordinaires* was entered as one of the sources of the *deniers extraordinaires* under the ministry of Pontchartrain. In Chamillart's period of control over the finances, under the *fonds extraordinaires* the term was shortened to *affaires extraordinaires.* At the time Boisguilbert was writing, the most disastrous abuse in connection with adding to the extraordinary revenue came from the sale of offices. So important was this among the *affaires* resorted to, that the sale of offices and affaires extraordinaires became almost synonymous. It was this abuse that Boisguilbert particularly deplored and attacked. He did not object to the practice of selling existing ancient offices. He himself had bought them, and he appeared to look upon the practice as constituting one of the legitimate investments of the time.[6] But he demanded a cessation of the practice of creating new ones, or reselling old ones under a new name, and of the disposal of them through traitants. The king would be better off, he says, if he were to borrow the sums required, as would any business man.[7]

[6] In practice, if not absolutely in law, since the reign of Henry IV, offices had been veritable properties, transmitted by inheritance. *Les préciputs,* they were called, just as land held in fee simple was referred to as *l'héritage.* Loans advanced for their purchase, and dealings in the offices, were among the common business practices.

[7] All the vocations, says Daire, were transformed into charges and sold for money. Voltaire speaks of them: "Counsellors of the king, controllers in the piling of wood, counsellors of police, offices of barbers-hairdressers, controllers-visitors of fresh butter, and tasters of salted butter were created. These extravagances make one laugh today, but then they made one weep." (*Siècle de Louis XIV,* Vol. II, p. 233.) In the case of judicial offices, new ones were created, and alternatives established. As the functions of the new offices were derived from the existing ones, not only was the value of the latter reduced, but the local administrative organizations were confused and disturbed.

The effect upon the people of the practice of selling offices was threefold. First, every office created gave the right to exact certain duties or fees from the public. Secondly, the exemption from most taxes other than those on the offices themselves usually being one of the prerogatives of their owners, it created a new body of exempts, and thus further increased the burden of those weighed down by the existing load.

> [This] exemption from *tutelle, curatelle, collecte,* billeted soldiers, and other public burdens, and often even exemption from the taille, [places] all these things on the rest of the people, as on an enemy country; and as it is the richest who buy these offices, it follows that all the weight falls on *les misérables*. This disproportionate burden among persons who ought to contribute equally to the public maintenance, has the same effect in a State as a load of one hundred thousand pounds suitable for forty horses to haul from Paris to Lyons, if it were [at first] placed upon only three. If, after [these first three] had succumbed at the end of the first day, the load should be replaced on another three in their team, it is certain that all [forty animals] would perish before the journey was half completed. Yet the blame could not be placed on the excess of the weight in relation to the forty horses, but only on the disproportionate [manner] of distributing it among the beasts of burden in relation to their number.

To Boisguilbert the practice was not only inhumanly unjust, but the essence of stupidity on the part of the government. It is with poverty, he says, as with diamonds:

> There are certain degrees where every increase doubles and triples its effect,[8] both for those who suffer and for the State. In truth, a farmer who has only a hundred écus with which to buy animals to equip his farm of a thousand livres of rent, cannot be deprived of them without being ruined, as well as his landlord, his creditors, and their creditors to infinity, because all the product of an estate depends upon fertilizer, [and] from the moment that it is no longer used expenses will not be made. Thus the levying of these hundred écus on this poor farmer for the expense of maintaining an office, causes a loss of five or six thousand livres to the body of the State; and that not only for one year, but for many years following, since a long time is required to bring a neglected estate back to its original condition.

[8] This figure may have been suggested by Sir William Petty's "Dialogue of Diamonds." See *The Economic Writings of Sir William Petty,* Cambridge, 1899, Vol. II, append. ii.

Finally, the new offices could not be created without diminishing the value of the old ones, which had been purchased in good faith. They constituted a tax on capital, and "there is nothing so pernicious as to take the capital of an individual for the needs of the prince." All told, says Boisguilbert, every ten thousand écus of revenue that the king receives from this source, cost the State as a whole more than a hundred thousand. By this expedient "a national debt has been created at a very high rate of interest." [9]

Louis XIV, himself, was not unaware of the disastrous effect of *affaires*. In the declaration of January 18, 1695, establishing the capitation, he declared that it was expected that its proceeds would permit the elimination of the former:

> We believe indeed, if the proceeds of the tax are as large as we have reason to expect, that it will be possible in the future to eliminate affaires extraordinaires, to which the exigencies of the time have caused resort. [We] promise, on [our] faith and word as King, to end this general capitation three months after the declaration of peace.[10]

These were false hopes, indeed, for the capitation was not established on principles which would insure its success.[11] It created a new burden on the masses and crippled them further. The proceeds in 1695 were 18,333,522 livres; those of affaires the preceding year had been 50,924,578 livres. The returns from the capitation had increased by less than 3,000,000 livres in 1697. It was discontinued following the peace of Riswick, to be reëstablished in 1701. But in 1704 affaires had increased to 69,057,000 livres.[12]

[9] *Le Détail*, pp. 235, 240, 257. "Few financial expedients have proved more ruinous," says Sir R. Lodge. The "sale of offices gave rise to a disguised national debt contracted on very disadvantageous terms."—Article on "Paulette," Palgrave's *Dictionary of Political Economy*, 1926.

[10] *Correspondance des contrôleurs généraux*, Vol. I, p. 566.

[11] *Le Détail*, p. 255.

[12] *Correspondance des contrôleurs généraux*, Vol. I, pp. 594–596; Vol. II, p. 605. Boisguilbert in *Factum* ridicules the capitation. It divided the population of the country into classes according to their quality or their degree, and taxed the members of a class or profession similarly. "It is certain and generally known," he declares, "that qualities and dignities no more denote the faculties of a man than his figure or the color of his hair. . . . Wealth or prosperity are not necessarily attached to any profession any more than

Boisguilbert remarked that vanity was a factor in the purchase of offices. That they continued to be bought regardless of the number created justified his statement as well as that attributed to Pontchartrain:

> Chaque fois que Votre Majesté crée un office,
> Dieu crée un sot pour l'acheter.

The Aides

The *aide* was originally a general sales tax granted and paid by the three estates to the king as an extraordinary source of revenue.[18] By the end of the seventeenth century the aides had become ordinary. Instead of a general sales tax, simple, equal, and at a low rate as originally, these taxes were on a few products only, and especially had become an onerous and stifling "duty levied on wine sold at retail and on that entering the closed places" in the pays d'élections. The result had been practically to destroy one of the important industries of the country. In some regions the tax was on the basis of the sixteenth, in some the twelfth, and in some cases of the fourth denier of the retail sale. To this, other duties were added, such as the "fourth part more" and the "right of gauge" which brought the taxes to one-third. But as the principal sale was in the closed towns

---

to any kind of figure or color of hair." Because an individual of a certain class or profession who has five hundred livres of income cannot be taxed as heavily as one who has five thousand livres, it necessarily follows that the latter is permitted to pay according to the tax placed upon the former, he declares. (*Factum*, p. 335.) The abbé de Saint-Pierre repeats the criticism made by Boisguilbert.—*Ouvrages politiques*, Paris and Amsterdam, 1729–1741, Vol. VIII, pp. 71–73.

[18] "One of the most ancient ordinances on the Aides—if it is not the first indeed, since it seems to create the Aide—is that of King John, dated at Paris on December 28, 1355. The comparison of that which it stipulates with that which existed in the time of Boisguilbert justified only too well the complaints and protests of the latter. It shows to what point, as to its nature, its total, its perception, its use, in every respect, in other words, this burden had been denatured in the course of two and one-half centuries. Again it makes clear in the most incontestable manner how little the arbitrariness in the levy and the expenditure of public money, which had become the rule under Louis XIV, is justified by history. This régime, on the contrary, was in flagrant opposition to tradition. This tradition was the voting, both of taxes and of their destination, by the legitimate representatives of the persons taxed." (Horn, p. 243.) This ordinance, which Horn reproduces in full, is worthy of study.

with their entrance duties for the king, *les hôpitaux*,[14] and the town, the whole made up a sum which, added to the others, constituted a total "very much exceeding the price of the merchandise, especially in the small containers." [15]

THE ADMINISTRATION

The duties of the aides having been placed on an exorbitant basis, one of two things was necessary: [dealers] either must completely abandon the commerce in liquors at retail, or deceive the [tax] farmers concerning the quantity sold. Both have been done in part. That is to say, this sort of consumption has been reduced to the quarter of what it was formerly, which is in itself an inestimable loss for the State, and for the little that it has been possible to continue to sell, it has been necessary to use fraud. This is done by means of secret cellars in which liquors are placed under false names. From there as much as is used during the day, or approximately so, is withdrawn at night in order to refill casks that have been declared in sale. Without this [ruse] the tavern keeper would lose considerably on the merchandise, even when he gives his labor for nothing.

As it was impossible for the farmers of the aides to prevent this disorder by the ordinary means, in verifying the frauds by witnesses, they have obtained edicts and declarations, which provide that the official reports of their agents, whatever they may be, are accepted as fact. And as no inquiry is made into the lives of the agents, or into their habits, at the time of their employment, and moreover, as they have for their individual profit the third of the fines and confiscations pronounced in consequence of their statements, they are absolutely [both] judges and litigants, and have at their disposition the property of all the tavern keepers in their districts. And if they do not cause all to perish at the beginning of their lease, it is because it is to their interest to do so only at the end. But they make use of another method for their own profit, [which] is equally damaging to the State. As by means of their official reports they are masters of all the property of the tavern keepers, they allow only those whom it pleases them to do so to sell, that is to say, those who buy liquors from them alone, at such prices as they ask. All the agents carry on a business in it, which was formerly forbidden by

[14] This term is not translated because the English expression has not altogether the same connotation. *Les hôpitaux* included institutions for the care of the indigent ill, insane asylums, almshouses, and workhouses. The nearest English equivalent for the meaning of the term at that time would be "charitable institutions."

[15] *Le Détail*, p. 194.

the ordinances. They ask an exorbitant price for these liquors, which they sell for three times what they have cost. Thus it is necessary for the tavern keepers to sell accordingly. This could not be done if everyone were in a position either to sell or to make his supply. But the agents take care to prevent the one or the other by the means just referred to and to which other [illustrations] are going to be added.

Agents cannot easily be kept all over the countryside to guard against fraud in the sale by visiting the cellars three or four times a day to see to what extent the number of casks has decreased. [To do so] would consume all the profit on the [tax] farm, hence it is the custom in the remote places to destroy as many of the taverns as are started. This has so successfully banished this kind of consumption in the country districts, that when one is not on a great highway, seven or eight leagues of road are traveled without finding a place to appease one's thirst. So, all the taverns being in the towns and great places, the agents are master of all the retail consumption. From these taverns they can draw no individual advantage without reducing them to the sixth part of what they were formerly. They have indeed done this, not only with respect to tavern keepers, but also with respect to [the number of] individuals [consuming the liquors.]

In effect, as it is usually necessary to go by wagon to acquire the wine in the place where it has been produced, there are edicts which require that declarations must be made before entering closed towns on the roads, and that certain duties be paid. At other [places it is] only [necessary] to show the permit to pass which has been taken from the first bureau. As it is to the interest of agents that no one except themselves carry on trade in wine, and, in order to reduce everyone to the necessity to go to the taverns, that there be as few as possible who make their own supply, and as it is almost always the same [tax] farmers who purchase the duties, everything is done in such a manner that when one has once gone over the road there will be no desire to return.

First, before starting a trip it is necessary to make one's declaration at the near-by bureau, and to get an attestation as to the quantity of wine that is going to be hauled. If one lives far from the bureau a day is lost in awaiting the convenience of M. the agent, which is never the time of the arrival of the wagoners; consequently it is necessary for the latter to fast or to eat at the tavern. Next, having gotten started, it is necessary to stop at the gate of the first closed town to present the declaration to see if it is satisfactory, and if the casks are of the gauge declared. M. the agent is often not at the house, or if he is there, he does not gauge any more. During this time the horses must be in the wind and rain, as there is no tavern keeper who is daring enough to give them cover until everything is finished. If the gaugers do not agree, as can happen, this means the confiscation of the merchandise and of the horses, or it is necessary to buy oneself off by a bribe to M. the agent, which exceeds three times the profit that can be made on the trip. Then if one of the horses casts a shoe on the way, which causes the place of declaration to be reached only a little late, one is told that the declarations are not accepted after the sun goes down.

The result is that days more must be used to cover the route than would be necessary if this disorder did not exist. The taverns are frightfully expensive on account of the exorbitant price of drinks; yet the keepers declare that at whatever price they sell wine they still lose, considering the heavy duties, and that it is necessary to cover their losses by raising the prices of other products, which are sold for four times their ordinary prices. Thus it follows that a single night away from home takes all the profit, even if all the inconveniences which have just been described did not exist. But there are duties to pay in *advance,* whether the wine that is carried has kept, or, as often happens, has spoiled. This [requirement] again retards extremely this kind of commerce, and breaks off that which could be made by exchange of merchandise for merchandise, considering that ready money is required. Furthermore the duties are taken on all the contents of the cask without any deduction for lees. The duties being so high and taking more than can be returned to the owner, in order to save them in part, the liquors are drawn off clear. And no longer nourished by the lees, the ciders of Normandy, especially, are easily soured, and cause sickness on the part of individuals who are under the necessity to drink them, as [is the case with] the poor. The result is that this sort of consumption is diminished still further.[16]

The Duanes

The duanes were the duties drawn from goods carried out of the kingdom, those brought in, or those which passed from province to province, no matter how short the distance.[17] The

[16] *Le Détail,* pp. 196–199.

[17] "For the collection of the duties, the kingdom was divided into many zones. The most important comprised Normandy, l'Ile de France, Maine, Anjou, Poitiers, Aunis, Perche, Berry, the Nivernais, Burgundy, la Bresse, the Bourbonnais, the Beaujolais, Touraine, Champagne and Picardy. These provinces were enveloped in a common line of duanes. The zone was called *l'Étendue des cinq grosses fermes* because the rights of perception had been farmed to five companies before having been let to a single one, as they were

provincial duanes Boisguilbert declared to be "odious and a disgrace to reason." On imports and exports, in extreme cases there were as many as twenty-six duties or declarations on a single shipment, to be made to as many different persons or bureaus before one could load or unload the merchandise.[18]

THE ADMINISTRATION

All the edicts made on the subject of the duanes and passage [over the highways] contain, in uniform phraseology, the obligation to declare, before the opening of the package, the quality, quantity, weight, measure, and diversity of merchandise which one wishes to ship or which one receives, the whole being subject to the penalty of confiscation and fines. If, after opening [the package], the verification which is made does not conform, article by article, to the declaration which has been placed in writing, all the goods are confiscated. To avoid the inconvenience of abandoning the merchandise when the shipment is examined, one is not permitted to pay such duties as [the collectors] might demand. The confiscated goods are divided into three parts: one-third goes to the least important agents who act as guards, one-third to the director or receiver, and the other third to the [tax] farmer, with this difference, that this last is at the discretion of the director, who puts himself to little trouble on the farmer's account provided he makes his own fortune. He never fails to make [this fortune] if only the duties of the duane are at a point so exorbitant that all consumption and commerce are ruined by them. Because if what is paid on products is an easy tax which does not interrupt trade, and [does not] as a consequence [reduce] the wealth of the country, the king, in truth, draws much advantage from this kind [of tax], but the director will never make his own fortune, nor will those who are employed in the raising of this tax. That is what is going to be made evident by facts so certain and so clear, that it will be impossible not to agree to this truth. But first let it be said that these positions of receiver or director are the first commissions that the princes always demand for theii

in 1661." (Lavisse, *Histoire de France*, Vol. VII[1], p. 201.) The provincial duanes had their origin when each province, belonging to separate princes, had its own system of customs duties. Those provinces which did not wish to submit to their reform in 1664 were thereafter known, from the standpoint of the duanes, as the provinces *reputées étrangères*. These, as listed by Daire, were "Brittany, Saintonge, la Marche, Périgord, Auvergne, Guyenne, Gascony, the generality of Auch, Roussilon, Provence, Dauphiné, Flanders, Artois, Hainaut, Franche-Comté and Lyons, that is to say, approximately half of the kingdom."—Daire note, *Factum*, p. 313.

[18] *Le Détail*, pp. 203, 209. *Factum*, pp. 313–314.

creatures. So these persons [have] high protection. And when the hand which gives them employment is not publicly visible, that is an indication that [the directors] only lend their aid to the powerful persons who draw from them that which is more useful. . .[19]

The duties of the duane, principally on the exports of the kingdom, having been placed on an exorbitant basis, the commerce in goods which are transported is extremely diminished by them, [and] the part which remains can subsist only as follows: either it is necessary completely to defraud the duanes by secret transport during the night, or to enter into an agreement with the directors to deceive the [tax] farmers. In either case the former profits, because if one risks trying to defraud it is impossible not to be caught sometimes, [in which event] by full right one-third of the confiscated product belongs to the directors. But very often they do not disclose [the amount] and come to an agreement [with the merchant] on the master's [i.e., the tax farmer's] part; [as for] the merchant, he is better off, even when he loses everything, if he has escaped the other consequences of confiscation.[20] The other method is at least as advantageous. This is, to address oneself first to [the directors] and, by means of a bribe, to treat in good faith the remission [in the duty] which the latter may wish to make. . . .

Thus, in one way or another it is necessary for the duties to be high. It is this which the protectors have care to watch, and to make a whole country perish rather than suffer the duanes to be such as the products can support without recourse to one of the two expedients. . . .

All the other means which are used to wear out the merchants are passed over in silence. Sometimes for six or seven days [the directors] cannot find time to receive the merchandise delivered, either, although they receive salaries, to exact a contribution for hurrying, or indeed to bring about the delay of the transport. Whatever method is used, no justice can be obtained from them, because, having high protection, they take no cognizance of ordinary judges, but have special ones whom they themselves name. It is in this way that the directors of the duanes are enriched in proportion to the diminution of commerce, both domestic and foreign, the same disorders being practiced in the transportation of goods from one province to another, which are practiced on goods leaving the kingdom.[21]

[19] One of the methods used to obtain this protection was a subtle and indirect form of bribery. The lands of the protector would be rented at a loss, that is, at a rent in excess of the real value of the property.—*Le Détail*, p. 173.

[20] That is, if the smuggler lost his goods, he at least avoided a fine by remaining quiet.

[21] *Op. cit.*, pp. 204–206.

THE ECONOMIC EFFECT OF THE AIDES AND DUANES

In effect the provincial duanes were like the aides. Both restricted the freedom of the roads; both made consumption "impossible." Great differences in prices in adjoining places were caused by the restriction of the markets. Burgundy wine, for instance, which sold in Orléans for one sou a measure, sold for twenty-four sous in Normandy and Picardy. The disorder of the aides was not the same throughout France, but all sections felt the effect on account of the decline of trade. Burgundy, for example, as a "pays d'états, enjoys exemptions from the aides to no avail.[22] Her nourishing manna, namely, her wines, with the aid, and from the surplus, of which she can procure her other particular needs, is equally ruined with a surplus as if she had these duties in her entrails." It was, then, to the interest of the regions not having the aides to help eliminate them elsewhere, for all parts of the kingdom suffered the same fate because of inability to carry on trade with the sections affected. Transportation costs had become prohibitive as a result of the loss of time in stopping for inspection and to pay duties, and from the inability to carry return loads of wine through fear of loss of the product, of confiscation of horses and wagons, and of fines. The trip of two hundred leagues from Provence to Normandy required three and one-half months, although normally it would have been possible to make it in four or five weeks. Products could not stand the expense of transportation. An army of the king, the ten thousand agents of the aides and duanes, had closed the roads of the kingdom, and caused each part of it to perish from an abundance of its own products and from an excessively high price for other products. "It is not necessary to consult the oracle to agree that France owes her ruin to such methods." The best provinces of France were reduced to such a state that it was "no exaggeration to say that the aides and duanes have injured property to the amount of twenty times as much as they have brought to the king." A great alembic was at work evapo-

[22] In general, but not absolutely without exception, the aides were confined to the pays d'élections.

rating the enormous wealth of France to obtain a small residue.[23]

If the aides and provincial duanes had so largely destroyed the domestic trade of the country, they had also ruined the foreign trade. For instance, in addition to a foreign trade in wine and wheat, Normandy had had a thriving manufacture in hats, playing cards, tobacco pipes, and whalebones, all of which she exported. Now that foreigners were banished from France, so to speak, they bought wheat and wines elsewhere at cheaper prices, and started their own manufactures of the other products they were accustomed to buy in France. What was equally serious, they took the French workmen. France, at the same time, was changed from a creditor country which she had been before, to a debtor country. Thus, by the very laws which had been made to conserve specie and to bring it into the country, she had been placed in a position to do neither. Moreover, the heavy export tax on wheat[24] produced effects that were generally unrecognized as resulting from this tax, but which Boisguilbert clearly perceived.[25]

The Grain Situation

The production of grain in France at the end of the seventeenth and the beginning of the eighteenth centuries was the nation's most acute economic problem. There was an alternation between famine conditions, which brought untold distress and starvation to the people, and excessive surpluses, which reduced the price

[23] *Le Détail,* pp. 181, 193, 200–201, 233–234, 239. *Factum,* pp. 312, 325–329. Cadet quotes the memoir on the generality of Paris written for the Duke of Burgundy as a verification of the picture drawn by Boisguilbert with respect to the aides. (Cadet, pp. 194–195, quoting *État de la France,* 1737 ed., Vol. II, p. 124.) Daire likewise quotes Le Trosne in corroboration of the earlier study. Le Trosne declared that to obtain thirty millions of revenue from the aides cost sixty millions to collect, and a loss of eighty millions to the national income, or a total loss one hundred and forty millions to obtain thirty millions for the treasury. (Daire note, p. 202, quoting *De l'administration provinciale,* 1779, Bk. III.) Adam Smith, writing on the restraints of domestic commerce, says, that "under such absurd management, nothing but the great fertility of the soil and happiness of the climate [*un excellent terroir et un climat heureux,* says Boisguilbert, indicating the probable origin of Smith's phrase], could preserve such countries from soon relapsing into the lowest state of poverty and barbarism."—*Wealth of Nations,* Bk. V, p. 386.

[24] See below, p. 265.

[25] *Le Détail,* pp. 203, 207–208. *Factum,* pp. 314–315.

to a level which ruined the cultivators.[26] To Boisguilbert, the cause was obvious and far-reaching in its results. It was left to him "to enlighten opinion, to take in hand the cause of the peasants, to show that the social crisis which was experienced proceeded from economic causes of which the most serious was the bad administration of grain." [27]

The grain situation was not the result of "indirect interests" as was the case of the aides, or of a "lack of attention to the general welfare" such as caused the disorders of the tailles, said Boisguilbert, but it was due to the "pious reflections" of those who thought that for everyone to be comfortable it was necessary for grains to be at low prices, notwithstanding that farmers could not meet their obligations.[28]

Boisguilbert saw that there was a relation between years of

[26] Boisguilbert states that in the thirty years prior to 1695 there had been four famines. There was also one in 1698–99, and again in 1709. These shortages were to recur during the eighteenth century—in 1740, 1767, 1771, 1775, 1784, and 1789.

[27] Frotier de la Messalière, *Boisguilbert et la liberté du commerce des grains*, Paris, 1903, pp. 41–42. Frotier, quoting Gustav Bond (*Histoire du blé en France*, p. 12), says that there was no settled policy in regard to trade in grain in France until the middle of the eighteenth century. It was in turn protectionist and free trade, with the object of preventing famine and maintaining grain at a low price. (Frotier, p. 7.) Cadet briefly summarizes the history of this policy for the hundred and fifty years preceding the time Boisguilbert was writing. Under Francis II, Charles IX and Henry III, prohibition of exportation had been the custom and the rule; free exportation had been only the exception and of short duration. This policy was exactly reversed during the reign of Henry IV, and continued to the famine of 1661. (Cadet, pp. 293–298. *Traité des grains*, p. 383. This was one of the reasons for Boisguilbert's admiration for Henry IV and Sully.) After 1661, besides the forbidding of exportation, other methods were used to maintain low priced grain. In 1661 merchants were forbidden to combine into societies for fear they would act to raise the price of grain. The government at times declared how much land must be placed in wheat. Maximum prices were fixed, and it was forbidden to use it for unusual purposes. Everything was done to prevent the dreaded shortage. This, says Frotier, was a survival of feudalism; it was the result of the belief that it was the duty of the king to see that his people did not lack subsistence. But it was more than that. It was partly a policy of fear. The Paris mob had been a factor to be considered since the Fronde. The cities were restless under want. The price of bread must be kept down at all cost.—Frotier, pp. 9–17, 29, 38–42.

[28] *Factum*, pp. 274–275. "Strange fatality of the monarchy," he exclaims, "to have, in order to be rich and happy, only to defend itself from the zeal and good intentions of those who govern it!"—Letter to Desmaretz, Nov. (no day given), 1704.

abundance and those of sterility such as France was experiencing. The one gave rise to the other. In the years of low-priced grain the poorer lands were gradually abandoned, and surpluses of grain were sacrificed and wasted. The ground was thus prepared for famine with the coming of the first bad year. The abasement [29] of the price of grain was the seed which produced it. But unfortunately the excessively high prices in famine years gave an undue impetus to production. If too low prices produced famines, so in turn famines produced low prices. France was enmeshed in a vicious circle. *Voilà le cadavre de la France.*[30]

The abasement of the price of grain is the greatest evil which can befall a kingdom, declared Boisguilbert. The so-called advantage to the poor is dearly bought. The price paid is the cessation of work, and a consequent inability to buy bread however low its price. The farmer must sell his grain to cover the cost of production. It then "flows tranquilly into the hands of *les misérables.*" He saw that a policy which did not consider the rights of the producers as well as those of the people, was a dangerous one.[31]

[29] *Avilissement.* Used by Boisguilbert in the sense of the reduction of the price below the cost of production.

[30] That Boisguilbert was not exaggerating when he stressed the widely varying prices of grain is shown by the record of average wheat prices per setier in the important grain market of Rosoy-en-Brie:

Year	Livres	Sous
1667–1691	9–10	..
1693	30	10
1694	39	3
1695	14	6
1698	21	12
1699	26	17
1701	15	16
1703	11	15
1706	8	..
1707	7	..

(Horn, pp. 145–147.) The year 1709, following almost a decade of low prices, saw a most disastrous famine. This occurred notwithstanding, or, as Boisguilbert would say, because of the fact that the laws causing grains to be at a low price had been rigorously enforced after 1699.

[31] *Factum*, pp. 286, 293, 325, 344. *Traité des grains*, pp. 359–360, 370, 377, 381–382. Frotier, pp. 41–42. Boisguilbert regarded famine prices as partly psychological. The spreading of a rumor of a shortage of grain made the evil worse than the condition called for as a result of the ignorance of the people, who lost their heads at the very suggestion of a shortage. Boisguilbert

Horn criticizes Boisguilbert for what the former calls his "unqualified demand" for high prices for the producers.[32] The criticism is not justified either by a careful analysis of Boisguilbert's reasoning, or by considering his theory as a whole. It is *vil prix* of which he ordinarily speaks. Vil prix he defines as a price which is less than the cost of production. It is against vil prix that he raises his voice. He is not talking, he points out, of an "excessive price of grain which always causes an infinite number of wretched beings to perish." His closeness of thought and carefulness of expression are shown when he defines famine as existing when prices are too high in relation to income.[33] If this definition is applied to the situation of the agricultural producers, it can be seen that he protested against the "famine" of other products which they were undergoing. The prices of the goods which they required were altogether too high in relation to the price of their own product from which their income was derived. They were as a consequence largely prohibited from consuming the goods of others. They suffered in the midst of an abundance of their own product as likewise did those who were unable to sell to them.

Again Horn wonders if the low price of grain was not as much the effect of *la misère* as the cause. Boisguilbert himself answers this in his *Dissertation on the Nature of Wealth.* No one has better understood the interrelation of cause and effect.

---

tried to get at the root of such behavior. He concluded that it was the result of the low food standards of the people which consisted largely of grain. They lacked, he said, the variety of diet of the English people of the same class. (*Traité des grains*, pp. 384–385.) Adam Smith in *The Wealth of Nations*, Bk. IV, pp. 27–28, essentially sums up the argument of *Traité des grains.*

[32] So also does Oncken say that what Boisguilbert sought was prices "as high as possible." See Appendix, pp. 343, 351.

[33] *Correspondance des contrôleurs généraux*, Memoir attached to letter of July, 18, 1703, p. 532. *Traité des grains*, p. 356. *Factum*, p. 285.

VII

THE POLITICAL SITUATION; ON COLBERT

It is only of God of whom one may wisely believe:
ipse dixit, et factu sunt.

HORN criticizes Boisguilbert for his failure to see that the conditions in France were partly the result of the political system. In considering Boisguilbert's attitude toward politics, it must be remembered that he was treading upon extremely dangerous ground in making such a scathing criticism of the fiscal system. No one who reads Boisguilbert's writings can doubt his courage. He was not pouring forth his criticisms as an *émigré* from the safety of a foreign land. Yet he wrote in such a manner as to show that he was far from being indifferent to what was taking place politically.

The supreme political question of the day was that of absolutism. Should the people have at least a restraining voice in government through the constituted authorities? Hinging around this was the question concerning the theory of the right to tax. With regard to absolutism Boisguilbert expressed himself in no uncertain terms. As to the right to tax, no diplomat could have expressed himself more adroitly, and it is only by reference to his ideas on the functions of assemblies and parlements, and by a careful consideration of his mode of expression that his real thought can be found.

In France in the seventeenth century theories of the right to tax were among the live issues of the day, as was inevitable in a country not completely emerged from feudalism. Among the theories evoked to legitimatize taxes were: 1. The necessity to maintain subjects in obedience. Taxes constitute a mark of subjection, a reminder of their subordinate rank. 2. Reasons of State: the prince is charged with governing and with assuring prosperity for which the subjects must supply the funds. 3.

Roman law: the king alone has the power to levy impositions; the king of France inherited the rights of the Roman emperors. 4. The Scriptures: render unto Caesar that which is Caesar's. 5. The king is owner of all the property in the kingdom; "everything that the subjects pretend to possess is in reality his, he only allows the enjoyment of it; when he levies a tax he simply takes back a part of his own property. The subject has no more right to refuse him than a farmer can refuse the rent to his landlord." [1]

It was upon the latter pabulum of absolutism that Louis XIV was nurtured from childhood by tutors, and later by the flatterers of his court and the eminent doctors of the Sorbonne. When the "Glorious Monarch" wished to oppress his people beyond the limit of human endurance, what could better ease his conscience than to throw the responsibility upon the doctors?

I am at the end of [my] resources, and I see that I oppress and that I ruin my people. . . . I spoke of it to my confessor, who told me that all the property of my subjects belonged to me, and that that which remained for them depended on me and that they only held it from me. I declare to you that I could not believe it, and my confessor, seeing that he could not reassure me, proposed that he consult at the Sorbonne. I was indeed glad to do it, and he has reported to me that the [result of the] consultation, signed by a dozen doctors, all the best ones, conforms to his advice. I avow to you that this has lifted a weight from me which crushed me. Now I shall be pained to cause unhappiness by the taxes, but as there is no more scruple and as everything belongs to me, that is indeed different.[2]

Sovereigns, says Boisguilbert, "are the first owners and the eminent possessors, to use a philosophical term, of all the land, and are rich or poor in proportion to its value." [3] But in the matter of securing revenue the "faculties" of the subjects must not be destroyed; that is, their ability to continue to pay in the future must not be impaired.

For this subject, it is necessary that the king regard France and all her wealth as being solely the property of himself, and that he consider all the possessors as his farmers, and finally that he be persuaded that everything that inconveniences them in their cultiva-

[1] Esmonin, pp. 7–10.
[2] Saint-Simon, *Mémoires*, Vol. XX, p. 370. Quoted by Esmonin, p. 11.
[3] *Dissertation sur les richesses*, p. 415.

tion, in their commerce and trade, is the same as if the damage were done to him personally in some property which he can own in certain provinces in the kingdom.[4]

To destroy his people is to destroy himself: "The king and the people are really one and the same thing." [5]

Boisguilbert made use of the same idea in a "truly comic discourse which he had the audacity to place in the mouth of Louis XIV, to sum up all the administrative ineptitudes of the epoch":

As the people can aid [the king] only by means of what they produce, and in proportion to what they produce, he must not consider his *états* other than [as] if all the lands belonged to him in person, as in Turkey, and as if his subjects were only simple farmers. Nevertheless, besides the reasons that have just been referred to, that one can pay him only from that which grows in the country, it is certain that there are many provinces from which he draws in many places much more than the owner. And in order to make clear how *a maxim* that would be so advantageous to [the king] is impaired, it is necessary only to consider how things go on. And [let us view the situation as] if, the land belonging to him really and in fact, the same [methods] were to be used with regard to his farmers as is done with the owners. We shall begin by ordinary taxes, such as the taille, the aides, and the duanes, and then we shall speak of the extraordinary.

If all the generality of Rouen belonged to the king in fact, as it did formerly in very great part . . . leasing it by contract to many individuals to farm, he would not ask them a certain rent, but he would say to them:

"When you wish a muid of wine, it will be necessary to pay seventeen duties at seven or eight separate bureaus, which are open only at certain hours and certain days. If you fail to pay me at the least of these bureaus, although you may have found it closed on your arrival, and although you may not be able to wait without great expense, your merchandise, wagon and horses, will be completely confiscated to the profit of the masters of the bureau, whose reports will be regarded as true against you when you do not agree as to the infraction. And going through the country to carry your merchandise it will likewise be necessary to make declarations at all the closed towns where you will pass, and wait to have them received as long

[4] *Factum*, p. 345.

[5] *Le Détail*, pp. 233–235, 240. *Factum*, p. 348. Memoir attached to letter of July 18, 1703.

as it pleases the agent to have you do so. Thus you will employ four times as much time as should be necessary to make such a trip. Moreover, when you wish to sell your merchandise to foreigners, who would ask nothing better than to buy at a reasonable price, I shall be free to levy a tax so exorbitant that they will be obliged to go elsewhere to buy. As a result, although nothing will be returned to me at all, your products will remain on your hands at a complete loss, with all the expenses that you have made in order to produce them. You will indeed often see them spoil, especially your liquors, without being able to obtain a denier, although one day's journey at the most from your home they are worth exorbitant prices. But if you should risk taking them there you might lose your trouble and your merchandise, because I have farmed certain duties to be raised on this road, for which there is required very much formality very difficult to observe, and in which those interested are [both] judges and parties, and however little one may be in error, all is lost. Although this may not return to me the tenth part of the wrong that this does to you and to your merchandise, nevertheless I am given to understand that it is to my advantage that things should be carried on in such a manner.

"Moreover it is necessary to pay me annually a certain sum or quantity of money, which will not be at all in proportion to the land that you hold from me, so that you who hold only five arpents will often pay me double that which another in the same parish pays on thirty. But it will be necessary for you to buy protection from the persons making the assessments . . . who are completely free to act without justice in this affair. You must not fail to remember to pay me regularly at the time the payment is due, because this [promptness] will be the means of ruining you, considering that those to whom I give these functions are interested that expenses be made to recover payments. Thus, although all such expenses are an evil, it is at the same time a less one than to be subject every year to an increase in the price of the farm, which is inseparable from the ease of payment. It is still necessary for you to keep yourself close, and if you have money to conceal or to bury it instead of trading, for fear of falling into these inconveniences from the increase in the rent of the farm. And indeed you must not place animals on your land to fertilize it. It is necessary to do likewise with regard to consumption. That is, in your expenses, either as to what you eat, or for your clothes or those of your family, it is necessary to affect a great show of poverty. Finally, as this rent is very badly apportioned and more badly paid, both from necessity and from affectation[6] it is necessary for you [in your turn as collector] to take four or five years to do

[6] That is, to pretend not to be able to pay.

the collecting. In this, if you are not ruined (as happens in innumerable cases), you will be much inconvenienced, for neither you nor your confreres being freed from your obligations by abandoning the farm and all your property [to me], often it is necessary to perish in prison because of inability to pay a rental four times too high, while you have neighbors who do not pay the twentieth part of what they should bear."

[Surely] his subjects would be able to say with reason: "Sire, although you wish only to be paid, and to receive as much money as possible, this manner in which you proceed seems to be invented to ruin us and yourself also. For, as our wealth and yours can come only from the sale of the products which grow on your land, that which you propose would make everything perish. But let Your Majesty count that which will come to you from the land in the manner that you set forth, and we will double it for you, provided we are given the liberty to sell and to consume what we wish. [To pay] this [sum] will be very easy for us, as we will have three times more sales in this manner than in the other."

However ridiculous this description may be, it is none the less true that it is exactly the present state of affairs, and although extremely damaging to the king and to the people, this part is preferred to the other, for reasons that are only too well known. And the terrible thing is that there is not the least product which may not be destroyed on account of the complete ruin of consumption. Thus, this picture has not been pushed as far as the original goes, nor does it even approach it. . . . So much for the *ordinary* revenues.[7]

Thus daringly did Boisguilbert satirize the actual operation of the leading political maxim of the Grand Monarch, in a manner which, as Cadet remarks, not even the "mordant irony" of Beaumarchais could have excelled. In effect he said to the king: I am willing for you to indulge in the fiction that the land belongs to you personally. But in that case let us see just what sort of a landlord you are. You must see that it is to your own interest to be a good one. You must aid rather than hamper your farmers in making your land as valuable as possible. Only in this manner can the yield be increased; only in this manner will you receive indefinitely the rent which is properly due to you. A different idea indeed from that which regarded ownership as the right to oppress and to destroy!

Boisguilbert asserted that in earlier times the domains had

[7] *Le Détail*, pp. 236–239.

sufficed for the ordinary needs of the king, with grants from his subjects for extraordinary requirements, such as war. This situation, he declared, had ceased to exist for two reasons. First, there was the alienation of a large portion of the crown domains to the Church. That this had occurred he resented strongly.[8] The second reason for taxes having become ordinary, at least after the domains had been diminished in extent, was the growth of governmental functions. Thus, Boisguilbert concluded, taxes are an evil, but they are necessary. They constitute a debt as legitimate as any other. Their payment is commanded by God. But while the "needs of the State require the people to aid with their property and with their person," it is never required "that some contribute all their property while others contribute much less."[9]

The levying of the king's tax was formerly the people's affair alone, declared Boisguilbert.[10] He no doubt was recalling the Norman Charter of 1313, article seven, which stated that taxes were to be imposed only in extraordinary circumstances. "Each 'aide' accorded was a 'gift' made for a single time only, 'from pure love and grace,' without obligating the persons taxed for the future." After the taille had become an ordinary source of revenue, subterfuges were used by the kings to evade the Norman Charter requirements. First, the Estates were called only after the taxes had been imposed to confirm what had already been done. Secondly, new taxes resembling the taille, which, like the taille, were levied "in the sol to the livre," were created without convoking the Estates. Finally, the Norman Estates

[8] *Le Détail*, p. 181. *Factum*, pp. 290–291. Likewise did he resent the Church having exacted gifts of land from individuals. It had grown rich, he felt, at the expense of the king and the people. It is interesting to compare Adam Smith on this point: "The rent of land, however, is, according to some, the sole fund, and according to others, the principal fund, from which, in all great monarchies, the exigencies of the state must be ultimately supplied. The more of this fund that is given to the church, the less, it is evident, can be spared to the state. It may be laid down as a certain maxim, that, all other things being supposed equal, the richer the church, the poorer must necessarily be, either the sovereign on the one hand, or the people on the other; and, in all cases, the less able must the state be to defend itself."—*Wealth of Nations*, Bk. V, p. 297.

[9] *Le Détail*, p. 244. *Factum*, p. 335. Memoir attached to letter of July 18, 1703.

[10] See above, note, p. 125.

were irregularly convoked between 1632 and 1657 and not thereafter, although never formally declared to be suppressed. Local protests were of no avail. Normandy was placed in the position of a pays d'élections "without anyone, after 1661, daring to make a complaint." [11]

One of the functions of the parlements was the registration of the edicts of the king, which was necessary before the edict became effective. But they also had the right, if for any reason the edict was disapproved, to make a formal protest before the registration took place. This was termed the right of remonstrance. Boisguilbert regarded the abrogation of this right [12] as the source of the growth of the power of the traitants and partisans, and the source of the abuse of the aides and duanes.[13] This right, he declared, had been the sole means which the French people had had to protect themselves against oppression after the suppression of the States General by Marie de Medici. For,

> whatever strong inclination these gentlemen [i.e., traitants and partisans] had to promote their affairs at the expense of the king and of the people, they were far from going to extremes (*taillassent en plein drap*); the will was always there completely, but the power was often lacking. The parlements and *compagnies* [14] had conserved to themselves the authority to make remonstrances concerning establishments which, having for their principles those which have just been noted, would have been too obviously injurious to the king and the people. There was the palladium or tutelary God which had conserved France since the suppression of the States General, which

[11] Esmonin, pp. 3–7.

[12] Literally speaking, the right of remonstrance was never actually abrogated. But in essence the right ceased to be an effective local check on central authority when the protest was not permitted except *after* the edict had been registered, and thus had become effective. For this reason the change is referred to as the abrogation of the right.

[13] *Factum*, pp. 315–316.

[14] Funck-Brentano lists the thirteen parlements in the order of their creation: Paris, Toulouse, Grenoble, Bordeaux, Dijon, Rouen, Aix, Rennes, Pau, Metz, Besançon, Douai, Nancy. Similar functions were performed in Artois, Roussillon, Alsace and Corsica by superior councils or *compagnies*. "The jurisdiction of the Paris Parliament extended over the entire ancient domain of the Kings, including, besides l'Ile de France, Picardy, Brie, Perche, Beaux, Maine, Touraine, Sologne, Berry, the Nivernais, Anjou, Poitiers, Aunis, Rochelais, Angoumois, la Marche, the Bourbonnais, Macon, Auvergne, the Forez, the Beaujolais and Lyons—ten million inhabitants."—*The Old Régime in France*, London and New York, 1929, p. 237.

had this function formerly, and which had acquitted itself so well that no monarchy, since the creation of the world, had been of so long duration or so flourishing. It furnished to the monarch, in his needs, three times more than the opposite method, namely, the use of partisans, has ever done in the most urgent necessity, as is the case today.[15]

The ruin which had threatened France for a century and a half, was thus finally achieved, Boisguilbert thought, through the final extinction of political liberalism; through the perfection of absolutism.[16]

The right of remonstrance was abrogated by the ordinance of 1667, which was renewed again in 1673.[17] Cadet says that "the right had already been taken away or rendered illusory in 1641 by Richelieu and in 1652 by Louis XIV." "Nevertheless, these edicts of 1667 and 1673 . . . gave free rein to despotism and arbitrary rule. 'Fiscal edicts fell upon France like a ravaging hail storm.'" "Boisguilbert did not cease to attribute to this political revolution the principal cause of financial disorder," Cadet declares, thus refuting Horn's statement that Boisguilbert failed to see that conditions in France were partly the result of the political system.[18]

On Colbert

Boisguilbert attributed the evils which had befallen France after 1661 to Colbert.[19] Her economic history, he thought, could be divided into two phases: before 1660 and after 1660. In this he was partly correct; yet there was, at the same time, a certain amount of injustice in it.[20]

[15] *Factum*, p. 308. [16] *Ibid.*, p. 315.

[17] The restoration of this right by an edict of September 15, 1715, was one of the first acts of the regent, the duke of Orléans.

[18] Cadet, pp. 134–139.

[19] In view of his guarded attacks upon absolutism, it appears reasonable to think that Boisguilbert placed solely upon the shoulders of Colbert all the blame that he would have preferred to lay in part upon the shoulders of Louis XIV had he dared to do so.

[20] With regard to Colbert, the Physiocrats seem to have unquestioningly adopted the view of Boisguilbert. Colbert's important apologists are Pierre Clément (*Histoire de l'administration de Colbert*, Paris, 1846), and Felix Joubleau (*Études sur Colbert, ou Exposition du système d'économie politique suivi en France de 1661 à 1683*, Paris, 1856). Even they, however, do not condone Colbert's grain policy.

Following the publication of *Le Détail de la France,* Boisguilbert was criticized for his attitude toward the Colbert régime. In *Factum de la France* he vigorously answered his critics. Colbert's personal integrity he did not impeach. "There was," he declared, "in 1660 or 1661, the assemblage of the two greatest contradictions which were ever encountered joined together, namely, a very great integrity in the minister, and a very great disorder in the administration."

Of what was the Colbert ministry guilty? First, he said, the taxes passing directly into the hands of the king from those of the people, such as the taille, were grossly neglected.[21] This neglect, Boisguilbert admitted, had begun in the previous administration. Secondly, affaires extraordinaires received a great impetus. But these, said Boisguilbert, were the least of the disorders. The great guilt of the administration lay in the fact that it had destroyed the proportions necessary for trade. To Boisguilbert, whose whole theory of commerce is built upon the necessity for balance or equilibrium among all economic forces, to have destroyed this basis of trade was sufficient to condemn the one responsible, however innocent and well-meaning the intention might have been. Finally it was in the Colbert régime that the one safeguard remaining to the people to prevent oppression, the right of remonstrance, had been abolished. There was no defense of Colbert possible in the eyes of Boisguilbert. France, he asserted, was flourishing in 1660. After that she had been at war with herself, as was shown by her desolated countryside.[22]

As Boisguilbert was attacked for his attitude toward the dead Colbert by his contemporaries, who were profiting from the existing order, so he was attacked a half century later by Voltaire:

> If the administration of Colbert is compared with all the preceding administrations, posterity will cherish this man whose body the senseless people wished to tear to pieces after his death. The French certainly owe to him their industry and their commerce, and as a consequence, this opulence, the sources of which dry up sometimes

[21] One of the proposed reforms of Colbert, never carried out, was to introduce the taille réelle throughout France.

[22] *Factum,* p. 308; chap. viii.

during war, but which always springs up again abundantly in peace. Nevertheless in 1672 [*sic*] people had the ingratitude to blame Colbert for the languor which began to make itself felt in the nerves of the State. One Boisguilbert, lieutenant general in the bailiwick of Rouen, had published at that time the *Détail de la France,* in two little volumes, and pretended that all had been in decadence from 1660. It was precisely the contrary. France had never been so flourishing as from the death of Cardinal Mazarin to the war of 1689; and even in this war the body of the State, beginning to be sick, was sustained by the vigor that Colbert had spread through all its members. The author of the *Détail* pretended that after 1660 the [income from the] lands of the kingdom had diminished by fifteen hundred millions. Nothing was more false nor less true. Nevertheless his captious arguments convinced those who wished to be convinced of this ridiculous paradox. So it is in England. In the most flourishing times one sees a hundred papers published which show that the State is ruined.

It is more easy in France than elsewhere to decry the minister of finances in the name (*esprit*) of the people. This minister is the most odious because taxes are always so. Moreover, as much prejudice and ignorance reign in general in finance as in philosophy.[23]

Boisguilbert's sword never dripped with such venom as did Voltaire's; he did not write with a poisoned pen. But with rapier-like thrusts of irony and satire he was a worthy match for the latter. He would have rejoiced in an encounter with Voltaire on a question of fact. The magistrate would have warned Voltaire that, in view of the case built up by the prosecutor, unsupported affirmation or negation were an insufficient defense. Certainly he would have asked Voltaire to support two statements: first, that "France had never been so flourishing as from the death of Cardinal Mazarin to the war of 1689;" and secondly, that "nothing was more false nor less true" than the prosecutor's summary of conditions.

The sage of Ferney, who, as Daire says, "complacently registers the names of the greater part of the courtiers and all the mistresses of the monarch," as a historian scorned the method employed by the contemporary historian of the latter part of the same reign. "It is not the function of history to examine how the people should contribute without being oppressed, and to mark

[23] Voltaire, *Siècle de Louis XIV,* Paris, 1785, Vol. II, pp. 220–221.

the precise point, so difficult to find, between the execution of laws and the abuse of laws, between taxes and thefts,"[24] said Voltaire, obviously with that one in mind who had recorded the everyday life of a people and outlined a science, but the reading of whose works had irritated him, and many of whose ideas he could not grasp.

Let us see what a modern historian who views Colbert with an admirable fairness has to say: "It was characteristic of Colbert's conservatism that he suggested no change in a system which was essentially erroneous, and which was liable to constant abuse." As to his policy:

it is impossible to doubt that the system which he adopted hindered the progress of those whose welfare he so much desired. Firm in the belief that the government knew what was for the interest of the citizens better than they did themselves, manufactures were protected, and industry and agriculture were regulated, until the manufacturer was bankrupt, the artisan was starving, and the peasant left his fields untilled, to live on acorns.[25]

Boisguilbert's great fault as a historian was that he idealized the past. Horn shows that in 1570 almost everyone who could pay the taille was exempt. Again he shows that France was in financial straits and the people poor, prior to 1660.[26]

On the other hand, Cadet says that Boisguilbert was right in his statement that France was prosperous in 1660. Agriculture was flourishing. The setier of wheat was around seventeen livres. "If the peasant paid much to the government, he drew much from the sale of his wheat, thanks to liberty in the grain trade. But the harvest having been bad in 1661, parlement, on August 21, enacted a famous and deplorable ordinance, which, under pretext of preventing famine in 1662, destroyed the foundations of this

[24] *Ibid.*, p. 239.
[25] Perkins, *France under the Regency*, pp. 99, 123.
[26] Horn, pp. 208–216, quoting Gerard du Haillan, *De Estat et succez des affaires de France*, Paris, 1570, and Feuillet, *La Misère sur la Fronde*, Paris, 1860. If Boisguilbert as a historian of times preceding his own is unreliable, as the historian of his own epoch "he may give the most precious light." As to the history of the past (which he, in the light of modern research, perhaps knew badly), "he allowed himself to be carried away by the warmth of his patriotism, and transfigured it for the need of his noble cause."—Cadet, p. 124.

essential commerce." Boisguilbert, he says, was hard on, and unjust to, Colbert; nevertheless he was right "in attributing the source of decadence to this fatal year." It was, however, a "formal injustice to confound in the same accusation Colbert and his successors. What the former did, which for him was only an expedient imposed by necessity, an expedient, moreover, that he submitted to the severe rules of his administration, became a doctrine for Pontchartrain and Chamillart, who readily gave over affaires extraordinaires to the hazards of foolhardy combinations." But "Boisguilbert, after all, is scarcely culpable except in following a too-rigorous logic, which, neglecting details, confines all this discussion to an argument which is not without value thus presented: The evil came from a political measure taken by Colbert; therefore whatever were the intentions of this very incorruptible minister, who let himself be deceived, the evil began with his ministry." This evil was "the growing invasion of men of money." [27]

Boisguilbert's second complaint against Colbert, continues Cadet, was that he failed to recognize the economic laws of society; that he did not raise himself above the prejudices of his time; that, through fear of famine and in a badly conceived compassion for the people, he had forbidden the free exportation of grain from the kingdom; that, in maintaining grain at a very low price, he ruined agriculture and thus produced the cruel alternative of extreme dearness and scarcity. With this indictment Cadet concurs. His criticism of Boisguilbert is that the latter saw only Colbert's errors; that he failed to mention the services which Colbert performed for France.

[27] Cadet, pp. 129–133, 140–141.

VIII

BOISGUILBERT'S PROPOSALS FOR REFORM

It is surely an evasion to prevent a thing, which, causing the general felicity of the people and the wealth of the king, would not by any means produce the same effect with regard to some other persons. Their number, not being the thousandth part of those whom this would enrich, ought not, therefore, to be permitted to stop so great a good.

TO "GET out of the present conjuncture," says Boisguilbert, considerable sums are needed. It is necessary to keep up the ordinary expenses, and to pay the arrears.[1] Thus the task he took upon himself was to show how the existing tax system could be reformed, the government be maintained as a going concern, and the deficit and loans be paid off.

Underlying his proposals are certain definite principles, which in turn have their root in his general theory of economic solidarity and in his theory of money. Taxes are a debt due from the people to the sovereign. Like any other debt they can be paid only from what the debtor possesses. But a wise creditor rather than destroy his debtor places him in a position to pay, so that he can profit through future dealings with him. As a recurring debt taxes cannot continue to be paid out of capital. They must be paid out of revenue, that is, out of what is sold and consumed. The sovereign cannot exact as much from poor subjects as from rich ones. But agriculture is the basic wealth of France upon which the prosperity of industry depends. Consequently, "poor peasants, poor kingdom; poor kingdom, poor king."[2] Therefore, for the king to be rich it is necessary for him to see to it that the agriculture of the country is prosperous. Instead, however, he is destroying it by means of the restraints upon the

[1] *Factum*, p. 341.

[2] The context of Quesnay's famous proverb, although never formulated as a proverb by Boisguilbert, constitutes, nevertheless, the background of his pages.

sale of its products, and by means of unjust taxation. To keep from impoverishing his subjects, the king must see to it that his taxes are certain and not arbitrary; that they are proportional to the ability to pay; that they are convenient in the manner of collecting; that they pass cheaply and directly from the hands of the people into those of the prince.[3]

In setting forth his reforms, Boisguilbert objected to being classed among "bearers of astonishing novelties." In *Le Détail de la France* he suggested the possibility of a *dime*,[4] but he thought that to create less "movement," the reorganization of the existing taille would be preferable. The taille was therefore to be retained as the core of the tax system; but the uncertainty of the arbitrary taille was to cease. Not the least disturbance was necessary to accomplish this, he stated. It was simply necessary to eliminate injustice in the assessments and to enforce the ancient and modern ordinances with regard to them. Ordinances "are worth nothing unless they are enforced." The payment was to be made by everyone in proportion to ability to pay.[5] The uncertainty of the tax would be abolished by making the rich pay as rich, and the poor, as poor, and by doing away with the solidarity of the taille. Agricultural life would take on a new aspect, he said, if a farmer knew that his property could not be seized for the taille of his neighbors, or his own tax raised out of proportion to others as soon as he displayed some sign of prosperity.[6]

Detailed directions were set forth for the administration of the tax. The arbitrary power of the intendants was to be eliminated. The local assessments also were to be reorganized, and the evils of the collection abolished. To speed up the payment, a discount

[3] These so-called Smith canons of taxation are repeatedly enunciated by Boisguilbert, and constitute the basis of his reforms.

[4] This was twelve years before Vauban's *Dime royale* was published. Boislisle well says that "Vauban was infinitely more revolutionary in the project for a dime royale than Boisguilbert in *le Détail de la France.*" The one only demanded an "exact and reasonable observation of ancient ordinances, based on the laws of nature." The other "wished to upset the financial system from top to bottom, and to substitute for empirical proceedings a unique form of imposition and perception. Dangerous chimera, of which its publication was indeed capable of complicating the political difficulties!"—*Projet de dime royale et la mort de Vauban*, p. 239.

[5] *Le Détail*, pp. 220–221. *Factum*, p. 321.

[6] *Le Détail* pp. 222, 242.

of two sous per livre was to be allowed on the tax if it was paid before the regular collection began. Especial severity was to be shown anyone favoring relatives or friends. Informers of cases of injustice or evasion were to be paid for the information. Finally, it "being necessary for industry to carry its part of taxes," towns were to be permitted to place their taille *en tarif*.[7] It "seems to be a natural law," Boisguilbert declared, for debtors to be allowed to acquit themselves in the manner most convenient to them as long as they do not injure others.[8]

Cadet criticized the plan because Boisguilbert laid too much stress on the pain of confiscation as a means of getting honest declarations, "as did the Physiocrats later. . . . He forgot that the traitants took advantage of confiscations, and that there was possibility of abuse." Horn complained that Boisguilbert would continue the exemptions of the taille.[9]

Boisguilbert is not sufficiently explicit with regard to exemptions in his directions for the reorganization of the taille. At one point he says that three or four months before the apportionment among the elections, all persons, exempt or nonexempt, shall be ordered to carry to the bureau in their election a correct declaration of all their property, whether they be landowners or farmers, with copies of their leases which they must sign as true, and that land shall be valued with due regard to neighboring property.[10] Again he says that every officer having received the apportionment, will make an estimate first of the property of all the non-privileged, both owners and farmers, without distinction, and will decide how much this will return.[11]

[7] Saint-Pierre, in his *Projet pour la taille tarifée*, adopted this principle proposed by Boisguilbert.

[8] *Le Détail*, pp. 191–192, 220–226, 228, 246, 254–256. *Factum*, pp. 321, 324.

[9] Cadet, pp. 326–327. Horn, pp. 346–347.

[10] Speaking of the Venetian land tax, Adam Smith says that "the landlord and tenant, for example, might jointly be obliged to record their lease in a public register. Proper penalties might be enacted against concealing or misrepresenting any of the conditions; and if part of those penalties were to be paid to either of the two parties who informed against and convicted the other of such concealment or misrepresentation, it would effectually deter them from combining together in order to defraud the public revenue. All the conditions of the lease might be sufficiently known from such a record."—*Wealth of Nations*, Bk. V, p. 315.

[11] *Le Détail*, pp. 222–223.

It appears probable that the latter reference to a distinction between privileged and non-privileged had to do with those who were legally exempt from the taille, namely, the clergy and nobles on their dwellings. Boisguilbert's intention that those who were legally obliged to pay should do so cannot be questioned. There was to be a return to the ancient ordinances. It has already been seen [12] that in the pays d'élections the lands of the nobles and those of the Church were legally subject to the tax, with the exception of the *taille d'occupation*. Boisguilbert specifically appealed to the self-interest of the exempts, to eliminate their objection to paying the tax, by showing that exemptions were ruining exempts as well as the nonexempts. Much of *Le Détail* and of *Factum* is devoted to such an exposition. In a letter of October 3, 1700, he complained that the farmers of the nobles did not pay the taille, and again on May 5, 1702, he contrasted the tax payments made by the English and the French nobility, leaving no doubt that he thought the latter should pay. And speaking of this injustice in the exemptions he suggested action by the king on the subject, because

> as this injustice is today so generally established that the more powerful a man is, the less taille his farmers must pay, which ruins him as well as the rest of the State, it is apropos that His Majesty himself have the goodness to explain to all the persons of his court, that, for their own interest, it is necessary that they act toward him as he acts toward them, in order that the relation be reciprocal, and as they themselves act toward everyone and especially toward the Church.[13]

And again:

> When God commanded that taxes be paid to princes, he had reference to everyone, and not only to the wretched and unprotected, who lack the power to exempt themselves from them. Otherwise, indeed, as can be said without impiety, this precept would have been useless, as there would have been no reason for it so far as the ones are concerned who would have been unable to do anything else.[14]

Ten years later he said that to make the taille and his capitation fall upon all the men in the kingdom, "*nobles, bourgeois et*

[12] See note, pp. 110–111.
[13] *Le Détail*, p. 220. [14] *Ibid.*, p. 221.

roturiers," would produce one hundred million livres of revenue, and this was the sum, eighty millions in excess of the existing capitation, that he expected to raise. Placing all the public burden on one group, he declared, is to act as if that group were a public enemy. Furthermore, it was clearly with exempts, as well as with traitants and partisans, in mind, that Boisguilbert stated the principle of the greatest good for the greatest number.[15] Whatever Boisguilbert's defects in his mode of expression, there is no question as to what he desired and thought necessary on the point of exemptions.

In *Le Détail* Boisguilbert would completely suppress the aides. The effect of their elimination, he said, would be for taverns to spring up over the country. Ten or twelve vocations depending upon them would revive, and a "million families would be placed in movement." [16] In *Factum*, written ten years later, there was not to be complete suppression. The "right of gauge" which was the source of so many confiscations, was to be done away with. "No container can be made with mathematical exactness, or its calculation be made with absolute accuracy." Furthermore, such duties as *parisis, sou-denier, travers, resve, haut-passage, grand, petit, nouveau droit,* which everyone had to pay, but which no one could understand, were to be combined into one tax and expressed in money. In place of the existing declarations, everyone conveying liquors by any method of transport was to be required to secure a *passe-avant* at the nearest bureau of aides, at a cost of ten sous, everything included. This would include the declaration of quantity and the place of destination, and would permit the load to proceed without being stopped at any place. The duties were to be reduced from one-fourth to one-eighth. Thus the aides were to be retained at a low rate for revenue, but the annoying restrictions which had destroyed the wine trade were to be ended.

As to the duanes, the provincial ones were to be eliminated. On imports duanes were to be retained for revenue only, "eliminating all the difficulties which bring nothing to the king, and

[15] *Le Détail,* pp. 231, 235. *Factum,* p. 346.
[16] *Le Détail,* p. 243.

only repulse foreigners." But "no quarter must be given to export duties, which are the greatest enemies of the king and the kingdom which they can ever have." [17] As a concession to public opinion indeed, Boisguilbert would permit the free exportation of grains to be prohibited in times of scarcity. But such a provision he thought to be unnecessary, even when their prices were exorbitant, "because they carry their prevention [of exportation] with them, by the rules of trade which do not permit one to make it at a loss." [18]

Affaires extraordinaires were to cease. To reëstablish the country by ceasing to sell offices would put the people in a position to traffic in the existing ones at high prices, part of which would go to the king. They buy things which give them enjoyment, he says, as soon as they can be afforded, and among these things *les dignités* hold the first place.[19]

In his treatment of the traitants Boisguilbert was eminently fair and moderate. They were the curse of France, he was certain, and they had grossly abused their privileges. But as a matter of temperament, and in part no doubt to reduce opposition to the minimum, he would not punish them for misdeeds. It was an institution which he fought, rather than men. In *Le Détail,* in which the aides were to be completely abolished and the duanes to be limited to duties on imports only, he suggested that the tax farmers be recompensed for their farms, with such profit as it would please the king to give them, or for the remainder of the lease both individual and general farmers of the aides and duanes might be made receivers of the tailles. But only the king and the people were to be interested in taxes, the king as receiver and the people as payers. "Honest wages" were to be paid to "those who serve the king in his finances," and no one was to be permitted "to profit by a denier through indirect ways." [20]

In *Le Détail,* Boisguilbert figured that the loss of income from the abolition of the aides, the provincial duanes and the export duties would amount to twenty-four millions. The increased

[17] *Le Détail,* p. 204. *Factum,* pp. 329–333.
[18] *Traité des grains,* pp. 368–369, 377–378, 381, 384, 388–390.
[19] *Le Détail,* p. 245. Letter of Dec. 31, 1701.
[20] *Le Détail,* pp. 219, 244, 251. Letter of Feb. 8, 1702.

revenue from import duties with the restoration of trade would cover seven millions of this, and the reorganized taille, returning to its old total, would add an additional twelve millions. There would remain five millions of ordinary revenue to be found. To obtain this, Boisguilbert proposed a chimney tax on those places and persons exempt from the taille, and upon the closed cities and towns which were to have their entrance duties on wines eliminated.[21]

To supply the extraordinary sums required for carrying on the war, and to take the place of affaires extraordinaires, the king was to borrow. To this end Boisguilbert lays down the requirements for the maintenance of the government's credit:

> And finally, besides all these resources, why should the king not provide for his needs as any business man would do? Let him borrow at the lowest rate that he is able to obtain. The two edicts referred to,[22] once published, would cause everyone to be eager to lend to him. Because, aside from the fact that that is a necessary consequence of the wealth of the people, which would increase considerably, the certain increase of the revenue of the king would assure in the minds of these same people both the capital and the arrears. And suppose that he might need fifty millions a year of extraordinary [revenue] until the end of the war, and that he might be obliged to borrow it all, which is unlikely. Should it last four more years, this would only be ten millions of *rente* for which he would be indebted, and for the people or State nothing at all,[23] not to speak of the reëstablishment of their wealth. But it is asked if, in the four years that the war has been going on, this has been the state of things? It is indeed certain that it costs more than a hundred millions of rente to the king, or to the State.

[21] *Le Détail*, pp. 226–228. This tax, including the method of its assessment, bears a definite resemblance to Sir William Petty's hearth or smoke tax. Cf. "Treatise of Taxes and Contributions," p. 94, and "Verbum Sapienti," pp. 106, 112, in *The Economic Writings of Sir William Petty*, Cambridge, 1899, Vol. I.

[22] That is, to free the roads and to establish just taxes.

[23] Daire note: "The vivacity of the author here defeats his habitual sagacity, because he has repeated often, and rightly, that the revenues of the king have no other source than those of the people, or of the State." Daire, it seems, is taking *rien du tout* too literally. In his conversational style Boisguilbert frequently uses the expression, but always in the sense of *very little*. For instance: *six deniers le livre, ce qui ne va à rien*. The latter had no misconception as to how government debts were to be paid. What is intended is to belittle the ten millions as a burden in comparison to the methods being resorted to, as is indicated by the remainder of the paragraph.

The day following the publication of these edicts, products taking on their former prices will re-create the revenues from which are formed the capitals of individuals who live from their incomes. And the end of the creation of new offices, eliminating, on the one hand, dealings in money at ten percent, the traitants valuing it on this basis (in which all the loss [resulting] from [an increase over] the ordinary rate fell again on the king), and, on the other hand, replacing all the offices in ordinary traffic, this will reëstablish things in their former course, which is to make the people flock to lend to the king.

But to maintain this relation, it is necessary to preserve good faith in this, for the interest, indeed, of His Majesty. The sovereign authority can introduce no especial jurisprudence concerning the repayment, as has been seen formerly, which would not be accepted between two private individuals. Loans are like armies. It is absolutely necessary to pay for supplies on the current basis, if one expects [armies] to subsist. For although nothing would be so easy as to have [the supplies] for nothing the first time, as by this conduct the purveyors would return no more, this would make all perish.[24]

Again, it would be necessary to have an especial bureau for the repurchase of this kind of rentes by the king himself, by which the owners would lose three months interest. This would be the means of collecting all the trusts in France, as well as the money of minors, in view of the fact that one would be assured of having the interest and of withdrawing one's capital without risk, whenever one wishes. Again, it would be fitting that these rentes might never be seized for the debts of the bearers, conserving neither succession (*suite*) nor hypothecation any more than money itself, so that every payment made and endorsed on the first instrument would be good and valuable, both for capital and interest, except in case of theft, or of hypothecation if stolen (*stellionat*), if there had been a preceding denunciation. It is certain that more would be offered than would be needed.[25]

[24] On this point Adam Smith says that "commerce and manufactures, in short, can seldom flourish in any state in which there is not a certain degree of confidence in the justice of government. The same confidence which disposes great merchants and manufacturers, upon ordinary occasions, to trust their property to the protection of a particular government; disposes them, upon occasions, to trust that government with the use of their property."—*Wealth of Nations*, Bk. V, p. 396.

[25] *Le Détail*, pp. 247–248. Daire note: "At the same time that these lines reveal a clear understanding of the conditions [underlying] *credit*, all that which precedes them shows that the author sees in this resource only an expedient to which necessity alone ought to cause recourse. Cf. these ideas of Boisguilbert with those expressed in the *Dime royale* on the same subject."

Ten years having elapsed after the publication of *Le Détail de la France,* and nothing having been accomplished in the way of reforms, Boisguilbert, in *Factum,* is somewhat more moderate and conciliatory in his demands. He explains to Chamillart that "in very great illnesses doctors do not at first give strong medicines for fear the indisposed person could not endure their violence." Thus the aides were not to be completely abolished, as has been said. They were to be reduced and all the vexations which stifled trade were to be removed. In *Factum,* therefore, at the beginning, he reiterates that the king need not dismiss or break any agreement which he has made with the traitants.[26] But it was difficult for him to adhere to such a conciliatory attitude very long. It is not necessary to suppress the tax farms or the farmers, "although this would be the greatest service that one could ever render to the State." In any case the functions of tax farmers must be reduced to a "less desolating ceremonial." They have been regarded as a sacred people, he continues, but they are far from deserving to be canonized.[27]

There are ten thousand taxes in France, Boisguilbert declares, raised by means of traitants and partisans; ten thousand judges having no other function than the handling of tax processes, and a hundred thousand collectors are required. But taxes should be few in number, and there should be no intermediaries. "Those princes are richest and the people least burdened where the taxes pass directly from the hands of the people into those of the monarch." Such direct payments require a small number of officers. There should be three or four kinds of taxes, one hundred to one hundred and fifty tax receivers, and no special judges. It would therefore be a cheap bargain to get out of the present condition by reëstablishing the wealth of the people, and that of the king as a consequence, regardless of the opposition of "persons to whom a general confusion means less, indeed, than their own hope of amassing a fortune, or the fear of losing an ill-gotten reputation from which they draw the same benefit as if they had fully merited it." [28]

[26] *Factum*, pp. 268, 287, 297. Letter of Dec. 28, 1704.
[27] *Factum*, p. 319.
[28] *Ibid.*, pp. 288, 290–292, 334, 342, 345–346.

Boisguilbert's proposals in *Factum* to supply additional revenue differ from, and are simpler than, those in *Le Détail.* In 1695, the year in which *Le Détail* appeared, a capitation was levied as an additional source of extraordinary revenue. In *Factum* Boisguilbert attacks the principles underlying the tax [29] which had defeated its purpose. But in order to form a simple tax system, he says, it is not necessary to do anything new. It is simply necessary to address oneself to the capitation. It has, he adds, the essential requirement of passing directly from the people to the prince without great expense. Furthermore, it is directed to the requirements of the prince in the present conjuncture, which is to provide the extraordinary revenue required and to eliminate affaires extraordinaires. The capitation has failed to do this, he states, although such was the intention expressed at the time of its establishment.[30] Instead of the existing division of individuals into classes for the purpose of assessing the tax, he proposes that it be paid in the tenth of the income by everyone. This tenth of the income was to be paid in money and not in substance, as Vauban proposed in his *Dime royale,* the principle of which Boisguilbert criticized as unfeasible.[31] The objection was anticipated that it would be difficult to get people to make a declaration of income. But in business, he says, this is practiced daily in a hundred other less important occasions, hence such an objection is without foundation.[32]

[29] See note, pp. 124–125.

[30] *Factum,* pp. 268, 334. Adam Smith says of capitation taxes that they "are levied at little expense; and, where they are rigorously exacted, afford a very sure revenue to the state. It is upon this account that in countries where the ease, comfort, and security of the inferior ranks of people are little attended to, capitation taxes are very common. It is in general, however, but a small part of the public revenue, which, in a great empire, has ever been drawn from such taxes; and the greatest sum which they have ever afforded, might always have been found in some way much more convenient to the people."—*Wealth of Nations,* Bk. V, p. 354.

[31] *Factum,* pp. 337–339.

[32] Adam Smith takes issue with this proposal for an income tax: "Capitation taxes, if it is attempted to proportion them to the fortune or revenue of each contributor, become altogether arbitrary. The state of a man's fortune varies from day to day, and without an inquisition more intolerable than any tax, and renewed at least once every year, can only be guessed at. His assessment, therefore, must in most cases depend upon the good or bad humor of his assessors, and must, therefore, be altogether arbitrary and uncertain.

"Capitation taxes, if they are proportioned not to the supposed fortune, but

The capitation or income tax was to be a temporary resource for four or five years, and in conjunction with other tax reforms and the increased prosperity resulting, Boisguilbert estimated that there would be an increase in revenue of not less than eighty millions annually in excess of that produced by the existing capitation, or one hundred millions in all. But,

When an increase of a hundred millions in an instant in the revenue is spoken of, it is not one hundred millions of new specie brought into existence, as in Peru [that is meant]; it is a hundred millions of bread, wine, meat, and other products, which being the sole sustenance of life, constitute likewise the sustenance of armies. [Specie] will be furnished to the extent of ten millions only, and even less, and the making of ten voyages and ten returns from the hands of the people to those of the prince, will result in this delivery of goods.[33]

Thus in *Factum* he proposes to raise the revenue necessary for the war by taxation rather than by borrowing. For the king to borrow

is the same thing as if the people themselves borrowed, since the burden of paying the capital and interest falls upon them just as certainly, although people are blind enough to believe the contrary, with the result that the debts that the prince contracts are regarded very indifferently. Thus it is preferred that the monarch obligate himself for a million of rentes at a frightful rate of interest, if only he does not demand an écu from each individual. But this person would be very much irritated at the same time, if he were wise, if he himself had to borrow for the arrears due on his debts, or for his ordinary expenses, since this conduct would send him immediately to the almshouse. Nevertheless, whether he or the king use this method is the same thing, although, to repeat, it may be that no one gives the least thought to this.[34]

---

to the rank of each contributor, become altogether unequal; the degree of fortune being frequently unequal in the same degree of rank.

"Such taxes, therefore, if it is attempted to render them equal, become altogether arbitrary and uncertain; and if it is attempted to render them certain and not arbitrary, become altogether unequal."—*Wealth of Nations*, Bk. V, pp. 351–352.

[33] *Supplément au Détail de la France*, pp. 265–266.

[34] *Factum*, pp. 298–299. "The public did not think at first that these borrowings would make a new burden for it: it did not see that it was it which contracted a debt when the sovereign borrowed. Nevertheless one alienated part of the taxes to pay the interest to the companies; and immediately afterwards, additional imposts were assessed to equalize the receipt and the

For Louis XIV to continue to borrow means "that after the end of the war the payment of interest on the money borrowed will cost the people more than the maintenance of the war, with the result that it will be a perpetual war that they will have to sustain." [35]

Boisguilbert declared that taxes must be borne by everyone in proportion to his faculties. Here, said Cadet, are the two essentials of taxation: universality and proportion. Horn also thought that Boisguilbert had in mind a progressive tax when he said that the "rich must pay as rich, and the poor, as poor." Although this statement in itself could indicate no more than proportional taxation, nevertheless Horn was quite correct. This is based upon the fact that Boisguilbert seemed to have had a clear conception of the diminishing utility of money. "Like all other kinds of debts," he said, "taxes are excessive or moderate, not in relation to the absolute amount of the sums which are demanded, but in their relation to the value of the property from which they are exacted." [36] And again: an "individual who pays one hundred francs of taille on a farm of one thousand livres, will be less burdened in paying two hundred if the farm can return two thousand livres, since this will be eight hundred francs that he will receive as pure profit, and he will be entirely discharged of his tax on the first one thousand livres." [37]

Horn was perhaps also right in saying that Boisguilbert did not seriously mean to exempt the poor when he repeated so often that the rich would profit by relieving them of taxation. Never-

---

expense."—Condillac, *Le Commerce et le gouvernement*, Amsterdam, 1776, p. 462.

[35] *Supplément*, p. 261. Adam Smith repeats this idea: "When funding, besides, has made a certain progress, the multiplication of taxes which it brings along with it sometimes impairs as much the ability of private people to accumulate even in time of peace, as the other system would in time of war. The peace revenue of Great Britain amounts at present to more than ten millions a year. If free and unmortgaged, it might be sufficient, with proper management and without contracting a shilling of new debt, to carry on the most vigorous war. The private revenue of the inhabitants of Great Britain is at present as much encumbered in time of peace, their ability to accumulate is as much impaired as it would have been in the time of the most expensive war, had the pernicious system of funding never been adopted."—*Wealth of Nations*, Bk. V, p. 412.

[36] *Supplément*, p. 265. [37] *Le Détail*, pp. 219–220.

theless, it would only have been the pushing to a logical conclusion his idea that there would be a greater gain for the rich from the increased consumption of the poor than from the reduction in their own taxes as a result of the payments by the poor. But for France to have procured even proportional taxation in the reign of Louis XIV would have been for her to obtain the quintessence of reform, and Boisguilbert, realist that he was in this matter, could not have hoped for more.

Talbot complained of a "serious omission in the theory of Boisguilbert. He explains very well what should be the form of the tax, the rules of apportionment and of perception, but he fails to speak to us of the amount of the tax. In what measure is it permitted the sovereign to tax his subjects? And what is the limit of the right to tax?" These questions, Talbot said, Boisguilbert failed to answer.[38]

The fault is not in Boisguilbert, but in Talbot, that he failed to find the answer. Speaking of the consumption of the country as fundamental to production, Boisguilbert declared that "it is that alone which can draw these goods from the bowels of the earth, because it is necessary for private individuals to absorb for their own usage ten times more than [is absorbed by] the sovereign if it is desired that this advance be permanent."[39] That is the definite statement that Talbot seemed to have sought in vain. But in *Le Détail,* Boisguilbert laid down a more general rule as to the limit of taxation than a definite percentage of national income. He referred to England, to the German States, and to Savoy. In all these countries the people paid *into the public treasury* more in proportion to their wealth than did the French, he asserted, but in none of them were the people reduced to beggary, or to the necessity of abandoning the cultivation of the land. It is permitted ministers, he continued, "to push the taxes of their masters as far as they can, as long as they give no blow to those two mammae of all the republic, agriculture and commerce." Here is a general principle of taxation which is applicable whether the functions of government be many or few.[40]

[38] *Les théories de Boisguilbert* pp. 115–116.

[39] *Dissertation sur les richesses,* p. 416. [40] *Le Détail,* pp. 216–217.

So, too, Horn criticized Boisguilbert for his failure to discuss the matter of expenditures. Horn regarded this as an indication of the general deterioration in thinking which had resulted from the absolutistic views and attitude of the reign. But minor writers were attacking the expenditures of Louis XIV and declaring them to be responsible in large measure for the evils of the time. Boisguilbert did not do so; on the contrary, he stated that the expenditures were not excessive with relation to the natural wealth of France, and had not risen in proportion to the changed price level. That he was not indifferent to expenditures, however, is shown by his reference to the extravagances of Catherine de Medici and of Henry III as leading to dealings with traitants, and by his approval of the control of expenditures under Henry IV.[41] But Boisguilbert was delving beneath the surface of things, and did not stop with the obvious. At the end of the seventeenth century, it was not the sum actually going into the treasury, but the amount which this sum directly and indirectly cost the people, which he regarded as the cause of the bankruptcy of France, and he discussed the actual and fundamental problems as he saw them.

Only once did Boisguilbert speak directly of the reform of the currency. In *Supplément au Détail de la France,* he asked: "Is it necessary to await peace in order to purge the State of paper money (*billets de monnaie*), which, by the disorganization it causes commerce, costs annually four times more than the value of all the sums for which it has been brought into existence, that is, four times more than the foreign war?" He then proceeded to state how it was to be gotten rid of: "Let the kingdom be recharged with it by a just assessment on the heads of individuals and communities. The *endorsement* that they will make thereon, payable in four years in four installments with interest, will make it circulate in trade without loss in the transferring." [42]

There was one especial point in his writings on which Boisguilbert was severely criticized by his contemporaries and which caused him to be regarded a visionary. This was his expectation

[41] See above, p. 39 and note, p. 121.
[42] *Supplément,* pp. 261–262. Boisguilbert's italics.

of a speedy effect from his reforms. Boisguilbert could not make himself understood with regard to a matter which he thought to be obvious. Strangely enough, with respect to this modern commentators have understood him little better than his contemporaries.

Dühring compared Boisguilbert's promise of quick results with Roger Bacon's pretense that he could teach in eight days all the mathematics that was known in his time. But one must be careful, he cautioned, not to regard Boisguilbert as a boaster. It was an "understandable illusion." He "judged the possibilities according to the inner and general essence of the matter." [43]

Indeed there appears to be something visionary in the reiterated statement that only two hours' work on the part of the ministers and three weeks' work on the part of the people would be necessary to give economic rebirth to France. Yet Boisguilbert strongly protested that he was no visionary. Certainly there was no need to have recourse to mysticism to explain what he meant. In matters of economic and fiscal science he was definitely a realist.

Boisguilbert was talking of the effect of the reëstablishment of credit and the increased circulation of money which would result from the return of confidence, and which in turn would restore trade. No one of his time so clearly understood the significance and the functioning of credit, its importance in everyday life, and the relation between private credit and the fiscal administration of the State. At least one-half of the income of the people, he asserted, was the result of the use of credit.[44] Yet it had become impossible for credit to be extended, he said, because credit depends upon solvency. The government had brought about almost universal insolvency by means of the aides, the duanes, and the tailles. In making it "impossible" for the people to sell or to consume, the government had made it impossible for the people to pay taxes. But along with the decreased revenue had come the increased expenditures because of the war. The unbalanced budget led to a resort to all kinds of expedients: to the

[43] *Kritische Geschichte der Nationalökonomie und des Socialismus*, Leipzig, 1879, p. 72. Unfortunately Dühring failed to explain what he meant by the "inner and general essence of the matter."

[44] *Supplément*, p. 261.

emission of short-time bills immediately discredited; to forced loans; to devaluation of the coinage. Boisguilbert perceived that by the use of such shifts hoarding had been increased, and the destruction of credit completed.

What was needed, he reiterated, was not that the State should act, but that it should cease to act. He proposed nothing new, he added, but simply a return to the ancient ordinances. The ministers needed to issue but two edicts: one to free the roads, and one to create just taxes. Their enforcement could begin at once, and the effect would be felt immediately,

> inasmuch as, between the permission to sell one's merchandise, when people are found in a position to buy it, and selling it, there is only an interval of twenty-four hours; and between having sold it and being richer than one was, there is no interval; and between being richer than one was and spending more, or buying lands, or cultivating them better, there is likewise no interval; and between doing these things and throwing money among the people there is no further interval. And from the moment that the people have money they consume the fruits that they have produced by their labor, and are in a position to pay the king in proportion.[45]

Although Boisguilbert may have been unduly optimistic about the speed of the revival of agriculture and commerce, nevertheless he clearly did not expect a miracle to happen with regard to the ordinary revenue. In *Le Détail* he showed how the government could bring about a revival of its credit and make legitimate use of loans. The effect of the reforms, he thought, would be felt within a year, and within two or three years the ordinary revenue would be sufficient to take care of the increased expenditures.[46] In *Factum* the capitation was to be an extraordinary resource for four or five years, at the end of which it would be possible to dispense with it.

Boisguilbert was confident that the principles set forth by him, and the reforms demanded, would so appeal to reason and common sense that their wisdom would be apparent and the result would be immediate adoption. These principles are "elementary truths and banalities" today, but they were not accepted in France in 1700. A revolution was necessary to make more than a start

[45] *Le Détail,* p. 256. [46] *Ibid.,* pp. 241–242, 246.

in ridding France of the evils which were apparent almost a century earlier. This "visionary" belonged to the future and not to his own generation. He was criticized by his opponents for wishing to "upset the State,"—"as if the State consisted," Boisguilbert retorted, "in those who ruin her land and her commerce, and thereby the king and his people." [47]

[47] *Factum*, p. 348.

IX

SOCIAL PHILOSOPHY: A PRECURSOR OF THE SOCIALISTS

In a perfectly harmonized choir, the individual cannot hear himself unless he makes a false note. . . . But alas! the foundation of existence, the common texture of our days, is made up of action, effort, struggle, and therefore dissonance. —AMIEL.

IF IN Boisguilbert there is to be found an important source of the orthodox theory which has dominated theoretical economic thinking to the present time, it is no less true that in him roots of modern liberal and radical thought are to be found. Almost alone among his commentators Skarzinski has sensed this trend in the Rouen magistrate. He says of him: "Here at the threshold of the science itself we find the germ of all the theories, the elements of all the philosophies of life conceived or developed later—a kind of preparatory step to the philosophy of political economy, which to date has not gone far beyond its original start." In Boisguilbert is found in germ, he asserts, Bastiat's economic harmony and Proudhon's economic contradictions peacefully existing together. "If we sum up briefly the theories of Boisguilbert concerning the solidarity and harmony of interests among the different classes, and if we strike a balance between the things which are practical and rational, and those which are idealistic and utopian, we find that in his confusion and in his gropings, Boisguilbert has instinctively touched about all the sides of the controversial problem which are yet unsolved; that he has grasped correctly the great law of the intimate relation, of the mutual reaction of the most diversified interests of society. But whether the interdependence of different classes would itself finally lead to harmony, or whether harmony would first have to be created, he has left unsolved." But from the sentence "'*pourvu qu'on laisse faire la nature.*'[1] we could pronounce the conviction, hinted at by Carey and others, that in fact no harmony is given by nature, but the possibility of such a harmony."[2]

Marx reproached Boisguilbert for his failure to see that the cause of the conditions in France was the existence of the institution of private property. The former's obsession against private property kept him from seeing that, if there were no other reason, the very existence of the wretchedness in France would have prevented Boisguilbert from adopting such a view. It was the maladministration of the government which Boisguilbert held responsible for the situation existing. It was the example before him which led him to declare that "the individual interest" is "always very much more perceptible and better managed than the general interest."[3] Seeing the manner in which those agents of the government, the intendants and traitants, managed affairs, Boisguilbert would have been the last person to suggest increasing their number or their sphere. It was not more, but less, government which he thought France must have if she were not to perish.

Measured by modern standards, Boisguilbert can certainly by no means be classed as a socialist. So far as is indicated by his writings, his dissatisfaction with the existing order did not lead him to desire to change its fundamental form, but primarily to bring about reforms in institutions, fiscal policies, and administration which would increase the general welfare. In essence he went far beyond such reforms. He was a Columbus charting a new sea; a Copernicus upsetting the thought of the world. Boisguilbert started a revolution in the social sciences by shifting the attention from the few to the many. In the name of humanity, others before him had attempted to ameliorate the condition of the masses. Fundamentally Boisguilbert fought a system—a system based upon the exploitation of one class or group by another. In doing so he established a theory based upon nonex-

[1] See below, pp. 250–251, for complete quotation.

[2] Witold von Skarzinski, *Pierre de Boisguillebert und seine Beziehungen zur neueren Volkswirthschaftslehre*, Berlin, 1873, pp. 62–66.

[3] *Le Détail*, p. 250.

ploitation and economic justice. It was upon such a foundation that later radical thought was to build.

From his utterances Boisguilbert must be given a definite place among the forerunners of the destroyers of the old régime. *Liberté, fraternité,* and not so much *égalité,* as *équité,* are implicit in his ideas. The old order feared their dangerous influence. One of its defenders, writing in 1761 to counteract the growing radicalism, attacked him:

> An anonymous author who wrote in 1707, and many morsels from whose book entitled *Le Détail de la France* have been copied since, seems to have written only to criticize most bitterly the operations of the ministry of finance from 1661 to his time. He spoke without sparing ministers; he was aroused to frenzy against the traitants and the persons employed in the levy of the taxes. He repeats at every instant words of rapine and vexation. Shall one take him for a guide? He does only injury.
>
> It is believed that he has since been invoked by the author of the *Réformateur,*[4] and that his soul, full of bitterness, has passed into that of this last author. Both, moreover, speak with the same confidence; both, nevertheless, have the same inability to propose any plan of administration. They have the same ignorance of the simplest parts of finance, of the product of the earth, of the arts, of manufactures. . . . I have often seen these two books in the hands of men little instructed, and in those of young people promptly and easily convinced of everything by the fire and by the ignorance of their age. Hatred against ministers, furor against useful men on the part of [men in] less distinguished ranks was the fruit of their detestable works.[5]

Boisguilbert was not a radical in his own eyes. He had small use for "bearers of novelties." His ideas, radical as they appeared to his contemporaries, and his humanitarian interests sprang from his protest against existing economic conditions, against institutions which produced such conditions, and against the corruption and self-interest which would ruin an entire State for personal advantage. His was a restless and inquiring mind coupled with warm human sympathy. The suffering of the people filled him with great pity, and with an extreme moral indignation. But he was not the passive type which could stop with

[4] Cliquot de Blervache, *Le Réformateur,* Amsterdam, 1756.
[5] Rivière (not Mercier), *L'Ami de la paix,* Amsterdam, 1761, pp. 112–114.

this. If the masses of France were enmeshed in hopeless poverty there must be a reason for it. He must find it. This accomplished to his satisfaction, he never thereafter ceased his efforts to bring about a change.

The Part Played by Nature

Boisguilbert decried the effect of civilization upon the well-being and security of man. To him civilization was synonymous with corruption. This corruption was due to defects or weaknesses of human nature, especially to self-interest, greed, and laziness. As a consequence, nature's plan for the organization of human society had been defeated. He extolled the "age of innocence," as he called primitive society. Liberty was then unfettered, he thought, and the lack of restrictions on trade and exchange produced the equilibrium which he saw as a part of the plan of nature. Man's wants were then simple, to be sure, but subsistence was never lacking.

> Barbarous people, who have been known in the last few centuries, and who are being discovered all the time, having no other laws and no other books than this same nature, are a certain proof of this truth. Nature, their guide, does not, to be sure, make for them repasts as magnificent or as delicate in some respects as are obtained in the refined and consequently rebellious countries. But in general very much is wanting before she will produce for them such bad ones, so that there is a balance, as it were, with respect to the two conditions.[6]

Protest against Economic Inequality

Another reason why Boisguilbert attacked the corrupting influences of civilization was because he thought civilization to be the cause of the inequality which led to so much human misery. Originally men were equal. Economic classes were the result of the exercise of might, which in turn resulted from an attempt to escape the consequences of divine punishment, namely, the condemnation to subsist by the sweat of the brow. This corruption had progressed until men, he said, are found divided into two classes: those who do all the work and have nothing,

[6] *Dissertation sur les richesses,* p. 411. In his idealizing an "age of innocence" or a primitive simplicity, Boisguilbert distinctly anticipated Rousseau.

and those who do nothing and have everything. As he expressed it:

> The condemnation which God pronounced against all men in the person of the first one, not to be able in the future, after his sin, to live or subsist except by work and the sweat of his brow, was punctually executed only as long as the innocence of the world lasted, that is, as long as there was no difference in the condition and state of men. Every individual was then his own servant and his own master, and enjoyed the riches and treasures of the earth in proportion to his personal talent to make them valuable. All ambition and all luxury were reduced to the procuring of food and clothing. The first two workers in the world, who were at the same time the two rulers of it, divided these two trades: the one worked the earth in order to have grain, and the other tended the flocks in order to clothe himself, and the mutual exchange they could make enabled them to enjoy one another's labor.
>
> But crime and violence existed even then. The one who was the stronger wished to do nothing and to enjoy the fruits of the labor of the weaker, thus violating entirely the orders of the Creator. And this corruption has come to such an excess, that today men are wholly divided into two classes, namely, one which does nothing and enjoys all the pleasures, and another, which, working from day until night, is found scarcely in possession of the necessities, or is deprived of them entirely.[7]

Extremes of wealth and poverty offended his sense of natural justice as not in the interest of national well-being. The great wealth of the few, he thought, did not compensate for the poverty of the many.[8] It was a negation of the equilibrium which he felt not only to constitute justice, but also to be eminently desirable at every point in the State. In a condition of greater balance, "if some persons would not be so magnificent, all the rest would not be so wretched, and by a just compensation there would be twenty times more well-to-do." [9]

Emphasis upon Consumption

It was a protest against a system which regarded a State as fortunate if it had impoverished masses to carry on production cheaply which, in part, led Boisguilbert to lay so much emphasis

[7] *Ibid.*, pp. 398–399.
[8] *Le Détail*, p. 177.
[9] *Dissertation sur les richesses*, p. 418.

upon consumption. He attempted to scotch this fallacy. All products "owe their birth, their limits, and their duration, only to the degree of power, more or less, that the country has, not only to produce, but to consume them. It is that alone which can draw these goods from the bowels of the earth. . . ." [10] Men will not work for nothing, and with fellow men who will not labor because they cannot consume, the mere ownership of property will leave its possessor unfortunate indeed.[11] Subsistence, at least, must be allowed for. But subsistence is not the end sought. It is the irreducible minimum only, which is essential if all production is not to cease. The maximum prosperity for the nation would only be attained, he thought, "if an untold number of men, who because of poverty consume almost nothing, either in the way of food or of clothing, were placed in a condition, which could easily be done, to be able amply to procure all their necessities, and even superfluities." [12]

Radical and presumptuous indeed must such a suggestion have been considered in France in 1700! But if this were radical, how much more so was his assertion that nature "loves all men equally and wishes them likewise to be able to subsist without distinction." [13] Such an opinion, not properly interpreted, could have fallen little short of *lèse majesté*.

The Consumption of the Masses, the Source of the Wealth of the Classes

Oppression of the masses in France especially took the forms of placing on them the burden of supporting an extravagant court, of carrying on wars, and of providing the sums required by a wasteful administration of the tax system. Boisguilbert regarded this not only as unjust, but as the result of an inexplicable blindness. It killed the goose that laid the golden egg. While the poor became wretched, the rich, strangely enough, found themselves growing poorer.

If the rich understood their own interest they would not weigh down the poor with proportionately heavier burdens. On the

[10] *Ibid.*, p. 416.
[11] *Ibid.*, p. 394.
[12] *Ibid.*, pp. 420–421. [13] *Ibid.*, p. 410.

contrary, they would relieve them wholly. This, to be sure, would constitute an immediate sacrifice, but a sacrifice comparable to an investment on which an immediate return is foregone in the expectation that a larger one will be obtained in the future. This would result from the following fact.

An écu with a poor man, or a very small merchant, has a hundred times more effect, or rather creates more revenue than with a rich man, on account of the continual and daily turnover which this modest sum undergoes with the former, which does not happen with respect to the rich, in whose coffers far greater quantities of money remain idle for months and whole years, useless as a consequence, either on account of the corruption of a heart blinded by avarice, or in the expectation of a better market.

But from this custody the king and the body of the State draw no benefit, and it constitutes so much theft from both.[14] [On the other hand] a thousand écus distributed among a thousand persons of small means, would pass through a thousand hands in less time than they would have resided in the coffers of a rich man. [Each écu] could only result, as a consequence, in bringing about a hundred écus for consumption. [On this total spent] the prince would have received the tenth part as his share, that is, he would have received the value of ten thousand écus on a sum with respect to which he has not received even a farthing because of the disturbance in the use which is made of it, and which is augmented and supported every day by those who falsely persuade him that it is to his particular advantage that both he and his people be equally ruined.

If, then, the rich understood their interests, they would wholly relieve the poor of their taxes, which would immediately create more well-to-do persons. This would result in a great increase of consumption which, spreading itself over all the mass of a State, would thrice indemnify the rich for their first advances. It would be analogous to a master who lends grain to his farmer in order to seed the land, without which he would have no harvest.[15]

Thus upon purely economic grounds Boisguilbert concluded that a more equitable division of wealth is more advantageous to society than extremes of wealth and poverty.

[14] By this statement that hoarding is theft, one is reminded of Proudhon's dictum that "property is theft." Incidentally it may be mentioned that Proudhon's thesis that equilibrium constitutes justice is also a major thesis in Boisguilbert's writings.

[15] *Op. cit.*, pp. 419–420.

Boisguilbert's Humanitarianism

Little of the misfortune that results from poverty seems to have escaped Boisguilbert's attention. There is his stern question in the *Supplément au Détail de la France,* for instance, in which he set forth the high mortality resulting from undernourishment and lack of physical attention:

Is it necessary to await peace in order to save the lives of two or three hundred thousand creatures, at least, who have perished in the years of poverty, above all in infancy; there not being half of them who can survive to the age of earning their livelihood, because their mothers lack milk, from want of nourishment, or from too hard labor; while at a more advanced age, having only bread and water, without beds, clothing or any remedy in their sickness, and deprived of sufficient strength for work, which is their sole revenue, they perish before having attained the middle of life? [16]

The lack of security caused by inability to save did not pass unnoticed:

Some, even many, find in the [savings of the] past, resources which aid them in the present, and even in the future. But such is not the case with many, almost an infinite number of others, unhappy creatures at whose throats poverty holds a knife continually, who can only prevent themselves from starving by working day and night. There is continually only a thread between their very frugal subsistence and their complete destruction. Everything hangs quite often on an écu, which by a continual turnover produces for them ordinarily for consumption, a hundred times its value during the course of a year.[17]

And that less attention should be paid to the welfare of men than to that of animals aroused a righteous indignation:

After all, are not men comparable to animals, and especially to horses? Who will make a horse work continually without giving it a measure of the necessary food unless one wishes it to die immediately? But can men, of whom continual toil is required, [and who] sweat blood and water in order to obtain only bread and water in the midst of a country of abundance, hope for a long life, or rather do they not perish before they have half run their course? And this does not take into account those who are prevented by

[16] *Supplément,* pp. 260–261.

[17] *Dissertation sur les richesses,* p. 412.

the poverty of their parents from living beyond infancy. They are, as it were, choked in the cradle.[18]

That the people should be so wretchedly poor was bad enough, but that this condition should be brought about or made worse by the action of the government was incomprehensible. In a beautiful and truly remarkable passage, Boisguilbert spoke of the poor who alone had reason to complain against taxes, but whose voices could not be heard above the plaints of the rich:

People cry out all the time in France about taxes, the rich more than the poor, as a result of this unhappy custom which has been introduced of having no justice in the apportionment of public charges. This places things on such a basis that whoever can, protects himself from them. [Thus] the more powerful a man is, the less [taxes] he pays, because he is more able to obtain exemption from them. And as among the means used to procure this privilege, noise and complaints are the most considerable, they are heard more clearly in the mouths of the rich than in those of the poor, which causes the latter always to be crushed. This, refalling by a counter-blow upon the rich, (as has been made clear,) eventually ruins both. A first minister ought not, then, to trouble himself much if people complain, but only if there is reason to complain.[19]

In particular he attacked the lack of humanity of the tax farmers, who, overreaching their authority, "would have us believe that the money they pay to the prince is important only in its quantity, and not in the manner in which it is raised on the people." [20] Then there was the injustice resulting from the unequal assessment of taxes, masked as it was by the intermediary of money:

How could one, of sound mind, place an ordinance on paper which would require every person who gathers a harvest of thirty setiers of wheat to pay forty in taxes; and another whose harvest amounts to two hundred be made to contribute only four, or even less, according to his credit? As such a demand, as well as its execution, would be a frightful sight, it is necessary to mask it, and it is that [masking] which money does marvelously well. It robs all the horror of such a measure from the influential persons who can order it done, because they have only a confused idea as to the detail, which

[18] *Ibid.*, p. 414.
[19] *Le Détail*, p. 243.
[20] *Dissertation sur les richesses*, p. 401. See quotation from *The Wealth of Nations*, above, note, p. 121.

can be understood only by [observing] the practice, that is, by the destitute existence [resulting], which is indeed far from their own situation. They wholly ignore the fact that no one, whoever it may be, can pay a sou either of taxes or other dues, except by the sale of goods which one possesses. Thus the demand for money has strict limits given by nature, which cannot be violated without producing a frightful monster.[21]

Again, there were the tax collectors, themselves facing ruin, and spreading ruin to avoid it. Like frightful monsters, in truth, they marched up and down the land, accompanied at times by detachments of soldiers to protect them from attack by an enraged people who saw their pitiful possessions seized. This additional handicapping of an already poverty-stricken populace brought forth another of the relentless questions of Boisguilbert:

Is it necessary to await peace in order that the tailles shall be justly apportioned throughout the kingdom, and that great estates shall not be taxed at little or nothing, while a wretched creature who has only his arms by which to maintain himself and all his family, after the sale of his poor personal property, or the implements with which he earns his livelihood, [a sale made] to provide for the billeted soldiers which is regulated according to the assessment of the taille, sees the doors and furnishings of his house taken to pay the remainder of a tax exceeding four times his ability to pay?[22]

As a climax there was the stupidity and the futility of imprisonment for debt.

And when all these means are exhausted, a man is guilty because he cannot do the impossible, and give what he does not have. He is dragged to prison, and he is held there for months, causing an increase in loss of goods, namely, the loss of his time and his work, which is his only revenue, as well as of the State and of the prince.[23]

Nor did he overlook the condition of the prisons themselves, where

it costs three sous, four deniers per person per day to sleep on straw; and it is necessary for their wives or children to bring them their food, sometimes from a distance of three or four leagues. And as it is often cold weather, and as the country prisons are in bad

[21] *Dissertation sur les richesses*, pp. 401–402.
[22] *Supplément*, p. 260.
[23] *Dissertation sur les richesses*, p. 402.

condition, they almost always return with diseases of weakness and undernourishment (*malades de fatigue et de misère*).[24]

The standard of living appears to have been equally low in town and country. "More than half of the people in the large cities, especially on this side of the Loire, and even in Paris and in the country, do not eat meat at all, and drink only water, which causes the loss of the greatest part of their strength, and as a result, of their work." [25] Their food is compared with that of similar classes in England:

It is certain, and no one denies it, that in France grains alone form almost all the food of the poor (*menu peuple*), without any aid either of drink or of vegetables, such as are consumed elsewhere, and still less meat and fish. In England, on the contrary, it can be said that bread has the least place in the ordinary pittance of the inhabitants. Meat and fish, which are very abundant there, and consequently very cheap, replace grains by more than three-fourths, and often even of all the functions that they have in France to nourish almost all the people. [In England] there is no country man so unfortunate as not to have his supply of salted meat and beer (which is a second food). Furthermore, they make no use of bouillon in which to cook the meats, although this is the most delicious food of the poor in France. They throw it in the street with the rest of the garbage, as well as the offals (*extrémités*) of animals, of which they do not make use at all, as everywhere else.[26]

Finally there is described the effect of a descent from one class to another.

A farmer, accustomed to live well with all his family, as was likewise his landlord when the farmer was able to pay the latter, is required by this same landlord to sell at a loss on account of the low price of grain. As a result of this [the farmer] is reduced to beggary, as is frequently the landlord also, or [they must] earn their living by manual labor. Not being accustomed to this (*à quoi n'étant pas faits*), or to the bad food, which is a necessary consequence, it can be said with assurance that the individuals scarcely fail to suffer the same fate as goods. The agony of spirit, the shame, the general desolation, make them and their families perish visibly. The evil commences with the children, who have need of aid in order to be brought up to the age when they will be able to gain a livelihood. This they cannot receive from parents who are denuded of

[24] *Le Détail*, p. 187.
[25] *Factum*, p. 347. [26] *Traité des grains*, p. 385.

everything. It can be said with certainty that more than half of them perish from lack of their needs, both while at the breast and during the first years of infancy. All the illnesses are mortal at this time from lack of care, of remedies, and of proper nourishment. . . .

It is only experience and close attention to entering personally into a very great discussion of all the unusual facts which could make all this believable, but it is not less certain than that an extreme necessity not only dries up all the tenderness of a nature, but even outrages nature on pressing occasions. . . . Since necessity knows no laws, she transgresses even the most sacred [laws], in proportion to the excess in which she is found. Let one not be at all astonished, then, at what is advanced, namely, that extreme poverty causes the diminution of families to be regarded as a blessing, and that this situation carries with it the means of procuring [the diminution].[27]

In truth, in Boisguilbert was food for a Rousseau.

The Concept of Economic Solidarity

The term "solidaire" referred, in the time of Boisguilbert, to the common obligation for the entire amount of taxes which the central government levied upon the communities. In the event that the portion subsequently assessed upon an individual could not be obtained from him, the amount was made up by an additional levy upon other contributors. Boisguilbert took over the term to express the economic interdependence which exists among the members of society. It is in this broader sense of oneness, of

[27] *Traité des grains*, pp. 367–368. An interesting contrast in the spirit underlying the treatment of a theoretical point and an actual condition is to be seen by a comparison of the above passage and the following one in *The Wealth of Nations*. In a country whose wealth is declining, says Adam Smith, "many who had been bred in the superior classes, not being able to find employment in their own business, would be glad to seek it in the lowest. The lowest class being not only overstocked with its own workmen, but with the overflowing of all the other classes, the competition for employment would be so great in it, as to reduce the wages of labour to the most miserable and scanty subsistence of the labourer. Many would not be able to find employment even upon these hard terms, but would either starve, or be driven to seek a subsistence either by begging, or by a perpetration perhaps of the greatest enormities. Want, famine, and mortality would immediately prevail in that class, and from thence extend themselves to all the superior classes, till the number of inhabitants in the country was reduced to what could easily be maintained by the revenue and stock which remained in it, and which had escaped either the tyranny or the calamity which had destroyed the rest."—*Wealth of Nations*, Bk. I, p. 75.

social unity, that the term has come to occupy an important place in economics, in sociology, and in philosophy.

The significance which the concept of economic solidarity has in Boisguilbert's theory was the result of his observation of the events in France taking place in his time. The aides, for instance, were only in a part of France, but the other part became poverty-stricken on account of an inability to carry on trade with the provinces of the aides. Likewise there was the injustice of the taille, in which "the evasion which the rich have made with respect to their just contribution, in order to make the burden fall upon (*en accabler*) the poor, having placed the latter in a position to be unable to consume *l'herbage*, to which reference has been made, [and] which may be used to signify all goods in general, it becomes a total loss to the owners, who have been completely ruined by this would-be privilege." [28]

From this he develops an organic view of economic life.

> Because there is a point to be made, to which no one has ever given thought, namely, that the body of the State is like a human body, of which all the parts and all the members must act together to maintain life, in view of the fact that the affliction of one part [of the body] quickly affects the rest of it, and causes the death of the individual. The parts not being of equal strength and vigor, it is this interdependence of the whole which causes the most robust to expose themselves, and even to present themselves to receive the blows that would be carried to the weakest and most delicate parts, which cannot stand the least attack. It is unnecessary to speak of the serpent which the Holy Scripture uses as a symbol of prudence, because when attacked it covers its head with all its body. Does not nature similarly teach men, on like occasion, to present the hands and arms in order to parry or receive the blows which are given to the eyes and to the head? [29]

In other words, just as "gangrene at the extremity of the members of the human body immediately causes the whole to perish, although all the parts far from the evil appear very sound and in good condition," [30] so, he thought, there would result a general loss of prosperity if reverses should come to any part of the economic body.

[28] *Factum*, p. 336. [29] *Loc. cit.*
[30] *Dissertation sur les richesses*, p. 400.

Out of this concept of economic solidarity came Boisguilbert's attack upon the folly of any individual or class attempting to further his or its interest at the expense of others. Any gain would be short-lived. But he goes beyond the purely negative necessity to refrain from injuring another group in his discussion of the rich and the poor. There must be protection given by the one to the other. Continuing his analogy between the economic body and the human body, he says:

> The poor in the body of the State are the eyes and the cranium, and as a result the most delicate and feeble parts; the rich are the arms and the rest of the body. The blows which are struck to obtain the needs of the State are almost imperceptible when they fall upon the strong and robust parts, but they are mortal when they strike the feeble, who are the poverty-stricken, and by a counterblow, those who refused them their assistance are in turn ruined.[31]

The Struggle between Employers and Employees

Boisguilbert noted the antagonism existing between employers and employees. This he saw as being due to the self-interest of each and to an unwillingness to treat one another fairly, whereas there should be a recognition of mutual dependence upon one another.

> Although they give birth to one another equally and reciprocally, as has been said, instead of conspiring together for their common maintenance as they should do, they work from morning to night to destroy and to clothe themselves with the very skin of one another. The workman would like to have the entire proceeds of the harvest for his labor without troubling himself about how the one who engages him will pay his landlord and his taxes, or in the least with the fact of the impotence in which the farmer would be placed to fertilize the land in order to give the workman another opportunity to earn his livelihood. Likewise the farmer in his turn would like to have the labor of all those whom he uses to cultivate his lands for very much less than these laborers need to support themselves and their families.[32]

The result is equally injurious regardless of which side wins. The laborer, for instance, may profit temporarily by forcing the

[31] *Factum*, p. 336.
[32] *Traité des grains*, p. 390.

employer to meet his demand, but he is ruined by the subsequent results of his shortsightedness:

The State suffers if either of the two has his way, because [in either case] the land remains [uncultivated], and commerce is not carried on. It is, then, only an equilibrium which may be able to save everyone. And nature alone, to repeat, can bring this about. But it is necessary not to keep her from acting. It is that, nevertheless, which is done when farmers are prevented from selling their grain to those who offer money for it. By this prohibition the cause of the worker is furthered for the time being, but it is lost ultimately.[33]

The source of the conflict is the changing price of grain. By every such change the situation of the farmer and the worker is affected. When the price falls, the income of the farmer is reduced, whereas the real wages of the laborer are increased, but he is unwilling to adjust his money wage to the changed condition.

Necessity alone, which controls these people, has lost the power which it had over them. If they earn the expenses of the whole week in a single day's work, far from adjusting their wages to the price [of grain], this situation encourages them to increase the poverty of the master by exacting a much higher wage, on account of the possibility of giving up work for a considerable time in case of his refusal. And since the cultivation of the earth must be done at the right moment, that is, if everything is not done at the day and the hour indicated by the seasons, everything is lost, the farmer can choose between perishing either from leaving everything undone, or from obligating himself for an expense for which he will not be reimbursed.

This situation spreads immediately throughout all the arts and vocations, where the same rebellion on the part of the workers with regard to the entrepreneur is seen, and [it influences] even the attitude of domestics toward their masters. The least word causes them, noting the low price of bread, to refuse the wages offered. Afterwards both workmen and servants pay dearly for their folly. When their savings are exhausted and their revolt is over, they can hardly ever obtain employment at the wages which they had refused, because the depression having become powerfully established, everyone is interested in dismissing people, and not in taking them on again.

[33] *Ibid.*, p. 390.

This proportion of interest is necessary then, among all sorts of dealers, and no one may draw a double share (*utilité*) when this reduces the portion of the other; otherwise all the harmony upon which the maintenance of the State depends is entirely destroyed. It is this, nevertheless, which occurs between these workmen and their masters when wheat is at a low price. This product being subject to variations in quantity from causes which are beyond the power of men [to control], such as the weather, the worker who claims to follow his right in case of an increase in price, as he does effectively, does not act with the same justice in the case of a fall in price, which is the cause of all the unhappiness to which reference has just been made, and of which one has had too much experience.[34]

Here, it will be noted, Boisguilbert gave the wages of labor a place in his proportionate price structure.

If he demanded that the farmer secure fair treatment in periods of falling prices, Boisguilbert was equally insistent that the worker should obtain fair treatment in the period of rising prices.

As a matter of fact, it is just to increase the wages of workmen when their work or their needs increase. Even on these occasions they do not appeal to the liberality of their masters, who would be no more reasonable than the workers themselves if everything depended upon their good will. But in these encounters, justice is brought about in such a manner that neither they, nor their masters, nor the State suffer any loss. As the abundance of commerce, which always brings in its train an increase in the price of products, especially of grains, as well as an increase in the silver which arrives every year in Europe, makes them hasten to secure workmen again, they capitulate regarding the increase in wages. This is not on account of the threats [of the workmen] to cease work, but [from their intention] to go elsewhere, where their demands will be granted. It is in this way that those who earned fifteen deniers a day one hundred and fifty years ago have had their wages increased to fifteen and twenty sous for the same work, because grains, which were worth twenty sous a setier at Paris at that time, as has been said, were [formerly] worth and should [now] be worth sixteen and eighteen livres, and it is the same with other products.[35]

[34] *Ibid.*, pp. 390–391. Cf. *The Wealth of Nations*, Bk. I, p. 85.

[35] *Ibid.*, p. 391. "In a year of sudden and extraordinary plenty, there are funds in the hands of the employers of industry, sufficient to maintain and employ a greater number of industrious people than had been employed the year before; and this extraordinary number cannot always be had. Those mas-

An increase in wages is "painless," in other words, when the increase accompanies or follows an increase in profits which results from the rising prices accompanying an increase in commercial activity, or following the influx of new metals. At such times the increase results, not from the kindness of heart of the employers, but from the competition of the latter for the available labor supply. As Boisguilbert expressed it elsewhere, when the price of wheat rises the farmers spare no effort to obtain a good crop. This "puts pressure upon the wage earners." The latter thereupon insist on higher wages, which the farmer accords "because there is still something to be gained." [36]

Boisguilbert had no patience with combinations of workmen for the purpose of increasing wages or resisting a decrease with falling prices. They simply increase that much more the tendency of workmen to upset the equilibrium, which means the destruction of all economic well-being. Describing the effect of such combinations, he said:

There is a spirit of rebellion so strongly established against justice on these occasions among workmen whose actions have been described, that in the commercial cities seven or eight hundred workmen in a single industry are seen to absent themselves suddenly and without notice. They leave the work unfinished because it is desired to lower their wages a sou a day, the price of their handiwork being lowered four times more, while the more mutinous use violence toward those who would listen to reason.

There are even statutes among them (for the most part among the nomadic and foreign workers), some written, which they pass from hand to hand. [In these statutes] it is provided that if one of the workers undertakes to lower his ordinary wage, he may immediately be forbidden to work his trade. Besides the vow made, which they make use of on such occasions, the master even suffers from a general forbidding of all the workmen ever to work for him. Well-to-do merchants have been seen to go into bankruptcy for the sole reason that they have been two or three years without being able to obtain anyone to work for them, although there might be

ters, therefore, who want more workmen, bid against one another, in order to get them, which sometimes raises both the real and the money price of their labour."—*Wealth of Nations*, Bk. I, p. 87.

[36] *Mémoire sur les blés*, p. 159. The last expression—*parce-qu'il y a encore à gagner*—is one which echoes down French economic literature, and could well have been an influence in the development of the concept of economic man.

any number of unemployed at that place belonging to the same trade.[37]

But reluctance to adjust themselves to a lower price level is not a characteristic of employees only. It is shared by dealers, who, as he said elsewhere, prefer bankruptcy to lowering prices by a single sou.

This excessive desire to maintain a price once attained is not at all limited to simple journeymen. All the arts and trades regard it as the safeguard and the sole maintenance of their vocations. They would rather sell one article at the fixed price than ten at a somewhat lower one, although the profit on the many exceed very much the diminution or the loss on the one. This is a thing concerning which they are incapable of listening to reason.[38]

An Attack upon Money

Superficially Boisguilbert's attitude toward money reminds one of the position taken by the French socialists in the second quarter of the nineteenth century. His attack upon it was the outgrowth of his reaction against the emphasis placed upon money as wealth under the mercantilist system, of the injustice in taxation covered by money, and of the breakdown in exchange which he witnessed.

It was the departure from the true idea as to what constituted wealth which, in part, was responsible for his views with regard to the evils of civilization. This error, he thought, had brought human misery in its wake. Gold and silver "were not wealth while innocence, or at least the following of the laws of nature persisted among the inhabitants of the globe, and an increase in widespread poverty has followed every degree of departure from this order." [39]

The difficulty arises from the fact that men fail to see the true nature and purpose of money. They make its possession an end to which everything is subordinated. Because it is unrecognized that money is required only in order to procure goods, "this cruel intermediary, as money may be called, destroys a . . . great quantity [of goods] through its fatal ministrations." That

[37] *Traité des grains*, p. 391.
[38] *Loc. cit.*
[39] *Dissertation sur les richesses*, p. 395.

is, by misuse, in making it an end rather than a means, or, as Boisguilbert said, in making it a god rather than a servant, money causes goods, and even men to be sacrificed to obtain it. It is the misuse of money, too, which creates such extreme inequalities in the distribution of wealth. At the same time it lends itself as an aid to all human weaknesses, namely, to "ambition, luxury, avarice, idleness, and laziness," as well as to "positive crime, both that which is punished by laws, and another kind which ignorance causes to crown all our days." [40] And so Boisguilbert made what Marx called the "first resolute polemic against gold and silver." [41]

But, he said, there is a way to end the tyranny of money:

> We have in use continually in Europe the easiest and cheapest device to bring the metals to reason, and, destroying their usurpation, place them in their proper sphere, which is to be the servants and slaves of commerce, solely, and not its tyrants. [This device] is to give them as competitors, not copper, not shells, not tobacco, as in the places mentioned, which cost trouble and work to obtain, but a simple piece of paper which costs nothing, and carries on, nevertheless, all the functions of money for millions in quantity for an indefinite length of time, that is to say, for as many hands as it may pass through, while the metals do not go at all from their natural state, and from the principles which called them into the world. . . .
>
> In this manner there would be a general prosperity, that is to say, a tremendous possession and consumption of goods, without the use of the least sum of money. Then, to repeat, the priests of this idol would not profit by making it a tutelary god of life, nor [could they] assert that men are happy or unhappy only in proportion as they possess more or less of this so-sought-after metal.[42]

In these greatly misunderstood paragraphs, which standing alone are capable of the most extreme interpretation, a paper substitute for the metals is visualized.

However, Boisguilbert was no visionary with respect to money. His "piece of paper" which would replace the metals was not something to circulate by fiat. Whatever the influence of this passage on the thinking of monetary experimenters, it refers

[40] *Ibid.*, pp. 398, 401, 418.
[41] *Gesamtausgabe*, Erste Abteilung, Band 3, p. 575.
[42] *Ibid.*, pp. 397–398.

only to sound bills of exchange, arising out of commercial activity.

Production for Use vs. Production for Profit

An interesting observation made by Boisguilbert pertains to that very modern problem of a conflict arising from the business requirement that production be for profit, and an underlying social demand that it be for use. Speaking of grains, he said:

> [In France they] have two interests and two faces. Both are encountered always in a continual combat, seeking only to destroy one another, because each party is persuaded that it can be happy only through the destruction of its enemy. These two parties are formed from the two effects which grains produce. The first of these is to nourish men in Europe, so that the failure of this manna makes them perish. The other comes from the possession of the land by the proprietors. To obtain from the land a greater quantity [of grain] than they need for their personal and individual use serves them as a means to procure for themselves, by the sale of the surplus, all the other things which the necessities, pleasures, or magnificence of life demand.
>
> The first interest requires that grains exist in the greatest possible quantity, and at a permanently low price. The other would be of the same sentiment with regard to the quantity if the excess did not depreciate the price. Since this always occurs, as experience has shown, [the latter] does not hesitate to favor its own interest, and to wish for, and to use all its effort to see them at a permanently high price, even should this mean a smaller quantity.[43]

Unwittingly Boisguilbert raised the problem of private property in land. Accepting the basic institutions of his time, this problem, as such, he did not discuss. But as society was organized, he saw the landowner holding the key position, and with him the economic structure rose or fell.

As to the conflict between production for use and production for profit, he proposed the only solution which to his far-sighted mind was logically justifiable and socially just. The two must be held in equilibrium. There must be a sufficient supply of grain to take care of the needs of humanity. But, he reiterated, the supply of grain does not appear like mushrooms and truffles; to

[43] *Quand même il devrait y en avoir moins. Traité des grains,* p. 369.

produce a crop requires a certain outlay of expenses in money. Furthermore, the land quickly becomes exhausted, and its fertility can only be maintained by continual fertilization; but the owner cannot and will not continue to apply fertilizer unless it pays him to do so. Grain prices which are below the cost of production, therefore, said Boisguilbert, are socially undesirable. In spite of the popular demand for the lowest possible prices, their ultimate effect is to exhaust the soil, restrict production, and bring about the famine which it is popularly thought that low prices will prevent. This is the thesis of *Traité des grains.*

The functions of the landowner and of the farmer, whose interests Boisguilbert saw as identical, then, is, according to this reasoning, not only to provide the supply of grain for the present, but also to husband nature's resources so that a future supply will be assured. This would be done, not so much from humanitarian motives on their part, but because it would be to their interest in the present continually to maintain the fertility of the soil. That this same result would be brought about through the foresight of the people as a whole Boisguilbert would never agree. With all his compassion for them he had a profound contempt for their very lack of foresight. "It is this confused multitude of people without heads and without brains which weaves the cord with which it is strangled." [44] Here, then, is the clue as to what would have been his attitude on the question of public, as opposed to private, ownership of land.

An Economic Utopia Visualized

Boisguilbert attacked the mismanagement of the existing economic system, the conditions which he regarded as an outgrowth of this mismanagement, and the social injustice resulting, with the utmost vigor. But he did not stop with this. Stone by stone as he tore down he attempted to rebuild. The result which he hoped to see attained, namely, prosperity based upon economic equilibrium, and the idealism of his proposals, make him not unworthy of a place among the utopians. Boisguilbert himself would have vigorously rejected such a classification. He would

[44] *Traité des grains*, p. 378.

have admitted that he saw the economic world remade through the application of justice and reason, but he would have rejected the idea that there was anything utopian or impossible of achievement about his ideas. Nevertheless it was utopian in that the fruition of his ideal remains in the realm of hope and desire, except, it may be added, in so far as it has existed in the minds of theorists engrossed with long-run results.

In considering Boisguilbert's ideas from the standpoint of a utopia, it should be noted that unlike other and avowed creators of utopias, he concerned himself with no other aspect of life than the economic, except in so far as social and political problems are interrelated with economic ones. Obviously he regarded man's problem of obtaining a livelihood as the dominant one. Consequently, he concerned himself with the solution of the economic difficulties of the individual, of the prince, and of the State.

The writings of Boisguilbert indicate that he possessed the same lofty moral ideas which characterized his great contemporary, Fénelon. Both envisaged an era of justice and perfection. But there are two reasons why Boisguilbert could not have subscribed to the ideal of communism which is dimly suggested in the romance *Télémaque*. The first is his concept of human nature. He saw man as dominated by self-interest, which would militate against the success of any plan for communism. Secondly, Boisguilbert's interest lay, not in a theoretical plan for the reorganization of society, to cure it of its economic ills, but in practical proposals which he was certain would bring about an immediate alleviation of the distress of France and her people. The difference in the ideas of the two men is the difference to be found in the views of a professional moralist and of an economist-statesman with a strong social bent. Boisguilbert was a political economist in the literal sense.

Boisguilbert proposed a system based upon what may be termed socialized-individualism. There must be, he thought, voluntary submission of the individual to the group. The foundation of his social philosophy is that the interest of the individual must give way to the general interest when the two come into conflict.[45] This subordination of self-interest to the general interest would be utilized to produce economic equilibrium. In essence his idea was that, although man is dominated by self-interest, in his ignorance of the fundamentals of economic principles he does not comprehend wherein his true interest lies. He thinks it is in the economic destruction of others, whereas in reality it lies in the saving of others from this annihilation. He must consider the interest of others in order to preserve his own welfare. Not only is this necessary, but he must not concentrate too greatly on the pursuit of wealth for himself alone, or attempt to monopolize it by the destruction of others, for this will only end in his own downfall.[46] Boisguilbert thus demanded the development of a new philosophy of economic relationships. Recognition of economic solidarity must take the place of the existing ideal of *sauve qui peut*.[47]

Though Boisguilbert was pessimistic about modern civilization from the standpoint of economic security, the concomitant of equilibrium, nevertheless he set forth the conditions under which he thought that modern economic society could be made to function on an even keel. There must be economic equality, in the sense that it is unnecessary for anyone to sacrifice goods for money. In this way, the conditions of the bargain would always be equal between buyer and seller. Neither would be compelled to deal at a loss and precipitate an economic upset. Defective economic institutions must be eliminated or modified. There must be free competition and liberty to trade in order to keep self-interest in check, and to equalize the distribution of products. Under these conditions, Boisguilbert thought, economic balance would be maintained, technical processes and skill would

[45] *Factum*, p. 307.

[46] *Traité des grains*, p. 355. *Dissertation sur les richesses*, p. 394.

[47] The classical error of Boisguilbert, which has been repeated by others, says Dühring, consists in assuming that it would only need a "moral decision of man," that is, for him not to desire to enrich himself at the expense of others, "to move in their relation on a basis of friendly furtherance and well-wishing reciprocity." This, he continues, is an impossible ideal. Boisguilbert assumes the possibility of economic justice and fairness without a knowledge of the natural laws which govern customs and moral relations "in which we have to figure with the tendencies of the conflicting parties."—*Kritische Geschichte*, pp. 79–80.

be improved, and economic well-being would be maximized.[48]

There was a further requirement. There must be a development of economic intelligence. Every individual must be made to see how the blind pursuit of self-interest will react upon him injuriously. Likewise the government must see the result of its own acts in upsetting the equality between individuals. In sum, a mistaken, short-sighted self-interest must be replaced by an enlightened self-interest. His highly ethical theory was inspired by the mandate to "do unto others as you would have them do unto you." [49] Everyone must be made to see, in other words, that attention to the interest of others is not visionary, nor the "reflection of religion which does not pass beyond theory." It constitutes, in the final analysis, attention to oneself. Every individual must recognize his dependence upon others, and understand that he draws his own prosperity from the prosperity of the whole of society.

Was Boisguilbert hopeful as to the outcome of his ideal of economic equilibrium? Paradoxically, it must be answered, yes and no. There was in him a strange mixture of optimism and pessimism. He had infinite belief in his economic ideas. In his attempt to develop the sympathy, justice, and understanding which must underlie self-interest in order to remake economic society, he laid great stress upon the publication of his writings. Yet he seemed to have been skeptical as to the possibility of being understood, for he said that "the people, who do not differ from beasts in their general reasoning, and who do not develop points of view beyond their personal and individual interests of the moment, will have difficulty in attempting to understand these principles." [50]

Thus there were two Boisguilberts: the one, an idealist; the other, a realist. He had an optimistic belief that the adoption of his reforms and his social philosophy could create a new world of security for everyone, but also a pessimistic disbelief that human blindness and stupidity could be overcome.

[48] *Dissertation sur les richesses*, pp. 402–404.
[49] *Ibid.*, p. 409.
[50] *Traité des grains*, p. 363.

X

THEORY OF ECONOMIC FLUCTUATION

A very dangerous malady in a State.

IN THE studies on Boisguilbert which have been published his theory has not been sufficiently considered as a whole, or rather, his theories have not been unified. He has been studied primarily for his theory of taxation, for his theory of money, for his theory of commerce in grain. There are two reasons for the failure to tie them together: first, his haphazard method of handling his material makes it extremely difficult to see that there is a single great plan behind the whole. Yet they are part and parcel of his explanation of the causes of economic fluctuations, and his proposals to bring about economic stability. The second reason is that those interested in his works have gone primarily to his most quoted and better known ones, *Le Détail de la France* and *Factum de la France,* in which it is less easy to see his essential unity of thought. Strictly speaking his works should not be considered separately in any case, but it is in his *Dissertation sur la nature des richesses, de l'argent et des tributs,* and to a less degree in *Traité des grains,* that his general theory of the interrelation of all aspects of economic life is more clearly discerned, and where, obscured by the groping to express new ideas and by his peculiar style, the "discovery" which was to bring him the fame of a Columbus or a Copernicus, as he thought, is to be found more generally set forth.

The facts with regard to France which Boisguilbert observed, and which form the background of his writings, were that the people were poor, the kingdom was poor, the king was poor; agriculture was well-nigh ruined and industrial life as a whole was almost in a state of collapse. Were these isolated phenomena, or were they related? What was the cause of it all, and how could the situation be changed? These were the problems which Boisguilbert set himself to solve.

Everyone has, he said, individually a desire to better his condition and to make it more secure. But as for wealth, "no one has ever considered the condition in its broader aspects (*en général*), although no one can be rich permanently, especially the prince, unless there is general prosperity (*l'opulence publique*)." [1] It was, then, to a study of this broader aspect of wealth, or the general prosperity, about which nothing was known, and in turn to its loss, that he gave his attention.

What is meant by general prosperity? What are its characteristics? How is it lost? What are the characteristics of the opposite condition, of *la misère moderne*—an "extreme poverty in the midst of an abundance of all things"? How can this state be ended and a return be made to prosperity? These are the questions Boisguilbert attempted to answer. There are dangers inherent in a complex economic structure, he thought.

> It is thus apropos to take up this matter in detail, and to show that, if this ample possession of all that which the mind can discover beyond necessities indicates true wealth, it is a most perilous situation which has the utmost need of management. Otherwise it may happen that that which has been instituted to make it possible to enjoy the superfluous, will serve, when measures are badly taken, only to deprive of the essential, throwing a State in an instant from the pinnacle of prosperity to the last degree of depression.[2]

[1] *Dissertation sur les richesses*, p. 408.

[2] *Ibid.*, p. 404. A word in regard to Boisguilbert's terminology is perhaps not amiss. There are those who object to modernizing the language of a writer of an earlier period. But in translating and interpreting Boisguilbert's writings the modern terms "prosperity" and "depression" have been used. He himself uses the term *la prosperité* once or twice. Ordinarily he uses the expression *temps d'opulence, l'opulence générale*, or *l'opulence publique*. The opposite state he refers to as *la misère, la misère moderne, temps de misère*. To translate these phrases as "time of wealth," or "time of opulence," or "state of poverty" would give the whole an atmosphere of obsolescence which the thought itself, in so many respects, scarcely deserves. After all, the external aspects of early trade disturbances and modern business cycles were similar. Furthermore, there is the precedent of Adam Smith, who, inspired, it may be, by Boisguilbert's remarks on the purchase of plate in times of prosperity, said that "the people, as they can afford it, as they have more commodities to give for it, will naturally purchase a greater and greater quantity of plate. The quantity of their coin will increase from necessity; the quantity of their plate from vanity and ostentation, or from the same reason that the

It is perhaps unnecessary to mention that the phrase "economic fluctuation" used in the title of this chapter carries with it no implication that it is being used in the present instance in the sense of what is known as business cycles. Although his descriptions and analyses are in large part applicable to business cycles, it was distinctly not recurring and self-generating cycles which Boisguilbert had in mind. On the contrary it was his belief that once attained, there would be no loss of prosperity, without the intervention of some fortuitous force, or, as he said, without some "unnatural" action to bring it about.[3]

As a matter of fact, Boisguilbert was concerned with two different economic movements. First, and constituting his primary interest, there was the question of secular trend. France, he said, had grown poorer since 1660. This he considered to be the result of the Colbertian policies which had interfered with the natural economic development of the nation. Agriculture had been virtually stifled, and with its decline had followed that of all economic life in France.

As to the national income, he maintained that

> the diminution is five hundred millions a year, because it is one-half of the income (*des biens*) of the kingdom, and that this same income from land only, whether real, as estates, or by accident, such as offices, bureaus, tolls and mills,[4] was formerly at seven hundred millions a year; thus these same revenues when they were doubled by the income from industry, were more than fourteen hundred millions a year, so that all being diminished by one-half, if

---

quantity of fine statues, pictures, and of every other luxury and curiosity, is likely to increase among them. But as statuaries and painters are not likely to be worse rewarded in *times of wealth* and *prosperity*, than in *times of poverty* and *depression*, so gold and silver are not likely to be worse paid for."—*Wealth of Nations*, Bk. I, pp. 188–189. My italics.

[3] Boisguilbert was by no means the first observer to try to explain the factors underlying economic depression. The quantity of early writings in this field is large. One of the most delightful studies, in economic literature, for instance, is John Hales' dialogue on the causes of conditions which literally caused grass to grow in the streets of English towns and cities in the sixteenth century. (*A Discourse on the Common Weal.*) But Boisguilbert's analysis is unique for two reasons: first, he attempted to analyze not only the phenomena characteristic of periods of depression, but those of prosperity as well. Secondly, he developed a theory which encompasses both prosperity and depression.

[4] Offices, etc., he said, had by legal fiction been classed as real estate.

there is an error in this supposition, it is that of not carrying the decrease far enough.[5]

In rejecting the popular explanation of the cause of this diminution in the national income, he went into the earlier secular trend of prices on the basis of government income and prices in general for which there were statistics available. Prior to 1660, he asserted, the income of both the king and of the people doubled approximately every thirty years, on account of the influx of gold and silver from the new world. The revenue of the king, which was then, in 1695, at about one hundred and fifteen millions, had not kept pace with the change in the price level, he said. When "in 1582 France brought thirty-two millions to the king he was much richer than he is today, because, as there is an increase of a tenth in [the size of] the domain of France, it was on the basis of thirty-five millions, which with respect to the price of things at that time in comparison with those of the present time, amounts to 175 millions today." [6]

[5] *Le Détail de la France*, p. 175. Ten years later, in *Factum*, especially, this estimate of loss is raised to 1,500 million livres, and the total normal national income to double this figure. There are several explanations for this increased figure of the loss of income. In the intervening time conditions had grown worse. The failure of *Le Détail* to accomplish anything undoubtedly led Boisguilbert to make out as strong a case as possible to induce action toward reform. Then there is the development of his economic ideas. In his later works he is estimating not only the loss actually resulting from the fall in prices, but also the loss of potential production—*tant produites qu'à produire*. Economically France was not developed as might have been expected considering the "fertility of her soil," her "happy climate," and her "industrious people." Finally, he was led to increase the figure of the loss of potential income by an estimate made of the national income of England at, says Boisguilbert, "nearly 700 million [livres] a year." This reference I have tentatively identified as being to Davenant's *Essay upon the Probable Methods of Making a People Gainers in the Ballance of Trade*, London, 1699. In Section IV Davenant gives the figure for England as 43,000,000 l. and for France as 81,000,000 l. The former, stated at 700,000,000 livres, would give a ratio of approximately 16 to 1 between the two currencies. Boisguilbert was writing *Factum* in 1703. In *The Desolation of France*, London, 1697, pp. 32 and 36, a ratio of 13 to 1 is indicated. In the interim between 1697 and 1703 the French coinage had been debased. What Boisguilbert sought to do was to emphasize the effect of bad government in France on the wealth of the country. Considering the natural character and the extent of the two countries, France, he declares, "governed by the same maxims" as England, would be four times as rich (*Factum*, p. 272), rather than twice, as she was considered to be in spite of her existing condition.

[6] *Le Détail de la France*, Pt. I, chaps. vi–vii.

While the facts upon which Boisguilbert based his conclusion may be open to question,[7] his method of approach to the problem shows an appreciation of procedure which today is still in process of development. Certainly it appears to have been the first serious effort at a definitely objective and factual approach to the problem, and is of sufficient significance to give Boisguilbert a place as the first statistician of economic fluctuations. Yet in spite of his accent on statistics he was not primarily concerned with them as such. On this point he said that

although the reduction of this loss or [its] estimation, to a certain sum (*prix*) be unimportant in itself, nevertheless it has been desirable to make the supposition in order to draw two advantages from it. In the first place, it makes [the condition] more real, and secondly, it makes clear and evident the interest to change conditions which the king himself has, not to speak of the public.[8]

Speaking from the standpoint of the average individual bewildered by circumstances which are not understood, Boisguilbert declared,

from what has just been said of France, it would be difficult to understand in what manner the revenues from land and industry can be diminished by so great a sum as five hundred millions a year, since there is still the same land, the same climate, the same inhabitants (or approximately so), and since there is neither lawyer, doctor, nor artisan who would not like to earn as much as he did thirty years ago; nevertheless, they do not earn half as much, as is well known.[9]

If, then, there was a progressive decline in the economic life

[7] Boisguilbert, says Dühring, like Vauban, was a poor statistician. But, he continues, if Vauban (an engineer) could be wrong in his facts and figures, it is not surprising that the Rouen magistrate was. (*Kritische Geschichte*, pp. 72–73.) Dühring's criticism is accurate as far as it goes. Yet in view of the difficulty of obtaining reliable statistics over two centuries later it seems to be expecting too much to demand accuracy before there was more than a start in the science of handling statistical data or in their collection. If the facts leave much to be desired, Dühring could well have paid a tribute to the method.

[8] *Le Détail*, p. 175.

[9] *Ibid.*, p. 173. It gives a finishing touch of modernity to Boisguilbert's approach to economic fluctuations to have him speak of "barometers" of general conditions. He enumerates them from time to time: tax rolls, purchase of offices and of buildings, activity of taverns, the number of tennis courts rented, defaulting of tax farmers, the evidence of registers, leases, and contracts.

of the nation which started, Boisguilbert believed, in 1660, how did it happen that he was able to describe so vividly not only periods of extreme stagnation, when, for instance, money moved "at the pace of a tortoise," but also periods when it ran "with the legs of a deer"?

It is clear from Boisguilbert's analysis that not all the years between 1660 and 1707, the date of the publication of the *Dissertation,* were bad years. Now and then there was a balance between agricultural prices and other prices, and temporary prosperity resulted. There was, in other words, the declining secular trend caused by laws and conditions which discouraged agriculture, hence, trade in general, and a secondary movement around this trend caused by the actions of nature. The price paid to secure the periods of temporary prosperity was a rather terrible one, but one which was successful temporarily. This price was the recurrent famines which France experienced. Famines, said Boisguilbert, are a violent method of restoring the balance between grains and other products. Thus, for example, after the famine years of 1693–1694 there followed five or six years of prosperity, which compensated for the evil. For, he said, the wretchedness produced by a long stretch of low-priced grain causes more to perish than die in a single year of famine. The famine is more dreaded, however, because, like "two persons stabbed," it causes a great "uproar and horror, and will draw a more violent pursuit than twenty others who will have perished by slow poison, secretly administered. In the latter circumstance there are doubts as to the true cause of death, and the greatest degree of uncertainty on the authorship of crime diminishes by half, all the fracas which ordinarily follows the other method of causing men to perish." [10]

As a result of this double movement, in which for short periods the decline in economic activity was broken, Boisguilbert has left us an analysis of two aspects of economic life, prosperity and depression, and the relation between them.

Agriculture and commerce, said Boisguilbert, are the two mammae of a country. Agriculture is the more important in

[10] *Traité des grains,* pp. 365, 368.

that it provides the fundamental needs, and it is only when these necessaries are adequately supplied that men can turn to the production of superfluities, and in turn exchange them for necessities. The flow of income thus starts from the land.[11] But in a civilized society, producing for the market, town and country, or industry and agriculture are completely interdependent. This interdependence is the result of money incomes. Thus, each exists by buying the other's products. When landlords and farmers, for instance, can no longer buy the products of industry, or the services of the professions, neither can those who are dependent upon industry or the professions continue to buy agricultural products. In this way a vicious circle is set up. Conversely, all vocations "form, as it were, a chain of opulence. [This chain] is of value only as a result of the assemblage of the links of which it is composed, and its value is lost, at least in great part, from the moment that a single link is detached from the chain." In other words, the interdependence of all economic life is so great and so complete, that although some vocations may provide the most unnecessary superfluities, once established, they form an integral part of the economic structure and cannot again be eliminated without destroying the whole.[12] From this it follows that "prosperity consists in the maintenance of all the vocations in a civilized and rich kingdom, which are sustained and made to move together reciprocally as the parts of a clock." But if, proceeding from a general cause, one vocation is affected, the resulting fall in consumption causes a slump in others, with endless reverberations. In other words,

all the professions, arts, and trades which compose a State, especially in France, where are found many more kinds and species than in any other place in the world, have their subsistence for an object, while procuring or furnishing that of others. This obliges each one to have recourse to others, and all to give employment reciprocally to one another. Nevertheless, not all have a function of

[11] Dühring said that Boisguilbert's recognition of the final dependence of industry upon agriculture was the most significant idea which he arrived at in his economic thinking.—*Kritische Geschichte*, p. 77.

[12] *Dissertation sur les richesses*, pp. 404–407. *Le Détail*, pp. 173–174, 201, 207, 217, 242. *Factum*, p. 285. *Traité des grains*, p. 355. *Rareté de l'argent*, pp. 171–173.

equal necessity, nor are they all equally indispensable. Some furnish the necessary, such as the primary and grossest subsistence, that is to say, bread and liquors; others, something more, such as the less important dishes; still others, meats, among which are encountered many different degrees [of usefulness], such as the delicate, the sensual, the superfluous, and finally the fantastic and the absolutely useless. All these different degrees, which are found not only in food, but also in clothes, in furnishings, in equipages, in spectacles, and finally in all the rest that is termed magnificence, and which gives life to more than two hundred professions, arts, and trades which are found in France, as has been said, take their birth from the fruits of the earth. If [the earth] became as sterile as the sands of Africa, [this sterility] would dismiss and cause to perish more than one hundred and seventy of these two hundred professions. Thus, to repeat, their interest is to maintain the cultivator, and to prevent him from perishing. But it is a certain maxim in commerce (*la méchanique*) that every trade must nourish its master, or that this master must immediately close his shop. Consequently, from the moment that the cultivator does not sell his wheat at a price which can cover the expenses of cultivation and all accessory charges, such as taxes and the different payments of the rent, which happens sufficiently often, it is certain that this farmer will abandon everything, or will not be able to pay what he owes to the proprietor. Behold from this moment, all the two hundred professions in peril, and if the fate of this farmer is common to many, which is inevitable, since the evil proceeds from a general cause, all classes suffer a considerable decline.

In truth, an owner of lands who is not paid can buy nothing, since one has nothing without money. The first blow (*grêle*) falls on the superfluous things; after that, if the disorder continues, one retrenches little by little, degree by degree, following the order that has just been noted. And as it is prosperity which gives them their birth, which is ordinarily only [that of] the fruits of the earth, [so] their fall drags everything with it.[13]

[13] *Traité des grains*, pp. 360–361. "If the loss of prosperity affected only the superfluous and the magnificent," says Boisguilbert, "it would not so much be regretted. But the workmen of these vocations exercise them only to procure necessities. So the one cannot be retrenched without the other being affected, which starts a new fall in the State." (*Ibid.*, p. 361.) It is difficult to think that this quotation from *Traité des grains*, including that which precedes and follows, may not have been the inspiration for the following famous passage in *The Wealth of Nations:* "But when by the improvement and cultivation of land the labour of one family can provide food for two, the labour of half the society becomes sufficient to provide food for the whole. The other half, therefore, or at least the greater part of them, can be employed in providing other things, or in satisfying the other wants and fancies of

The result is that when all producers are able to procure such prices as will permit them to remain in their vocations and to buy from others, there is general prosperity. This prosperity is both the cause and the effect of the consumption which can then take place.[14]

These prices upon which general prosperity rests are termed variously *prix proportionnels, prix proportionnés,* or *prix de proportion.* There is in them, it should be noted, both the connotation of adequacy and of relationship. As producers are consumers of one another's products, there is a necessary relation among all prices and costs. By a change in the price of one product, the requirements which must be covered by the prices of others are necessarily altered. Once established, then, the proportional price structure must not be disturbed in any of its constituent parts. It must remain stable as a whole, or the parts must move together. If increased expenses come to one product or to one set of producers and the price cannot be increased accordingly, either the expenses will press against profits or the various expenses will not be met or the capital will be impaired; but the price of this product will not increase as needed. On the contrary, the increased need for money on the part of any producer will cause him to offer his goods at a sacrifice (*jeter à la*

---

mankind. Cloathing and lodging, houshold furniture, and what is called Equipage, are the principal objects of the greater part of those wants and fancies. The rich man consumes no more food than his poor neighbor. In quality it may be very different, and to select and prepare it may require more labour and art; but in quantity it is very nearly the same. But compare the spacious palace and the great wardrobe of the one, with the hovel and the few rags of the other, and you will be sensible that the difference between their cloathing, lodging, and houshold furniture, is almost as great in quantity as it is in quality. The desire of food is limited in every man by the narrow capacity of the human stomach; but the desire of the conveniencies and ornaments of buildings, dress, equipage, and houshold furniture, seems to have no limit or certain boundary. Those, therefore, who have the command of more food than they themselves can consume, are always willing to exchange the surplus, or, what is the same thing, the price of it, for gratifications of this other kind. What is over and above satisfying the limited desire, is given for the amusement of those desires which cannot be satisfied, but seem to be altogether endless. The poor, in order to obtain food, exert themselves to gratify those fancies of the rich, and to obtain it more certainly, they vie with one another in the cheapness and perfection of their work."—*Wealth of Nations,* Bk. I, pp. 164–165.

[14] *Dissertation sur les richesses,* pp. 402, 406–407, 411–412, 420–421.

tête). The effect of this fall in price in any one market, especially in the case of grain, is gradually felt in an ever widening circle, until within a few weeks an entire kingdom, and even other countries feel the impact. The producer will not long continue to produce if he cannot gain a livelihood from his trade. Concerned with a dynamic theory, Boisguilbert did not pass over the situation to say what would happen in the long run. He was concerned to analyze the immediate effect. The result of this, he said, is a decreased ability to consume upon the part of those who depend upon this product for an income. This means that certain other industries which have sold to these consumers are adversely affected, and so, because of the interrelation of all the parts of economic life, soon there is general economic stagnation. It was for this reason that Boisguilbert called the necessity which each dealer has to obtain his expenses "the first law of trade." Trade, in other words, must be profitable if it is to continue without interruption.[15]

This uninterrupted exchange of products, that is, the circulation of income, is the essence of wealth or of prosperity.

Wealth, then, is only this continual exchange (*mélange*) from man to man, from trade to trade, from region to region, and even from kingdom to kingdom. It is a frightful blindness to seek the cause of depression elsewhere than in the cessation of such commerce brought about by the disorganization of proportion in prices. [Such prices] are not less essential to the prosperity (*la prospérité*) of all States than to the very maintenance of their existence.[16]

The interdependence of economic life, which Boisguilbert described so well, and which occupies the central place in his theory, is referred to as the solidarity which exists among all products and among all producers, and between producers and consumers. It is due to this interdependence that any change in one part of the economic structure spreads to other parts. As a result, the economic well-being of everyone tends to rise or to fall together.[17] The maintenance of economic well-being thus depends upon the maintenance of economic equilibrium. "The equilibrium [in the

15 *Dissertation sur les richesses*, pp. 400, 406–407, 409–412. *Traité des grains*, pp. 357–359.

16 *Dissertation sur les richesses*, p. 408.

17 *Ibid.*, pp. 400, 403–407, 410. *Le Détail*, p. 201.

prices] of all products," is, then, the "sole conserver of general prosperity." If this equilibrium is lost,

a kingdom is seen filled up with goods while the people lack them entirely. . . . This one perishes because his cellars are full of wine and he lacks everything else; that one is in the same position with regard to his grain; and finally, all the others living by industry languish equally, not being able to procure bread and liquors by the fruit of their labor, which again reacts upon the possessors of these products (*mannes*), as they cannot exchange a part of their products for their other needs, such as clothing, shoes, and all the rest.[18]

The general price disturbance need not start with agricultural products; yet, "this justice [i.e., the payment of remunerative prices] which, being the natural law, must be observed in the exchange of even the least important products unless each is to destroy the other, is an indispensable obligation in the trade of grain with all [other products]," [19] because, being the source of all the requirements of life, and starting the flow of income, those who obtain their income from the land deal continually with the producers of all other products, so that any change in the ability of this farm group to buy quickly affects the prices of all other products. Nevertheless, Boisguilbert says, it is agricultural products that are peculiarly subject to change in prices. Unlike manufactured products, "almost all [of which are] works of the hands of man, and as a consequence more subject to his laws," they are almost totally determined by nature herself, and are especially subject to fluctuation in quantity in any one region.[20] The price of agricultural products thus occupies, he thinks, a central or strategic position in the economic organization.[21]

[18] *Dissertation sur les richesses*, p. 411.
[19] *Ibid.*, p. 410. [20] *Loc. cit.*
[21] Boisguilbert was not rigidly inflexible in the matter of agricultural products being the starting point of the flow of income. What he really had in mind is raw materials or natural products, the "fruits of the country" or *denrées primitives*, as he called them. In Peru, for instance, this would be silver. But in France they are "grains principally," "liquors," "animals" (skins and wool) and "cloth." In naming the latter he was presumably thinking of the growing of flax and the cultivation of the silkworm, as he referred to the "cultivators" of these products. Again he was not absolutely doctrinaire with respect to raw materials as the basis of wealth for all nations, because he saw in the case of Holland an exception. He regarded her wealth as being

Since all economic well-being depends upon the stability of the proportional price structure, it is essential that stability be maintained. But how can this be accomplished? There are two requirements.

When prosperity is reached, said Boisguilbert, there is a certain accumulation of goods of a definite composition. This stock must not be altered. The relation between production and consumption must be maintained. The equilibrium between them must not be disturbed. If a change occurs at either point the result is disastrous. The total mass of goods and its constituent parts must be kept unchanged, because,

> from the moment that someone wishes to derogate this rule of justice, in order to put more in, or to carry away less than one's share, lack of confidence occurs, as well as disorganization in the proportion of prices, the mass is spoiled, and the individuals who no longer obtain their subsistence from it are obliged to gain their livelihood by strange means, which are very destructive, and almost always criminal at the same time.[22]

But it will occur to anyone that this assumes a strictly planned economy, which, to be successful, must be carried out by means of a system in which there is a regimen of production and consumption.

Planned, yes, or, as Boisguilbert said, a return to the laws of nature. For the carrying out of the plan, in his optimism he relied upon the education and the intelligent action of government, of producers, and of consumers. All must learn what the laws of nature are and then apply them. The significance of proportional prices in the well-being of State and of society must be recognized. Such prices are obligatory if commerce is to continue. No one should wish to consume at prices which are below the cost of production and which do not include a profit. Everyone must understand that to do so means that no one will for long be able to consume at all.[23] Both government and individuals must recognize the danger of being dominated by the

---

based upon the commerce of the country and the commercial skill of the people.

[22] *Dissertation sur les richesses*, p. 422.

[23] *Ibid.*, p. 406. *Traité des grains*, pp. 357–358.

interest of the present moment, and the result of the failure to coöperate with nature.[24]

The second requirement to maintain the price structure is that the "profit must be divided" between the buyer and the seller. If the buyer must pay too much, his expenses are increased and his own price requirement is thereafter disturbed; if he pays too little, the seller suffers. In order to bring about fair division of the profits, first, the buyer and seller must be equally matched in every bargain, that is, neither must be more necessitous nor more eager than the other; and secondly, each must be dominated by the sole desire for profit. As long as this situation exists there will be no change in price to start the ball of misfortune rolling. Boisguilbert assumes that they are not in "cities pressed by a long siege." In other words, there must be free competition.[25]

The equality in the bargain, which is essential to the maintenance of proportional prices, in turn is maintained by them. Each producer is then keeping his capital intact, is paying all his expenses, and has a profit for himself. None is then in a position to have to sacrifice goods for money when he trades with another. He is then free to enter the bargain motivated solely by the desire for profit.

The fact that both parties to the bargain are equally alert to grasp any advantage offered, that is, that they are both dominated by self-interest, is the next crucial factor in bringing about a division of profits. On account of their economic interdependence, it would eventually be fatal for either one to have all the profit; nevertheless, each one, in his blindness, is determined to have it all. The bargain thus becomes a battle without quarter being given on either side. But neither one can secure all the profit if each has an equal necessity to buy or sell. Under such circumstances, provided nothing has happened to eliminate competition, if one should take advantage of the other, the latter, seeing the attempt, will be free to break off this bargaining and deal with another. This threat, or possibility, causes the one who

[24] *Dissertation sur les richesses,* pp. 402, 406.

[25] *Ibid.,* p. 409.

seeks to gain by unfair methods to capitulate, so that he will stand to lose as much as he would like to gain, because of his sheer desire to propitiate the other. But this division of profits is obtained by nature only "at the point of the sword," as it were. The more intelligent method would be for the buyer, for instance, to recognize that the seller is only the steward or agent for the buyer, and the "latter must keep an exact account with him as a factor with a merchant, allowing him all his just expenses disbursed, and paying him for his own work. Unless this rule is observed no more work will be done, and as a consequence there will be no more profit for the master." [26]

What is it that destroys proportional prices? Obviously it is anything which destroys the equality in the bargain, or that eliminates the profit motive. It may be the short-sighted self-interest of those individuals who take advantage of a situation to destroy others in order to promote their own immediate advantage; it is likewise anything that reduces at any point, or breaks off the flow of, income or consumption. It is, for example, restraint upon the free exchange of goods. Extremes of too much or too few products are dangerous, and it is essential that there be an averaging of the two conditions in order to maintain price stability. This will be done naturally by exchange between different vocations and regions concerned, if there is freedom of trade.[27]

As long as proportional prices are maintained, money is desired for no other purpose than to obtain goods, and anyone can get it who has an excess of his product of which to dispose. It moves rapidly from person to person; a little of it brings about a large number of exchanges or carries on a great deal of production and results in much consumption.[28] Just as soon as a change occurs in any part of the price structure and its inevitable effect upon other prices begins to be felt, the entire situation changes. Lack of confidence results and the value of property depreciates. Credit vanishes and since everyone now either wants or needs the metals, products are offered for what they will bring in order to obtain them. Money comes to be desired for its own sake, and

[26] *Ibid.*, pp. 409–410.
[27] *Ibid.*, pp. 408, 411, 416, 420. [28] *Ibid.*, pp. 397, 417.

when it is obtained no one wants to let it go. Since so much of it has been hoarded, and since its substitutes are no longer used there is complaint of a shortage of money. As is to be expected, money becomes very much overvalued because of its increased importance. It goes into the coffers of the rich where it produces no income. The lower classes with their great collective consuming capacity can no longer buy; others fear to do so. Trade and exchange languish in the meantime, and poverty is experienced everywhere.[29]

So money is a complicating factor which contributes toward the destruction of proportional prices. It helps to bring this destruction about whenever there is occasioned an unusual demand for money, to procure which, goods must be offered at a sacrifice. When this occurs the two requirements of the bargain, equality and the profit motive, which bring about a division of profits (which in turn supports the price structure), will be eliminated. For example, a spendthrift may be willing to sell his products for what they will bring now rather than to wait for the greater sum to be derived by marketing his products in the usual and orderly manner.[30] Through force of circumstance, bankrupts, also, and others sacrifice products for money.[31] In each case the market is spoiled because the seller entered the bargain without either the ability or the intention to hold out for all the profit that might have been procured.

The worst offender, however, is the government itself. Having set up barriers which prevent freedom in the sale of goods,

[29] *Ibid.*, pp. 413–414. *Causes de la rareté de l'argent*, pp. 166–167.

[30] *Dissertation sur les richesses*, p. 399.

[31] Boisguilbert recognized two different classes of bankruptcies, the isolated and the general, as they may be termed, and three types of bankrupts. An individual may be ruined, he said, by too much expense or other causes. But in this case his property simply changes hands without affecting the State as long as the property involved produces the same amount of products and their price or sale is not affected. This he regarded as one of the ways in which wealth is redistributed. (*Le Détail*, p. 179.) Then there is the dishonest creature, who, establishing his credit in some manner, buys goods on credit, at whatever price is asked, knowing he will never pay the debt, and quickly sells at any price he can get for ready money. This is secreted, and bankruptcy declared. (*Dissertation sur les richesses*, p. 400.) Finally there are those who, through no fault of their own, fail in large numbers as a result of general conditions. Having stocked their shops, and sales fall off, they perish from lack of credit to carry them through.—*Traité des grains*, p. 362.

although only by sales can money be obtained, it then proceeds to demand money for the payment of taxes. The payer of the taxes is now prevented from entering the bargain on the basis of the necessary and customary equality between buyer and seller. If it is the seller who is affected, he must sell his goods for what is offered; if it is the buyer, he must refrain from buying as much as he otherwise would have bought. In either case the price falls. This producer makes no profit and is unable to meet his expenses; he ceases to produce or to consume. Others are suffering from this same general cause. Those dependent upon the industry concerned can no longer consume. This affects other industries, and the whole economic structure begins to collapse.[32]

These, then, are the chief ways in which money is changed from its natural position as the "slave" of commerce into a "tyrant" or "god," which requires everything to be sacrificed to it.

The equilibrium among proportional prices and that between production and consumption having been destroyed, how can it be built up again? One must proceed on the "reasoning furnished by philosophy or by nature, that when the cause ceases, the effects immediately experience the same fate."

In France these causes were trade barriers, unequal taxation, and a bad tax system. They brought about the invasion of *la misère*. "A bridge of gold must be built" to facilitate its retreat.[33] To free the channels of trade and to create a just tax system would build this bridge. Hoarding would cease. The masses must be placed in a position to consume freely not only necessaries, but even superfluities. Not on the exploitation, but on the liberal consumption of the masses rest the luxuries of the classes, Boisguilbert warns.

"It can be set forth as a *principle,*" says Boisguilbert, that *"consumption and revenue are one and the same thing."*[34] He gives an example:

France is especially injured because the disorder of the taille and the excess price of liquor at retail produce their greatest effect

[32] *Dissertations sur les richesses*, pp. 401, 403, 410.
[33] *Le Détail*, p. 212.
[34] *Ibid.*, p. 193. Boisguilbert's italics.

upon persons of small means. It is they who have the least defense, and who make the least supply [of wine]. Yet at the same time it is they who carry on the greatest consumption because they are of the greatest number. In truth, a dayworker has no sooner received his day's wage than he goes to drink a liter of wine, when it is reasonably priced. The tavern keeper selling his wine rebuys it from the farmer or vineyardist. The vineyardist pays his landlord, who gives employment to the worker, and satisfies his passion either to build, or to buy offices, or to consume in some manner, whatever it may be, in proportion as he is paid by those who cultivate his lands. Thus, if this same wine which was worth four sous the measure, rises suddenly, through an increase in the tax, to ten sous, as we have seen it do in our days, the workman, seeing that that which would remain of his day's wage would not be sufficient to nourish his wife and children, is reduced to drink water, as almost all [workmen] do in the good-sized cities, and by that breaks off the circulation which was accustomed to furnish his day's wage. By this he is reduced to beggary. . . . It is the same with all the other products. There is none of them of which the destruction of consumption, caused by the disorders noted heretofore, may not first make cease ten or twelve kinds of trades, which depend upon this first principle.[35]

While Boisguilbert stresses consumption by the ultimate consumer, it must be pointed out that throughout *Le Détail, Factum,* and *Traité des grains* he also uses the term "consumption" in the sense of what may be called productive consumption: the ability to keep up the fertility of the soil, and to keep the land stocked and equipped. By this term he also refers to the sale of products to other countries.

Finally, there must be flexibility in the price structure, including wages, to meet changed conditions. When the price of one commodity falls, the costs of others are reduced. There must be a general price readjustment, a willingness to meet this situation. Economic activity would then simply be carried out on a changed price level. But if there is resistance in meeting the fall in the price of the first commodity, particularly so significant a commodity as grain, then the price must be artificially sustained if necessary in order to maintain the circulation of income. This would be required in the general interest.[36]

[35] *Ibid.*, p. 212. [36] *Traité des grains*, pp. 391–392.

Boisguilbert summarizes what may be called his economic credo: "the wealth of a State consists in a continuous commerce, so that neither land, nor workers, nor works, are ever in a moment of repose, [a condition] which produces the same [inactivity] with respect to money." Or to state it differently: the "sole and only interest of France, as well as the other kingdoms of the world, is that all the land shall be perfectly cultivated . . . that all kinds of commerce shall be as valuable as possible; that all men whose work is their sole resource for their subsistence shall never lose a moment of time and never be idle." [37]

Because his writings are so largely devoted to the matter of taxation it is easy to regard it as having been Boisguilbert's major interest. Yet to do so is to fail to grasp the significance of his writings or of his purpose. His tax proposals were a means to a definite end. He considered himself the pleader for all the cultivators and for all the business men in the kingdom. He pleaded for a system which would bring prosperity to them, without which he thought there could be prosperity for no one.

Just as all vocations were seen as interdependent, so he saw public and private finance as inseparably connected. The prince must inevitably be rich or poor in proportion to the wealth or poverty of his subjects; but the wealth or poverty of the people will be determined by the wisdom or the errors of those who govern.

In this manner, in his *Dissertation on the Nature of Wealth, Money, and Taxes,* Boisguilbert weaves them all into a unified theory.

He had found, he thought, the cause of that most bewildering of all forms of poverty, in which able-bodied men are eager to work, but are not permitted to do so; in which factories [38] are idle, though the owners wish them to run; in which farmers

[37] *Ibid.*, pp. 389, 391–392.

[38] Vauban, in proposing a capitation tax in 1694, estimated the number of industrial plants in France at that time as follows:

"Il y a au moins quinze mille foulons, huileries, battoirs à chauvre, moulins à papier, à écorce, à scier du bois et autres usines de cette nature.

"Il y a quelque dix mille fayanceries, poteries, tuileries, briqueteries, etc.

"On suppose qu'il y ayt en France cinq cent forges, martinets ou fonderies de fer, cuivre, ou autres machines de cette nature."—*Correspondance des contrôleurs généraux* Vol. I, append. ix, p. 564.

work from morning to night with no return for their labor; and in which there is want in the midst of plenty. He had found the secret of endless prosperity, he thought, in the concept of economic equilibrium, based upon such prices to producers as would permit economic life to function in all its parts without interruption, and consequently would permit a high degree of consumption on the part of all men. In this prosperity the government would share without oppressing anyone, since taxes, like "all kinds of debts, are excessive or moderate, not in absolute amount, but in [relation to] the resources of those who pay." Such was the "discovery" which was his justification for comparing himself to Copernicus and Columbus.

XI

ON MONEY AND CREDIT

It is unnecessary for the slave to become the master.

BOISGUILBERT'S contributions to the theory of money are his observation of the fact that it is a means to an end and not an end in itself, that its behavior is the result and not the cause of the changing activity of commerce, that its quantity is a matter of indifference, and his recognition of the importance of the velocity of circulation. In writing about money his concern was to combat two ideas: first, that the wealth of a country consists in the money which it possesses; and secondly, that the disturbances which France was undergoing were due to the scarcity of specie. These were the widespread notions of the time. It was the latter idea which caused Boisguilbert to pose a riddle or paradox which so irritated Chamillart, the controller general. This paradox was, that the scarcer money is in France, the more there is of it. To Boisguilbert there was nothing mysterious about such a statement; it was simply an explanation of the behavior of the precious metals.

Boisguilbert did not discuss the quantity theory as such. He accepted the fact that the general level of prices rose or fell with the change in the quantity of money in a country, or rather in the commercial world.[1] But he dismissed this change in the general price level as of no moment as long as the same quantity of goods is exchanged.

Money is not wealth, he preached to a world convinced that it alone was wealth, or at least that it was wealth of a superior kind.

> [To] produce much revenue in a country rich in products, it is not necessary that there be much silver, but only that there be very

[1] He saw a necessary relation among the prices in different countries exchanging goods with one another.

much consumption. One million [livres] will have more effect if the consumption is great than ten millions when there is no consumption, because this million circulates (*se renouvelle*) a thousand times, and will produce much revenue at every step, whereas the ten millions kept in a coffer are no more useful to a State than so many stones.[2]

In his earliest writings Boisguilbert attempted to clear up the part played by money and to show its place in the national economy. In passages noteworthy for their perspicacity, he dedeclared that,

[the] great diminution in the revenues of France [is not due to the lack of gold and silver,] which are now in greater abundance in the kingdom than when the revenues were more considerable. And though this truth be very certain, since it might seem to be a paradox to those who are accustomed to say when they see prosperity diminish in a country, that there is no more money, it is fitting . . . to say a word concerning the nature and the qualities of gold and silver, whether as money or as substance, and to have understood the position which money holds in the world.

It is very certain that it is not a good in itself, and that the quantity has nothing to do with the prosperity of a country considered as a whole, provided there be enough to sustain prices contracted by the products necessary to life. Likewise it cannot prevent the places whence one obtains it from being very poverty-stricken, and in those countries [it cannot prevent] a man who has two écus to spend each day from passing his life with more difficulty than another, who, as in Languedoc, has only six sous for his maintenance. And indeed one can say that the richer a country is, the more it is in a situation to dispense with specie, since there are more people for whom it can be represented by a piece of paper under the name "bill of exchange."

Money (*l'argent*), then, is an incorruptible pledge that all men have agreed to give and to take reciprocally from one another on the current basis in order to obtain as much goods as they need; because the one who receives the money is certain that it will produce for him the same effect with respect to the things of which he has need. No one in the world receives it to consume it or to hoard unless this be done in order to wait for a greater quantity so that it may be used more effectively. As a result, if all products necessary to life had, as has silver, a stable price, and if they were not perishable, or if the more or less considerable degrees of perfection

[2] *Le Détail* p. 212.

that each in particular has did not detract from the true estimation of them, so indeed that they might always have a current price that would be required to use them [as money], it can be said that gold and silver would be no more valuable than all the other most common metals, and they would even yield to them in value, being less fit for the other uses. Exchange would then be made directly, as was done at the beginning of the world, and is still done with respect to some kinds of merchandise at wholesale after they are evaluated.

From these principles it follows, that in wealth, which is nothing other than the power to procure the easy maintenance of life, both for necessities and superfluities [the one or the other] being a matter of indifference at the end of the year to the one who has passed it in abundance, as he considers whether he has procured his commodities with little or much money, money is only the means and the way to an end, whereas goods useful to life are the purpose and the end. A country can be rich without very much money, and that one which has only silver, very poverty-stricken if it can be exchanged only with difficulty for these [necessities and superfluities]. Thus the ships of Spain no sooner reach Europe than it is necessary to carry all the silver to the countries whence products have been obtained, to carry into those where the mines are situated. And this silver produces by a continual circulation (*révolution*) the same effect in these countries that it has produced in [the country of] its birth, making more or fewer circulations and recirculations (*tours et retours*) as it changes masters more or less often, that is to say, as more or less commerce or consumption is made.

But countries such as France, which produce products necessary to life, have this advantage over those from which silver is obtained: exchange is made in a very advantageous manner, considering that silver, not being consumed at all by use, produces utilities without limits and without end for the country to which it is carried; whereas the goods which are given in counter-exchange are useful only a single time, perishing through use. But while silver has the quality of being unalterable by time and accidents, it has at the same time that of not increasing by keeping as does other merchandise. And it is useful not when it is in the coffer, but when it is conserved as little as possible. And as it is consumption, of which it is only the slave, which leads its movement, from the moment that [consumption] ceases it stops also, and dwells immobile in the hands where it is found when the disorder commences to make itself felt. In this way, if when commerce is active the worst situation of a merchant is to have his money useless in his coffer, because it produces nothing, it is to his advantage when commerce is inactive not to have it out, considering that if he earns nothing, he loses nothing, for he risks losing on account of bankruptcies, inseparable from the cessation of commerce.[3]

And what is said of the merchant is equally true of all persons who live on their incomes, either from lands or from lending. Such persons, receiving payments, cannot reinvest (*reconstituer*) for lack of security, because the most ordinary disturbances occurring on the land, the products [of the land] diminish daily and perceptibly on account of the destruction of consumption. Consequently they prefer to lose interest rather than to risk capital, reducing expenses to a minimum, which increases the evil for the whole body of the republic. In this manner all the revenues of industry cease completely, and silver, which produces as much revenue as it circulates, not going out of strong hands [i.e., out of the coffers of the rich], completely stops its ordinary course. This paralyzes the State in all its parts, and causes it to be poverty-stricken in the midst of an abundance of all sorts of goods. The poor feel the effects first, but they are communicated next imperceptibly to all the other parts of the State, even to the most noble (*relevé*). . . .[4]

Boisguilbert believed that the "importance" of money "is not at all subject to ordinary laws."[5] What did he mean by this statement? He explained it in one of his letters on money and trade.

[The] less money is seen in France, the more it exists and is kept; likewise, the more it appears in commerce, the less there is and the more it is lost. This . . . has need only of a word, concerning which none of those who are exposed to the revolutions of one fortune and the other is ignorant, but which is little known to others, especially at Paris, where people live with very little understanding of the manner in which the people live and procure for themselves both money and their needs in the country. There is then, dead money and live money. The first is that which, being motionless and

[3] Speaking of the two ways in which capital can be made to yield an income or profit to its employer, Adam Smith says: "First it may be employed in raising, manufacturing or purchasing goods, and selling them again with a profit. The capital employed in this manner yields no revenue or profit to its employer, while it either remains in his possession, or continues in the same shape. The goods of the merchant yield him no revenue or profit till he sells them for money, and the money yields him as little till it is again exchanged for goods. His capital is continually going from him in one shape, and returning to him in another, and it is only by means of such circulation, or successive exchanges, that it can yield him any profit. Such capitals, therefore, may very properly be called circulating capitals."—*Wealth of Nations*, Bk. II, pp. 261–262.

[4] *Le Détail*, pp. 209–211. [5] Letter of Sept. 21, 1704.

concealed, is no more useful to the State than if it were stones, or than if it were in the bowels of the earth, and the other, that which is alive, moves always and is never a moment in repose. Only the latter is of significance in a State, since it alone creates all the harmony and makes all the classes subsist by its circulation from hand to hand. . . . It is consumption which leads the march; [money] stops, dislodges, and runs along with consumption. Thus [when there is] very much consumption, a little silver, on account of its frequent appearances, passes for a very great quantity of specie; [consumption] diminishing, silver stops immediately and causes it to be said that there is no more of it.[6]

Boisguilbert saw that the character and functioning of the medium of exchange is one thing in times of prosperity, and another in times of depression. What he saw was a change in emphasis from money as a current medium of exchange, to money as a future medium of exchange, or as a store of value. As a legitimate function he recognized the former only. This can be explained by the fact that he was explaining hoarding with its resulting accentuation of the breakdown in trade.

In prosperous times there is, he says, "beneficent" money. This is subordinated to products and serves commerce. It is a means and not an end in itself. It is a convenience only, which facilitates trade. No one wishes to keep it, and it moves rapidly from hand to hand and from place to place. A single écu is used in many transactions daily, and permits much consumption. All economic life flourishes. Money substitutes, bills of exchange and book accounts (*la parole*), arise. Solvency is general because proportional prices exist and yield a profit to producers.

In times of depression all is changed. The former "beneficent" money is changed into "criminal" money, which takes precedence over products, and is an end in itself, a "god" to which all forms of property and even human beings are sacrificed. It becomes "paralytic," and settles down in one place and can scarcely be "pried loose" whatever the means used. When it does move it is "at the pace of a tortoise." Trade declines for want of a medium of exchange. Prices are low because no one can consume. Due to their increased importance, the metals become much overvalued. Money substitutes cease to exist because their

[6] Letter of July 1, 1704.

bases, property values, have been destroyed and insolvency is widespread.[7]

Causes de la rareté de l'argent, et éclaircissement de mauvais raisonnement du public à cet égard is a brief but choice work belonging to the history of monetary theory which deserves to be better known. In this Boisguilbert declares that the error in the thinking of the people with respect to silver comes from the fact that in France silver is regarded as a fruit of the country and as a source of wealth, as it is, indeed, in Peru. In France, it is only the "bond of trade, and the pledge of mutual exchange which can no longer be made directly on account of the multiplicity [of products]."[8] He then proceeds to show that, notwithstanding the use of money, the essence of the transaction is an exchange of goods for goods, though only after the intervention of the numerous vocations which make up the modern State. He modifies his statement as to money as a pledge by adding that in times of prosperity silver is only the guarantee of exchanges "and of the faithful execution of the intention of the contracting parties when [the exchange] cannot be effected directly."

In the conjunctures of prosperity when all things are at a good price, silver is not at all the source of the prosperity, and it is even eliminated from the greater part of its function of guarantee, since only the poor have need of caution, and innumerable individuals being rich in proportion to their estate, their bills pass as money, and maintain this continual circulation and exchange that specie formerly carried on. [This the bills do] with even more ease and satisfaction on account of the convenience of the transfer which this sort of money has as one of its qualities (*par devers elle*), and on account of an assurance against violent seizure.[9]

[7] *Dissertation sur les richesses,* pp. 417–418. Speaking of these passages in the *Dissertation,* Durand says: "Dans ce procès de l'argent . . . dans ses grandes lignes, Boisguilbert n'est pas seulement l'avocat; son réquisitoire voisine avec la plaidoirie du défenseur. Il commence par vauter les qualités de l'argent bienfaisant, qui facilite le commerce tant qu'il en demeure l'esclave; mais, le moraliste apparait vite et tonne avec force contre les crimes du vil métal." It is not a moralist whom one should see here, but the acute observer with an intensely vivid and poetical imagination, which leads him to personify money and dramatize its behavior.

[8] *Causes de la rareté de l'argent,* p. 163 (1707 edition of *Le Détail de la France*). [9] *Ibid.*, pp. 165–166.

Boisguilbert ridicules the idea that everything is the result of money just because money is so precious in times of depression. It is overabundant in times of prosperity, he declares, when silver is almost unnecessary in commerce. The large dealers make it almost wholly with bills, and the small ones make it with credit.

The workmen, because of the sustained value of their reciprocal products, have no need of other guarantee than the products themselves, and silver has no other function at all than to serve as a caution in their absence, thus it remains, to repeat, almost useless to everyone, which causes it to be turned to strange uses. These uses are, for instance, for magnificence, in which the goldsmith's [art] holds the first place, then in manufactures and the embellishment of temples and houses. To all this is added the consumption of oriental merchandise, which can be obtained only by shipping specie into countries whence it never returns. [All this] absorbs very much more than the amount which is assumed to have passed into Italy and Germany during these last years. But the conjunctures of scarcity of this metal, such as [we have] today, not only stops these uses (*détours*), but brings back into commerce all which is available or which is not completely destroyed. Thus [so far as the quantity of silver is concerned] there is a balance, all this at least equaling the transportation which is assumed to have carried it out of the kingdom on account of the war.[10]

To say that the stoppage of trade and the low prices, which do not cover the cost of production or rent and taxes, are the result of lack of specie comes from failure to understand how the use of credit and the rapidity of circulation reduce the quantity of silver in use. But now, Boisguilbert says, it is in vain that shops are full of goods. The lack of sales ruins the credit of the shopkeepers. Rent absorbs their few sales. Thus there is need of silver. The man living on his rents, fearing that they may not be paid in the future begins to reduce his expenditures, and consequently reduces the circulation of silver. All this has its beginning in the destruction of the prosperity of the farmer.[11]

"Silver is scarce, not from lack of existence, but because, circulation being always a prerequisite for prosperity, all men are today reduced to the cruel necessity to give it up only in the last

[10] *Ibid.*, pp. 166–167. [11] *Ibid.*, pp. 170–171.

extremity." Silver is scarce because it alone is having to carry the burden of existing exchanges, whereas it is usually assisted by "paper and parchment." Silver is scarce because so great is the preference given to it that it alone can be called wealth. Silver is scarce because war is made against it, and people wish to carry it off against the will of the possessor. It is like men: "if they are taken by force, they conceal themselves in retreats and caverns." [12]

The controller general and the director of finances, Desmaretz, would not accept the thesis that the so-called scarcity of money was effect and not cause. It was the reasoning of a "quack" and not that of a reputable physician.[13] As a further effort to convince them, Boisguilbert attempted to explain the aid given by, and the functioning of, credit, in a letter to Chamillart which is worthy of being quoted in full, not only for the analysis itself, but also for the picture of the commerce of the times which the letter contains.

Rouen, July 4, 1704

My Lord,

The so-called scarcity of money, or lack of specie, is the first objection that you have taken the trouble to make in [the letter] which you have done me the honor to write to me. Yet my last [letter, it] seems, [ought] to have shown you sufficiently that there is error in this thought, and that money is the valet of consumption, stopping, walking, and even running with it according to its movements, the same money passing indefinitely in review and passing for so much new money. It is nevertheless still apropos to call your attention to an increase in, and a coadjutor to, specie that prosperity and consumption bring into commerce, namely, bills, which are preferred to money when the solvency of business men is almost general. This is a kind of money which is brought into existence (*se bat*) hourly and at little expense, as you know, and which moves much more quickly than silver. But from the moment that this solvency is brought to an end, [a condition] which results from the cessation of consumption, the greater part of these bills (*espèces*) are destroyed (*mises au billon*), and the mints which manufacture them, namely, the business men, are completely at a standstill. Furthermore, money in essence, which is almost wholly

[12] *Ibid.*, pp. 174–175.

[13] See Chamillart's letter to Boisguilbert, above, p. 56.

in small business where that in paper can have no currency, is immediately withdrawn from it in order to take the place of that which no one any longer wishes to receive, although a moment before it was very valuable.

This [substitution of credit for silver] goes so far in these times of consumption, that a business man being approached for a loan by another whose solvency is not nearly so well established [as that of the first man] if [the former] wishes to accommodate him, although he may have no money, he gives a bill payable at term which the other negotiates immediately. But from the moment that consumption stops, from which many bankruptcies are inseparable because of the lack of sale, this kind of business ceases completely. These revolutions are so sudden and change so greatly and so completely in a moment, that even the Sieur le Gendre, with his great wealth, which I believe reaches more than four million livres . . . had a sad experience ten years ago in [one of] these unexpected cases. It was only two days after he had lent three hundred thousand livres, when he received news [that] two hundred and fifty thousand livres of letters of exchange drawn by him on Lyons [had been] protested on account of two or three bankruptcies. As money was wholly lacking on the exchanges at Rouen as well as elsewhere, he has avowed to me many times that he spent one entirely sleepless night. The same thing happened to Sieurs le Couteulx, the most famous bank in France. In the same moment all the money, that is, its circulation, having dried up completely, everyone wished to draw out specie. The Sieurs le Couteulx of Rouen had two hundred thousand livres belonging to various individuals in the city, all of whom came to demand them at the same time, and they were on the brink of ruin. They had twenty thousand livres of mine. One of them came to find me with tears in his eyes, saying he could not pay me. This [payment] I did not exact, along with some others, judging indeed that such a time would pass, as it did. At the death of one of [the firm] three or four years ago, it was found that he had more than two million livres of property.[14]

Shall one say, my Lord, that these different revolutions are the effect of the lack of specie, and that it has disappeared suddenly, or that it has ceased to exist in order to be reborn a moment afterwards? Nothing such as that, if you please. It is its movement which has ceased, not its existence. Thus take care, if you please, not to blame money any more, or to believe that there is not enough

[14] This last, and apparently irrelevant sentence should not be regarded as a meaningless insertion. It is cited as evidence of the fact that the embarrassment was temporary in nature. Incidentally this is quite characteristic of Boisguilbert's method.

of it in France to form eighty million livres of increase [in revenue] for the king. I maintain not only the contrary, but that even in an instant you can cause to recirculate, not to be reborn, a sufficiently great quantity to permit an increase of four hundred million livres of consumption. After all, all the money that is desired, and that the king must have, is exacted only to procure the necessary products. By this function it is not consumed, but can be found continually on foot to render everywhere the same service, as well as its substitute, which is a piece of paper or a bill of exchange, of which the amount very much exceeds that of silver when consumption takes place.

It is with such money that the prosperity of Holland subsists. The town hall of Amsterdam owes more than one hundred million livres; that of Middleburg, around ten million livres, upon which neither pays any interest. Everyone voluntarily carries his funds there for the facility and security of business, and far from exacting anything, two percent is given in pure loss. And when one wishes to exchange these bills for silver, instead of a demand for it at these town halls the two percent that had been given is refunded. You know, my Lord, that the people do not do exactly the same thing with the king, although this ought to be [the case] with more reason. But it is not your fault. It is certainly [the fault] of those whom corruption, ignorance, or personal interest have exalted to the skies, in spite of the unhappy state in which they have left France. They have spoiled relations between the king and his people, and you pay dearly for the folly. They do to the prince as do the lions in the fable, when the animals were hunting at the common expense on condition of equally dividing the prey. Nevertheless, the lion took all under divers pretexts, of which the first was: *Quia sum leo.* The evil is not without remedy, otherwise I should not give myself the honor to speak to you of it.

The summary then, if you please, of all this, is that money is both the child and the father of consumption; that one can have it only by the sale of goods; that the ruin of this sale is today the most liquid revenue of almost all the court; but that the reëstablishment hangs only by a thread, and as a consequence that of the circulation of money without it being necessary to make it come from abroad. This last is not speculation at all, but the grossest experience, although it may become theory in the sight of those who are neither merchants nor farmers.

I am, with a very profound respect, my Lord, your very humble and obedient servant, Boisguilbert

The apparent scarcity of money can be overcome only by creating a situation which will make it willing to show itself. When a lender can lend with confidence that he will be repaid; when a borrower can borrow without fear of being ruined thereby; when people dare to spend, then the circulation of money will begin. All this will be made possible by reforming the ruinous tax system and its more ruinous administration. The effect would be as if

> one were to announce to many very poverty-stricken individuals that they had just inherited very valuable property. Although no rent would be due for a year, nevertheless they would not fail to be conscious of it from that very moment, because everybody would lend to them very readily, seeing the certainty of being reimbursed, both as to capital and to interest at the end of the year at the most. . . . [A] farmer would be seen easily to borrow on all sides in order to stock his farm with animals. . . . [As] this would produce fertilization, which is always followed by a good harvest, he would be in a position to share the profit with those who would have aided him. The artisan . . . would immediately place a horse on foot in order to carry on his trade, half on credit, as is always the case, and half otherwise . . . and all of them having made some profit, then would no longer fear to feed and clothe themselves according to their faculties, which is a very natural thing. This, redounding to the profit of the merchant and artisan of the cities, would place the latter in a position to consume the products arising from cultivation, and thus reëstablish the circulation which maintains States whose land is fertile, but of a wholly useless fertility when it is impossible or forbidden to cultivate it, as is held to be the case in more than half of France today. It is that which causes her poverty.[15]

One fundamental criticism has been made of Boisguilbert's theory of money. It is based upon his frequent statements that money is not wealth; that money is of no use in itself. From these statements Horn was led to believe that Boisguilbert regarded money as having a purely conventional and arbitrary value. Combining this with his statement that silver can be replaced by "a simple piece of paper," Horn was somewhat uncertainly of the opinion that Boisguilbert must be relegated to the John Law class of monetary theorists.

These criticisms are the combined result of Boisguilbert's method of expressing himself and a failure to read him with

[15] *Le Détail*, p. 242.

sufficient care. In combating the popular idols with regard to money, Boisguilbert had a tendency to make extreme statements; furthermore he had the regrettable habit of failing to include qualifying phrases at every step. They are due, further, to the failure to see that Boisguilbert was discussing hoarding, and that he was considering it, not in its relation to the hoarder, but to the people as a whole.

Boisguilbert was under no misapprehension as to gold and silver having intrinsic values. His comment on the German silver mines shows that he regarded silver to be subject to the laws of supply and demand as were other commodities.[16] And again, while silver, he says, "has the quality of being unalterable by time and accidents, it has at the same time that of not increasing by keeping as does *other* merchandise." [17] Furthermore, in times of prosperity its value decreases (*devient absolument à rebut*), "which causes it to be turned to strange uses, namely, to magnificence, in which the goldsmith's [art] holds the first place, then to manufactures and the embellishments of temples and houses." [18] But wealth he defines as "nothing more than a complete enjoyment, not only of all the necessaries of life, but even of all that which forms the voluptuous and the magnificent." This would seem to dispose of Horn's final conclusion, that "while recognizing that silver is not superior to all [other] merchandise, as it was considered at his epoch, he failed to perceive that it is their equal." "He thought he had said everything in repeating that money is only the guarantee, the pledge for the future delivery of the object which the seller had in view in giving up his own product."

Horn failed to see that Boisguilbert makes a scholastic-like distinction between gold and silver as metals or their products and gold and silver as money, and between money as such and

[16] See below, note, p. 233.

[17] *Le Détail*, p. 211. My italics.

[18] *Rareté de l'argent*, pp. 166–167. Such uses, he says, bear only the least resemblance to hoarding, although they may result from "the expectation that the metal would be needed sometime." But "this aid would not be resorted to unless the State were sick, and had such a frightful indisposition, that, if it were long, the remedy would be of less duration than the disease, the extremity of which is known by the desire for, or dearness of, gold and silver."—*Dissertation sur les richesses*, p. 405.

its circulation. Silver, *étant réduit en monnaie,* he says, "cannot furnish any of the needs of life," that is, it cannot be consumed. Not money, as such, but the quick circulation of money (*des jambes de cerf*) "is the sole source of the wealth of the people." [19] In other words, goods are worthless unless they are consumed; it is only when they are exchanged that they can be consumed; consumption he defines as wealth; money hoarded is neither magnificence nor subsistence; therefore it is only the circulation of money, bringing about exchange and thereby consumption, which is a source of wealth. Boisguilbert's purpose was to emphasize the function of money as a tool, a means. Hoarded, it adds nothing to the general prosperity. It was not individual wealth which it was his concern to analyze, but the general prosperity "to which everyone must look for his own well-being."

Boisguilbert's ideas as to "paper" and "parchment" seem sufficiently clear.

> It is not necessary to believe, as does Horn, that Boisguilbert was a partisan of the replacement of metallic money by paper money, as the trial was made of it some years later under the inspiration of Law. Boisguilbert speaks only of bills of exchange underwritten by merchants who have a powerful credit; he speaks only of the system of clearing employed already at that epoch at the great commercial centers such as that of Lyons.[20]

Another says:

> Far from blaming Boisguilbert for thinking of the rational utilization of the effects of commerce, which have become the most common commercial medium of exchange in our days, we can only felicitate him for having understood *at his epoch:* (1) the letter of exchange; (2) payments by off-sets. . . . The author of *Le Détail* had, then, a century at least before a slow and difficult realization in his own country, a sufficient and exact conception for his time of the famous clearing houses.[21]

One other criticism remains to be disposed of. A favorite device of the controller general resorted to by Pontchartrain especially, for the easing of difficulties of the treasury, was the manipulation of the currency. Although, Talbot says, "it is not nec-

[19] *Supplément,* p. 265. *Factum,* p. 277.
[20] Talbot, p. 86.
[21] Durand, pp. 45–46. Durand's italics.

essary to speak too certainly," nevertheless he is inclined to infer from Boisguilbert's silence upon the matter of the devaluation of the coinage a tacit assent to this procedure. To assume such approval is to accuse Boisguilbert of a lack of clarity in his thinking and of inconsistency in his reasoning with regard to money on a point which he appears to have understood exceptionally well, or else it is to accuse him of temporizing concerning a subject on which he thought most strongly. Such approval upon his part would have involved denial of one of his major premises with regard to money: that its quantity and, hence, price levels, are matters of indifference. It would have been in complete conflict with his notion that the action of money is determined by consumption, rather than that the quantity of money determines consumption. To Boisguilbert devaluating the currency would have been not only futile, but worse than useless. It was not money which was lacking, he saw, but confidence. It was lack of confidence which was causing money to be hoarded. To throw new money into circulation as was done in the melting down of silver objects is useless, he declared. It quickly follows the rest into hiding.[22] Speaking of the sums needed by the king, he said that "they never move except at the order of consumption," and "reside whole years in retreats from which all the machines in the world cannot draw them. Furthermore, *all the measures which are taken serve only to hold them there more firmly.*"[23] Indeed, Boisguilbert may be said to have remonstrated with Pontchartrain on his procedure. In *Le Détail,* published while the latter was still controller general, he says, apropos of the reëstablishment of the government credit and the creation of a willingness upon the part of the people to lend to the king, that "it is necessary to preserve good faith in this, for the interest indeed of His Majesty. The sovereign authority can introduce no especial jurisprudence concerning the repayment [of debts] such as has been introduced heretofore, which would not be accepted between two private individuals."[24]

There is another point. Boisguilbert was quick, eager indeed,

[22] *Le Détail,* p. 213.
[23] *Supplément,* p. 266. My italics.
[24] See above, p. 155, for the complete passage.

to commend the controllers general for any action which he could in the least approve. It was almost pathetically as if he did not wish always to be regarded in the light of a carping critic. He wrote Desmaretz in 1708:

It is said, indeed, that you have taken the position (*parti*) of having the coinage of the newly arrived specie made at the expense of the king. By this you permit it to be understood that you do not approve throwing seed on unproductive soil (*terre perdue*), but, on the contrary, on the most productive (*mise à usure*), and that the future is to you as dear as the present.[25]

In the next year, the terrible year of 1709, in which Desmaretz succumbed to the temptation to devaluate the coinage, Boisguilbert sent but one letter, which accompanied a project to re-establish the judiciary in France. Even in this he could not refrain from warning Desmaretz that the latter's sole guide must be *la justice, la raison.* His silence, we may believe, was not that of assent to the methods used, but of final despair. No more was to be expected from Desmaretz than was obtained from those who preceded him.[26]

[25] Letter of Sept. 16, 1708, *Correspondance des contrôleurs généraux,* Vol. III, p. 50.

[26] For further discussion of the subject of money and credit, see pp. 47–52, 162–163, 182–184, 202–204, 292–304.

XII

ON VALUE AND PRICE

The contest . . . is between the sellers of grain and the ones who buy it.

FUNDAMENTALLY all of Boisguilbert's writings may be considered studies in values and prices. Practical writer that he was, his concern was with prices, and it is around prices that he carried on his discussion. But when he asserted that money is a means and not an end in itself; when he eliminated the quantity of money from consideration by stating that the general price level is a matter of indifference; when he reduced the circulation of money to an effect and not a cause, he entered essentially into the realm of value. No one has more clearly enunciated the fact that every purchase and sale is an exchange of goods in which money is only a convenient way of carrying out the exchange than Boisguilbert in *Causes de la rareté de l'argent.* His real concern was not for prices as such, but for the basis upon which all goods and services are exchanged.

Boisguilbert's fundamental thesis with regard to trade is that there can be no general prosperity, which to him connoted continuous production, continuous exchange, continuous distribution, continuous consumption, unless prices are proportional. Proportional prices he defines as prices which permit all goods sold to cover the cost of production. That is, the exchange value of each product in relation to all other products must be such as will leave all producers without loss. This will enable them to maintain themselves, to employ, and to pay all contracted or other charges. There will then be no impediments to consumption and no discouragement to production. Thus he saw that by means of an equilibrium among all exchange values all the economic processes could be integrated. Conversely, with a disturbance of this equilibrium of values, or loss of price parity, this integration would be destroyed. This loss of integration would result in a breakdown in exchange, in payments, and a consequent lack of coördination between production and consumption—*la misère* or depression. Economic fluctuation thus becomes a matter of relative values, their maintenance and their destruction.

There is a wealth of suggestion in Boisguilbert's fantastic illustration of conditions in France in his day:

Everyone perishes, as has been said, from an excess of one product and a dearth of another, which throws all individuals reciprocally into poverty, whereas exchange of these surpluses would make them very happy.

The result is as if some prince, abusing his authority . . . in order to torment and cause many subjects to perish in a grotesque manner, had ten or twelve chained a hundred feet from one another. One being quite naked, in spite of the extreme cold, would have an enormous quantity of meat and of bread near him, ten times more than he would be able to consume before perishing, which he would soon do because he would lack everything else, and especially liquors, of which he would not have a drop within reach. Another, chained at the fixed distance, would have probably twenty pieces of clothing about him, three times more than he would be able to use in many years; but he would be without any food to sustain his life, and would be prevented from having it furnished to him. At a similar distance a third, and so on to the end, would be found surrounded by many measures of liquors, but without any clothes or food. It would be true to say after they perished, which they would inevitably do if the extremity continued to the end, that they had all died of hunger, of cold, of thirst, from lack of liquors, bread, meat, and clothing. Nevertheless, it would be very certain that, taken as a whole, they did not lack either food or clothing, and that each of them could have been, without *force majeure,* well equipped and well fed.

[Had they been] unchained, which would have required only a moment, they would immediately have made one another happy by a mutual exchange which would not have been delayed for a moment.[1]

No better illustration of the interrelation of utility, value, wealth, and exchange could be devised.

That it is a disturbance in values, and not a high or low price level, which causes the difficulty is shown in the illustration of the

[1] *Dissertation sur les richesses,* pp. 422–423.

shoemaker and the farmer. In the reign of Francis I, when the price level was low,

> [the] cultivator who sold his wheat for only twenty sous, and the shoemaker his shoes for five sous, both received their expenses from these sums, because proportional prices existed. But if wheat were worth fifteen francs, as it is today, the shoemaker would die of hunger with his shoes at five sous, while conversely, the cultivator would be in the same situation, if selling his wheat at twenty sous, he or his master should be obliged to buy shoes at four francs.[2]

Boisguilbert was interested in grain for several reasons: first, because of the general situation in France; secondly, its fate, he thought, determined the fate of other products; again, the price of wheat was accustomed to undergo distressingly great variations in France; and finally, he saw its price to be subject to certain forces not encountered in the case of other products. His analysis of value, or of price, was for these reasons restricted to this commodity.

The value of a commodity at any time he saw to be determined by the interaction of the forces of supply and demand. As to the latter, there is the essence of the concept of diminishing utility in his statement that any product fit for nourishment, "whatever its quantity," would be preferred to money if the latter could not be exchanged for other things.[3] It is not scarcity alone, nor is it the cost of production which gives value to products. The ultimate factor is the demand for the product: "all the most exquisite fruits of the earth and the most precious products are only dung from the moment they are not consumed." [4] As to supply, grains differ from "other products, which are almost all the works of the hands of man and as a consequence more subject to his laws." [5]

> The weather (*le ciel*), which is not always equally favorable to the earth in bringing about the perfection of her fruits, or rather is never the same, takes the first place in determining the quantity of grains. A long drought, a great abundance of rain, a rude and hard winter without snow, which is an excellent cover for grains against

[2] *Factum*, p. 279.
[3] *Dissertation sur les richesses*, p. 396.
[4] *Factum*, p. 282.
[5] *Dissertation sur les richesses*, p. 410.

the rigors of cold, and finally a little fungus growth (*pluie emniellée*), which ordinarily attacks the cavity (*tuyau*) a little before maturity, making it absolutely impossible for the grains in the head to be nourished, are so many enemies that this primitive manna of men in Europe must suffer, [enemies] that they cannot combat other than by their prayers (*voeux*).[6]

Speaking of the conflict between production for profit and production for use,[7] Boisguilbert said,

The contest, then, is between the buyers and sellers of grain. It is unquestionable that, in a certain sense, commerce in grain resembles that of all other products, in which the buyer would like to have the merchandise for nothing, and the seller, to obtain from it four times his cost. It is not less true, however, that it differs very much in another respect. In an ordinary negotiation, the cupidity of the merchant is restrained, first, by the certainty that his neighbor, whose shop is as well supplied as his own, will always sell according to reasonable conditions, and next, by the circumstance that the buyer is not in an absolute necessity to acquire the things which he has to sell. But these two things which act as a regulator (*la police*) in the traffic of all other products, will fail to do so in the grain trade. The cultivator can no more refrain from selling his grain, than that one who wishes to eat can refrain from providing himself with it. And these are the two requirements which cause the disorder, and bring it to pass that in this traffic the two parties just referred to [i.e., buyers and sellers], are continually at war. But there is something more to be said: any degree of advantage that the one has over the other is a contagious fever, which spreads quickly and visibly, and places everything in such an excess that one party quickly vanquishes the other, which brings ruin to the State, regardless of which side secures the victory."[8]

Boisguilbert thus raised the problems arising from the two distinguishing characteristics in the grain trade: the inelasticity of demand which tends to move the price from one extreme to another out of all proportion to the change in the supply, and the inability of man to control the production and marketing of grain as he does other products.

In a passage which foreshadows marginal theory, he says,

it suffices that a considerable diminution [in price] make itself felt

[6] *Traité des grains*, p. 379.
[7] See above, pp. 184–185.
[8] *Traité des grains*, p. 369.

in some part of any product in order to communicate this evil to all [the product] by a necessary participation in the dearness or the cheapness that all merchandise of the same sort has, especially in the same State, with respect to the dealer's price. Thus, for example, if there are two sacks of wheat beyond what is necessary for the usual consumption, which the dealer is obliged to sell at whatever they will bring, this will lower the price for all the grain sold in the market; and if the same thing happens in the following markets, this evil continues always while increasing, and after being communicated to the country, it reaches the farthest regions.[9]

Boisguilbert excellently describes the effect of distress merchandise, which, when offered at such a low price, spoils the market for other products of the same kind:

When a producer or merchant sees his affairs in disorder and that on account of lack of sales he cannot satisfy those to whom he is in debt when the debts are due, he "makes finance," as it is called, in order to escape beggary. That is, he disposes of everything at a ruinous (*vil*) price, and at a loss, not to himself, but to his creditors, and placing the key under the door of his house, he takes flight with the money in his pocket. He takes leave of the country, to reappear no more, or only after he has obtained considerable reduction from those to whom he is in debt. Aside from the disorder which this causes to all the State, it forms an even more frightful one, in that this sale at so low (*vil*) a price and at a loss of merchandise which ought to be dearer by its nature, reduces to nothing that of all the other sellers who can never hope that the buyer will be sufficiently liberal to buy their products at a higher price than they can be obtained elsewhere.[10]

There cannot be, in other words, two prices for the same product in the same market, and that portion of the product which is offered at the lowest price determines the price at which the remainder will sell.

It was the cause of extreme variations in the price of wheat which were peculiar to France which Boisguilbert was eager to clear up. A difference of seven or eight degrees in price, he says, does not indicate a difference of seven or eight degrees in quantity. In times of scarcity the cultivator is seven times less pushed to sell, and in times of abundance he is seven times more

[9] *Le Détail*, p. 201. [10] *Traité des grains*, p. 362.

pushed to sell by the landlord and others. He proceeds carefully to analyze the factors producing famine prices: on rumor of a shortage in the crop, first, in the hope that the evil will increase, the sellers refrain from making their ordinary sales, using every means to get their creditors to wait for payment. Secondly, the buyers, who ordinarily buy their supplies of grain from week to week or month to month, hasten, in panic, to supply their needs as soon as possible for the entire year. The result is that the markets are less amply supplied than usual, and the demand greater than ordinary. Equilibrium between demand and supply is disturbed in a violent manner, for "it is the markets alone which are sovereign on this occasion, and not the quantity of grain, whatever that may be, which exists either in the granaries or in the barns of the farms." [11]

To maintain a balance between an excess supply or an excess shortage, that is, between a too high or a too low price for grain, requires careful management:

[These two parties,] [12] which are such great enemies of each other, must always be in equilibrium, otherwise the State suffers regardless of who holds the advantage. Markets where the grains are sold publicly bring about a balance. These markets decide the fate of the people in one way or another with respect to the price of grain. As a matter of fact, a market or public staple house, where there are ordinarily sold five hundred setiers of grain a week, cannot have an alteration above twenty only, without an increase or a very considerable diminution [in the price] of these same grains, which augments in a moment, and which doubles and triples, by the least increase, all the preceding [price changes]. It is like a balance suspended in equilibrium because the weight is equal in each of the two scales. A hundred pounds of any material whatever cannot receive an increase of even two pounds in one of the two scales without destroying the equilibrium.[13] This, then, is precisely what takes place in the market with regard to the price of grain. To repeat: an increase or a diminution of twenty sacks at the market or staple house above or below the ordinary supply of five hundred sacks

[11] *Ibid.*, pp. 379–380.
[12] That is, the producer and consumer, or supply and demand.
[13] "Without destroying the equilibrium" is a free translation of the following: "sans que l'autre ne soit emporté entièrement, et ne descende aussi bas, en faisant remonter celui qui a perdu le contre-poids aussi haut, que s'il n'y avait rien du tout, et que toute la charge fût en un seul."

offered (*d'apport*) every week, destroys (*emporte*) the balance, and makes it fall immediately on one side. And as from the evil on these occasions there comes evil, so either a fall in the price of grain, or its rise, is cumulative.[14]

A slight shortage, or a slight surplus of grain, in its effect upon price, Boisguilbert thus saw magnified in importance out of all proportion to the absolute quantity. A *denrée délicate,* he called it, referring to this delicate response to demand and supply. Either the shortage or the surplus was harmful to the State. The one created a hardship upon those for whom bread constituted a large part of the diet; the other, in its effect upon economic life as a whole, ruined rich and poor. Low prices, consequently, were even more to be dreaded than famine prices. They lasted longer, were more difficult to correct, and produced a general economic debacle.

Boisguilbert saw the maladjustment between prices and costs as correcting itself temporarily in the long run by the forcing of the high cost producers out of production. Thus while demand might be the fundamental factor underlying value,[15] and while the interaction of demand and supply might determine it at a given time, nevertheless, in the long run, the cost of production must be covered if the product is to continue to be produced. But in France at that time, the dropping out of producers did not represent a permanent solution. It brought on famine, and the excessively high prices, again encouraging production, started the vicious circle of circumstances over again. Hence Boisguilbert's conclusion:

It is easy to see, from all that has just been said, of what consequence it is in a country, to maintain abundance therein, to prevent any merchandise from being worthless (*à rebut*), which is the means to make it dry up. Causing the entrepreneurs to lose, they cease their traffic entirely, which causes a high payment (*qui fait payer la folle enchère*) for the preceding abasement of the product.[16]

Here is presented a lesson in value which gives Boisguilbert a not unworthy place among the precursors of Alfred Marshall.

[14] "L'avilissement des blés produit l'avilissement, et la cherté le haussement continuel de prix."—*Traité des grains,* pp. 378–379.

[15] See above, p. 225. [16] *Op. cit.*, p. 389.

XIII

ON THE RENT OF LAND

Grains come from the land through the work of men and the influence of the climate.

CURIOSITY is aroused to see how closely, if at all, Boisguilbert, supremely interested in the land both as a practical farmer and as a theorist, may have come to the theory of rent.

In 1700 agricultural production in Normandy was essentially similar to that in England in the days of Anderson and of Ricardo. There was an agricultural population composed of four groups: landlords (*les maîtres*); farmers (*les laboureurs* or *les fermiers*) paying a money rent (*le fermage*);[1] workers paid by the day (*les ouvriers* receiving *les journées*), and servants (*les valets* receiving *les gages*) who appear to have differed from the day laborers only in that they were regularly employed.[2]

THE VARYING QUALITY OF LAND

Boisguilbert laid great stress on the varying quality of the land and refers to it repeatedly. It is certain that there are more than a hundred degrees of difference between the most fertile and the most favored by nature, and the least, which seems to

[1] At no place does Boisguilbert discuss *les métayers* or *le métayage*. In addition to rent-paying farmers there were small peasant proprietors rapidly losing their land. Condorcet says that "it is necessary to observe that there are two methods of cultivating: in the one, the proprietor gives only his land, and the cultivator makes all the advances; in the other, the cultivator, who is called *métayer*, gives only his labor and his care. The proprietor furnishes the rest and the fruits are shared. More than the half of our provinces is still abandoned to this second method of cultivating." ("Réflexions sur le commerce des blés" [1776]. In *Oeuvres*, Paris, 1847, Vol. XI, pp. 116–117.) *Le métayage* appears to have been more common in the south of France, in contrast to the money rent in the northern part.

[2] Norman serfs had been free since the eleventh century. The term *valet* is a survival of the days of feudalism, deriving from the low Latin *vassalus* meaning vassal. The old French forms are *vaslet* and *varlet*.

have been created only to form the contour of the world, since it furnishes nothing, either for cultivation or for pasture.[3] Elsewhere he was more specific: "It is very certain that there are lands that are never cultivated . . . others that in fifteen years [produce] only once or twice; others every seven or eight years, and almost all [the remainder] rest at least one year in three."[4] But he repeatedly said, the "best land in the world does not differ in any respect from the worst when it is not cultivated."[5]

The Difference in the Cost of Production and the Part Played by Nature

The significant thing about the varying quality of the land, Boisguilbert asserted, is the difference in the cost of production and the abundance of the harvest. The best lands produce at little cost and produce an abundant harvest, whereas the worst ones produce very little and that with uncertainty and at a large cost that may or may not be covered by the return from the harvest. These dissimilarities are due to the difference in the aid given by nature. In some cases she helps much, and in other cases she aids man little in his efforts to obtain the fruits of the earth. There is at the top of the list, the situation of the land in Egypt.

> [The Nile provides] both the expenses of four workers [per *arpent*] who are necessary almost everywhere else to prepare the ground, and those of the fertilizer and improvements that must be given it, so that it is only necessary to throw the seed on the mud and without fear of cold, frost, or storm, wait for it to return its value with usury. It is this which caused that country formerly to be called the granary of the Romans, and causes the dispositions of the weather (*le ciel*), which are most important almost everywhere else, to be counted for nothing in that country.[6]

Something of the same sort, he said, is true in Muscovy, "where the snow, remaining on the earth for eight or nine months, after melting, leaves in the soil a salt, which, with the aid of a simple

[3] *Traité des grains,* p. 359.
[4] *Ibid.,* p. 375.
[5] *Le Détail,* p. 193.
[6] *Traité des grains,* p. 371.

and very easy labor, replaces all sorts of fertilizers, and a very abundant harvest is obtained only two months after the seed is sown." [7]

In contrast to Egypt and Muscovy, "land in France does not give grains, but sells them very dearly in most places." Nevertheless, people in France, Boisguilbert declared, have the impression that they grow there like "mushrooms and truffles." If this were true it "would be the pure effect of [the land's] liberality, which would exact no expense or care for culture. So that it being only necessary for everyone to wait for its purely gratuitous bounty, attention or work would have no part in the size of the harvest." [8] But such an error is due to the lack of knowledge of the practice of agriculture.

Because, far from the lands there being nearly so liberal, one can be assured that they are all, or the greater part of them, very rebellious to the hand of the cultivator, and withal very niggardly,[9] giving nothing for nothing, and [producing] only in proportion to the care and fertilizer that is lent to them. And indeed, often when the weather is not favorable, many of them are encountered which cause bankruptcy, allowing their fatal term to expire, or the harvest season [to come] without returning interest or capital, that is to say, the seed.[10]

But in educating the French public in the mystery of agricultural production, Boisguilbert was not content with vague generalities. As was his custom, he went into the details of production on the best and on the worst classes of lands, paying particular attention to the latter, in a manner that few modern agricultural economists have surpassed. At the same time he gives a valuable picture of agricultural production for comparative purposes.

Some [land] is seen, although of very small quantity, where two poor horses only can exploit up to a hundred arpents [11] a year, and cultivate (*renfuir*) or turn two arpents a day without any need of fertilizer. This makes all perish by a too great product, and does

[7] *Loc. cit.*
[8] *Ibid.*, pp. 370–371.
[9] *Intéressées*—literally, "selfish."
[10] *Op. cit.*, p. 371.
[11] The quantity of land in an arpent differed in the various provinces from one and three-fourths acres to two acres.

not permit the payment of the usury on the sowing at twenty to one.[12] This it does without ever resting, contrary to the practice with almost all the lands. But there is found on the other side, and in much greater amount, [land] that it is necessary to force to produce, and that by continual work, such as fertilizing and increasing the number of horses, the land resisting at every step. And with all that it is necessary to give them rest at least once in three years, and even more often. Some produce a crop every seven or eight years, and some only once in fifteen years, in proportion to the belief that the price of grain is such that the product (*la culture*) will support the expense.

An arpent of land of the least degree of perfection rented at three livres,[13] [a price which] is encountered many times and even below, which makes six livres, considering the year of rest, cannot be exploited without a strong seeding, that is to say, a setier worth approximately eight livres. Four workers are necessary, at least, and often five, whom one never pays less than three livres, ten sous each, and even more for the worst lands, which are ordinarily stony, and which, as a consequence of the destruction that they cause to the plowshare, requires it to be taken often to the forge for resharpening (*recharger*). Thus, there are again fourteen francs of expense, at least. It is necessary to manure it, which will require not less than a dozen small loads, or other measure in proportion, which is still another dozen francs. There is the expense of the harvest in order to profit on the field, which amounts to three livres. That is, there are more than thirty-eight francs sown on the land. And when the harvest is four setiers, which almost never happens on such land, one regards oneself as very fortunate. But the poor lands make the seed deteriorate, and always make it lose its perfection, contrary to the excellent, as in Hungary, where *seigle* becomes *froment* at the

[12] Boisguilbert clearly recognized the effect of an increased supply from a superior source. He says that the "silver mines in Germany which supplied the whole world before the discovery of the Indies, were destroyed from the moment that this metal became more common. They could no longer support the expense that it was necessary to make in Europe to draw it from the bowels of the earth." (*Le Détail*, p. 233.) Adam Smith repeats the idea: "After the discovery of the mines of Peru, the silver mines of Europe were, the greater part of them, abandoned. The value of the silver was so much reduced, that their produce could no longer pay the expense of working them, or replace, with a profit, the food, cloaths, lodging and other necessaries which were consumed in that operation." (*Wealth of Nations*, Bk. I, p. 169.) What necessity did in Germany with respect to silver, Boisguilbert says, stupidity did in France with respect to grains.—*Le Détail*, p. 207.

[13] Elsewhere he says that in the case of the best land, the landowners "sell the harvest to the farmers" in some cases "even at thirty and thirty-five francs."—*Mémoire sur les blés*, p. 153.

end of three years. And if the wheat one has sown cost eight francs the setier, the grain from this poor land is sold at the most for only six francs. Thus the cultivator and the landlord have a considerable loss, which obliges them to leave the land uncultivated, which regularly occurs. There are large sections uncultivated, formerly cultivated, which cannot occur without reducing the landlord and the farmer to extreme poverty; whereas if the wheat were valued at eleven or twelve livres the setier, as it could easily be, the landlord and the farmer, the servants and the workmen, would all have profited.[14]

From this it is seen that in France lands normally cultivated varied in their production from fourfold or less when prices were not artifically reduced by forbidding exportation, to twentyfold, and that there was a distinctly inverse relationship between costs and productivity. Incidentally to show the difference in productivity, Boisguilbert, in his imaginative way, referred to the return on the better land as a return with "usury," and that on the mediocre or poorer lands, as "interests."

Boisguilbert saw a money rent contracted in advance by the cultivator as a form of expense to him which could be met with difficulty when the price of the product fell. Rent along with taxes, constituted the last or final expense, as it were.[15] Nevertheless he did not include rent in the cost of production unless in a very special manner as differing from ordinary costs. In speaking of the farmers' difficulties as results of the excessively low prices, the problem of covering costs and paying rent were referred to separately—"the expenses of their culture, together with the payment of the rent."

Most conclusive is his calculation of the expenses of production on the poorest land under cultivation. Here it is obvious he did not include rent in the expenditures. "An arpent of land of the least degree of perfection, rented at three livres . . . cannot be exploited without a strong seeding," etc. These enumerated expenditures are:

Seed	8 livres	(approximately)
Four or five men ...	14 francs	(at least)

[14] *Traité des grains*, p. 359.
[15] *Mémoire sur les blés*, pp. 155–157.

Manure	12 francs (at least)
Harvest	3 francs
	37 francs

Boisguilbert says the total expense is thirty-eight francs. This difference of one is either the result of an error in his addition, or a slight difference between the "livre" and the "franc," terms which he apparently uses indiscriminately. In any event, the three, or six, livres of rent are not included and were clearly not intended to be. No doubt is left, however, when he definitely states that

> what has been said of poor lands being a loss to the farmer and the landlord when wheat is at a low price, is equally true of the return from those of the first degree of excellence; because if the expenses of production are less, the profit belongs to the landlord, who leases his lands at a proportional price; [and this price] not being attained by the harvest, when wheat is very cheap, it produces the same effects that have just been noted, and toward just as many persons.[16]

Here, said Horn, "either everything deceives us, or there is in germ the doctrine of the rent of the land." Strangely enough this very significant paragraph was overlooked both by Daire and by Marx.

The Importance of Price

PRICE DETERMINED BY SUPPLY AND DEMAND

It should be recalled that Boisguilbert did not discuss production under static or long-run conditions. He was striving to bring about a situation in France in which the price obtained for grain would cover the cost of production on the worst land which was accustomed to produce. But what he saw was a great variation in prices which continually changed the conditions of production on both poor and mediocre lands and which affected the income on the better lands. Such changing prices were solely the effect of the interplay of the forces of supply and demand without reference to costs on any class of land.[17]

[16] *Traité des grains*, p. 360.
[17] *Ibid.*, pp. 362–363, 369. *Le Détail*, p. 201.

THE EFFECT OF PRICE ON THE QUALITY OF LAND CULTIVATED AND ON RENT

The best land does not differ from the worst if it is not cultivated. But however rich and well cultivated, land is more useless to the cultivator than if he had grown nothing if its products are not sold, for there is no "point of culture" which does not require some expense.[18] In other words, agricultural products have a money cost independent of the price obtained. The low price of grain does not allow poor lands to cover their costs; for this reason they are abandoned and if this price continues to fall it causes the mediocre lands to suffer the same fate, and the best ones to be neglected.[19]

> [All lands] are more or less liable to see their fate for cultivation determined wholly by the price of grains. As not all things can be carried to their perfection unless the interest of the worker or of the entrepreneur is obtained, there are more than half the lands that one would not be able to provide with the necessary fertilizer, in proportion to the ingratitude of the land, good wheat being at nine to ten francs at Paris, that is, five to six for small grain in the provinces. . . .
>
> Thus one cannot dispute the fact that the price of grain is an unfailing barometer which causes the culture of the lands to rise or fall in proportion as it increases or diminishes.[20]

In a passage in which he speaks of the "empire" which price has over the fate of grains, he says it is the "price alone" of wheat and grains which "seeds the lands, from the worst which in memory man has ever seen grow anything, to the best favored by nature." [21]

As to the relation between rent and price, the former is the result of the latter and rises and falls with it. For example, "the six consecutive years after 1694 saw wheat almost always at double the price which prevails today. As a consequence, all the estates, both good and bad, were well cultivated. . . . The pro-

[18] *Le Détail,* p. 193.
[19] *Ibid.*, p. 174. *Factum,* p. 351.
[20] *Traité des grains,* p. 371. It is unnecessary to add that Boisguilbert has here misused the word "barometer."
[21] *Ibid.*, p. 374.

prietors were well paid, and all things valuable." [22] But after 1700 the situation changed: "The price [did] not cover the expenses of cultivation in many places, [and was] very far from satisfying the payments due to the proprietor and taxes. It [was] this which occasioned, aside from the loss of five hundred millions of reduction of rent in the kingdom . . . the abandonment of a great amount of land of difficult exploitation." [23]

Likewise, comparing the situation in 1695 with that of thirty years earlier, Boisguilbert stated that lands formerly paying one thousand livres of rent had been reduced to five hundred livres because of the fall in price.[24]

Protesting against a policy which kept grain prices low for the sake of the poor, and which eventually produced famine, he declared that "all the classes seed the land, and it is not the cultivator alone who has this commission, although this has grossly been assumed." [25] Here is a foreshadowing of the concept of rent as a social product.

Rent of Situation

Boisguilbert clearly recognized the advantage accruing to the lands situated close to great urban centers. This advantage was sufficiently great to bring about a "violence" to waste land in causing to be made highly productive land which originally was not destined to such an end.

> It is very certain that there are lands that are never cultivated, through the lack that has just been noted; others that in fifteen years [produce] only once or twice; others every seven or eight years, and almost all [the remainder] rest at least one year in three. But worse ones are encountered of which naturally one would demand nothing, which are cultivated every year, and which produce even as much as two harvests in one summer.
>
> The reason for this difference is, that there is none of them which, put to the test, can resist the quantity of fertilizer possible and necessary to make them fertile. From the moment that those of this type are found situated in places where one can procure for them this advantage at a price which is not above that of the fruits of the

[22] *Ibid.*, p. 365.
[23] *Factum*, p. 274.
[24] *Le Détail*, pp. 173–174. [25] *Traité des grains*, p. 363.

harvest, such measures are always taken with regard to them. Such are those which are found at the gates and in the environment of great cities, which, notwithstanding their defect of being stony or sandy, are all developed into truck gardens (*potagers*) and even produce grains every year, without ever having a moment of rest. The reason for this is that the sewage of the city having no other interest than that of being carried away, at the most, the nearby land has the preference in the transportation because of the proximity, which also produces the facility for the sale of the fruits of this land made good in spite of nature. And this violence that one does to it stretches out and gains the country around in proportion to the price of grains, until farmers two leagues from a maritime city have been seen to maintain two horses and a servant all the year only to go and obtain two loads a day of certain wastes, moistened with salt-water sprays, which have the virtue of tripling the effects of all other kinds of fertilizer. That is, these farmers spend eight hundred francs a year in having their horses make eight leagues a day to enrich only fifteen or sixteen arpents of land, and that profitably, when wheat is at sixteen or eighteen francs at Paris. On the other hand, at nine or ten francs it is at a loss, or rather this activity [of the farmers] is left off.[26]

Here is the first germ of the Ricardian theory, said Daire, and Karl Marx agreed.[27]

Summary

Referring to Boisguilbert, Du Pont de Nemours said that except for two points, upon which the Physiocrats laid great stress, he would have to be given the "honor of the invention of economic science." One of these points was that he did not "recognize the existence of the net product." [28] It is true that Boisguilbert did not recognize what may be termed the philosophical abstraction known as the "net product," but it cannot be said that he did not recognize a differential payment made to the landowner which was not a cost of production to the farmer, and which was the result and not the cause of price. He saw, indeed, that rent occasioned no "variation in the relative value of commodities independent of the quantity of labor necessary

[26] *Ibid.*, p. 375.
[27] *Gesamtausgabe*, Berlin, 1932, Erste Abteilung, Band 3, p. 582.
[28] See below, p. 324.

to produce them," which was the particular problem Ricardo set out to determine.

It is clear that Boisguilbert, in his discussion of agricultural production, included all the elements necessary to make up the so-called Ricardian theory. One feels that had he read Ricardo on rent he would have responded, "But that is obvious!" His objection would have been with reference to price as determined by the cost of production at the margin. The price, he thought, should be sufficient to cover the cost on the worst land under cultivation at a given moment. As it was, he saw that price determined the margin of cultivation, and that there was a lag between the two which complicated the situation. As is said elsewhere, what static economics assumes as a *fait accompli* he saw as an ideal to be achieved.

The question naturally arises: Why did Boisguilbert not sum up his facts and state them as a full-fledged explanation of the phenomenon of rent? The answer should be apparent. That was not his purpose, and with all his digressions he included nothing which was not pertinent to his purpose. He was not engaged in a theoretical exposition as such. His objective in writing on agriculture was to show the ministers and the people of France "who thought that the farmers could make less, but that they could never lose," that the existing agricultural policy was ruining the nation. To accomplish this he attempted to make clear the intricacies of agricultural production and commerce in grain. It was only incidental to this end, and due to his natural tendency to clarify underlying principles, that he set forth the points enumerated as essential to the understanding of those whom he sought to enlighten.

XIV

THE RELATION OF BOISGUILBERT'S CONCEPT OF ECONOMIC EQUILIBRIUM TO STATIC THEORY

It is necessary for all things and all products always to be in equilibrium.

THE classical dramatist sometimes got himself so involved with a character that the latter could not be resolved into the play as a whole. A common expedient in such cases was to kill off the character and go on with the play.

A casual reading of Boisguilbert may leave the impression that, similarly, in an *impasse* he used nature or the natural law as a means of evading a difficulty into which he got himself in his reasoning; but a careful study shows that he had a definite conception of nature and natural law. He conceived of nature as dominated by equilibrium or balance, the maintenance of which was the function of her laws.

Boisguilbert's writings bear the earmarks of a deeply religious nature. The Bible became the point of departure for his theory. He perceived the original equality of men as destroyed by departure from the injunction that they were to live by the sweat of their brows. He saw a balance between life and its needs, for nature "cannot love men less than she does beasts, and she does not put in the world a single one of the latter that she does not assure its pittance at the same time. She deals similarly with men where they uphold her judgment."

Because of his knowledge of its uncertainty and insecurity he became enamored of the concept of this balance in economic life. From it he developed a theory of economic equilibrium based upon the operation of natural law.

Balance or equilibrium is the rule of nature, but it is disturbed in social life by the action of men or governments seeking to serve their immediate aims by defeating her. Out of this defeat grows the inability of men to procure their livelihood from their labor, which they can do only in a state of equilibrium. Nature intends the trades of men to sustain them. She intends them to divide their labor and to exchange the products resulting from it. This exchange is a requirement of nature, because, while she does not always provide for all needs in one place, she does so considering large areas as a unit.

In his analysis of what is essential in order that wealth may be created, that is, that men may be permitted to consume freely as a result of their labor, he saw this balance functioning in all aspects of economic life. There is need, for instance, of equilibrium in value between goods and money so that exchanges can take place without delay. The division of profits between buyer and seller, which sustains proportional prices, he refers to as an equilibrium, the result of which would make it impossible for fortunes to be obtained except by means of work and ability. Likewise the equal necessity to buy and to sell which exists in all trades is an equilibrium or balance, which is sustained by the desire for profits on the part of all traders. There is necessity for equality between sales and purchases, and an equal necessity to buy and sell. It is necessary, in other words, for "all things and all products to be continually in equilibrium, and to maintain proportionate prices in relation to each other and to the expenses necessary to produce them." This equilibrium among all goods is the sole conserver of public prosperity. It must be maintained, else a country will be filled up with goods which the people will lack entirely.[1]

What are the elements which go to make up this proportional price, or the natural price, as we may term it, since it is the price necessary to carry out the plan of nature that all men be sustained by their labor? This price must be sufficient to cover all outlays. These include the maintenance of the capital used, that is, the land, utensils and implements; then there are wages to the laborer and rent to the landlord. In addition to these elements there is the profit, the "honest recompense" with which

[1] *Dissertation sur les richesses*, pp. 399, 404, 409–411.

the entrepreneur must maintain himself, which must also be included in the price obtained. Interest is not specifically referred to, although the ruin which a high rate brings to the individual as well as to the State is mentioned.

These, then, are the elements which proportional prices must cover. In prosperous times such prices are obtained; but unfortunately there are times when the actual prices for which goods are sold will not cover them, and at such times agriculture and industry decline, and consumption cannot go on.

So we find in Boisguilbert's theory two prices, a natural price which covers all necessary outlays including profit, and a market price which may or may not coincide with the former.[2]

Let us now see what Adam Smith had to say about price. Referring to wages, rent, and profit, he said:

> In every society the price of every commodity finally resolves itself into some one or other, or all of those three parts; and in every improved society, all the three enter more or less, as component parts, into the price of the far greater part of commodities.
>
> In the price of corn, for example, one part pays the rent of the landlord, another pays the wages or maintenance of the labourers and labouring cattle employed in producing it, and the third pays the profit of the farmer. These three parts seem either immediately or ultimately to make up the whole price of corn. *A fourth part, it may perhaps be thought, is necessary for replacing the stock of the farmer, or for compensating the wear and tear of his labouring cattle, and other instruments of husbandry.* But it must be considered that the price of any instrument of husbandry, *such as a labouring horse,* is itself made up of the same three parts; the rent of the land upon which he is reared, the labour of tending and rearing him, and the profits of the farmer who advances both the rent of this land, and the wages of this labour. Though the price of the corn, therefore, may pay the price as well as the maintenance of the horse, the whole price still resolves itself either immediately or ultimately into the three parts of rent, labour, and profit.[3]

Here, it will be observed, Adam Smith included three of Boisguilbert's elements of price, while he rejected his fourth, namely, the maintenance of capital, as not constituting another special or distinct element. The reference to the horse, for in-

[2] *Ibid.*, pp. 402, 404, 406, 417, 421.
[3] *Wealth of Nations,* Bk. I, p. 52. My italics.

stance, comes directly from Boisguilbert: "the master of a carriage horse gives it food before taking the profit which he draws from its service, else he will lose its service, or he will lose the animal altogether, which would ruin him without anyone pitying him or doubting that the cause of it was his own carelessness." [4]

But, as Boisguilbert would say, it is not yet time to finish with Adam Smith. Let us glance at his well-known natural and market prices.

> When the price of any commodity is neither more nor less than what is sufficient to pay the rent of the land, the wages of the labour, and the profits of the stock employed in raising, preparing, and bringing it to market, according to their natural rates, the commodity is then sold for what may be called its natural price.
>
> The commodity is then sold precisely for what it is worth, or what it really costs the person who brings it to market; for though in common language what is called the prime cost of any commodity does not comprehend the profit of the person who is to sell it again, yet if he sells it at a price which does not allow him the ordinary rate of profit in his neighbourhood, he is evidently a loser by the trade; since by employing his stock in some other way he might have made that profit. His profit, besides, is his revenue, the proper fund of his subsistence. As, while he is preparing and bringing the goods to market, he advances to his workmen their wages, or their subsistence; so he advances to himself, in the same manner, his own subsistence, which is generally suitable to the profit which he may reasonably expect from the sale of his goods. Unless they yield him this profit, therefore, they do not repay him what they may very properly be said to have really cost him.
>
> Though the price, therefore, which leaves him this profit, is not always the lowest at which a dealer may sometimes sell his goods, it is the lowest at which he is likely to sell them for any considerable time; at least where there is perfect liberty, or where he may change his trade as often as he pleases.
>
> The actual price at which any commodity is commonly sold is called its market price. It may either be above, or below, or exactly the same with its natural price.[5]

So here we find that Adam Smith's two prices correspond to those of Boisguilbert. For Smith did not reject the latter's fourth element in price; he simply resolved it into the other three

[4] *Dissertation sur les richesses,* p. 417.
[5] *Wealth of Nations,* Bk. I, pp. 57–58.

elements. Whereas Smith said that unless the goods sold yield a profit they cannot be said to repay him what they have cost him, Boisguilbert said that if the trader does not profit it is as if he had not sold at all.[6] Smith asserted that a dealer will not sell his goods for any considerable time below the natural price, "at least where there is perfect liberty, or where he may change his trade as often as he pleases," while Boisguilbert said that nature "has established the rule that it is necessary for each trade to nourish its master, or that he must close his shop and procure himself another one." [7]

Thus far, except for the superior and more connected reasoning of Smith, which is to be expected following three-quarters of a century of reasoning on the subject, we find little difference in the thought of the two economists; but there was a significant difference in their mode of attack, a difference which was to affect the course of economic reasoning for a century and a half.

With Boisguilbert economic equilibrium, or the maintenance of proportional prices, or the natural price of each product, as we may call it, was an ideal. It was occasionally attained, but the economic and social pathology resulting when it failed to be, was not to be ignored, and it was this condition which made the necessity to attain and maintain the goal of equilibrium so significant.

With Smith the concept of equilibrium, and departure from it, took on a completely new aspect:

> The quantity of every commodity brought to market naturally suits itself to the effectual demand. It is the interest of all those who employ their land, labour, or stock, in bringing any commodity to market, that the quantity never should exceed the effectual demand; and it is the interest of all other people that it never should fall short of that demand.
>
> If at any time it exceeds the effectual demand, some of the component parts of its price must be paid below their natural rate. If it is rent, the interest of the landlords will immediately prompt them to withdraw a part of their land, and if it is wages or profit, the interest of the labourers in the one case, and of their employers in the other, will prompt them to withdraw a part of their labour or

[6] *Dissertation sur les richesses*, p. 404. [7] *Ibid.*, p. 409.

stock from this employment. The quantity brought to market will soon be no more than sufficient to supply the effectual demand. All the different parts of its price will rise to their natural rate, and the whole price to its natural price.

If, on the contrary, the quantity brought to market should at any time fall short of the effectual demand, some of the component parts of its price must rise above their natural rate. If it is rent, the interest of all other landlords will naturally prompt them to prepare more land for the raising of this commodity; if it is wages or profit, the interest of all other labourers and dealers will soon prompt them to employ more labour and stock in preparing and bringing it to market. The quantity brought thither will soon be sufficient to supply the effectual demand. All the different parts of its price will soon sink to their natural rate, and the whole to its natural price.

The natural price, therefore, is, as it were, the central price, to which the prices of all commodities are continually gravitating. Different accidents may sometimes keep them suspended a good deal above it, and sometimes force them down even somewhat below it. But whatever may be the obstacles which hinder them from settling in this center of repose and continuance, they are constantly tending toward it.

The whole quantity of industry annually employed in order to bring any commodity to market, naturally suits itself in this manner to the effectual demand. It naturally aims at bringing always that precise quantity thither which may be sufficient to supply, and no more than supply, that demand.[8]

In these paragraphs, the abstract quality which was to become so characteristic of English economics, the "long-run tendency," may be said to have had its birth. Economic stability, that is, price equilibrium, is here not a goal to be achieved, as with Boisguilbert, but it is something of a theoretical actuality. The significance of the departure from natural price is passed over as of no moment simply because this same natural price has become recognized as a central tendency.[9]

[8] *Wealth of Nations*, Bk. I, pp. 59–60.

[9] It will be recalled that Cantillon, like Smith, carried out his reasoning upon a single plane. But, unlike Smith, there is no exposition of an underlying philosophy of a central tendency over a long run. It is rather for the sake of simplicity and convenience of treatment. "I do not consider here the variations in Market prices which may arise from the good or bad harvest of the year, or the extraordinary consumption which may occur from foreign troops or other accidents, so as not to complicate my subject, considering only a State in its natural and uniform condition." (*Essai sur la nature du*

Compare the impersonal character of the withdrawal of land, capital, and labor from the market as described by Smith, with Boisguilbert's treatment of the situation in which the landowner, the dealer, and the laborer find rent, profit, and wages insufficient. Unless the land can be made to pay all its expenses "there will be nothing for anyone in the world." If the person or his capital is seized for the difference between the market price and expenses, there is "no other remedy" than "to give up the cultivation in question. . . . Besides that, the evil, being communicated to all other products by a kind of solidarity of interest which exists among them, causes this same destiny to affect almost all other kinds of goods." [10] The producers "must never be expected to supply products from their liberality, or from their prudence, when they, themselves, must all die of hunger." [11]

[It is necessary, then, that] commerce continue without interruption, and at a price which is obligatory . . . namely, a price which prevents the merchant from losing, so that he is able to continue his trade with profit; otherwise it is as if he did not sell at all; and with his destruction it will be like the case of those grappling vessels (*vaisseaux accrochés*), in which one places fire to the powder of the other, which causes both to blow up.[12]

Boisguilbert had great understanding of, and compassion for, men who labor without adequate recompense.

[Any loss borne] by the poor causes the suppression of their necessities, of which they cannot be deprived without perishing, as is too well known. After all, are not men comparable to animals, and especially to horses? Who will make a horse work continually with-

---

commerce en général [1737], London, 1931, Pt. I, p. 65.) Again, apropos the complications of the foreign exchanges, he said: "My subject does not allow me to enlarge on the effects of these accidental causes: I confine myself always to the simple views of commerce lest I should complicate my subject, which is too much encumbered by the multiplicity of the facts which relate to it." (*Ibid.*, Pt. III, p. 265.) He is, in other words, adopting a method of treatment which would lead him to avoid the defects of Boisguilbert, who "complicated" his subject by the "multiplicity of the facts which relate to it." The latter, who placed such emphasis upon the practical necessity to understand all the facts of economic life regardless of the effort required, would have heartily condemned such an artificial simplification, as he would have regarded it, of these facts for the sake of style.

10 *Dissertation sur les richesses* pp. 402–403.

11 *Ibid.*, p. 421. 12 *Ibid.*, p. 404.

out giving it a measure of the necessary food unless one wishes it to die immediately? But can men, of whom continual toil is required, and who sweat blood and water in order to procure only bread and water in the midst of a country of abundance, hope for a long life, or rather do they not perish before they have half run their course? And this does not take into account those who are prevented by the poverty of their parents from living beyond infancy. They are, as it were, choked in the cradle. . . . [To deprive them of subsistence] is an outrage to religion, to humanity, to justice, to statesmanship, and to the crudest reasoning.[13]

Not that Adam Smith reacted to social phenomena merely as a logical machine. On the contrary. Strangely reminiscent of Boisguilbert is his statement that the laborer's wage must be at least sufficient to maintain him, and that this rate is "evidently the lowest which is consistent with common humanity." While "poverty, though it does not prevent the generation, is extremely unfavourable to the rearing of children. The tender plant is produced, but, in so cold a soil and so severe a climate, soon withers and dies." [14]

Adam Smith not only saw central tendencies in economic processes; he dealt also with their changing character under dynamic conditions. For instance: "First, I shall endeavour to explain what are the circumstances which naturally determine the rate of wages, and in what manner those circumstances are affected by the riches or poverty, by the advancing, stationary, or declining state of the society." [15] He would do likewise for profits and for rent, and it is this with which his Book III is concerned.

But when Ricardo came to *The Wealth of Nations* his mind was intrigued, not so much with the above, but with this:

The market price of any particular commodity, though it may continue long above, can seldom continue long below its natural price. Whatever part of it was paid below the natural rate, the persons whose interest it affected would immediately feel the loss, and would immediately withdraw either so much land, or so much labour, or so much stock, from being employed about it, that the quantity brought to market would soon be no more than sufficient to supply

[13] *Ibid.*, pp. 414, 417.
[14] *Wealth of Nations*, Bk. I, pp. 70, 81. [15] *Ibid.*, Bk. I, p. 65.

the effectual demand. Its market price, therefore, would soon rise to the natural price. This at least would be the case where there was perfect liberty.[16]

With Ricardo the die was cast. The natural price became the normal price, and the endless fluctuations characterizing economic life became mere deviations from the normal.

To summarize: Boisguilbert, who painstakingly analyzed economic processes both in periods of *l'opulence* and of *la misère,* or in periods of "prosperity" and "depression" as we would call them, came to the conclusion that economic equilibrium must be maintained to eliminate the evils of the latter. This economic equilibrium hinged upon the sustaining of prices which would carry out the design of nature to permit everyone to live by his own labor. This natural price which Boisguilbert endeavored to show how to achieve, became in *The Wealth of Nations* a central tendency over the long run, although Smith gave attention to society in its advancing, stationary, and declining aspects. For Boisguilbert economic processes were purely dynamic with the ideal of stability. For Smith there was, as it were, a conflict between a dynamic view and a propensity to see only long-run tendencies. With Ricardo the static view of economic processes may be said to have been wholly achieved.

16 *Ibid.,* p. 64.

XV

LAISSEZ FAIRE

It is for nature who produces her favors to distribute them.

WHERE does this theorist belong who has aroused such a controversy with regard to the principle of liberty that he is declared by some to be an adherent of laissez faire, and by others, of protectionism? [1] What is the thought of the man who used the expression, "laisser faire," yet, who, according to Oncken, did not use it? Certainly he cannot be left dangling astride a fence, as it were. If it is possible he must be lifted to a comfortable position on one side or the other, or the reason for his anomalous situation made clear.

In its usual form, laissez faire, the first use of the slogan is found in D'Argenson. Boisguilbert used it only in the infinitive and the subjunctive. But in considering the origin of the expression, one factor must not be overlooked: Boisguilbert, the phrase maker. His expressions cling to the memory. They lend themselves to quotation. Furthermore, there is in his writings a progression in the use of this particular phrase. In *Le Détail* he asserted that *Il est seulement nécessaire de laisser agir la nature. . .*[2] In *Factum* this was developed into *Il n'y avait qu'à laisser faire la nature. . .*[3]

It thus appears apropos to give in its setting the first recorded use of a term which occupies so important a place in the history of economic theory.

Having stated that it is not the general price level which is of

[1] For Oncken's view as to the origin of the maxim "laissez faire," and a criticism of it, see Appendix, which is suggested as an introduction to the present chapter.

[2] *Le Détail,* p. 239.

[3] See below, p. 326.

significance in the prosperity of a nation, but the proportion among all prices, Boisguilbert proceeded:

> It is, therefore, proportions which create all wealth, because it is by their means alone that exchanges, and as a consequence, commerce, can be carried on. It would be ridiculous to make a distinction between two equally good meals because one had cost very much more and the other very much less, and at the same time pretend to establish a higher degree of felicity in that one for which more had been expended. And it is by the disturbing of this harmony that the 1,500 millions of income, vanished from France since [the year] 1660, have been lost. This justice, which must exist between two dealers who trade only with one another, must extend likewise over the two hundred professions which today are to be found in France. All of them have a common interest to maintain it, because from it alone can they obtain their subsistence and their maintenance. It must not be disorganized in the least of its parts, that is to say, the least important workman (*chétif ouvrier*) [must not] sell at a loss, for his destruction, like a contagious fever, corrupts the whole. It must exist, not only from man to man, but also from region to region, from province to province, from kingdom to kingdom, and even from year to year, in aiding or furnishing reciprocally that which they have in excess, and receiving in counter-exchange the things of which they have a shortage. Nevertheless, by a frightful corruption of the heart, there is no individual at all, although he obtain his well-being only from the maintenance of this harmony, who does not work from morning to evening and use all his efforts to ruin it. There is not a single worker who does not try with all his power to sell his merchandise for three times more than it is worth, and to buy that of his neighbor for three times less than it costs to produce it. It is only at the point of the sword that justice is maintained in these encounters. It is the function of nature, or Providence, nevertheless, to bring this about; and as she has provided feeble animals retreats and means in order that they may not all become the prey of those which, being stronger or born armed in some manner, live by killing, likewise in the commerce of life she has established such an order that, provided she is let alone (*pourvu qu'on la laisse faire*), it is not at all in the power of the most powerful in buying the product of the most wretched, to prevent the sale from providing the subsistence of the latter. It is this which maintains prosperity, to which both are equally indebted for the subsistence proportioned to their estate.

Quoting himself, he said:

It was said *pourvu qu'on laisse faire la nature,* that is, that she is given her liberty, and that one mix in this commerce only in order to provide protection to all and to prevent violence. Nevertheless, just the opposite has been done. There are no means, however frightful they may be, that one has not believed not only legitimate, but even the mark of the most superior policy, [which have not been taken] to ruin this harmony, in attacking or weakening all products specifically, one after another, by means of partisans. When one kind of goods had been destroyed under pretext of bringing money to the king, although he did not receive the hundredth part of the evil caused, so that the entrepreneurs[4] had nothing more to do, deceiving MM. the ministers, the same measures were brought to other kinds of goods which were not yet destroyed. The result is that that one who has most ruined the country, and as a consequence the king, is the one who has had the most to do with its affairs.[5]

Of the chapter in *Factum de la France* containing this paragraph, Mirabeau said: "The chapter is admirable in the profundity, the clarity, and the distinctness of the views, and in the simplicity of the enunciation."[6] The author of *Le Détail de la France* "recognized . . . the advantages of the liberty of commerce." So said Du Pont de Nemours,[7] indicating that the Physiocrats regarded him as an exponent of the principle of laissez faire.

So much for the origin of the term itself. Did the concept have the same connotation with Boisguilbert that it has come to have, and that it had, indeed, with Adam Smith?[8] It must be recognized that there has been a change. There has been a formalizing, a crystallizing of the idea, or, it may be said, a progression or a degeneration as one prefers. Karl Marx, writing on Boisguilbert, recognized the change which had come into the meaning. With Boisguilbert, he said, "as later with the Physiocrats, this theory still had some humanity and significance."[9]

[4] That is, tax farmers and partisans.
[5] *Factum*, pp. 279–280.
[6] "Notes inédites sur Boisguilbert par le Marquis de Mirabeau—publiées par G. Weulersse," *Revue d'histoire de doctrines économiques*, 1910, p. 128.
[7] See below, p. 324.
[8] Adam Smith, as is well known, does not use the French expression. Instead he usually refers to occurrences under conditions of "perfect liberty." The only case in which he may be said to use the phrase itself is the English equivalent of "laissez faire la nature." See below, pp. 325–327.
[9] *Gesamtausgabe*, Erste Abteilung, Band 3, p. 575. For the best example of laissez faire economics run riot, as it were, and to contrast its spirit with

With Boisguilbert the expression meant not so much *laissez-nous faire,* but literally *laissez faire la nature.* It was nature's plan for the functioning of economic society which must not be interfered with by any *ministère étrangère.*[10] Just what did he regard as nature's plan for mankind? It was that all men should be able to gain a livelihood from their labor "or that of their ancestors." Immediately, it was anything which served to bring this about and did not tend ultimately to destroy this ability upon the part of others, and thus, in turn, of oneself. It is in this way that the term may be said to have included just taxation as well as freedom to trade. The oppression of unjust taxation interfered with the ability to gain a livelihood or to improve one's condition as certainly as restrictions on the ability to trade. Laissez faire meant the "mutual aid" of man and nature: that products be moved from the place where they were superfluous to the place where products were lacking. It meant freedom to sell under conditions of equality with the buyers. There are two reasons why Boisguilbert stressed freedom to sell. The first is because at the time he was writing France was limiting the competition for the purchase of her grains to the home market, and the aides prevented the movement or sale of wine. From this situation and the condition resulting, he developed his theories of the basic position of agriculture in the national economy, of the solidarity of interests, and of prices. The second reason for his emphasis upon selling is that he saw buying as inevitably resulting from selling. It is but natural, he said, that as the incomes of individuals increase they increase their consumption, progressing from the barest subsistence to the utmost magnificence in food, clothing, shelter, and equipage. The essential requirement at the time he was writing was to increase

---

that of the origin of the doctrine, see the evidence of W. G. Sumner before a Select Committee of the House of Representatives relative to "Causes of the General Depression in Labor and Business," etc., 45th Congress, 3d Session. House of Repr., Misc. Doc. No. 49. Washington, 1879.

[10] Incidentally, Boisguilbert does not use this expression in its literal sense, but in the sense of "outside intervention." One of the difficulties in understanding his exact thought is his figurative use of terms. As Daire, who did not himself always understand the exact significance of what Boisguilbert was saying, said, he must be read for his thought, not for his style.

the income which would permit the desired consumption. But under the conditions then existing, the basic need was to obtain permission for sales to take place, without which there was no money income.

To Boisguilbert laissez faire meant, fundamentally, unrestricted economic opportunity for everyone; but it was here that he took a long-run view. Permanent security for everyone meant taking into consideration the economic solidarity of society. Therefore the freedom to pursue one's own economic interest must be tempered on the part of the individual by economic justice to others. There was, in other words, in his ethical theory of laissez faire a personal obligation for every man to be his brother's keeper in the sense of not destroying him. It was a renunciation and a denunciation of the *sauve qui peut* which has come to be regarded as the essence of the principle.

A belief in freedom from restraint in the exchange of goods was for Boisguilbert the logical corollary of his definition of wealth, his emphasis upon consumption, and his belief in a Divine Providence. Wealth, he said, consists in an abundance of consumable goods. But nature has not equally supplied all places with her wares, and from this is evolved the necessity to exchange if such wealth is to exist. For its unbounded enjoyment "it is necessary for all these two hundred trades to carry on a continual exchange among themselves, in order to aid one another with that of which they have too much, and to receive in counter-exchange those things which they lack. And this must be done not only from man to man, but even from region to region, and from kingdom to kingdom." [11] Self-interest will cause conflict to arise.

> Authority is necessary in order to have peace and the laws of men observed among a large number of men, who seek only to destroy them and to deceive and circumvent one another from morning to night, and who aspire continually to establish their wealth on the ruin of their neighbors. But it is nature alone who can create order and maintain peace among them. *All other authority spoils everything when it mixes in affairs, however well-intentioned it may be.*

[11] *Factum*, p. 284.

. . . Her first intention is for men to live comfortably by their labor. . . .

Thus finally, in order that this design may be effected, it is essential for everyone, in selling or buying, equally to profit. . . .

It has been said, and it is repeated again, that, in order that this happy situation may exist, it is necessary for all things and all products to be continually in equilibrium and to maintain proportional prices in relation to one another, and in the expenses which must be made in order to produce them. But it is known that from the moment anything which is in equilibrium, as a balance, receives the least increase on one of the sides, the other is immediately carried as high as if there were nothing there at all.

The same thing is true of all kinds of commerce. *It is all that one commodity can do to defend itself from pressure by another, even when there is no outside aid extended to its enemy;* but from the moment that aid is given, as is only too well known, it can be said immediately that all is lost, both for the product which profits from the misfortune of the other, and for the one which suffered it.[12]

Boisguilbert continued the subject and shows that he thought that economic boundaries transcend political ones.

[Nature] loves all men equally and likewise wishes them to be able to subsist without distinction. But in this manna of grain she is not always as liberal in one region as in another. She gives it in profusion in one province and even in a kingdom, while she deprives another wholly. But she intends that by mutual aid they shall create a balance [which is] mutually advantageous, and that by averaging these two extremes of extraordinary dearness or of undue cheapness of grain there will result a condition which will create public prosperity, which is nothing less than the maintenance of this equilibrium so essential to, or rather the sole principle of, wealth, although this is unknown to those who are concerned only to theorize.

In this, [nature] does not know different countries, or different sovereigns; and she does not concern herself with their friendliness or enmity, or with their warfare, provided they do not declare war against her. If that occurs, although through sheer ignorance, she scarcely hesitates to punish the rebellion that is made against her laws, as has been only too well found out through experience.[13]

Continuing, he said, that "in the Roman empire,"

[as] is authentically attested by Seneca, the philosopher, in his writings, almost all the known world recognized only one domina-

[12] *Dissertation sur les richesses,* pp. 408–409. My italics.

[13] *Ibid.,* pp. 410–411.

tion. As a result, diversity of sovereignty did not place any prince in this so-called and fatal interest of revolting against the laws of nature with regard to grain, so contrary to the situation which has since been experienced when there has been no desire to defer to her judgment. [But Seneca] also remarks in formal terms that never had nature, in his time, although he was very old, or in antiquity, of which he had a perfect knowledge, refused men, even in her greatest anger, the necessaries for their subsistence. If he had lived in these later times he assuredly would not have spoken in that manner.[14]

In other words, "it is for nature who produces her favors to distribute them, otherwise she takes her leave, which does not differ from a general upset." [15]

Here Boisguilbert expressed an ideal of economic internationalism; an internationalism which has its basis in the territorial division of labor. Out of this natural exchange of goods taking place freely and without interference, would come, he thought, the economic equilibrium which he regarded as the basis of prosperity. Here laissez faire is erected into a theoretical principle, just as the term itself is expressed in *Factum de la France.* The *Dissertation sur la nature des richesses* was Boisguilbert's final work. It is at the same time the most abstract and theoretical. At no point is any suggestion of restraint expressed. It seems reasonable to think that it may have represented his purest thought.

There are other indications that Boisguilbert had completely shaken off mercantilist thought, and that he was not a protectionist in principle. To show this there are, for instance, a few pertinent questions which may be answered: (1) How did he expect the exports of grain to be paid? (2) Was it his idea that foreign trade should be at the expense of foreigners?

[14] *Ibid.*, p. 411. Distinctly reminiscent of this is the following passage in *The Wealth of Nations:* "Were all nations to follow the liberal system of free exportation and free importation, the different states into which a great continent was divided would so far resemble the different provinces of a great empire. Among the different provinces of a great empire the freedom of the inland trade appears, both from reason and experience, not only the best palliative of a dearth, but the most effectual preventative of a famine; so would the freedom of the exportation and importation trade among the different states into which a great continent was divided."—*Wealth of Nations,* Bk. IV, p. 41.

[15] *Dissertation sur les richesses,* p. 414.

(3) Would he restrict the imports of other products than grain? (4) What was his general attitude toward other regulations and prohibitory measures? (5) Did he favor the Colbertian policy of artificially encouraging manufactures by means of protective measures?

(1) Boisguilbert, as has just been shown, saw all commerce as fundamentally an exchange of the surpluses of different areas. Money he regarded as playing a small part in such exchange except upon the part of a specie-producing country, which would necessarily use this product of the country to obtain other needs, just as any other country used its special product or products. It will be remembered that although he was begging Chamillart for permission to export grain, along with his other reforms, the latter complained of the plans because they carried with them no principle of obtaining specie from other countries.[16] Boisguilbert appeared to have regarded such importation as an incident which would naturally occur in the course of trade, and never as the specific object of it. France was spoken of very simply as having gotten her share of the specie of the new world.[17] As for France,

> Her power comes from the fact that, producing in quite great abundance all sorts of things necessary to life, not only sufficient to nourish the great number of inhabitants which she contains, but even to provide part for those who lack them, she is found surrounded at the same time with neighbors, who, not having the same advantage, exhaust their countries, in order to find some things fit for delicacies and luxuries, so that they may exchange with her for the necessaries. And this still not sufficing for their needs, they are constrained to make use of waggoners and seek in the farthest countries these same superfluities with which to obtain these same necessaries.[18]

Again, referring to the inability to export grain, he said, "far from a tax which has caused so general a ruin having brought some utility to the king, it is quite the opposite, as never having received a sou from it, he has lost the import duties on the *merchandise that the foreigners brought in [formerly] in coming to acquire our wheat.*"[19] Not that Boisguilbert failed to

[16] See above, pp. 64, 217.
[17] See above, pp. 48–49.
[18] *Le Détail,* p. 172.
[19] *Ibid.,* p. 208. My italics.

see the individual seller as receiving money from the sale of his goods, or the individual buyer as giving money. This was done by both. But it was merely the convenient intermediary between two dealers who could not immediately make use of one another's products. In this connection there is a passage which can easily be misunderstood by a casual reading isolated from his works as a whole:

Foreigners have gone to buy at Danzig and at Hamburg. And the too great quantity [of grain] which has remained in this country has caused the cultivation of the mediocre lands to cease, and the best ones to be neglected in many places. By this means there has been created a famine in silver not less injurious to the body of the State than that which has happened to wheat.[20]

Standing alone, this would appear to imply that the famine in money came from the fact that foreigners were no longer bringing money into the country; but that is not the meaning at all. It means that, because of the failure to sell the surplus grain, proportional prices were destroyed between grain and other products, which, affecting trade, took money out of circulation.

Talbot quoted a remark by Boisguilbert which he regarded as indicating that the latter had not completely rid himself of mercantilistic ideas.[21] Said Boisguilbert:

A country can be rich without very much silver and that one which has only silver, very poverty-stricken if it can be exchanged only with difficulty for these same products [i.e., necessities and superfluities]. Thus the ships of Spain no sooner reach Europe than it is necessary to carry almost all the silver to the countries whence one has obtained products to carry into the ones where the mines are situated. And this silver in these countries produces by a continual circulation the same effects that it has produced in [the country of] its birth, making more or less circulations and recirculations as it changes masters more or less often, that is, as more or less commerce or consumption is made.

But countries such as France, which produce products necessary to life, have this advantage over those from which silver is obtained: exchange is made in a very advantageous manner, considering that silver not being consumed at all by use, produces utilities without limits and without end for the country to which it is carried; whereas

[20] *Ibid.*, p. 207. [21] Talbot, pp. 76–78.

the goods that are given in counter-exchange are useful only a single time, perishing through use. But while silver has the quality of being unalterable by time and accidents, it has at the same time that of not increasing by keeping it as does other merchandise. And it produces utility not when in the coffer, but when it is hoarded as little as possible.[22]

In quoting only the first sentence of the second paragraph, Talbot had not sufficiently considered it in relation to the entire thought with which it is connected, or with Boisguilbert's thought as a whole. The latter never assumed that a country can do without a medium of exchange. Fundamentally he saw that goods buy goods. But they are exchanged indirectly by means of an intermediary. In a money economy "one can have nothing without money." But one buys money with goods, and goods with money. What Boisguilbert was emphasizing is the consumption of goods; but the circulation of money is essential to consumption. It is by means of its circulation that money "produces utilities without limit"; it is by means of rapidity of circulation that a country may be rich without much money. To become rich by spending silver, which was Boisguilbert's idea, was the very antithesis of the mercantilist idea of becoming rich by keeping silver. Furthermore, what Talbot overlooked, is that if Boisguilbert conceded a superior quality to the money one receives in exchange from a silver producing country, so did he concede a superior quality likewise to the merchandise which is given in exchange.

As a result of this passage Talbot, inferring that Boisguilbert desired to see silver enter the country, also thought that he failed to understand that the rise of prices within a country would make it impossible to continue to sell products abroad. Boisguilbert did not discuss this point, but the inference is quite in favor of his understanding the fact. For instance, speaking of the reason for the breakdown in trade, he said that it was because grains had not been permitted to rise in proportion to the increase in the prices of other products which had occurred as a result of the influx of new specie. This disturbance of proportional prices, he declared, had made it impossible for those deriving their income from the land to continue to buy

[22] *Ibid.*, pp. 210–211. The italics are mine, and constitute Talbot's quotation.

from other producers. Yet when he spoke of proportional prices as a requirement of trade, he included prices "from kingdom to kingdom."

(2) One of Boisguilbert's fundamental contributions to economic theory was a recognition that exchange can be profitable both to buyer and to seller. Indeed he declared that it must be profitable to both if commerce is to continue. Proportional prices must exist from kingdom to kingdom, and they are by definition such prices as permit profit for both parties to a bargain. In the matter of principles of trade he made no distinction between foreign and domestic transactions. "One country carries on business with another just as one merchant does with another." [23] To him domestic trade was of supreme importance from the standpoint of its proportionately greater amount. Foreign trade could never be more than a small part of the total trade of a country.[24] But Boisguilbert regarded this small amount as important because it determined the fate of the surpluses which ruined domestic trade and industry. Like any other trade it increases the wealth of the country by increasing the ability to consume. From this it results that the other country would have the same advantage.[25]

(3) Among his reforms of the duanes, concerning import duties, Boisguilbert would "conserve them in the state they are in, *for the sums only, while smoothing away the difficulties,* which return nothing to the king, and only repulse foreigners." From this it appears that Boisguilbert was chiefly interested in the duty as a fiscal measure. He did not object to customs duties as such; but he insisted that such taxes be "proportioned to the things on which they are levied," and that they should not be

[23] *Factum,* p. 327.

[24] See above, p. 50.

[25] The deprecation of the significance of foreign trade which is found in Boisguilbert, is by D'Argenson turned to scorn of it. "Depuis cette pestilentielle invention du Nouveau-Monde, le délire du commerce étranger s'est emparé de tous les gouvernemens, et, l'art étouffant la nature, on s'est nui à plaisir par faux raisonnemens. Les législateurs s'y sont creusé le cerveau, et à nous des tombeaux." "Laissez à ces petites républiques à être voituriers et courtiers: c'est le métier des pauvres petites gens; mais nous, état riche et abondant, demeurons chez nous."—*Mémoires et journal inédit,* Vol. V, pp. 370–371.

"four times more than the merchandise can bear." [26] Indeed, one of his fiscal discoveries was that an increase in a tax rate does not necessarily produce a corresponding increase in revenue, because it tends to suppress the thing taxed. He gave a historical example which shows that his ideal for trade was duties for revenue and not for protection:

So far as they have been moderate, they have caused no disorder; but as soon as they have been carried to an exorbitant height, they have been equally damaging to the king and to the State, since they have banished all foreign commerce. The people of other countries have been constrained to learn our manufactures while drawing our workmen, and to go to seek more cheaply our natural products, such as wheat and wine, in other countries which are enriched at our expense, and have learned to become good managers since we have ceased to be. Yet it seems, however, that this disorder should have been avoided more than all the others, after what happened in the time of Henry IV on the subject of the duanes, the recital of which, found in a contemporary history (*historien*), proves all that might be brought to bear on this subject. At the peace of Vervins although one of the articles of the treaty provided that import and export duties on merchandise in the States of the kings of France and Spain should remain as they had always been, without power to be raised reciprocally; nevertheless Philip III, newly arrived on the throne, being perhaps dissatisfied with the peace, wished to attack it through some infraction. In his ports he raised extremely all the import and export duties, and France having done likewise by way of reprisal, although the price of the farm [of the duties] had not been increased at all, the [tax] farmers were bankrupted completely, and could not satisfy their contracts, on account of the great diminution which this brought to consumption and to commerce.[27]

The test of such taxes, in other words, was whether or not the flow of goods was stopped.

(4) Some indication as to Boisguilbert's general attitude toward regulations and restrictions may be discerned in his attitude toward matters having nothing to do with imports and exports. There is, for instance, an atmosphere of toleration wherever religion is mentioned. "The new religion" and not "the so-called reformed religion," he had the courage to say. In this

[26] *Le Détail*, pp. 216, 254. *Factum*, p. 329. My italics.
[27] *Le Détail*, pp. 203–204.

connection there is his apology for *MM. les ministres,* and indirectly for heretics, as amusing as it is full of insight. Referring to the "mistakes" of ministers surrounded by selfishness and corruption, he said that they had resorted to the means used because "it was as impossible to act otherwise as it would have been for a subject born in error to embrace and to profess the Catholic religion in a country where there were only heretics." His liberality and his difficulties as a censor of the press have been mentioned. Likewise did he protest against forbidding those who live in the country to flee to the towns where the taille had been placed *en tarif.*[28]

So also did Boisguilbert speak disapprovingly of combinations among workmen to raise or sustain wages in time of a falling cost of living. Simple soul that he was, he thought each side, employer and employee, should see that it was mutually advantageous to deal justly with one another.[29] Although lieutenant of police, he likewise expressed himself as opposed to police regulations in the sale of grain by farmers in time of shortage. It only augmented the evil, he declared. He protested against the heartlessness of grain speculators and dealers; yet he did not suggest that any curb be placed upon them except by the importation and exportation of grain to equalize the supply. Finally he opposed limiting trade in grain to grain merchants, "organized as a body, with statutes of the Council."[30] Liberty, justice, and reason—everywhere one can discern the spirit of the man, there is adherence to these principles.[31]

(5) Boisguilbert did not speak directly of the encouragement Colbert gave to stimulate manufactures by means of protective measures; but in a letter to Chamillart he indicated what one

[28] *Le Détail,* p. 192. *Factum,* p. 318.
[29] See above, pp. 178–182.
[30] *Traité des grains,* pp. 355–356, 380–381. Letter of Aug. 30, 1708, *Correspondance des contrôleurs généraux,* Vol. III, No. 153, p. 49.
[31] One may contrast the spirit of Boisguilbert with that of D'Argenson, who, in comparison with the former, rendered lip service to the principle of liberty; who would enact "lois somptuaires contre les dépenses excessives; que chacun vive avec ordre et frugalité. Punir les dépensiers, récompenser les économes"; who would "bien régler les ordres de l'État et de supprimer les moyens trop faciles d'en sortir et de changer sa condition."—*Mémoires et journal inédit,* Vol. V, pp. 354, 373.

may regard to be his view. Referring to Colbert, he said, that "the *contrôle des exploits* . . . is almost the only fiscal edict (*édit bursal*) that can be said to have been advantageous to the people." [32] Now Cossa said that "Colbert's fiscal reforms . . . created French manufactures." [33] Thus one may infer that Boisguilbert did not approve of policies which had artificially stimulated manufactures; that of Colbert's tendency to regiment and control, the only advantage he saw was the system of checks against fraud and dishonesty in governmental affairs.

Practical Limitations on the Principle of Liberty

The fact remains, however, that if one attempts to sustain the view that Boisguilbert was not protectionist in principle, one must explain the reason for his position on two points: First, when he proposed eliminating export taxes, why did he not also suggest eliminating or reducing those on imports? Secondly, how can one account for the following paragraph which is responsible for Oncken's regarding Boisguilbert solely as an agrarian?

> The wheats of Barbary, as soon as they are excluded from Provence, will return to Languedoc six times this increase in tax, and to Provence likewise. If this province, producing very little [wheat] herself, buys grains at a dearer price, she will regain triple by the sale, augmented both in price and quantity, of her oils, olives, grapes, and dried figs, which one knows often to be valueless (*à rebut*) there. They are in that miserable state only because the provinces whose grains serve as counter-exchange to procure the remainder of their needs, are unable to do so on account of their abasement. This using [34] of the wheats of Barbary cannot at all be good except in times of sterility. There is nothing so harmful as its continuation in ordinary times. This continual import (*maintien*) is indeed only the effect of the special and personal interest of the army purveyors (*munitionnaires*), who, in order to gain on their sales by obtaining their supplies as cheaply as possible, put themselves to little trouble for the general good of the king and the people. To this [must be] joined the individual advantage of the tax farmers (*entrepreneurs*), who are taken care of in this commerce by protection bought at a money price.

[32] See above, p. 39.
[33] *An Introduction to the Study of Political Economy*, London, 1893, p. 207.
[34] *Établissement.* Literally, "exploitation."

To admit foreign grains except in times of sterility, especially in a fertile country such as France, is a great error in policy. England [who understands this,] pays a bounty on their exportation. Spain, who, on account of the almost continual abandonment of the cultivation of the greatest part of her best lands, would seem to be excusable in committing it, considering that dearness is more common than a reasonable price, understands at the same time so well the horrible inconvenience of abasing a product of this nature in the years of abundance, that, since the union of the two monarchies in the royal house of Bourbon, she has begged us not to carry wheat to her on these occasions, although it would profit the poor, to speak the erroneous language that has reigned in France for so long.[35]

Does not this passage, and the fact that Boisguilbert appeared to have been primarily concerned with the elimination of export duties on grain indicate that his interest was simply to raise agricultural prices, and to favor farmers and landowners? Certainly he wished to raise such prices; certainly he wished to aid farmers and landowners. Nevertheless, before accepting the view that this was his only concern it is essential to see whether there is any reason for his attitude on grain importation, and for the paradox of one who declared that "nature breathes only liberty," and that it is necessary to "leave her alone," desiring at the same time to restrict the importation of grain.

It was stated above that in what may be considered Boisguilbert's only purely theoretical work he did not speak of keeping out exports. It is not without significance that in the works which contain his practical proposals there should be found the limitation on the principle of liberty. It is essential to repeat what should by this time be remembered, namely, that the enunciation of theoretical principles was with Boisguilbert incidental to practical proposals for reform. His concern was to make proposals which would be acceptable.

Boisguilbert wrote after an interval of forty years following Colbert's introduction of the principle of the protection of manufactures. Although he appeared to have disapproved of the principle, he accepted the situation as inevitably established. There is a significant passage which indicates this very fact.

The two hundred vocations which today enter into the composition

[35] *Factum*, pp. 343-344.

of a civilized and opulent State, which begin with bakers and end with actors, are, for the most part, first called into existence, the one after the other, by voluptuousness only. *But once they are introduced, or have taken root in some fashion, they become thereafter a part of the substance of a State, and they cannot again be disjointed or separated without immediately altering the body. From the least or the least necessary they are all like the Emperor Augustus, of whom it was very justly said that he should not have been born, or that he should not die.*[36]

In view of the fact that the manufactures introduced by Colbert were those of luxuries for which France was to become so famous, it is impossible not to regard this paragraph as referring directly to the result of his policy. It throws further light on Boisguilbert's attitude toward Colbert. It was the growing complexity of economic life, the multiplication of vocations, which Boisguilbert regarded as rendering a State susceptible to what he called *la misère moderne*—want in the midst of plenty. Colbert it was who had changed a simple economic organization into a complex one. He had forced nature; he had disturbed the balance in the economic life by introducing the artificial, and the unnecessary, and by subordinating the natural products of the State to them. To Boisguilbert, Colbert had not been the friend, but unwittingly the enemy of the State; he had subjected it to hazards which it otherwise would have escaped.

This passage explains the retention of the import duties. They would not be increased or decreased. The industries which owed their existence to them at their existing height would be allowed to continue undisturbed. According to Boisguilbert's theory it would have been fatal to do otherwise. There is indication that he had thought out the matter of the transfer of labor, at least, from one employment to another. But in view of the nature of his writings, which was to promulgate an immediate policy, and in view of the fact that he was combating the opposition of his enemies who declared that he wished to upset the State, he would not have dared to make such a proposal either for capital or for labor had his ideas developed to such a point. It would have been

[36] *Dissertation sur les richesses*, p. 404. My italics.

impolitic for him to go further, and would have made more certain the defeat of his ideas.

As to export duties, the emphasis in *Le Détail* was not on their complete elimination; the demand was rather that products subjected to the duanes be taxed according to what they could bear. Nor did he suggest keeping out Barbary wheat. In *Factum*, published twelve years later, Barbary wheat was to be kept out, and "no quarter" was to be given to export duties. The difference in emphasis and in policy must have been due to the changed conditions. From 1693 to 1700 the price of grain was high, and France was importing rather than exporting it. The country as a whole was prosperous, Boisguilbert said, from 1696 to 1700; but thereafter came a marked change. Encouraged by high prices, the production and surplus of grain increased. The price fell until that of small wheat in the provinces was only six livres per setier "at the most." [87] Yet the surplus could not be exported. The export tax of sixty-six livres per *muid* prevented it. Such a rate amounted approximately to five and one-half livres per setier, or at the existing price of small grain in the provinces, it was almost 100 percent. It was obviously something in the nature of a strong protest against such absurd taxation which led Boisguilbert to demand that "no quarter" be given to export duties.

Why did Boisguilbert specify Barbary wheat as necessary to be kept out of the country? It seems reasonable to think that this wheat represented a peculiar problem which influenced him in the formulation of his grain policy. Did he regard it as constituting fair competition with that of Languedoc? What he had to say with regard to the Moors leads one to conclude that he did not. Speaking of their promise to make the sterile lands of Provence and those around Bordeaux as fertile as artificially-made soils around great cities, if, on their expulsion from Spain, they would be permitted to come into France, he said: "as there would have been no difference on the side of nature, but only of the expenses, the harvest, *sustained by the frugality of the people,*

[87] See note, p. 134, for changes in the price of grain at Rosoy.

would have compensated them, which would not be the case with the people of the north, who eat very much more, and wish to make more expense." [38] Certainly Boisguilbert, with his emphasis upon the importance of consumption, would have frowned upon the army purveyors for buying this cheap supply which could undersell the grains of Languedoc resting upon higher living standards. Furthermore, Languedoc constituted a better, and a natural market for the surplus products of Provence. Barbary's products, with the exception of grain—her oils, grapes, olives, and figs were also those of Provence, hence there could not be between Provence and Barbary a natural exchange of surplus products. As it was, all the advantage of the trade was going to two special groups: the army purveyors and the tax farmers. But there is another fact to be considered. Bâville, one of the principal opponents of Boisguilbert's reforms,[39] was intendant in Languedoc. One can conceive that the paragraph on Barbary wheat was in part a bid to gain his support, or at least to reduce his opposition. It can be assumed that Boisguilbert was compelled, by the urgency of the situation and the extent of the opposition, to stoop to the rôle of politician, as well as rise to that of economist and statesman.

There was another disturbing factor in the wheat situation which could have led Boisguilbert to declare that it was "a great error in policy" for France to import grain except in time of shortage. England was dumping wheat. Obviously referring to this, he said that Holland, "producing almost no necessaries of life, has them in abundance, and cheaper than at the place where they grow." [40] Evidently Boisguilbert was prepared to take defensive measures against an import which could further demoralize the agricultural situation in France. Indeed, he has a passage which leads one to think that this was occurring in the years after 1700. The English, he said, "give money at a pure profit

[38] *Traité des grains*, p. 376. My italics.

[39] See above, pp. 70–73.

[40] *Le Détail*, p. 171. Adam Smith quotes Sir Matthew Decker, "an excellent authority," as saying that the English bounty "enables foreigners, the Dutch in particular, not only to eat our corn cheaper than they otherwise could do, but sometimes to eat it cheaper than even our own people can do upon the same occasions."—*Wealth of Nations*, Bk. IV, p. 15.

to those who sell grains abroad. [They sell them] *even to their greatest enemies,* considering that it would be necessary to sell them to the demons themselves if they should wish them." [41] Boisguilbert declared that the importation and exportation of grain in "a country as fertile as France" was of no "consideration for the kingdom in relation to its subsistence." Its purpose was "to equilibrate the balance and the supply." [42] France normally had an excess over her requirements, and her periodical shortages were the result of a swing in the opposite direction induced by the disturbed equilibrium between the forces of supply and demand. It was this disturbance which he sought to eliminate. But it should be noted that he was not making an especial rule for France alone. It was a general rule, applicable to any agricultural country which must try to maintain economic stability, which he set forth.

Boisguilbert was an agriculturist, and this may have led him to emphasize, in his theory, the place of agriculture in the national economy. While he must have been supremely interested in maintaining it in a healthy state for its own sake, yet the certainty and the sincerity of his interest in the well-being of all France cannot be doubted. His interest in her economic problems extended back to the time when he personally was prospering in his own agricultural undertakings. One must go deeper than either personal or class interest to find the explanation of his interest in agricultural problems, of his insistence upon unrestricted exportation, and of his desire to restrict the importation of grain.

There are, indeed, five well-defined reasons for this emphasis.

(1) Boisguilbert was dealing with the actual social and economic problems of the country. Yet at the time he was writing the outstanding fact in France was the decay of agriculture. It was inevitable that any book on economic or social problems should center upon this theme. It was, for instance, for the relief of those on the land, as well as to relieve the king's purse,

[41] *Traité des grains,* p. 374. My italics. France and England were at war at the time this was written, and certainly France was the greatest enemy of England at the time.

[42] *Ibid.,* p. 381.

that Vauban proposed his *dime royale.* It is the reconstruction of life in the countryside which forms the underlying theme of Fénelon's *Télémaque.*

(2) Discrimination against agriculture had existed since the famine of 1661. Its ruin was not an accident, but the result of a policy deliberately pursued, if not by Colbert, certainly by his successors. Boisguilbert was struggling to show the error and the effect of such a policy. Comparing prices prior to 1660, he said that since then, as a result of the policy adopted,

> [prices of] all products except grains, have *doubled* due to very natural causes (which are simply the quantities of silver which daily arrive in Europe), and concerning which an especial chapter will be written. All kinds of products are tranquilly permitted to take their quota of increase in price, as they have always done since the discovery of the New World. This justice is refused to grains alone. It is believed that everything has been gained in obliging a farmer, or his landlord, who are only one and the same thing, or a like interest, to give their grains at the same price which they had fifty years ago, while they are constrained to buy all products, both for personal needs as well as the things necessary for agriculture, at double [such prices].[43]

In other words, if agricultural prices were emphasized, it was because there was a definite reason for it.

(3) Boisguilbert was combating popular prejudices against the exportation of grain.

> In order to explain still more clearly the rôle of foreign commerce in grain, both exportation and importation, one can say that everything about it is violent and extreme, because everything is exposed to the impetuosity of the public, or rather of a blind and tumultuous troop which does not understand what is advantageous and what is harmful to it. The only thing which counts is that the people are in a seditious mood. And as they take alarm at the exportation of a very little quantity of grain, a thousand times less than that which the low price has caused to be destroyed, either because of the neglect of the cultivator, or because of the wasteful consumption, [so] they believe themselves to be menaced by a famine on the arrival of a little quantity of foreign wheat.[44]

The trouble was, he said, that it was not known how much

[43] *Traité des grains*, p. 357. Boisguilbert's italics.
[44] *Ibid.*, p. 381.

grain was consumed in the country and how much was produced, and consequently how much could be exported, all of which he attempted to estimate.[45] What he wished to do was to convince the *éclairés* that they did not "merit paradise" in thinking grain should be at a low price for the sake of the poor, and to conjure the "panicky terror of the people which causes them to throw themselves headlong into a very deep and rapid stream, in order to flee from an enemy which has neither feet nor legs with which to reach them, nor arms to harm them." [46]

(4) Boisguilbert's emphasis upon grain, and his making an exceptional case of it, was inherent in his theory itself. Agriculture he regarded as the starting point in the flow of income. Furthermore, he observed from his analysis of the value of grain, that there were certain peculiar characteristics which differentiated the behavior of its price from other prices. Its price was so susceptible to variations that an especial effort must be made to maintain an equilibrium between demand and supply. England used a bounty on exportation, and Holland destroyed a portion of her supply of pepper in years of abundance to keep the price from sinking below the cost of production. Boisguilbert approved what he thought to be the principle back of each of these policies, although he never suggested such policies for France. But he would have brought about the evenness of supply which nature fails to give in any country or place, by permitting free exportation and permitting importation to act as a balance in time of shortage. He gave an explanation which must indeed have bewildered his contemporaries:

It is easy to see, by all that has just been said, of what consequence it is in a country, to maintain abundance therein, to prevent any merchandise from being superabundant (*à rebut*), which is the means to make it dry up. For, causing the entrepreneurs to lose, they cease their traffic entirely, which causes a high payment (*qui fait payer la folle enchère*) for the preceding abasement of the product.[47]

[45] See Horn, pp. 184–187, for a criticism of Boisguilbert's statistics on this point.

[46] Condorcet, in his *Réflexions sur le commerce des blés,* devoted chapter iv ("Des préjuges du peuple sur le commerce des blés,") of Part II of this subject.

[47] *Traité des grains,* p. 389.

Boisguilbert saw the pendulum, price, motivated by the continual changes in supply, swing back and forth as a form of perpetual motion. It must be induced to come to rest.

(5) The final point with respect to what appears to be a departure from laissez faire principles has to do with the inflexibility in the prices of all things for which those living from the land must make expenditures. When it was a question of their fall, the change was resisted by everyone, from the laborer who must be hired, to the wig and carriage maker.

> One has set forth this detail with respect to the price which grains must have because the prosperity of a State consists in a continual commerce, so that neither land, nor workers, nor works, be ever in a moment of repose, which produces the same effect with respect to money. This interruption or this disturbance comes only from their abasement after one has put a price on products on the rise of grain [prices], which is not at all followed when the situation changes. *But as it is impossible to make all the parties concerned of whom one has just spoken, understand reason, and lower* [*their prices*] *when grain increases* [*in quantity*], *it is necessary to support the price that grain has once attained,* and not to destroy the gaiety of the heart, as one can say has been done for forty years under pretext of giving pleasure to the poor, although that ruins them entirely, as has been made clear.[48]

Economic perfection Boisguilbert recognized as an ideal, which, he said, is scarcely to be found except in Holland and China. But he would not give up the ideal because perfection is recognized from the start as an impossibility. "It is necessary, then, to do as nature does: when she cannot produce a perfect subject, she forms a less perfect one." [49]

Conclusion

Boisguilbert would have denied that the principle of liberty would be annulled by the exception he had made. There was

[48] *Ibid.*, pp. 391–392. My italics.

[49] *Ibid.*, pp. 389–390. May one not say that Adam Smith echoes this sentiment when he says apropos the English bounty of 1688: "So far, therefore, this law seems to be inferior to the ancient system. With all its imperfections, however, we may perhaps say of it what was said of the laws of Solon, that, though not the best in itself, it is the best which the interests, prejudices, and temper of the time would admit of. It may perhaps in due time prepare the way for a better."—*Wealth of Nations*, Bk. IV, p. 45.

only one way, he thought, that all men could live by their labor, namely, in the maintenance of proportional prices, which he attempted to bring about. In any case, he was statesman as well as economist. His interest was in men rather than in theories as such, and he was doctrinaire only about the necessity to obtain practical results.

All in all, it would seem to be as unreasonable to deprive Boisguilbert of a place in the history of laissez faire because in practical application he would limit the theoretical principle, as it would be to declare that Turgot did not believe in liberty in the exportation of grain because he gave liberty only in the internal trade when he became controller general. Turgot, the statesman, dared not allow the freedom of exportation which Turgot, the economist, would have approved, because to have proposed so radical a measure would have endangered such other reforms as might be undertaken.

It may be added that there is a fundamental agreement between Boisguilbert's views and those of Adam Smith and Ricardo on the relationship of liberty and equilibrium. *If* there were no restrictions on trade, said Boisguilbert, every producer would attain his costs. What he proposed as a method of securing this desirable situation was the starting point of Smith and Ricardo. *Assuming* conditions of perfect liberty, they stated as the basis of their reasoning, then natural, or normal, or cost-covering prices would obtain.

Certainly it cannot be gainsaid that if Boisguilbert failed to live up to his principle of liberty, he at least expressed the ideal. It must not be forgotten that his objective was not to outline a science, but to promulgate an art of harmonious economic relationships. He wrote for a given time in the world's history. If his ideals are universal in their application it is because, basically, economic problems change little from era to era. Economic justice for the masses, and freedom to trade were the urgent needs of France in 1700. Boisguilbert championed both principles.

It is perhaps fitting to add that although Boisguilbert loved France and sighed over her state, there was nothing chauvinistic about him. He thought quite dispassionately that her natural equipment was superior to that of the other countries of Europe, but he thought that, excepting Spain, none used their resources so badly. England and Holland were his ideals among the contemporaneous States.[50] He admired their commercial acumen, the liberality of their governments, and their political institutions under which the people "jealous of their liberty" determined their own fates. In his impetuous manner he idealized them accordingly. He would have had France model herself after them.

[50] It is scarcely necessary to recall that Boisguilbert's views with regard to France, Spain, Holland, and England were shared by Adam Smith.

XVI
THE PROTOTYPE OF THE WEALTH OF NATIONS

Tout le monde veut être riche.

IN A preceding chapter an attempt has been made to show the relation between Boisguilbert's concept of economic equilibrium and the development of static theory. In the following chapters the similarity between the fundamental ideas of Boisguilbert, as presented in his *Dissertation sur la nature des richesses, de l'argent et des tributs,* and those of Adam Smith in *The Wealth of Nations* will be set forth.

In no place did Smith refer to Boisguilbert by name; but in the following paragraph he made a remark which, it must be assumed, referred to Boisguilbert and to Vauban. Speaking of Colbert, Smith said:

The industry and commerce of a great country he endeavoured to regulate upon the same model as the departments of a public office; and instead of allowing every man to pursue his own interest in his own way, upon the liberal plan of equality, liberty, and justice, he bestowed upon certain branches of industry extraordinary privileges, while he laid others under as extraordinary restraints. He was not only disposed, like other European ministers, to encourage more the industry of the towns than that of the country, but, in order to support the industry of the towns, he was willing even to depress and keep down that of the country. In order to render provisions cheap to the inhabitants of the towns, and thereby to encourage manufactures and foreign commerce, he prohibited altogether the exportation of corn, and thus excluded the inhabitants of the country from every foreign market for by far the most important part of the produce of their industry. This prohibition, joined to the restraints imposed by the ancient provincial laws of France upon the transportation of corn from one province to another, and to the arbitrary and degrading taxes which are levied upon the cultivators in almost all the provinces, discouraged and kept down the agriculture of that country very much below the state to which it would naturally have risen in so very fertile a soil and so very happy a climate. This state of discouragement and depression was felt more or less in every part of the country, and *many different inquiries were set on foot concerning the causes of it.* One of those causes appeared to be the preference given, by the institutions of Mr. Colbert, to the industry of the towns above that of the country.[1]

The Thesis and the Title

Boisguilbert called the work with which we are here chiefly concerned, a *Dissertation on the Nature of Wealth, Money, and Taxes.* In it he attempted to determine what it is that makes a nation, its people, and its prince, rich or poor. Adam Smith called his great work *An Inquiry into the Nature and Causes of the Wealth of Nations.* Boisguilbert, in other words, seventy years before *The Wealth of Nations* appeared, posed the question and attempted the analysis which Smith later was to complete, from the outline which Boisguilbert had drawn up. From the content of his work Boisguilbert could have used Smith's title. Conversely, from its content, Smith could have called *The Wealth of Nations* a *Dissertation on the Nature of Wealth, Money, and Taxes.* Finally, their ideas are in agreement as to what creates and constitutes the wealth of a nation. Wealth, said Boisguilbert, consists of the necessities, and the superfluities of life which a nation consumes. This wealth, he said, is the result of the labor of the masses, made possible and increased by the interchange of superfluous products. Smith combined these ideas in the famous first sentence and paragraph of the Introduction to *The Wealth of Nations:*

> The annual labour of every nation is the fund which originally supplies it with all the necessaries and conveniencies of life which it annually consumes, and which consist always either in the immediate produce of that labour, or in what is purchased with that produce from other nations.[2]

[1] *Wealth of Nations,* Bk. IV, p. 162. My italics. Smith, in this paragraph, again uses the expression "so very fertile a soil and so very happy a climate" to which attention has been called as closely resembling a phrase in *Le Détail.* See note, p. 132.

[2] Although Boisguilbert in his definition of wealth never speaks of the *annual* consumption, yet all his calculations and references to the diminution of wealth in France are "per year."

The Purpose

Boisguilbert's ideas were the outgrowth of the conditions existing in France during his lifetime. In a predominately agricultural country he saw the decline of agriculture, the stagnation of industry and trade, and with it all an impoverishment of all classes. His attempt to analyze the underlying causes led inevitably to his theory of the interrelation of agriculture and industry, to his emphasis upon the importance of exchange of products, to the consumption of the masses, and to his negation of the importance of the precious metals. Theoretically he demolished the mercantile system. His purpose, however, was not to enter into theory, but to influence the practical policy of France. That his writings took on the significance of economic generalizations was a by-product of this desire to influence policy by giving explicit reasons for his ideas. Abstract thought appears in no place to have been deliberately pursued for its own sake.

Adam Smith, on the other hand, was preoccupied with his generalizations, and with the reasoned and deliberate destruction of the theory of mercantilism. But, like Boisguilbert, he proposed a method whereby the wealth of nations would be increased. So far, however, as *The Wealth of Nations* can be regarded as a handbook for a nation's policies, this function or purpose must be regarded as subordinate to the purely academic interest in ideas and thought for their own sake.

The Method

Each author relied upon the historical method combined with logical reasoning. In Boisguilbert the tendency to abstract thought and generalizations from the conditions described and analyzed was halting and at times indistinct. In Smith both were well defined and fully developed. Boisguilbert's early interest in the classics led him to make frequent allusions to the economic conditions of antiquity. At the same time he ranged far and wide over contemporary history to illustrate his points. Chiefly, however, he looked to earlier conditions in France—especially to the reign of Henry IV, the king, who, in Boisguilbert's eyes, could do no wrong—in his attempt to interpret the conditions of his time. In comparison with *The Wealth of Nations* enriched with its store of historical references, the *Dissertation on the Nature of Wealth* appears in many ways childlike and naïve today. Yet, economically speaking, in the latter is set forth the technique of a Van Mander which was to culminate in the art of a Rembrandt.

The Form

The resemblance in form of the two studies is not without significance. Each begins with a description of conditions in the natural state. The conclusions with regard to the advantages and disadvantages of this state in contrast to a state of civilization are, however, diametrically opposed. There follows in each book a disquisition upon the division of labor and exchange. The third portion of each work is devoted to money. Boisguilbert stated that "it is apropos to make an especial chapter for gold and silver, in order to show whence this disorder has entered into the world." [3] Speaking of "the universal instrument of commerce," Smith said that he would "now proceed to examine . . . the rules which men naturally observe in exchanging" goods "either for money or for one another." [4]

Boisguilbert devoted chapter four to a description and analysis of economic conditions in times of prosperity. He ended this with the remark that "enough has been said of prosperity; it is now necessary to come to the depression, although the explanation of the one includes the picture of the other." [5] Chapter five was devoted to the condition of society at such a time. Smith stated, "I shall endeavour to explain what are the conditions which naturally determine the rate of wages, and in what manner those circumstances are affected by the riches or poverty, by the advancing, stationary, or declining state of the society." [6] Likewise he proposed to do the same for rent and for profits. Here is to be found, in a sense, the major distinction, between Boisguilbert and Smith. Smith minimized Boisguilbert's em-

[3] *Dissertation sur les richesses,* p. 395. [4] *Wealth of Nations,* Bk. I, p. 30.
[5] *Dissertation sur les richesses,* p. 407. [6] *Wealth of Nations,* Bk. I, p. 65.

phasis upon economic change, or periods of prosperity and depression. Instead of devoting chapters or a book to this subject, he reduced the importance of economic fluctuations by considering them as temporary departures from central tendencies, and in themselves of insufficient importance for prolonged analysis. Hence we find him substituting for Boisguilbert's chapters analyzing periods of prosperity and depression, a book devoted to the historical review "Of the Different Progress of Opulence in Different Nations." But it is scarcely necessary to point out the suggestion of similarity even here. Finally, after this divergence, each one ended with a study of the manner in which the policies of the sovereign can add to, or detract from the wealth of the nation.

In general, then, to summarize, the two works follow this plan of development:

Topic	*Boisguilbert*	*Smith*
1. The natural state. 2. The division of labor and exchange.	Chaps. i–iii	Bk.I, i–iii
3. The use of money in exchange.	Chaps. ii–iii	Bk.I, iv–xi
4. *Boisguilbert:* An analysis of conditions in a nation in times of prosperity and depression.	Chaps. iv–v	Bk.II
Smith: Of the Different Progress of Opulence in Different Nations.		Bk.III
5. The policies of the sovereign as a factor in adding to or hampering the development of national wealth.	Chap. vi	Bks.IV–V

This outline appears to be an oversimplification of so complex a work as *The Wealth of Nations.* It is intended, indeed, to reduce it to its lowest terms. Objection may be made, for instance, to the inclusion of the chapters on value and the shares of distribution in Book I, chapters iv–xi, under the heading of the use of money in exchange. But on second thought it will be remembered that Smith was proceeding in a very logical manner with the analysis of the use of money, and that this led him naturally, but as a digression, indeed, to the phenomenon of the price of commodities, which in turn led him into an analysis of the nature of value, of the real basis upon which goods are exchanged, and finally he was led into distribution through an attempt to analyze "the component parts of the prices of commodities." In the same manner one may regard Book II, "Of the Nature, Accumulation, and Employment of Stock," as a digression on, or, if preferred, an amplification of, the subject of money.

Finally, it is essential to note that while each work follows the general order of subject matter given here, each writer was addicted to the grievous habit, from the standpoint of style, of creating a *mélange* out of his work. While very much less marked in Smith, on account of his greater clarity of expression, in his work there is likewise to be found the same disorderly treatment of material which particularly characterizes Boisguilbert's writings.

The Content

THE SIGNIFICANCE OF THE LABOR SUPPLY

Adam Smith began *The Wealth of Nations* with the following statement:

> The annual labour of every nation is the fund which originally supplies it with all the necessaries and conveniencies of life which it annually consumes, and which consist always either in the immediate produce of that labour, or in what is purchased with that product from other nations.

Boisguilbert stressed the labor supply less than did Smith. He was more concerned with showing the dependence of production upon consumption and exchange. Nevertheless, the importance of the labor supply was frequently brought out.

Speaking of the inability of a poor creature to carry a disproportionate burden of taxes, he said that "he is dragged to prison and is held there for months [causing] an increase in loss of goods, namely, the loss of his time and his work, which is his only revenue, as well as that of the State and of the prince."[7] And again, referring to the inability to consume in times of depression, he said:

This situation being encountered by innumerable subjects, one sees by that the loss which it has cost the masses, who alone, in spite of the error of the rich, are those who can procure for them their wealth in the profit of the sale which is made, while this écu apart from a powerful man would never have been anything but an écu, both with respect to the individual and all the body of the State.[8]

Boisguilbert and Smith saw that only a portion of the potential labor supply is utilized in the production of goods. But beyond that there is a fundamental difference in their views. Boisguilbert, contrasting primitive and civilized conditions, declared that "today men are wholly divided into two classes, namely, one which does nothing and enjoys all the pleasures, and another, which, working from morning to night, is found scarcely in possession of the necessities, and is indeed often deprived of them entirely."[9] Smith repeated the first part of this idea:

Among civilized and thriving nations, on the contrary . . . a great number of people do not labour at all, many of whom consume the produce of ten times, frequently of a hundred times more labour than the greater part of those who work; yet, [he adds] the produce of the whole labour of the society is so great, that all are often abundantly supplied, and a workman, even of the lowest and poorest order, if he is frugal and industrious, may enjoy a greater share of the necessaries and conveniencies of life than is possible for any savage to acquire.[10]

The mordant philosophy of one who saw individuals helpless in the grasp of circumstances, was succeeded by a strictly individualistic point of view. Smith saw man master of his own economic destiny through frugality and industry to a far greater extent than Boisguilbert would have conceded always to be possible.

[7] *Dissertation sur les richesses*, p. 402.
[8] *Ibid.*, p. 412.
[9] *Ibid.*, p. 399.
[10] *Wealth of Nations*, Introduction, p. 2.

THE DIVISION OF LABOR AND EXCHANGE

This division of labour, from which so many advantages are derived [said Smith] is not originally the effect of any human wisdom, which foresees and intends that general opulence to which it gives occasion. It is the necessary, though very slow and gradual consequence of a certain propensity in human nature which has in view no such extensive utility; the propensity to truck, barter, and exchange one thing for another.[11]

Smith did not know, he said, whether this is an inherent characteristic, or simply the result of the faculty of reason and speech. Boisguilbert in his simple description did not commit himself as to cause and effect, but throughout his writings there is an attitude that anything which interferes with the exchange of products, which in turn interferes with the division of labor, is an interference with the laws of nature. He has original man engaging in each process:

The first two workers in the world, who were at the same time the two rulers of it, divided these two trades: the one cultivated the earth in order to have grain, and the other tended the flocks in order to clothe himself, and the mutual exchange that they could make enabled them reciprocally to enjoy one another's work.[12]

Boisguilbert saw the division of labor as developing from an abundance of agricultural products:

These two hundred vocations which constitute the perfection of the most civilized and productive States are all children of the fruits of the earth. The extent to which it is in condition to produce with abundance and to make [it possible] to consume . . . is what gives birth to them, commencing with the most necessary, such as the baker and the tailor, and ending with the actor, who is the last work of luxury, and the highest mark of an excess of the superfluous.[13]

Smith expressed the same idea in a slightly different manner:

But when by the improvement and cultivation of land the labour of one family can provide food for two, the labour of half the society becomes sufficient to provide food for the whole. The other half, therefore, or at least the greater part of them, can be employed in

[11] *Ibid.*, Bk. I, p. 15.
[12] *Dissertation sur les richesses*, p. 399. [13] *Ibid.*, p. 405.

providing other things, or in satisfying other wants and fancies of mankind.[14]

Smith emphasized the fact that

it is the great multiplication of the productions of all the different arts, in consequence of the divisions of labour, which occasions, in a well-governed society, that universal opulence which extends itself to the lowest ranks of the people. Every workman has a great quantity of his own work to dispose of beyond what he himself has occasion for; and every other workman being in exactly the same situation, he is enabled to exchange a great quantity of his goods for a great quantity, or, what comes to the same thing, for the price of a great quantity of theirs. He supplies them abundantly with what they have occasion for, and they accommodate him as amply with what he has occasion for, and a general plenty diffuses itself through all the different ranks of the society.[15]

Corresponding with this in thought is Boisguilbert's fantastically exaggerated picture of the importance of exchange, as shown through its breakdown: "Everyone perishes, as has been said, from an excess of one product and a dearth of others, which throws all individuals into poverty, whereas exchange of these products would have made them very happy." [16]

But Boisguilbert also spoke positively of the advantages of the division of labor.

[Individuals] who are so completely devoted to possessing all the earth and [who would procure] all its wealth, would end by being poor wretched creatures if they could not enjoy the labor of their fellow men. And would they not prefer the condition of beggars in an inhabited world? Because, in the first place, aside from the fact that it would be necessary for them to produce all their requirements, far from serving their luxurious desires by that, it would be an outstanding achievement, if, by continual work, they could reach the point of procuring necessaries; moreover, with the least illness they would perish from lack of assistance, or rather from despair.[17]

Here is pictured a man unable to exchange his products for lack of a market; as a consequence he is compelled to forego

[14] *Wealth of Nations*, Bk. I, p. 164.
[15] *Ibid.*, Bk. I, pp. 12–13.
[16] *Dissertation sur les richesses*, p. 422. See above, p. 224, for complete quotation.
[17] *Ibid.*, p. 394.

the benefits of the division of labor. This paragraph could well have inspired the following and much quoted passage in *The Wealth of Nations:*

> As it is the power of exchanging that gives occasion to the division of labour, so the extent of this division must always be limited by the extent of that power, or, in other words, by the extent of the market. When the market is very small, no person can have any encouragement to dedicate himself entirely to one employment, for want of the power to exchange all that surplus part of the produce of his own labour, which is over and above his own consumption, for such parts of the produce of other men's labour as he has occasion for.[18]

Boisguilbert explained how the use of money in exchange arises.

> Commerce and exchange can no longer be made from hand to hand as in the age of innocence. The seller of one product does not often trade with the seller of another product for which he actually has a need, and for the obtaining of which he gives up his own. Money then comes to the aid, and the receipt of it which he procures from his buyer, is an evidence, with guarantee, that his demand will be effective in some place where the seller of the product which he desires is found. He will obtain as much [of this product] at the current price as is commensurate with his own product which he has previously relinquished.[19]

Smith developed the idea in his paragraph on the inconvenience of the double coincidence of barter:

> But when the division of labour first began to take place, this power of exchanging must frequently have been very much clogged and embarrassed in its operations. One man, we shall suppose, has more of a certain commodity than he himself has occasion for, while another has less. The former consequently would be glad to dispose of, and the latter to purchase, a part of this superfluity. But if this latter should chance to have nothing that the former stands in need of, no exchange can be made between them. The butcher has more meat in his shop than he himself can consume, and the brewer and the baker would each of them be willing to purchase a part of it. But they have nothing to offer in exchange, except the different productions of their respective trades, and the butcher is

[18] *Wealth of Nations,* Bk. I, p. 19.

[19] *Dissertation sur les richesses,* pp. 396–397.

already provided with all the bread and beer which he has immediate occasion for. No exchange can, in this case, be made between them. He cannot be their merchant, nor they his customers; and they are all of them thus mutually less serviceable to one another. In order to avoid the inconveniency of such situations, every prudent man in every period of society, after the first establishment of the division of labour, must naturally have endeavoured to manage his affairs in such a manner, as to have at all times by him, besides the peculiar produce of his own industry, a certain quantity of some one commodity or other, such as he imagined few people would be likely to refuse in exchange for the produce of their industry.[20]

Adam Smith was less of a realist than Boisguilbert. This difference was doubtless in large measure the result of the difference in their backgrounds. Smith was the sheltered academic thinker; Boisguilbert lived in the midst of men gaining their livelihoods in agriculture and trade, whose differences it was his function as magistrate to resolve. Their dissimilarity in this respect was also in part the result of the difference in the periods in which they lived. At the end of the seventeenth century and at the threshold of the eighteenth century, France was suffering from the disturbances of wars, a burdensome and unjust tax system, and an impoverished agricultural class. She was undergoing a period of secular decline, with a consequent drag upon any revival of trade. On the contrary, throughout the eighteenth century, England was sweeping forward with an economic vitality which would necessarily tend to shorten and to minimize any temporary setbacks. The result was that Adam Smith saw nothing but good in the division of labor. He idealized it and waxed little short of lyrical with regard to it. Boisguilbert, on the contrary, was for once the more balanced of the two. Like Smith he was enthusiastic over the theoretical and practical advantages of the division of labor and its concomitant, exchange. But he saw one thing far more clearly than did Smith: that is, the highly integrated and interdependent character of economic life. The potentialities for harm, as well as for good, and the consequences as he observed them, oppressed him. It was his

[20] *Wealth of Nations*, Bk. I, pp. 24–25. Professor Cannan notes a close resemblance between this passage and Harris, *Money and Coins*, Pt. I, §§ 19, 20.

theoretical view with regard to the division of labor and exchange and his practical experience in an everyday world which led Boisguilbert into an *impasse* in his thinking which he seemed never to have resolved to his complete satisfaction. It was this conflict between the theoretical and the practical which led him to question the relative advantages and disadvantages of a simple state and a highly developed state of civilization. The conflict was tied up with his concept of wealth and with his emphasis upon consumption. Wealth, he said, consists in the ability to consume abundantly, thus it depends upon the development of the division of labor and exchange, which increase with the progress of civilization. Up to this point all is highly desirable and good.

But there is a fly in the ointment. The result of this division of labor and exchange in a highly civilized state, is a delicately interrelated and interdependent mechanism, which reacts quickly to adverse factors which disturb any of its parts, with a consequent collapse of the economic structure. Observing alternations between want and plenty, Boisguilbert concluded that they are socially less desirable than the ability to consume less, but with certainty. His view that a simple state is more desirable than a highly civilized one was obviously reached reluctantly. It indicates an unwilling admission to himself, that, although he regarded it as possible, it was improbable that men would be wise enough to manage a complex economic structure in such a manner as to prevent its occasional collapse. In his view we see common sense, as it were, gaining the ascendancy over idealistic enthusiasm. He apparently perceived limits beyond which the division of labor, or the multiplication of vocations could not safely go. On the contrary, Smith, more optimistic, saw no practical limit to the extension of the division of labor except that occasioned by the requirements of the market itself.

This is the conclusion to be expected on the part of each one, in view of the fact that the vision of one was distorted by too close attention to the existing conditions, and that of the other by a tendency to be preoccupied too exclusively with long-run conditions. Smith correctly took issue with the view that the savage state gives the individual greater security, yet at the same time he turned loose upon the world an equally great error in his pronouncement that frugality and industry are sufficient to supply man abundantly with the necessities and conveniences of life in a civilized state.[21] This orthodox view which regards the security and well-being of labor as dependent solely on the individual's own efforts, was to dominate social thought for a century and a half, and was to hamper the development of social machinery necessary to add to the security of labor in an unstable economic world.

DEFINITION OF WEALTH; THE EMPHASIS UPON CONSUMPTION

In taking up the views of Boisguilbert and Adam Smith, wealth and consumption, and indeed the function of money, cannot well be treated separately. To each one these three topics were inseparably interrelated, and to each one they were the result of protests against the mercantilistic ideas dominating their times. But likewise they were part and parcel of the ideas of both with regard to the division of labor and exchange. In dealing with them, therefore, a certain overlapping, a certain repetition, is unavoidable. This is a difficulty, incidentally, which both Boisguilbert and Smith experienced which was inherent in the development of their ideas, and accounts for much of the apparent disorder of their subject matter.

Fundamentally, each one saw that there was a "mistake in the idea as to what constitutes wealth." [22] "True wealth," said Boisguilbert, "consists of a full enjoyment, not only of the necessaries of life, but even of all the superfluities, and all that which can give pleasure to the senses." [23] The liberality of this definition must have startled a world which considered wealth to consist primarily in treasures of gold and silver. But the fanciful idea of this visionary was repeated three-quarters of a century later: "Every man is rich or poor according to the degree in which he can afford to enjoy the necessaries, conveniencies, and amusements of human life." [24]

[21] *Wealth of Nations,* Introduction, pp. 1–2.
[22] *Dissertation sur les richesses,* p. 394. [23] *Ibid.,* p. 403.
[24] *Wealth of Nations,* Bk. I, p. 32. Professor Cannan quotes Cantillon's definition of wealth: "'La richesse en elle-même n'est autre chose que la nourriture, les commodités et les agréments de la vie.'" Cf. Boisguilbert.

But this full enjoyment of material and immaterial goods cannot be obtained for and by oneself alone. To repeat,

those who are so completely devoted to possessing all the earth, and [who would procure] all its wealth, would end by being poor wretched creatures if they could not enjoy the labor of their fellow men. And would they not prefer the condition of beggars in an inhabited world? Because, in the first place, aside from the fact that it would be necessary for them to produce all their requirements, far from serving their luxurious desires by that, it would be an outstanding achievement, if by continual work, they could reach the point of procuring necessaries; and moreover, with the least illness they would perish from lack of assistance, or rather from despair.[25]

Smith proceeded in the same vein, and out of this concept of wealth arising from the division of labor and exchange, he developed his labor theory of value:

But after the division of labour has once thoroughly taken place, it is but a very small part of these [necessaries, conveniencies and amusements] with which a man's own labour can supply him. The far greater part of them he must derive from the labour of other people, and he must be rich or poor according to the quantity of that labour which he can command, or which he can afford to purchase. The value of any commodity, therefore, to the person who possesses it, and who means not to use or consume it himself, but to exchange it for other commodities, is equal to the quantity of labour which it enables him to purchase or command. Labour, therefore, is the real measure of the exchangeable value of all commodities.[26]

But the consumption of the superfluous is possible only through an excess of necessities:

It has been said in general, at the beginning of these memoirs, of what true wealth consists, namely, a full enjoyment, not only of the necessities of life, but even of all the superfluities and all that which can give pleasure to the senses, on which the corruption of the heart invents and refines all the time. Whatever the condition, however, it is possible to procure the superfluities only in proportion to the excess of necessities.[27]

Or, as Adam Smith said, "when we are in want of necessaries we must part with all superfluities." [28]

[25] *Dissertation sur les richesses,* p. 394.
[26] *Wealth of Nations,* Bk. I, p. 32.
[27] *Dissertation sur les richesses,* p. 403.
[28] *Wealth of Nations,* Bk. I, p. 191.

No modern writer adhering to the belief that economic ills spring in large part from underconsumption has put the case more strongly than Boisguilbert. So strongly did he stress consumption that he declared that it and revenue are the same thing.[29] If ability to consume constitutes wealth, so does wealth spring from this very consumption. It is necessary to consume the goods produced if production is to continue. To produce and not to be able to sell (a term which he used as equivalent to "consume") is the same as if one had not produced, or worse, because "all production has a money cost." In such a case there will be no revenue for the producer and consequently no ability to consume the products of others.

But consumption will not keep pace with production unless the aid of the masses is obtained in consuming what is produced. The wealth of the nation itself depends upon this liberal mass consumption. Thus it is not only a matter of concern to the masses themselves that they be able to consume freely; it is equally a matter of interest to the rich and to the sovereign, in view of the fact that the income of both depends upon goods sold. A market for all products, in other words, is essential if profitable prices, which in turn sustain prosperity, are to be maintained, and the consumption of the masses provides an unlimited market.

Smith, like Boisguilbert, regarded it as a matter of abstract justice that the masses should consume freely. But he lacked the enthusiasm for ample consumption that is so characteristic of Boisguilbert. He qualified, as it were, the extent to which he was willing to commit himself:

> Is this improvement in the circumstances of the lower ranks of the people to be regarded as an advantage or as an inconveniency to the society? The answer seems at first sight abundantly plain. Servants, labourers, and workmen of different kinds, make up the far greater part of every great political society. But what improves the circumstance of the greater part can never be regarded as an inconveniency to the whole. No society can surely be flourishing and happy, of which the far greater part of the members are poor and miserable. It is but equity, besides, that they who feed, cloathe and

[29] "It can be set forth as a principle, says Boisguilbert, that consumption and revenue are one and the same thing."—*Le Détail*, p. 193.

lodge the whole body of the people, should have such a share of the produce of their own labour as to be themselves tolerably well fed, cloathed and lodged.[30]

Both men, then, regarded liberal mass consumption as representing both wisdom and justice. If Smith showed a certain lack of enthusiasm with regard to increasing the standard of living of labor, it was due to the fact that he thought it could not be permanent. "Every species of animals naturally multiplies in proportion to the means of their subsistence," [31] and this increase in numbers would reduce wages because the market would become overstocked. This fall in wages would again act as a corrective of excess numbers. "It is in this manner that the demand for men, like that for any other commodity, necessarily regulates the production of men; quickens it when it goes on too slowly, and stops it when it advances too fast." [32] Nevertheless, the high wages were held to be desirable: "The liberal reward of labour, therefore, as it is the effect of increasing wealth, so it is the cause of increasing population. To complain of it is to lament over the necessary effect and cause of the greatest public prosperity." [33]

Boisguilbert and Smith agree that prices would rise with the increase in consumption. Aside from the inherent justice in being permitted to consume liberally that which one has produced, to raise the price of agricultural products was the avowed purpose of Boisguilbert. Smith declared that "the increase in the wages of labour necessarily increases the price of many commodities, by increasing that part of it which resolves itself into wages, and so far tends to diminish their consumption both at home and abroad." [34] Boisguilbert's view was that without prices which are sufficiently high to induce producers to continue to produce and to employ labor, there will be no consumption. It is not so much

[30] *Wealth of Nations*, Bk. I, p. 80. Professor Cannan notes at this point in *The Wealth of Nations* Berkeley, *Querist*, 5th ed., 1752, qu. 2, where it is asked "'whether a people can be called poor where the common sort are well fed, clothed and lodged.'"

[31] *Ibid.*, p. 81.

[32] *Ibid.*, p. 82.

[33] *Ibid.*, p. 83.

[34] *Ibid.*, p. 88.

the fact that the cost of living has risen which is of concern to the worker, he stated, but his inability to find work.[35] He would, therefore, have dismissed as of no practical importance the fine point raised by Smith.

Smith's use of the phrase "subsistence wage" reminds one of Boisguilbert's frequent use of the term "subsistence" in discussing the needs and conditions of the people. Both are in agreement that "there is . . . a certain rate below which it seems impossible to reduce, for any considerable time, the ordinary wages even of the lowest species of labour. A man must always live by his work, and his wages must at least be sufficient to maintain him." [36] Boisguilbert, protesting against the excessive taxation of the people and the sacrifices which had to be made by them, declared,

> it is necessary indeed that this subsistence take precedence over all kinds of payments, through a justice that is due even to beasts, which God mentions in the first law that he gave to man. . . .
>
> The supposition or the practice of the contrary is an outrage to religion, to humanity, to justice, to statesmanship, and to the crudest reasoning.
>
> Why, then, in a naturally very fertile country does one see a sovereign who does not have armies as numerous and as well equipped as he would wish, and as his needs would seem to require? It is because there is not enough bread, wine, meat, and all the other products to distribute.
>
> And why this deficiency? It is because the lands of his kingdom, which could amply produce all these products, are either untilled or very badly cultivated.
>
> And why, finally, this disorder? Because, against divine precept, the mouths, not only of beasts, but of men have been bound while they were working in the field.
>
> Their life and their subsistence have been refused them and they have abandoned work.[37]

Or, as Adam Smith said, repeating an old proverb, it is better to play and starve than to work and starve. With Boisguilbert's implication that the product of labor increases with an increase in the returns to it, Smith concurred: "The liberal reward of

[35] *Mémoire sur les blés*, p. 159.
[36] *Wealth of Nations*, Bk. I, p. 69.
[37] *Dissertation sur les richesses*, p. 417.

labour, as it encourages the propagation, so it increases the industry of the common people." [38]

So also they agree as to the part played by the land in the creation of wealth. "The real wealth of the country," said Smith, is "the annual produce of its land and labour." [39] Referring to the Spanish conquistadors, and their suffering with the land of a continent at their disposal, as well as its treasure of gold and silver, Boisguilbert remarked:

> It is, then, not the extent of the country which is owned, or the quantity of gold and silver, which the depravity of the heart has erected into idols, which make, absolutely, a man rich and prosperous. . . . [They] can only permit their possessor to perish miserably when the one is not cultivated at all, and when the other cannot be exchanged for the immediate needs of life, such as food and clothing, which no one can do without. These are, then, those things which alone can be termed wealth.[40]

Boisguilbert and Smith were each of the opinion that a country cannot be prosperous without a prosperous agriculture. Boisguilbert explained how it comes about by means of purchases on the part of those deriving income from the land of the goods and services of other producers. In the following paragraph Smith not only repeated this idea, but he may be said to have summarized the underlying thesis which Boisguilbert attempted to sustain in all his writings:

> The contrary circumstances, the neglect of cultivation and improvement, the fall in the real price of any part of the rude produce of land, the rise in the real price of manufactures from the decay of manufacturing art and industry, the declension of the real wealth of the society, all tend, on the other hand, to lower the real rent of land, to reduce the real wealth of the landlord, to diminish his power of purchasing either the labour, or the produce of the labour of other people.[41]

Boisguilbert was enthusiastic over the prospect of a remunerative price for agricultural products. This was not on account of the cultivator alone, but because he saw this as the

[38] *Wealth of Nations,* Bk. I, p. 83.
[39] *Ibid.,* Bk. I, xi, p. 240.
[40] *Dissertation sur les richesses,* pp. 394–395.
[41] *Wealth of Nations,* Bk. I, p. 248.

certain means by which prosperity would be brought to the country as a whole.

And immediately this same nature, released and reëntering into all her rights, will reëstablish commerce and the proportion of prices among all products. And this being accomplished, it will cause each product to bring about an increase in the others, and to support one another continually, until out of a perpetual misfortune there will be created a general prosperity, from which everyone will draw in proportion to his work or to his domain. And this continuing always while increasing at the same time, until the earth from which everything springs can furnish no more, one can imagine what abundance of wealth would be seen if all things, agricultural land as well as everything else, were as valuable as it is possible for nature to make them. For after all, there is no region so wild and sterile as it is thought to be, which could not easily be made very productive if the price of the products which could be harvested there did not lack all guarantee in relation to the expense that must be made to produce them.[42]

Adam Smith was not far behind in his enthusiasm over the same prospect:

The lands of no country, it is evident, can ever be completely cultivated and improved, till once the price of every produce, which human industry is obliged to raise upon them, has got so high as to pay for the expense of complete improvement and cultivation. . . . This rise in the price of each particular produce, must evidently be previous to the improvement and cultivation of the land which is destined for raising it. Gain is the end of all improvement, and nothing could deserve that name of which loss was to be the necessary consequence. But loss must be the necessary consequence of improving land for the sake of a produce of which the price could never bring back the expense. If the complete improvement and cultivation of the country be, as it most certainly is, the greatest of all public advantages, this rise in the price of all those different sorts of rude produce, instead of being considered as a public calamity, ought to be regarded as the necessary forerunner and attendant of the greatest of all public advantages.[43]

And again he declared,

if this rise in the price of some sorts of provisions be owing to a rise in the real value of the land which produces them, to its increased

[42] *Dissertation sur les richesses*, pp. 420–421.
[43] *Wealth of Nations*, Bk. I, p. 227.

fertility; or, in consequence of more extended improvement and good cultivation, to its having been rendered fit for producing corn; it is owing to a circumstance which indicates in the clearest manner the prosperity and advancing state of the country. The land constitutes by far the greatest, the most durable part of the wealth of every extensive country. It may surely be of some use, or, at least, it may give some satisfaction to the public, to have so decisive a proof of the increasing value of by far the greatest, the most important, and the most durable part of its wealth.[44]

THE RÔLE OF MONEY

Boisguilbert and Smith were concerned not only to tear down the popular notion as to what constitutes wealth, but also to build up a new conception as to the function of money. That misconceptions as to the true nature of wealth and money should have arisen was inherent in the situation that had existed in the four or five centuries preceding the opening of the eighteenth century when Boisguilbert was writing.

Medieval economy was adjusted to a shortage of the precious metals. A manorial or rural economy resting upon service payments and exchange by barter could get along with a small amount of such a highly specialized medium of exchange. However, the Crusades ushered in a new epoch. Service payments broke down, new products were introduced, new wants were developed, and new industries were established. The development of towns, which was to accelerate all economic life, received a great impetus. This quickening of the economic life of Europe had as its concomitant an increased demand for funds with which to carry on exchange if the embryonic industrial expansion were not to be stillborn due to a secular decline in prices already low. The major source from which to add to the supply of the precious metals was the treasure of the East. In the trade carried on between the old and settled East and the developing Europe, one would expect to find that the balance of trade favored the East. A young Europe, economically speaking, must have had a greater demand for the goods of the rich and productive East than the converse. It was to be expected, therefore, that, throughout the period from the thirteenth cen-

[44] *Ibid.*, p. 240.

tury to the sixteenth century, there would have been a tendency for the already limited supply of the precious metals in Europe gradually to be drained to the East.

Politically the breakdown of feudalism also increased the demand for specie. When equipped and provisioned knights and yeomen were not at beck and call, others had to be equipped and provisioned to replace them. The process, throughout this early period of struggle between kings and nobles, was an expensive one. The right to tax, well-developed tax systems, and borrowing power, did not arise fully developed to take the place of the old system. There was a logical and sound reason, therefore, for the emphasis upon the accumulation of a royal hoard or treasure of specie. It constituted a necessary phase in fiscal and political development.

Thus, in its need for specie, the economic life of Europe at the end of the fifteenth century must have presented a picture analogous to river trade where traffic is threatened with being stopped as the stream runs lower and lower. Trade, if it were not to be halted, due to the scarcity of the means of carrying it on, required relief and encouragement. It had survived, not on account of the ease of sustaining it, but from the sheer strength of the underlying impulse. That it developed to the extent it did must have been due in great measure to the meeting of the situation by the use of a money substitute, bills of exchange, which aided in economizing the available supply of specie.

The discovery of America brought the flood which was needed to relieve the situation. European trade acted as a sponge to absorb the almost limitless silver of the new world. Like men dying of thirst, maddened to see one individual gulp down the available supply of water, so the nations of Europe must have felt to see Spain monopolize almost the whole source of the precious metals. The impatience for specie was too great to wait for its orderly distribution through the process of trade. It was perhaps not only national rivalry, but the outgrowth of an intensely felt need, which turned the English, for instance, into a nation of buccaneers, preying upon Spanish bullion-laden galleons.

By the opening of the eighteenth century a money economy was fairly well established. But, though there was now an excess of specie rather than a shortage, as measured by the change in the price level, the mania to possess it persisted. Values expressed in terms of money had led readily to an emphasis upon the representative rather than upon the things represented. Men had become enamored of a common denominator. It was inevitable that prophets should appear whose function it would be to destroy the false god, money. The way had to be pointed back to the time when wealth was enumerated as so many horses, sheep, or oxen. Boisguilbert was among the first of these prophets, but his preaching fell upon deaf ears. His mantle descended upon Adam Smith.

"There is," Boisguilbert maintained, "a mistake in the idea as to what constitutes wealth, as well as with respect to money."[45]

> Heaven is not so far from the earth as the distance between the true idea that one should have of money, and that which corruption has established concerning it in the world, and which is almost so generally received that the other is scarcely known. Yet this ignorance (*oubli*) is so great a degeneration (*dépravation*) that it causes the ruin of States, and brings about more destruction than the greatest foreign enemies can ever cause by their ravages.[46]

"Silver," he insisted, "is a source of wealth only to Peru, because there only it is the fruit of the country, which far from meriting envy, maintains its inhabitants very wretchedly in the midst of kegs of this metal."

Smith explained how the notion that money is wealth arose: "That wealth consists in money, or in gold and silver, is a popular notion which naturally arises from the double function of money, as the instrument of commerce, and as the measure of value." [47] While Boisguilbert declared that "a god has been made of these metals for a long time; and departure has been made from the object and the intention for which they were called into commerce, which was to serve as tokens in exchange and in the reciprocal delivery of goods." [48] In the meanwhile,

[45] *Dissertation sur les richesses*, p. 394. [46] *Ibid.*, p. 396.
[47] *Wealth of Nations*, Bk. IV, p. 396.
[48] *Dissertation sur les richesses*, p. 395. In the *Dissertation on the Nature of*

it is hoped that after the discovery of the source of the evil, it will not take so long to determine the remedy, and that this will cause men to come back from their blindness, [and keep them] from destroying every day an unlimited quantity of goods, fruits of the earth, and commodities of life, alone fit to make men subsist, in order to obtain a product, which, being of absolutely no use in itself, was called to the service of men only in order to facilitate exchange and trade, as has already been said.[49]

So Smith stated that the "great wheel of circulation is altogether different from the goods which are circulated by means of it. The revenue of the society consists altogether in those goods and not in the wheel which circulates them." [50]

Boisguilbert pointed out that money "is at the most, and has always been, only a means to procure goods, because it itself is acquired only by a preceding sale of goods. This intention to procure goods is generally as characteristic of those who receive money as of those who part with it." [51] And, he said, it "should follow, and not precede consumption, as a valet follows his master."[52] In agreement as to both of these points, Smith declared

goods can serve many other purposes besides purchasing money, but money can serve no other purpose besides purchasing goods. Money, therefore, necessarily runs after goods, but goods do not always or necessarily run after money. The man who buys does not always mean to sell again, but frequently to use or to consume; whereas he who sells, always means to buy again. The one may frequently have done the whole, but the other can never have done more than the one-half of his business. It is not for its own sake that men desire money, but for the sake of what they can purchase with it.[53]

Wealth Boisguilbert repeatedly refers to this use of money as its sole function. That he recognized its function as a measure of value, however, is indicated throughout. In *Le Détail de la France* he refers to this function specifically: "Considering that, as gold and silver are not, and have never been wealth in themselves; [that they] are valued only by a relationship, and are worth only as much as they can procure of the things necessary to life, for which they serve only as a pledge and a valuation, it is a matter of indifference to have more or less of them, provided that they can procure the same effect," that is, provided the same quantity of goods is exchanged.—*Le Détail*, p. 178.

49 *Dissertation sur les richesses*, p. 395.

50 *Wealth of Nations*, Bk. II, pp. 272–273.

51 *Dissertation sur les richesses*, p. 396. 52 *Ibid.*, p. 417.

53 *Wealth of Nations*, Bk. IV, p. 405.

Boisguilbert noted that in times of prosperity, when substitutes for money are plentiful and its velocity greatly increased, the value of money decreases, and "in order not to remain idle, it is obliged to offer its service to the household, and to display and to have recourse to the goldsmith and to other works." [54] Or, as Smith expressed it:

When . . . the wealth of any country increases, when the annual produce of its labour becomes gradually greater and greater, a greater quantity of coin becomes necessary in order to circulate a greater quantity of commodities: and the people, as they can afford it, as they have more commodities to give for it, will naturally purchase a greater and a greater quantity of plate. The quantity of their coin will increase from necessity; the quantity of their plate from vanity and ostentation, or from the same reason that the quantity of fine statues, pictures, and of every other luxury and curiosity, is likely to increase among them.[55]

Both Boisguilbert and Smith, as has been shown, emphasized the fact that money is a means and not an end. What makes a man rich or poor is his ability to command goods and services. What in reality is sought is power over these. What is of importance, therefore, is not money as such, but purchasing power. Boisguilbert spoke of purchasing power chiefly with respect to the sovereign. Money, he said, has the same function for princes as for the people, namely, to procure goods and services.[56] Consequently, "an écu from their viewpoint is worth only as much as those who are in their pay can procure bread, wine, or other produce with it." [57] And so,

the one or the other . . . is a matter of indifference to the sovereign, as it is likewise to all those who are in his pay, and above all to his soldiers, who have no sooner received their pay than they convert it into food and other needs of life, so that it would be the same to them to receive these things immediately without the intermediary of money, as is practiced in many places.[58]

While Smith said:

Thus if a guinea be the weekly pension of a particular person, he

[54] *Dissertation sur les richesses*, p. 405.
[55] *Wealth of Nations*, Bk. I, pp. 188–189.
[56] *Dissertation sur les richesses*, p. 417.
[57] *Ibid.*, p. 415. [58] *Ibid.*, p. 401.

can in the course of the week purchase with it a certain quantity of subsistence, conveniencies, and amusements. In proportion as this quantity is great or small, so are his real riches, his weekly revenue. His weekly revenue is certainly not equal both to the guinea, and to what can be purchased with it, but only to one or other of those two equal values; and to the latter more properly than to the former, to the guinea's worth rather than to the guinea.[59]

Boisguilbert and Smith agree that the quantity of money in a country is a matter of indifference. Such a view is a necessary corollary to the concept that wealth consists of goods rather than of money, and to the idea that money itself is a commodity which, like any other commodity, is to be obtained in exchange for commodities. Money, therefore, being a commodity, a "fruit of the earth," as Boisguilbert called it, its value will change with a change in its quantity in relation to other commodities. In exchange, simply more or less of other products will be offered for it. If, as Smith said, we have more of it, assuming no change in the amount of other products, we must simply become accustomed to carrying shillings instead of groats in our pockets. Boisguilbert declared that "it is a matter of indifference" if "things be at a high or at a low price," provided that they all change together.[60]

Boisguilbert and Smith were likewise of the opinion that the total amount of money in a country forms only a small part of the entire capital of the country. The former stated that, "in a country of great resources, [money] ought not, naturally, to form more than the thousandth part of its resources, assuming all of the ordinary value of the latter." [61] While Smith declared that "money, no doubt, makes always a part of the national capital; but it has already been shown that it generally makes but a small part, and always the most unprofitable part of it." [62]

The quantity of money in a country adjusts itself to the need which is required by the wealth of the country. Boisguilbert stated it negatively: "No one will ever enjoy, easily and for a long time, bread, wine, meat, or clothing of the most superfluous

[59] *Wealth of Nations*, Bk. II, pp. 273–274. [60] *Factum*, p. 279.
[61] *Dissertation sur les richesses*, p. 414.
[62] *Wealth of Nations*, Bk. IV, p. 404.

magnificence, unless these things are in the country, and even abundantly so. [If they are not plentiful,] land will come to nothing, and money will flee without power to return." [63] Smith entered into the matter of the flight of money and of its return:

> The same quantity of money . . . cannot long remain in any country in which the value of the annual produce diminishes. . . . But having no employment at home, it will, in spite of all laws and prohibitions, be sent abroad, and employed in purchasing consumable goods which may be of some use at home. . . .
>
> The quantity of money, on the contrary, must in every country naturally increase as the value of the annual produce increases.[64]

But must not governments be concerned with preserving and increasing the amount of the precious metals in order to carry on foreign wars? And does not this contingency negate the theory that the quantity of money in a country is a matter of indifference? Smith discussed the question.

> Others admit that if a nation could be separated from all the world, it would be of no consequence how much, or how little money circulated in it. The consumable goods which were circulated by means of this money would only be exchanged for a greater or a smaller number of pieces; but the real wealth or poverty of the country, they allow, would depend altogether upon the abundance or scarcity of those consumable goods. But it is otherwise, they think, with countries which have connections with foreign nations, and which are obliged to carry on foreign wars, and to maintain fleets and armies in distant countries. This, they say, cannot be done, but by sending abroad money to pay them with; and a nation cannot send much money abroad, unless it has a good deal at home. Every such nation, therefore, must endeavour in time of peace to accumulate gold and silver that, when occasion requires, it may have wherewithal to carry on foreign wars.[65]

He gave his own opinion, differing from that of Sir Thomas Mun and his school, as he had set it forth above:

> It is not always necessary to accumulate gold and silver, in order to enable a country to carry on foreign wars, and to maintain fleets and armies in distant countries. Fleets and armies are maintained, not with gold and silver, but with consumable goods. The nation

[63] *Dissertations sur les richesses*, p. 408.
[64] *Wealth of Nations*, Bk. II, p. 322.
[65] *Ibid.*, Bk. IV, p. 397.

which, from the annual produce of its domestic industry, from the annual revenue arising out of its lands, labour, and consumable stock, has wherewithal to purchase those consumable goods in distant countries, can maintain foreign wars there.[66]

This was the view of Boisguilbert.

The outcome of a foreign war, which goes on two hundred leagues from these regions . . . depends absolutely on justly or badly contrived measures that are taken within a State. . . .

All the things which are destroyed are alone the means of sustaining war, and they constantly play the principal part in determining its outcome; [and] the perfect understanding that enemies can have that this sole resource of armies will be more or less permanent with the nations opposed in relation to their own situation regarding these same provisions, is the only thing which brings them to listen to peace, which ought to be the object of all wars, however holy and just they may be.[67]

Again he went into the subject, this time in greater detail:

If the people have a large quantity of grain on account of the cultivation of much land made possible by a price which covers all expenses of production, the prince will assuredly have the means to give bread to numerous troops. In the same way [he will have] wine, clothes, meat, horses, rigging for ships, wood for buildings, metals with which all sorts of arms are made, and, in short, all the commodities with which armies and fleets are raised and supported. These things receive their birth, their limits, and their duration only from the degree of power, more or less, that the country has, not only to produce, but to consume them. It is that alone which can draw products from the bowels of the earth. . . And if the prince has need of a quantity of goods, for instance, such as materials of which vessels and their armaments are constructed, to a degree which exceeds the consumption of his subjects, so that he would need more of them than usual, this is made up by the exchange which he makes of other things which he receives in greater quantity than he requires.[68]

With his emphasis upon the change in economic conditions, Boisguilbert gave especial attention to the difference of velocity with which money moves at different times. Aside from this stress on changing velocity, his views and those of Smith were

[66] *Ibid.*, Bk. IV, p. 407.
[67] *Dissertation sur les richesses*, p. 418.
[68] *Ibid.*, p. 416.

essentially similar. As a part of his emphasis upon the importance of the consumption of the masses, he stated that "an écu with a poor man or a very small merchant has a hundred times more effect, or rather creates more revenue than with a rich man, on account of the continual and daily turnover which this modest sum undergoes with the former." [69] Smith substituted the difference between wholesale and retail trade for Boisguilbert's differentiation between rich and poor:

> The circulation between the dealers, as it is carried on by wholesale, requires generally a pretty large sum for every particular transaction. That between the dealers and the consumers, on the contrary, as it is generally carried on by retail, frequently requires but very small ones, a shilling, or even a halfpenny, being often sufficient. But small sums circulate much faster than large ones. A shilling changes masters more frequently than a guinea, and a halfpenny more frequently than a shilling. Though the annual purchases of all the consumers, therefore, are at least equal to those of all the dealers, they can generally be transacted with a much smaller quantity of money; the same pieces, by a more rapid circulation, serving as the instrument of many more purchases of the one kind than of the other.[70]

Having finished with the circulation of the funds of the poor, Boisguilbert launched an attack upon hoarding by the rich: The "continual and daily turnover" which is seen in the funds of the one "does not occur with respect to the other in whose coffers far greater quantities of money remain months and whole years idle, and useless as a consequence, either on account of the corruption of a heart blinded by avarice, or in the expectation of a better market. But, on this custody, the king and the body of the State draw no benefit, and it constitutes so much theft from both." [71] In a note in his edition of Boisguilbert's works, Daire shows a lack of historical perspective by criticizing this statement on the ground that it is in conflict with the accepted view with regard to savings. Daire's error was a failure to remember that, if we leave out of account the accumulation of stocks of goods, the savings made in 1700 largely took the form of hoarded specie, on account of the lack of opportunity for invest-

[69] *Ibid.*, p. 419.
[70] *Wealth of Nations*, Bk. II, p. 305.
[71] *Dissertation sur les richesses*, p. 419.

ment except in land, and the lack of development of deposit banking. An ardent disciple of Smith, he doubtless had in mind the latter's statement that "what is annually saved is as regularly consumed as what is annually spent." [72] But Daire should have looked further. Here is a view, which, again substituting the dealer for the rich man, coincides with that of Boisguilbert: "That part of his capital which a dealer is obliged to keep by him unemployed, and in ready money for answering occasional demands, is so much dead stock, which, so long as it remains in this situation, produces nothing either to him or to his country." But, Smith added, "the judicious operations of banking enable him to convert this dead stock into active and productive stock; into materials to work upon, into tools to work with, and into provisions and subsistence to work for; into stock which produces something both to himself and to his country." [73]

It will be recalled that Boisguilbert was especially emphatic in his insistence that the complaints of a scarcity of money heard on every side in times of depression were not the result of less money in the country, but the result of the fact that money had gone out of circulation and into hoarding, and that it could not be borrowed because of the collapse of credit. Its behavior is, by him, completely tied up with the economic conditions existing at a particular time. Smith discussed the same problem:

No complaint, however, is more common than that of a scarcity of money. Money, like wine, must always be scarce with those who have neither wherewithal to buy it, nor credit to borrow it. Those who have either, will seldom be in want either of the money, or of the wine which they have occasion for. This complaint, however, of the scarcity of money, is not always confined to improvident spendthrifts. It is sometimes general through a whole mercantile town, and the country in its neighbourhood. Over-trading is the common cause of it. Sober men, whose projects have been disproportioned to their capitals, are as likely to have neither wherewithal to buy money, nor credit to borrow it, as prodigals whose expense has been disproportioned to their revenue. Before their projects can be brought to bear, their stock is gone, and their credit with it. They run about everywhere to borrow money, and every body tells

[72] *Wealth of Nations*, Bk. II, p. 320.
[73] *Ibid.*, Bk. II, p. 303.

them that they have none to lend. Even such general complaints of the scarcity of money do not always prove that the usual number of gold and silver pieces are not circulating in the country, but that many people want those pieces who have nothing to give for them. When the profits of trade happen to be greater than ordinary, overtrading becomes a general error both among great and small dealers. They do not always send more money abroad than usual, but they buy upon credit both at home and abroad, an unusual quantity of goods, which they send to some distant market, in hopes that the returns will come in before the demand for payment. The demand comes before the returns, and they have nothing at hand, with which they can either purchase money, or give solid security for borrowing. It is not any scarcity of gold and silver, but the difficulty which such people find in borrowing, and which their creditors find in getting payment, that occasions the general complaint of the scarcity of money.[74]

As a part of his effort to dethrone money from its position as sovereign of men's imagination as well as of commerce, Boisguilbert erected a "strong" case for the substitution of credit.

We have in use in Europe all the time the easiest and cheapest device to bring the metals to reason, and, destroying their usurpation, place them in their proper sphere, which is only to be servants and slaves of commerce and not its tyrants. [This device] is to give them as competitors . . . a simple piece of paper which costs nothing, and carries on, nevertheless, all the functions of money for millions in quantity for an infinity of times, that is to say, for as many hands as it passes through, while these metals do not go from their natural state,[75] and from the principles which called them into the world.

It is asked . . . if the bills of a celebrated merchant, whose credit is powerfully established by a certain known wealth, of which there exists more than one example in Europe, are not worth as much and are not preferred to ready money; and if, having all the value, and all the efficacy, they have not particular advantages over the metals, because of the ease of guarding and transferring them without fear of violent theft?

It may also be added that these bills will never be presented for payment as long as they are only in the hands of a good and upright individual who wishes to make only a prudent use of them at any time. This means that he will not divest himself of his wealth, es-

[74] *Ibid.*, Bk. IV, p. 404.

[75] By the natural state of the metals Boisguilbert means their subordination to products, that is, their use as a means rather than an end.

pecially of a considerable sum, except to procure for himself the equivalent, either in immovables or movables, if he is a merchant, and not to consume it in ordinary expenses, either now or hereafter, which is the sole case where the bill is of no more use. If these things are not done, after passing through an infinite number of hands, which it would have enriched while guaranteeing future delivery of that which could not be furnished immediately, it would be returned to its first drawer, where only a compensation would be due.

In this manner, there would be a general prosperity . . . without the intervention of the least sum of money.[76]

Allowing for its more temperate tone, for the passage of time and the development of banking, and the substitution, consequently, of banking and bankers for the "celebrated merchants" of Boisguilbert's day, a remarkable similarity, point by point, is discerned in Smith's introduction of the subject of credit.

The substitution of paper in the room of gold and silver money, replaces a very expensive instrument of commerce with one much less costly, and sometimes equally convenient. Circulation comes to be carried on by a new wheel, which it costs less both to erect and to maintain than the old one. But in what manner this operation is performed, and in what manner it tends to increase either the gross or the neat revenue of the society, is not altogether so obvious, and may therefore require some further explication.

There are several different sorts of paper money; but the circulating notes of banks and bankers are the species which is best known, and which seems best adapted for this purpose.

When the people of any particular country have such confidence in the fortune, probity, and prudence of a particular banker, as to believe that he is always ready to pay upon demand such of his promissory notes as are likely to be at any time presented to him; those notes come to have the same currency as gold and silver money, from the confidence that such money can at any time be had for them.

A particular banker lends among his customers his own promissory notes, to the extent, we shall suppose, of a hundred thousand pounds. As those notes serve all the purposes of money, his debtors pay him the same interest as if he had lent them so much money. This interest is the source of his gain. Although some of those notes are continually coming back upon him for payment, part of them

[76] *Dissertation sur les richesses*, pp. 397–398. *Compensation* has been translated here literally "compensation," as Adam Smith in his day certainly would have read it. As Boisguilbert used it, however, it in reality refers to set-offs, or clearing.

continue to circulate for months and years together. Although he has generally in circulation notes to the extent of a hundred thousand pounds, twenty thousand pounds in gold and silver may, frequently, be a sufficient provision for answering occasional demands. By this operation, therefore, twenty thousand pounds in gold and silver perform all the functions which a hundred thousand could otherwise have performed. The same exchanges may be made, the same quantity of consumable goods may be circulated and distributed to their proper consumers, by means of his promissory notes, to the value of a hundred thousand pounds, as by an equal value of gold and silver money. Eighty thousand pounds of gold and silver, therefore, can, in this manner, be spared from the circulation of the country; and if different operations of the same kind should, at the same time, be carried on by many different banks and bankers, the whole circulation may thus be conducted with a fifth part only of the gold and silver which would otherwise have been requisite.[77]

Or, as Boisguilbert said, the richer a country, the more it is in a position to dispense with specie.[78]

THE DESTRUCTION OF THE WEALTH OF NATIONS

Having shown what the wealth of nations consists of, and having reduced money to its proper place, both Boisguilbert and Smith noted the way in which this wealth is destroyed. The factors bringing this about are the same, and treated in the same order. The first of these is private prodigality:

A voluptuous man, who has hardly enough time in all life to satisfy his pleasures, scorns to keep his house and his warehouses filled with grain and other fruits of the earth to be sold at the current price in time and season. This care, this waiting, and this anxiety, are not adapted to his manner of life; a half as much ready money, even a quarter, promotes his affairs better, and his sensual pleasures are served by it with more secrecy and diligence.[79]

Their reasoning upon the subject was altogether different, to be sure. Smith condemned the prodigal because he encroaches upon his capital, and because he maintains unproductive rather than productive labor:

[77] *Wealth of Nations,* Bk. II, pp. 275–276.
[78] See above, p. 209.
[79] *Dissertation sur les richesses,* p. 339.

Whatever, therefore, we may imagine the real wealth and revenue of a country to consist in, whether in the value of the annual produce of its land and labour, as plain reason seems to dictate; or in the quantity of the precious metals which circulate within it, as vulgar prejudices suppose; in either view of the matter, every prodigal appears to be a public enemy, and every frugal man a public benefactor.[80]

Boisguilbert condemned the bankrupt, as well as the prodigal, because both spoil the market for the legitimate dealer, and anything which disturbs price balance constituted a "crime" in his sight.

But it is not yet time to finish with the use which crime makes of this unique money, and which would be prevented by other kinds of goods, if they did not have this unhappy representative. Bankrupts, who wholly disorganize commerce, destroying the confidence of everyone, and preventing the trading with credit and with bills, could almost never steal with impunity from everybody as they do daily.[81]

Not that Boisguilbert saw all bankruptcy as the result of deliberate pillage. Some individuals are caught in the net of circumstance:

Nevertheless, some of these crimes, such as bankruptcy, take their origin from a more remote source, namely, necessity caused by a preceding disorganization of the State, [and] which is not at all wholly the result of a deliberate brigandage or highway robbery.[82]

With his temperate touch Smith turned the "crime" of bankruptcy into "misconduct":

The effects of misconduct are often the same as prodigality. Every injudicious and unsuccessful project in agriculture, mines, fisheries, trade, or manufactures, tends in the same manner to diminish the funds destined for the maintenance or productive labour. In every such project, though the capital is consumed by productive hands only, yet, as by the injudicious manner in which they are employed, they do not reproduce the full value of their consumption, there must always be some diminution in what would otherwise have been the productive funds of the society.[83]

[80] *Wealth of Nations,* Bk. II, p. 323.
[81] *Dissertation sur les richesses,* pp. 399-400.
[82] *Ibid.,* p. 400.
[83] *Wealth of Nations,* Bk. II, p. 323.

But the greatest source of the desolation of nations lies in the conduct of governments themselves.

Let us look, then, at another cortege, namely, those who are entrusted with collecting the taxes of princes. . . . It will be shown that there is many a prince who does not procure a liter of wine for any of his soldiers that twenty, or even a hundred more than he receives are not destroyed. . . .

There are those who would over-reach their authority, who would have us believe that the money which they pay to the prince is important only in its amount, and not in the manner in which it is raised on the people. . . . Capital (*préciputs*), which ought to be considered before the tax, and even all sorts of requirements, such as, for instance, the expenses of production, are sacrificed first, as well as the utensils and implements necessary to succeed. And the certainty which this makes of the abandonment of all the land in the future, which would be a thousand of loss for one of profit, is of no importance to people who are dominated by the interests of the present moment, whether they are pressed by the necessity of acting in this manner because otherwise they would be subject to similar ruin, [a possibility] which is only too well known, or whether their individual fortune is promised to them only at this price, [a condition] which is likewise very common.[84]

As Boisguilbert stated it elsewhere, the wealth of a nation is determined as truly by the wisdom or the errors of those who govern as by the quality of the soil and the climate. Such was the view of Adam Smith:

Great nations are never impoverished by private, though they sometimes are by public prodigality and misconduct. The whole, or almost the whole public revenue, is in most countries employed in maintaining unproductive hands. Such are the people who compose a numerous and splendid court, a great ecclesiastical establishment, great fleets and armies, who in time of peace produce nothing, and in time of war acquire nothing which can compensate the expense of maintaining them, even while the war lasts. Such people, as they themselves produce nothing, are all maintained by the produce of other men's labour. When multiplied, therefore, to an unnecessary number, they may in a particular year consume so great a share of this produce, as not to leave a sufficiency for maintaining the productive labourers, who should reproduce it next year. The next year's produce therefore, will be less than that of the foregoing, and if the same disorder should continue, that of the third year will

[84] *Dissertation sur les richesses*, pp. 400–402.

be still less than that of the second. Those unproductive hands, who should be maintained by a part only of the spare revenue of the people, may consume so great a share of their whole revenue, and thereby oblige so great a number to encroach upon their capitals, upon the funds destined for the maintenance of productive labour, that all the frugality and good conduct of individuals may not be able to compensate the waste and degradation of produce occasioned by this violent and forced encroachment.[85]

Thus did Boisguilbert and Smith see the same elements as causes of economic disorder. Private prodigality, bankruptcies, and the action of the State—these are the factors destroying the wealth of nations. There the similarity ends. Smith's reasoning lacks the realism of that of the lieutenant of police. He had been tainted with the abstractions of Physiocracy. Smith thought this injury to result from the maintenance of unproductive labor; to Boisguilbert the destruction came from the disturbance of values and the upsetting of the economic equilibrium in each case.

FUNDAMENTAL CONCEPTS OF BOISGUILBERT AND SMITH

Certain fundamental concepts in *The Wealth of Nations* are so much a part of it that they have come to be regarded as veritable "Smithisms." Such, for instance, are his assumption of divine providence, earthly abundance, and harmony of interests,[86] and his emphasis upon self-interest and the desire to better one's condition, and upon natural liberty. While these concepts are associated with Smith, it is not pretended that they were all original with him. It is recognized that they are to be found in the works of various writers of the seventeenth and eighteenth centuries, and that they were simply combined into an integrated system by Smith. That they were combined three-quarters of a century earlier by Boisguilbert, and that the latter's works were written before many of the writers appeared who were to receive credit for originating certain of the concepts is less well known.

Underlying everyday economic activity Boisguilbert saw certain fundamental factors, the operation of which, he thought,

[85] *Wealth of Nations*, Bk. II, pp. 324–325.
[86] See J. R. Commons, "Institutional Economics," in *American Economic Review*, Vol. XXI, Dec. 1931, p. 650.

determined or modified its course. That they are likewise found to occupy an important place in *The Wealth of Nations* is not without interest.

Original Equality.—In the "innocence of the world," said Boisguilbert,

> every individual was then his [own] servant and his [own] master, and enjoyed the riches and the treasures of the earth in proportion as he had personally the talent to make them valuable. All ambition and all luxury were then reduced to procuring food and clothing. The first two workers in the world . . . were at the same time the two rulers of it.[87]

Here Boisguilbert stood, as it were, at the parting of the ways. He could have developed his subject either from the economic or from the political standpoint. He chose the former, and led into the field which intrigued his interest, namely, the division of labor and exchange. The "rulers," he continued, "divided these two trades: the one worked the earth in order to have grain, and the other tended the flocks in order to clothe himself, and the mutual exchange that they could make enabled them to enjoy one another's work." Had he not been concerned to utter the protest which follows the above, and which explains the loss of this equality, Boisguilbert could also have seized this opportunity to speculate as to the basis upon which this exchange took place. This, however, was left to Smith, who repeated the idea of original economic equality. "In that original state of things, which precedes both the appropriation of land and the accumulation of stock, the whole produce of labour belongs to the labourer. He has neither landlord nor master to share with him." [88]

Self-Interest, Divine Providence, Earthly Abundance, and Harmony of Interests.—The first sentence in *The Wealth of Nations* is a significant one, consisting as it does of an ungloved attack upon the popular conception of the nature of wealth. In this it resembles the opening sentence in the *Dissertation on the Nature of Wealth,* which likewise is an opening assault upon mercantilism. "Everyone wishes to be rich, and most persons

[87] *Dissertation sur les richesses,* p. 399.
[88] *Wealth of Nations,* Bk. I, p. 66.

work night and day in order to become so; but a mistake is usually made in the route taken in order to succeed in it." Here Boisguilbert wished to emphasize the stress placed upon money. But incidentally he set forth an assumption which was to occupy an important place in his theory, namely, the desire of every man to better his condition. "Every individual understands what it means to be wretchedly poor, because everyone works from morning to night in order not to become so, provided his senses have not blinded him, or in order to cease to be so if he is sufficiently unhappy on finding himself in this situation. . . . All have, then, this disposition individually." [89]

There is, however, a complete interdependence among men, and "those who are so completely devoted to possessing all the earth, and who would obtain all its wealth, would end in being poor wretched creatures if they could not enjoy the labor of their fellow men.[90] Nevertheless, men "must never be expected to supply products to others as a result of their liberality or their prudence." [91] Or, as Adam Smith combined the two ideas, "man has almost constant occasion for the help of his brethren, and it is in vain for him to expect it from their benevolence only. . . . It is not from the benevolence of the butcher, the brewer, or the baker, that we expect our dinner, but from their regard to their own interest." [92]

It may be that a dealer is producing at a loss, "so that the surrender of the whole product will not at all clear the seller of his obligations, and it is necessary for his person and his other property to answer for the balance. This is not absolutely without example in some countries in Europe, and it is an evil for which no other remedy has been found than to give up the cultivation of the product in question, finally to get rid of the loss on this one kind of goods." [93] This he does because nature "has established the rule that it is necessary for each trade to nourish its master, or close his shop and procure himself another

[89] *Dissertation sur les richesses*, p. 408. Here the concept of economic man begins to make its appearance.

[90] *Ibid.*, p. 394. [91] *Ibid.*, p. 421.

[92] *Wealth of Nations*, Bk. I, p. 16.

[93] *Dissertation sur les richesses*, p. 403.

one."[94] Or, as Adam Smith developed the idea: "Every individual is continually exerting himself to find out the most advantageous employment for whatever capital he can command."[95]

By this self-interest the general good is promoted. "All men cherish night and day this wealth as a result of their self-interest, and form at the same time, although this is unrecognized, the general well-being, whence, in spite of themselves, they must look for their individual advantage."[96] And Adam Smith agreed that "every individual necessarily labours to render the annual revenue of the society as great as he can. He generally, indeed, neither intends to promote the public interest, nor knows how much he is promoting it. . . . By pursuing his own interest he frequently promotes that of the society more effectually than when he really intends to promote it."[97]

To understand how Boisguilbert saw the public interest served by the self-interest of the individual necessitates referring to his theory of proportional prices, and to their effect upon general prosperity. Proportional prices, it will be remembered, are composed of a general price schedule which permits all producers to produce with profit and hence to maintain employment and expenditures necessary to carry off the goods produced. A fall in the price of one product so that costs cease to be covered reduces the consumption of those dependent upon this industry, and in this way disorder spreads throughout the economic world. Assuming that there is no outside force interfering to cause a producer to sacrifice his product for cash, his self-interest can be depended upon to make him hold out for the maximum price obtainable; but an increase in price which has no basis in increased costs is equally disastrous. The seller, however, will not be able to get the maximum price desired because the self-interest of the buyer will cause him to go elsewhere to deal. As long as one is free to sell in the best market possible, and the other, to buy of someone else, their self-interest will cause them, as Boisguilbert said, "to divide the profit," or, to state it differently,

[94] *Ibid.*, p. 409.
[95] *Wealth of Nations*, Bk. IV, p. 419.
[96] *Dissertation sur les richesses*, p. 408.
[97] *Wealth of Nations*, Bk. IV, p. 421.

the product will be sold at such a price as to permit the seller to obtain his costs, and likewise as not to disturb the costs of the buyer. Self-interest, then, is a vital factor in the maintenance of the equilibrium in prices which Boisguilbert regarded as essential to prosperity, and is an integral part of his theory.

The ideas of the two men differ at this point in a way which deserves mention. Smith stated that "by pursuing his own interest [a man] frequently promotes that of the society more effectually than when he really intends to promote it. I have never known much good done by those who affected to trade for the public good. It is an affectation, indeed, not very common among merchants, and very few words need be employed in dissuading them from it." [98] To this view Boisguilbert would never subscribe. He distinguished clearly between a short-sighted self-interest, which eventually defeats itself in ruining others, and an enlightened self-interest, or, as Boisguilbert would call it, self-interest tempered with justice. This conception of self-interest is part and parcel of his concept of the interdependence and solidarity, or harmony of interest, of mankind. It was his belief that no one can be permanently prosperous unless there is general prosperity. This in turn rests upon his conception of the circulation of income. The prosperity which results from an unbroken circulation of income, or the uninterrupted exchange of goods, depends upon the maintenance of proportional prices. Boisguilbert's point of view is shown in the case of the shoemaker and the farmer:

A shoemaker wishes to sell his shoes for four francs if this has once been the price. He will never come down by a sou unless he should become bankrupt. Yet he wishes to buy wheat from the farmer at that price which abundance, joined to a forbidding of exportation, forces the latter to offer it for, that is to say, for less than it costs to produce it. And so it is with the others. But the unhappy shoemaker never notices that he is bringing about his own ruin, because this farmer is thereby placed by the shoemaker in the situation of not being able to pay rent to his landlord, and the landlord, as a consequence, is unable to buy the shoes of the shoemaker. Thus, as a result of the two or three sous that the latter is able to gain on food, he puts his family, as well as himself, in the almshouse.

98 *Wealth of Nations*, Bk. IV, p. 421.

However, it would be a sheer waste of time to attempt to make him understand the above, by showing him that his shoes had sold for four francs because grain was at a proportional price, so that each of the dealers could trade with profit; but that now the one having fallen [in price] it is necessary that the other should do the same.

One day when [the shoemaker] feels less need to sell his wares than the farmer, who is pushed by taxes, or by the landlord, the former laughs at these reasons, and all his concern is to have the grain at the best possible bargain. And he is sufficiently stupid to thank God for [having obtained] it. [But God] is assuredly not at all the author of this situation, because he is never evil, only permitting it, though there are those, who, through ignorance give him credit for this fatal felicity.[99]

But in spite of the requirement for prosperity that producers shall not sell at a loss,

not much higgling takes place, as is seen in all kinds of bargains before they are concluded, without attention being drawn to this rule of justice: each dealer, whether on a large or a small scale, would like to have the profit of the sale for himself alone, even if it would take all the goods and even the life of his compatriot, instead of having it divided as it must be. To think that that is the ruin of the State, the same as if trade were made with false weights or measures, enters into the mind of no one, although one might well apply to this conduct the maxim of the Evangel, which is "let it be done unto others, as it would be done unto you." [100]

If prosperity persists, it is, in reality, in spite of, rather than because of, such short-sighted self-interest on the part of individuals, because,

on account of a frightful blindness, there is no trader of any kind who does not work with all his power to disconcert this harmony. It is only at the point of the sword, whether in buying or in selling, that it is maintained; and public prosperity, which furnishes a livelihood for all the people, subsists only by a superior Providence, who sustains it as she makes agricultural products thrive, there not being a moment or a single market where it may not be necessary for her to act, since there is not a single encounter where war is not made against her.[101]

[99] *Dissertation sur les richesses*, pp. 411–412.
[100] *Ibid.*, p. 409.
[101] *Ibid.*, p. 404.

But if dealers are not so short-sighted as to disturb proportional prices, self-interest is an unmitigated good.

As long as things remain in this equilibrium, there are no other resources with which to enrich oneself, whatever one's condition in life, than through force of work and capacity beyond one's neighbor, not in order to deceive him in trying to have his goods at a vile price, but in order to surpass him in skill.

And as this emulation becomes general on account of the despair of enriching oneself otherwise, all the arts are perfected, and prosperity is carried to the highest possible point.[102]

Boisguilbert thus saw a purely short-sighted self-interest as the source of economic friction which is only offset by a Divine Providence. To him it is ignorance or stupidity or blindness which prevents individuals from seeing that their economic welfare is advanced by the prosperity of others. Economic waste and conflict can be prevented by a rational policy of attention to the ultimate effect of present conduct. A social point of view is called for, in other words, not for the sake of others, but on one's own account.

Immediately, Boisguilbert and Smith seem only in superficial agreement with regard to self-interest; that the former considered it as the foundation of an economic and social philosophy, whereas in the theory of the latter it appeared to constitute little more than a human attribute underlying the desire for gain. Nevertheless, the moral indignation which Smith felt and expressed in *The Theory of Moral Sentiments* for Mandeville's theory of self-interest[103] indicates that in extolling the effect of self-interest on the general good in *The Wealth of Nations,* Smith had in mind the doctrine of a modified self-interest utilized by Boisguilbert, rather than the grosser theory of Mandeville. But there is a further agreement. In the theories of both Boisguilbert and Smith, self-interest is tied up with the concept of equilibrium. The former thought self-interest should promote equilibrium, and that as long as equilibrium exists it constitutes a general good. Smith extended this idea. With him self-interest

[102] *Loc. cit.*

[103] *Essays, Philosophical and Literary, by Adam Smith,* Ward, Lock and Co., London (no date), pp. 272–278.

does produce equilibrium, in that it acts to cause an increase or decrease in production according to the needs of the market, hence, according to the return obtainable.

With Boisguilbert, Providence plays a more important part than in simply acting to counteract the destruction wrought by short-sighted self-interest. She rewards with prosperity those nations which are not dominated by a short-sighted policy with regard to trade, or which have not a mistaken national self-interest:

> Thus it can be seen . . . what a frightful error it is to mistrust the liberality or prudence of a goddess who knows how to produce immense wealth in the most sterile country for men who wish indeed to accept her terms for the fructification of their work, while she leaves in extreme poverty those to whom she gave much more at first, but who only show their gratitude by wishing to reduce her to slavery. In this, however, they never succeed in the end without making themselves unhappier than slaves.
>
> Nevertheless, she is so beneficent, and she loves man so greatly, that at the first sign of repentance she forgets all the past indignities, and overwhelms him with all her favors, as has been said.[104]

As in the case of self-interest, the harmony of interests of the various economic classes was with Boisguilbert an integral part of his theories. It is indeed his fundamental theory. Like the chant of a litany there runs monotonously through his writings the thought or the expression *tout y étant solidaire.* The prince cannot be prosperous unless the people are; the producer cannot thrive unless the consumer is in a position to buy; but consumers are those who earn wages, the landlords and other producers, and they cannot buy unless they are able to sell their services or products. In other words, Boisguilbert could not see any class permanently prosperous except through the prosperity of all other classes. Yet he made one exception. There were "entrepreneurs" whose interests were opposed to the general interest. These were the tax farmers and partisans who battened on the misery of society.

Concerning this Smith and Boisguilbert are at variance. Of the three great orders of society, the former saw the interest of the

104 *Dissertation sur les richesses,* p. 421.

wage earner and the landowner as identical with that of society as a whole, while that of the entrepreneur was regarded as conflicting, because

> the rate of profit does not, like rent and wages, rise with the prosperity and fall with the declension of the society. On the contrary, it is naturally low in rich, and high in poor countries, and it is always highest in the countries which are going fastest to ruin. The interest of this third order, therefore, has not the same connection with the general interest of the society as that of the other two. . . . The interest of the dealers, however, in any particular branch of trade or manufactures, is always in some respect different from, and even opposite to, that of the public. To widen the market and to narrow the competition, is always the interest of the dealers. To widen the market may frequently be agreeable enough to the interest of the public; but to narrow the competition must always be against it, and can serve only to enable the dealers, by raising their profits above what they naturally would be, to levy, for their own benefit, an absurd tax upon the rest of their fellow-citizens.[105]

Boisguilbert, who carried on his observations in a country "going fastest to ruin," would have regarded Smith's reasoning as unsound at this point. The "rate of profit" might be higher, but not the total profit, in the opinion of Boisguilbert who saw that the largest gain did not come from selling a few units at a maximum price, but many units at a lower price;[106] who saw a prosperous business possible only through the existence of prosperous customers; and who saw the monoplist eventually shutting off his own sales. He would never have agreed that it is to the ultimate interest of the producer to oppress the consumer; but he would have agreed that the producer, not always realizing what constitutes his ultimate interest, would regard it to his apparent or immediate interest to act in such a manner as to destroy the consumer.

LAISSEZ FAIRE

Boisguilbert's position with regard to laissez faire has been given. His conception of liberty has a humaneness, a gentleness, almost, which resulted from his proposing the principle of laissez

105 *Wealth of Nations,* Bk. I, pp. 249–250.
106 See above, p. 182.

faire as a means of relieving a people crushed because of its absence.

Adam Smith's theory evinced a beginning of that harshness which grew until finally, it may be said, man was subordinated to the principle originally introduced to serve him. The lack of humanity in the concept of which Marx justly complained, arose from the very nature of the long-run view of economic processes. It strikes, and necessarily offends, those who see and are concerned with the period of economic and social chaos intervening before the eventual adjustment to a new set of conditions. Adam Smith wavered upon this very point, and discussed it at considerable length. For instance:

> The case in which it may sometimes be a matter of deliberation, how far, or in what manner, it is proper to restore the free importation of foreign goods, after it has been for some time interrupted, is, when particular manufactures, by means of high duties or prohibitions upon all foreign goods which can come into competition with them, have been so far extended as to employ a great multitude of hands. Humanity may in this case require that the freedom of trade should be restored only by slow gradations, and with a good deal of reserve and circumspection. Were those high duties and prohibitions taken away all at once, cheaper foreign goods of the same kind might be poured so fast into the home market, as to deprive all at once many thousands of our people of their ordinary employment and means of subsistence. The disorder which this would occasion might no doubt be very considerable. It would in all probability, however, be much less than is commonly imagined.[107]

But Smith, in an emphasis upon the adaptability of individuals to change, quickly shifted to the long-run view. He soon lost sight of the fact that this group with little resources lives in the present rather than in the future. He compared laborers with discharged soldiers:

> The manufacturer [i.e., the laborer] has always been accustomed to look for his subsistence from his labour only: the soldier to expect it from his pay. Application and industry have been familiar to the one; idleness and dissipation to the other. But it is surely much easier to change the direction of industry from one sort of labour to another, than to turn idleness and dissipation to any. To the greater part of manufactures besides, it has already been observed, there are

[107] *Wealth of Nations*, Bk. IV, p. 433.

other collateral manufactures of so similar a nature, that a workman can easily transfer his industry from one of them to another. The greater part of such workmen too are occasionally employed in country labour. The stock which employed them in a particular manufacture before, will still remain in the country to employ an equal number of people in some other way. The capital of the country remaining the same, the demand for labour will likewise be the same, or very nearly the same, though it may be exerted in different places and for different occupations. Soldiers and seamen, indeed, when discharged from the king's service, are at liberty to exercise any trade, within any town or place of Great Britain or Ireland. Let the same natural liberty of exercising what species of industry they please, be restored to all his majesty's subjects, in the same manner as to soldiers and seamen; that is, break down the exclusive privileges of corporations, and repeal the statute of apprenticeship, both which are real encroachments upon natural liberty, and add to these the repeal of the law of settlements, so that a poor workman, when thrown out of employment either in one trade or in one place, may seek for it in another trade or in another place, without the fear either of a prosecution or of a removal, and neither the public nor the individuals will suffer much more from the occasional disbanding some particular classes of manufactures, than from that of soldiers. Our manufacturers have no doubt great merit with their country, but they cannot have more than those who defend it with their blood, nor deserve to be treated with more delicacy.[108]

If Smith would not treat labor with "more delicacy" than soldiers and sailors, he laid himself open to the charge that he would treat the enterpriser with more consideration than he would labor:

The undertaker of a great manufacture, who, by the home markets being suddenly laid open to the competition of foreigners, should be obliged to abandon his trade, would no doubt suffer very considerably. That part of his capital which had usually been employed in purchasing materials and paying his workmen, might, without much difficulty, perhaps, find another employment. But that part of it which was fixed in workhouses, and in the instruments of trade, could scarce be disposed of without considerable loss. The equitable regard, therefore, to his interest requires that changes of this kind should never be introduced suddenly, but slowly, gradually, and after a very long warning.[109]

One cannot reproach Adam Smith with having deliberately

[108] *Ibid.*, pp. 434–435. [109] *Ibid.*, p. 436.

favored capital more than he did labor. He simply thought that that portion of capital which is fixed in plant is less adaptable to changed conditions, less mobile than labor. He forgot his adage that "man is, of all sorts of luggage, the most difficult to be transported."

Aside from the difference in the interpretation of the spirit of laissez faire which began to be manifested in Adam Smith, there is another marked, and indeed almost amusing, distinction between him and Boisguilbert. This has to do with the difference in their views on the value of grain.

Boisguilbert's limitation on the principle of laissez faire arose from his study of the causes and the effects of the fluctuating value of grain. In contrast to this, Smith refused to accept any limitation of the principle on this point on account of his conception of its value.

Speaking of the country gentlemen who had imposed the high duties on the importation of foreign corn and established the bounty, Smith declared that they "did not perhaps attend to the great and essential difference which nature has established between corn and almost every other sort of goods." [110] With this Boisguilbert would have agreed; he made almost the same statement himself.[111]

In the case of limitation of the importations of manufactures, continued Smith, you really encourage those manufactures.

> But when by the like institutions you raise the nominal or money-price of corn, you do not raise its real value. You do not increase the real wealth, the real revenue either of our farmers or country gentlemen. You do not encourage the growth of corn, because you do not enable them to maintain and employ more labourers in raising it. The nature of things has stamped upon corn a real value which cannot be altered by merely altering its money price. No bounty upon exportation, no monopoly of the home market, can raise that value. The freest competition cannot lower it.[112]

Boisguilbert contended that no one should attempt to theorize about agriculture and its commerce who is unacquainted with

[110] *Ibid.*, Bk. IV, p. 16.
[111] See above, pp. 225–226.
[112] *Loc. cit.*, Bk. IV, p. 17.

their practice. To do so, he declared, "produces monsters." He would have regarded Adam Smith as having sired one at this point. The peculiarities which Boisguilbert saw to differentiate the production and commerce of grain from other products were an inelastic demand and an uncontrollable supply. Whatever the ultimate or real value of grain might be, he would have declared that it is upon its money price that its producers depend for their requirements which they must purchase from others. Whereas Smith stated that the "average money price of corn regulates more or less that of all other commodities," Boisguilbert declared that it *should* do so.[113] But thinking in terms of a given time Boisguilbert saw that such was not the case, and that, on the contrary, an effort must be made to adjust the prices of agricultural products to other prices. To Boisguilbert who saw an increase in the production of grain and the building up of surpluses in times of high prices, there would have been something inexplicable in Smith's statement that by raising the "money price" you "do not encourage the growth of corn." The long-time swings between a large production and famine conditions the former observed to be the inevitable reactions to the changes in the money price of the product. In short, it must be confessed, there is a realism about Boisguilbert's discussion of grain which is completely lacking on the part of Smith's treatment of the same subject, whether one regards it from an immediate or from a long-run point of view.

OF THE REVENUE OF THE SOVEREIGN

Book V of *The Wealth of Nations* shows fewer marks of the thinking of Boisguilbert than any other portion of the work. This occasions a certain surprise, in view of the fact that in the opinion of scholars Boisguilbert has perhaps been more generally associated with public finance than with any other field of economics. Nevertheless, there is a trace of Boisguilbert even here. The so-called "Smith canons of taxation" were directly enunciated by Boisguilbert. Smith's discussion of tax farming—its cost in money to the people, its severity, the ostenta-

113 See above, p. 270; also *Traité des grains*, p. 355.

tious mode of life on the part of the tax farmers who wax rich—follows closely paragraphs scattered throughout *Le Détail, Factum,* and *Dissertation sur la nature des richesses.* Likewise his description of the French taille summarizes parts of *Le Détail.* On public debts, Smith's view approaches that of Boisguilbert. Finally, in the following quotation he may be said to summarize Boisguilbert's thesis as to the dependence of the sovereign for his financial well-being upon that of the people, and his duty toward them: "In almost all countries the revenue of the sovereign is drawn from that of the people. The greater the revenue of the people, therefore, the greater the annual produce of their land and labour, the more they can afford to the sovereign. It is his interest, therefore, to increase as much as possible that annual produce." [114]

[114] *Wealth of Nations,* Bk. IV, p. 136.

XVII

THE PROTOTYPE OF THE WEALTH OF NATIONS: EXTERNAL EVIDENCE

What if I lend mine ears, somewhat more attentively unto bookes, sith I but watch if I can filch something from them, wherewith to enammell and uphold mine?
MONTAIGNE.

AN EXAMINATION OF EXTERNAL EVIDENCE UPON THE MATTER IN QUESTION

THREE questions arise as a result of a comparison of the ideas of Boisguilbert and Adam Smith. Did the two derive from common sources? Is the similarity of thought the result of the indirect influence of Boisguilbert on Smith through the intermediary of Cantillon, the Physiocrats, and other eighteenth century writers? Did Smith derive directly from Boisguilbert? The first is doubtless probable to a limited extent. The second is conceivably possible. On the other hand it is difficult to explain all the points of similarity between the two as the result of a common or of a wholly indirect influence.

Smith did not mention Boisguilbert, as has been said, and none of Boisguilbert's writings is listed in the catalog of Smith's library. The latter, however, is not conclusive, as Professor Bonar made no pretense that it was a complete catalog of the library, but only as complete as it was possible to determine the content a century after the library itself had been dispersed. Yet there appears to be circumstantial evidence that Smith was familiar with the writings of Boisguilbert. It is this evidence which will be examined.

There is, first, the reference given above from *The Wealth of Nations.*[1] For further clues we must go to the life of Smith as given by Dugald Stewart and by John Rae.

[1] See above, pp. 273–274.

First of all we are told by Stewart that, according to his friend Dr. Maclaine, Smith's favorite studies at Glasgow were mathematics and natural philosophy.[2] Thereafter, Stewart said, Smith began to devote himself almost wholly to social science during his residence at Oxford.[3] Smith passed seven years at Oxford. In this period he seemed to have devoted all his time to reading, and he must have become familiar with a goodly portion of such part of the library as may have engrossed his attention. We are further told that Smith made a practice, during his residence there, *of translating, especially from the French,* with a view to improving his style.[4] One would hesitate to say that Smith would have been apt to translate Boisguilbert's writings to improve or develop his style;[5] but he could have read no work that would have been more likely to develop an intense interest in the social sciences, or one less likely to escape his efforts at translation, once this interest had been aroused. On this, the matter is resolved to some extent into that of the content of the library of Balliol at the time of Smith's residence,[6] as well as those of Glasgow and of Edinburgh, with which he was familiar.

There being no separate edition of the *Dissertation sur la nature des richesses,* Smith could not have known it without a knowledge of the remainder of Boisguilbert's writings. There is indeed reason to think that he was familiar with them all, and furthermore that he knew a particular edition of 1707. This was the first complete edition, which appeared "without name of

[2] "Account of Life and Writings of Dr. Smith," in *Essays on Philosophical Subjects,* Dublin, 1795, p. xii. All references to Dugald Stewart's life of Smith will be from this edition.

[3] *Ibid.,* p. xiii.

[4] *Ibid.,* p. xiv.

[5] Yet in spite of his difficulties and defects there is a charm, a freshness, and a frankness of expression in Boisguilbert similar to the qualities which characterize *The Wealth of Nations.*

[6] The writer is unaware of the extent to which a student at Oxford at that time would have had access to the libraries of colleges other than the one of which he was officially a resident. It must be remembered that there was keen desire both in England and in France, who were at war with one another at the time Boisguilbert was writing, to obtain publications which would throw light on one another's condition. Furthermore, England, as well as Holland, was the place of refuge of innumerable *émigrés,* who would be interested in obtaining such writings.

place or of author." Of the two complete editions published in 1712, the one carried Boisguilbert's name as author. The other (as well as the second edition in 1707), was published under the title of *Testament politique de M. de Vauban.* If the anonymous edition of 1707 was the one with which Smith was familiar, it explains, at least in part, his failure to give credit to Boisguilbert for any ideas he may have received from him. Thus far, then, it would seem that if Smith had in his own library a copy of Boisguilbert's writings, or any part of them, in all probability it was in the form of a manuscript translation from an unknown author, or else notes thereon, and may have been among the papers which so greatly disturbed his peace of mind until they were destroyed.

The question as to Adam Smith's originality arose during his lifetime, as well as immediately after his death. Smith, as has been shown by Dugald Stewart, was peculiarly, and, in the light of modern psychology, it may be said, suspiciously sensitive about it. The question centered around the principle of freedom of trade. Stewart said, that "his doctrine concerning the freedom of trade and of industry coincides remarkably with that which we find in the writings of the French Oeconomists, appears from the slight view of their system which he himself has given." [7] But Stewart asserted that Smith did not get his doctrine from the Physiocrats. They "appear, with respect to him, to have been altogether original, and the result of his own reflections." The "economical writers," he said, simply had the "start of him in publishing their doctrines to the world." The fundamental principles of his *Inquiry,* he continued, were in his lectures, delivered as early as 1752 or 1753, "at a period, surely, when there existed no French performance on the subject, that could be of much use in guiding his researches." [8] It is true that at this time Quesnay had not published his *Tableau économique,* nor was Cantillon's *Essai* yet in print. But Dugald Stewart in writing this shows that he himself had never read *Le Détail de la France,* in which the descriptions and analyses of the effects

[7] *Essays,* etc., p. c.
[8] *Ibid.,* p. ci.

of restraints on trade in France, and the protestations against it, were sufficient to start a new school of economic thought.

Stewart manifested a strange carelessness in his own scholarship. To substantiate his statement that in 1752 or 1753 there existed "no French performance" from which Smith could have drawn, he cited the "Notice abrégé des différents écrits modernes qui ont concouru en France à former la science de l'économie politique," in *Éphémerides du citoyen,* Tome premier, [January], 1769. In this article Du Pont de Nemours cites Montesquieu, Melon, Dutot, and Vauban, as the French writers of any importance in the field of economic thought preceding 1754–1755. Thus far Stewart was correct. There was nothing here which could have influenced Adam Smith's economic analysis to any great extent. But Du Pont, like Stewart, was careless. Had the latter read the entire series of articles in *Éphémerides,* of which the January number was only the first, a doubt would certainly have entered his mind. In the ninth number, September, 1769, Du Pont makes a most abject apology. In this final number of the articles, presumably at the instigation of Mirabeau, he said:

> We just now recall a book that it is indeed astonishing that we should have forgotten, as it is one of the first that we have read and as we possess two copies of it. This book is *Le Détail de la France,* by M. Pierre le Pesant, Seigneur de Bois-Guilbert, attorney general of the Court of Aides in Normandy. This work, of which the title, it is true, is not very clear, and of which the reading is a little fatiguing because the style is incorrect and diffuse, is, nevertheless, singularly precious on account of the sagacity with which the author understood all that of which the world in his time was ignorant: the necessity to respect the advances of useful labor, and *the advantages of liberty of commerce.* If he had seen that land and waters were the sole sources from which the labor of man can obtain wealth, and that labor of conservation, of manufacture, of exchange, etc., that have been quite improperly confounded under the generic term of industrial labor, did nothing except to exert itself on wealth already produced without adding anything thereupon; if he had recognized the existence of the net product, and distinguished it from the costs of reproduction; if he had combined these truths with the others that he sensed, the honor of originating the principles of economic science would be due him.[9]

[9] "Notice abrégé," etc., *Éphémerides du citoyen*. September, 1769, pp. 8–10. My italics.

But these "defects" which Du Pont deplored in Boisguilbert's reasoning, are the very points on which Smith also was to differ from the Physiocrats. Du Pont continued to discuss Boisguilbert, devoting more space to him than was given to any writer with the exception of the Physiocrats themselves. With a knowledge of this eulogy Stewart would not have made the statement he did. In any case, Adam Smith, the scholar, the economist, must have been an avid reader of the current numbers of *Éphémerides*. Certainly he had read Quesnay and Mirabeau, who specifically mention Boisguilbert. Surely he had read Vauban's *Dime royale* wherein the author of *Le Détail de la France* is lauded. Furthermore, it may safely be assumed that Smith was familiar with all the works of Voltaire, who referred to Boisguilbert eight times. Surely Smith's curiosity would have led him to become acquainted with the writings of a man who had so irritated Voltaire that the latter had declared "it is not the function of history to examine how the people should contribute [to taxes] without being oppressed." In view of all the chances he had to learn of Boisguilbert's existence, it is difficult to think that Smith, with his intellectual curiosity, failed to know his writings by 1770, if he had not made their acquaintance twenty years earlier.

Dugald Stewart carried the subject of Adam Smith's originality still further.

There exists, however, fortunately, a short manuscript drawn up by Mr. Smith in the year 1755, and presented by him to a society of which he was a member; in which paper, a pretty long enumeration is given of certain leading principles, both political and literary, to which he was anxious to establish his exclusive right; in order to prevent the possibility of some rival claims which he thought he had reason to apprehend, and to which his situation as a Professor, added to his unreserved communications in private companies rendered him peculiarly liable. This paper is at present in my possession. . . . *Many of the most important opinions in* The Wealth of Nations *are there detailed;* but I shall quote only the following sentences: "Man is generally considered by statesmen and projectors as the materials of a sort of political mechanics. Projectors disturb nature in the course of her operations in human affairs; and *it requires no more than to let her alone* . . . that she may establish her own designs."

[He continued to quote Smith:] "Little else is requisite to carry a state to the highest degree of opulence from the lowest barbarism, but peace, easy taxes, and a tolerable administration of justice; all the rest being brought about by the natural course of things. All governments which thwart this natural course, which force things into another channel, or which endeavour to arrest the progress of society at a particular point, are unnatural, and to support themselves are obliged to be oppressive and tyrannical. A great part of the opinion (he observes) enumerated in this paper is treated of at length in some lectures which I still have by me, and which were written in the hand of a clerk who left my service six years ago. They have all of them been the constant subjects of my lectures since I first taught Mr. Craigie's class, the first winter I spent in Glasgow, down to this day, without any considerable variation. They had all of them been the subjects of lectures which I read at Edinburgh the winter before I left it, and I can adduce innumerable witnesses, both from that place and from this, who will ascertain them sufficiently to be mine." [10]

Having delivered these lectures so soon after his return to Scotland, it would seem that Adam Smith had left Oxford with the outline of the ideas later to be developed in *The Wealth of Nations* fairly well fixed in mind. One must be grateful to him for writing this paper, and to Dugald Stewart for recording excerpts from it, for it contains an important piece of evidence with regard to the originality which Smith was trying hard to establish. The first passage in which Boisguilbert used the expression "laisse faire" has already been quoted.[11] But again in *Factum* he said:

Il n'y avait qu'à laisser faire la nature, comme partout ailleurs, et la liberté, qui est la commissionnaire de cette même nature, n'aurait pas manqué de faire une compensation avantageuse, qui aurait formé un très-grand bien de deux très-grandes misères.[12]

Leaving out of consideration the similarity of the thought in general to the quotation from Smith, there could be no better translation of the phrase *Il n'y avait qu'à laisser faire la nature* than Smith made when, speaking of nature, he said, "it requires no more than to let her alone." Substitute the antecedent "na-

[10] *Essays on Philosophical Subjects,* pp. ciii–cv. My italics.
[11] See above, pp. 250–251.
[12] *Factum,* p. 286.

ture" for the pronoun "her"—"it requires no more than to let nature alone"—and the probable source of the expression is apparent.

In his *Life of Adam Smith* John Rae continued the history of the controversy. In all the discussion as it is set forth there is no mention of the name of Boisguilbert. Of Cantillon, and of Tucker, yes. But there seemed to be no knowledge of an older source. Rae quoted the Marquis of Lansdowne, whom Smith had long known as the Earl of Shelbourne, as having said in a debate in the House of Lords in 1793:

> With respect to French principles, as they had been denominated, those principles had been exported from us to France, and could not be said to have originated among the population of the latter country. The new principles of government founded on the abolition of the old feudal system were originally propagated among us by the Dean of Gloucester, Mr. Tucker, and had since been more generally inculcated by Dr. Adam Smith, in his work on the *Wealth of Nations*.[13]

Boisguilbert, incidentally, was bringing out two editions of his complete works in 1712, the year in which Josiah Tucker was born![14]

Speaking of the paper read before the Glasgow Economic Society by Smith, Rae said,

> Mr. James Bonar suggests that this manifesto of 1755 was directed against Adam Ferguson, but that is not probable. Ferguson's name, it is true, will readily occur in such a connection, because Dr. Carlyle tells us that when he published his *History of Civil Society* in 1767 Smith accused him of having borrowed some of his ideas without owning them, and that *Ferguson replied that he had borrowed nothing from Smith, but much from some French source unnamed where Smith had been before him.*[15]

Adam Ferguson's frankness is both refreshing and enlighten-

[13] *Life of Adam Smith,* London, 1895, p. 291.

[14] Nevertheless, in a very definite way, the concept of the principle of liberty "was exported" from England to France. Fundamentally there were two major influences which determined Boisguilbert's thinking. First, there were the conditions resulting from bad government in France; secondly, there was the different course of political, economic and social events in England. His positive theory may be said in a very real sense to have been simply a rationale of what he thought to be the English way of life, a way of life he would have the French adopt.

[15] *Op. cit.*, p. 65. My italics.

ing. This reply, as quoted by Dr. Carlyle, lends itself to two interpretations. It can mean, first, that Ferguson failed to state what the source was, which appears to be the obvious meaning. But it may mean that Ferguson referred to an *anonymous* French source into which both he and Smith had dipped.

Ferguson, like Smith, made no direct reference to Boisguilbert. It remains, then, to examine his *History of Civil Society* for traces of the influence of the latter. If they can be found, then the evidence is plain that Ferguson was laughing up his sleeve at Smith's protestations of originality, but was gentleman enough to remain quiet for the benefit of his friend's reputation until he himself was, presumably, accused of borrowing from the latter.

The fact is that Ferguson's *History of Civil Society* does show the influence of Boisguilbert's ideas. In a sense Ferguson may be said to have grasped what we may call the ultimate ideas of Boisguilbert, that is, the ideas of Boisguilbert, the social philosopher, rather than of Boisguilbert, the economist, to an even greater extent than did Smith in *The Wealth of Nations.*

What is here termed "the ultimate ideas of Boisguilbert" refers to his ideal of social perfection, and to his belief in the necessity for the voluntary subordination of the individual to the group in order to promote the general welfare. It is upon these ideas, particularly, that much of the reputation of Ferguson rests. They are the basis for his reputation as a precursor of the sociologists.

In giving the following quotations from Ferguson as an indication of his ideas, corresponding ones from Boisguilbert will not be quoted. It is assumed that the reader now has sufficient acquaintance with the fundamental ideas of the latter to recognize them in the writings of another.

In his statement that "Mankind are to be taken in groupes [*sic*], as they have always subsisted." [16] Ferguson stated not only his basic idea, but also that of Boisguilbert. He continued:

> Man is, by nature, the member of a community; and when considered in this capacity, the individual appears to be no longer made

[16] *An Essay on the History of Civil Society,* 2d ed., London, 1768, Pt. I, p. 6.

for himself. He must forego his happiness and his freedom, where these interfere with the good of society. He is only part of a whole; and the praise we think due to his virtue, is but a branch of that more general commendation we bestow on the members of a body, on the part of a fabric or engine, for being well fitted to occupy its place, and to produce its effect.[17]

The recognition of this relationship as a working principle is the basis of virtue:

A person of an affectionate mind, possessed of a maxim, that he himself, as an individual, is no more than a part of the whole that demands his regard, has found, in that principle a sufficient foundation for all the virtues.[18]

Ferguson explained the source of self-interest:

Although the consideration of interest is founded on the experience of animal wants and desires, its object is not to gratify any particular appetite, but to secure the means of gratifying all; and it imposes frequently a restraint on the very desire from which it arose, more powerful and more severe than those of religion or duty. It arises from the principle of self-preservation in the human frame; but is a corruption, or at least a partial result of those principles, and is upon many accounts very improperly termed *self-love*.[19]

This self-love must be subordinated to the higher qualities of the individual.

It is somewhat remarkable, that notwithstanding men value themselves so much on qualities of the mind, on parts, learning and wit, on courage, generosity, and honour, these men are still supposed to be in the highest degree selfish or attentive to themselves, who are most careful to animal life, and who are least mindful of rendering that life an object worthy of care. It will be difficult, however, to tell why a good understanding, a resolute and generous mind, should not, by every man in his senses, be reckoned as much parts of himself, as either his stomach or his palate, and much more so than his estate or his dress. The epicure, who consults his physician, how he may restore his relish for his food, and by creating an appetite, may increase the means of enjoyment, might at least with an equal regard to himself, consult how he might strengthen his affection to a parent or a child, to his country or to mankind; and it is probable that an appetite of this sort would prove a source of enjoyment not less than the former.[20]

[17] *Ibid.*, Pt. I, pp. 86–87. [18] *Ibid.*, Pt. I, p. 57.
[19] *Ibid.*, Pt. I, p. 18. [20] *Ibid.*, Pt. I, pp. 19–20.

Both Ferguson and Boisguilbert, then, were intent upon the development of consideration on the part of the individual for the group. Each would do it through an extension of the concept of self-interest. Here is also shown an essential difference between their ideas. Ferguson enlarged the concept to include consideration for spiritual development as well as for physical welfare; the practical Boisguilbert, on the other hand, who took no flights into the ethereal, would obtain results by having the individual recognize that in the end his own economic interest is bound up with that of the group.

For Ferguson, as for Boisguilbert, public interest is served by the self-interest of the individual. "The public interest is often secure, not because individuals are disposed to regard it as the end of their conduct, but because each, in his place, is determined to preserve his own."[21] Nor must there be public interference in the pursuit of this self-interest.

> Men are tempted to labour, and to practice the lucrative arts, by motives of interest. Secure to the workman the fruit of his labour, give him the prospect of independence or freedom, the public has found a faithful minister in the acquisition of wealth, and a faithful steward in hoarding what he has gained. The statesman in this, as in the case of population itself, can do little more than avoid doing mischief. It is well, if, in the beginnings of commerce, he knows how to repress the frauds to which it is subject. Commerce, if continued, is the branch in which men committed to the effects of their own experience, are least apt to go wrong. . . .
>
> If population be connected with national wealth, liberty and personal security is the great foundation of both: and if this foundation be laid in the state, nature has secured the increase and the industry of its members; the one by desires the most ardent in the human frame; and the other by a consideration the most uniform and constant of any that possesses the mind. The great object of policy, therefore, with respect to both, is, to secure to the family its means of subsistence and settlement; to protect the industrious in the pursuit of his occupation; to reconcile the restrictions of police, and the social affections of mankind, with their separate and interested pursuits.
>
> In matters of particular profession, industry, and trade, the experienced practitioner is the master, and every general reasoner is a novice. The object in commerce is to make the individual rich; the

[21] *Ibid.*, Pt. III, p. 196.

more he gains for himself, the more he augments the wealth of his country. If a protection be required, it must be granted; if crimes and frauds be committed, they must be repressed; and the government can pretend no more. When the refined politician would lend an active hand, he only multiplies interruptions and grounds of complaint; when the merchant forgets his own interest to lay plans for his country, the period of vision and chimera is near, and the solid basis of commerce withdrawn. He might be told, that while he pursues his advantage, and gives no cause of complaint, the interest of commerce is safe.

The general police of France, proceeding on a supposition that the exportation of corn must drain the country, where it had grown, had, till of late, laid that branch of commerce under a severe prohibition. The English landholder and the farmer had credit enough to obtain a premium for exportation, to favor the sale of the commodity; and the event has shewn, that private interest is a better patron of commerce and plenty, than the refinements of state.[22]

Here, in almost every sentence, the views of Boisguilbert are to be found. "In matters of particular profession, industry, and trade, the experienced practitioner is the master, and every general reasoner is a novice." When he wrote that, was Ferguson thinking of Boisguilbert's remark with regard to Vauban uttered in *Factum de la France* (as well as in his correspondence), as when he declared, following the above quotation, that "I willingly quit a subject in which I am not much conversant, and still less engaged by the views with which I write"?

If so, it explains why Ferguson followed and developed the ideas of Boisguilbert along purely sociological, rather than economic, lines as did Adam Smith. Ferguson did not know about things commercial, and cared little, and following Boisguilbert's advice he left the field to others.

There are, however, a few other points of similarity in their views to which attention may be called. There is, for instance, the development of Boisguilbert's theme as to how the "corruption of the hearts" of individuals, that is, over-attention to their immediate interest, rather than to the welfare of the group, leads to a disorganization in the economic life of a country.

Men, in fact, while they pursue in society different objects, or

[22] *Ibid.*, Pt. III, pp. 219–221.

separate views, procure a wide distribution of power, and by a species of chance, arrive at a posture for civil engagements, more favourable to human nature than what human nature could ever calmly devise.

If the strength of a nation, in the meantime, consists in the men on whom it may rely, and who are fortunately or wisely combined for its preservation, it follows, that manners are as important as either numbers or wealth; and that corruption is to be accounted a principal cause of national declension and ruin.

Whoever perceives what are the qualities of man in his excellence, may easily, by that standard, distinguish his defects or corruptions. If an intelligent, a courageous, and an affectionate mind, constitutes the perfection of his nature, remarkable failings in any of those particulars, must proportionally sink or debase his character.

We have observed, that it is the happiness of the individual to make a right choice of his conduct; that this choice will lead him to lose in society the sense of personal interest; and, in the consideration of what is due to the whole, to stifle those anxieties which relate to himself as a part.

The natural disposition of man to humanity, and the warmth of his temper, may raise his character to this fortunate pitch. . . . He may entertain, toward the different ranks of men with whom he is yoked in the state, maxims of respect and of candour: he may, in the choice of his actions, follow a principle of justice, and of honour, which the considerations of safety, preferment, or profit, cannot efface.

From our complaints of national depravity, it should notwithstanding, appear, that whole bodies of men are sometimes infected with an epidemical weakness of the head, or corruption of the heart, by which they become unfit for the stations they occupy, and threaten the states they compose, however flourishing, with a prospect of decay and of ruin.

A change of national manners for the worse, may arise from a discontinuance of the scenes in which the talents of men were happily cultivated, and brought into exercise; or from a change in the prevailing opinions relating to the constituents of honour or of happiness. When mere riches, or court-favour, are supposed to constitute rank; the mind is misled from the consideration of qualities on which it ought to rely. Magnanimity, courage, and the love of mankind, are sacrificed to avarice and vanity, or suppressed under a sense of dependence. The individual considers his community so far only as it can be rendered subservient to his personal advancement or his profit: he states himself in competition with his fellow creatures; and, urged by the passions of emulation, of fear and jealousy, of envy and malice, he follows the maxims of an animal destined to preserve his separate existence, and to indulge his caprice or his appetite, at the expense of his species.[23]

Again, there is Ferguson's explanation of the meaning and function of luxury, which corresponds to Boisguilbert's view in regard to what he termed *le superflu*.

With all this diversity in our judgments, we are generally uniform in employing the term [luxury] to signify that complicated apparatus which mankind devise for the ease and convenience of life. Their buildings, furniture, equipage, cloathing, train of domestics, refinement of the table, and in general, all that assemblage which is rather intended to please the fancy, than to obviate real wants, and which is rather ornamental than useful.

When we are disposed, therefore, under the appellation of *luxury*, to rank the enjoyment of these things among the vices, we either tacitly refer to the habits of sensuality, debauchery, prodigality, vanity, and arrogance, with which the possession of high fortune is sometimes attended; or we apprehend a certain measure of what is necessary to human life, beyond which all enjoyments are supposed to be excessive and vicious. When on the contrary, luxury is made an article of national lustre and felicity, we only think of it as an innocent consequence of the unequal distribution of wealth, and as a method by which different ranks are rendered mutually dependent, and mutually useful. The poor is made to practice arts, and the rich to reward them. The public itself is made a gainer by what seems to waste its stock, and it receives a perpetual increase of wealth, from the influence of those growing appetites, and delicate tastes, which seem to menace consumption and ruin.[24]

Then there is the comparison of man to animals in relation to the part played by nature so like Boisguilbert: "Nature, therefore, we shall presume, having given to every animal its mode of existence, its dispositions and manners of life, has dealt equally with those of the human race." [25]

And there is the same attitude toward the corrupting influence of the commercial state on the human spirit, as contrasted with a simpler existence: "If the savage has not received our instructions, he is likewise unacquainted with our vices. He knows no superior, and cannot be servile; he knows no distinctions of

[23] *Ibid.*, Pt. VI, pp. 364–366.
[24] *Ibid.*, Pt. VI, pp. 375–376.
[25] *Ibid.*, Pt. I, p. 6.

fortune, and cannot be envious; he acts from his talents in the highest station which human society can offer, that of counsellor, and the soldier of his country." [26] But as to the other state, "it is here, indeed, if ever, that man is sometimes found a detached and solitary being: he has found an object which sets him in competition with his fellow creatures, and he deals with them as he does his cattle and his soil, for the sake of the profits they bring." [27]

For the most part in another direction, Adam Ferguson, in his *History of Civil Society,* showed the earmarks of the influence of Boisguilbert, in many respects less distinctly, because he pursued a different sequence of ideas, but as certainly as did Adam Smith. Each found in his writings that which brought a response according to his own taste and inclination; each, for the most part, took a different route in pursuit of the ideas obtained. Thus from a common source there diverged two roads: one was to lead to the conception of man as an economic animal, concerned only with the pursuit of gain; the other was at least to point the way to man's position and responsibility as a member of a community. But both were to fail to grasp the fact that Boisguilbert had made the roads converge again; that he had tried to reconcile the apparently irreconcilable conflict which exists between individual and social interest. This he did through his long-run view of self-interest, when he declared and attempted to show, that no one can be permanently secure in his position except through the stability of the whole, and that in his own interest, therefore, man dare not neglect to give attenion to the welfare of others.

Conclusion

In spite of their common intellectual equipment in the way of judicial attitude and sound logical thinking, even a casual reading of *The Wealth of Nations* and any of the works of Boisguilbert reveals immediately the difference between his temperament and that of Adam Smith. The one was eager, impatient, intuitive, alert; the other calm, meticulous, slow, and painstaking. The

[26] *Ibid.*, Pt. IV, pp. 285–286.
[27] *Ibid.*, Pt. I, p. 29.

one was a practical yet studious type of great originality, penetrating thought, and natural brilliance; the other scholarly and academic, well fitted to develop and coördinate the ideas of others. Only in his last two books does Smith rise to something approaching the restrained impatience, the fighting mood, indeed, which is so characteristic of Boisguilbert.

The result is an aroused, though closely reasoned, exposition of protest on the one hand, and a calm and seasoned presentation of a thesis on the other. Each attempted to explain the economic phenomena of his day. Boisguilbert had an especial handicap in having to a great degree to forge his own tools of thought. Smith had the advantage of these original implements, and the improvement resulting from their whetting and development through a half century of use.

The difference in accent, if one may so call it, in the works of the two men, is the expression of the difference in their backgrounds. In his economic analysis it was inevitable that Boisguilbert as a practical man of affairs should attempt to deal in a very realistic manner with the dynamic character of economic life. It was likewise inevitable that the passing of the subject matter into the hands of an academic philosopher should result in a tendency to convert this everyday realism into a philosophical abstraction. So too, the disturbed economic conditions in the closing years of the reign of Louis XIV imperatively demanded a dynamic analysis; conversely, the prosperity of England in the third quarter of the eighteenth century and before, lent itself to a minimizing of economic change, and to long-run analysis. Each man expressed, and was the expression of, his times.

In essence, one may say that Adam Smith took the *Dissertation sur la nature des richesses, de l'argent et des tributs* as his text for *An Inquiry into the Nature and Causes of The Wealth of Nations*. This text Smith approved, disagreed with, expanded, and added digressions, until he had produced a notable and perfected work bearing his own imprint. In the one, there is, as Daire has said, "economic science in the cradle." To have brought the infant to maturity deserves scarcely less credit than to have given it birth.

APPENDIX

CRITICISM OF ONCKEN'S HISTORY OF THE ORIGIN OF THE MAXIM LAISSEZ FAIRE

But there is still more to be said.

Origin of the Slogan according to Oncken

The origin of the phrase "laissez faire" is obscure. An attempt to trace its history was made by Professor August Oncken.[1] In view of the fact that his is the standard work upon the subject, and presumably definitive; that a thorough-going study of Boisguilbert necessitates a review of the maxim; and finally in view of the character of this presumably authoritative work with relation to Boisguilbert, it would seem to be advisable to give a somewhat full summary of the pertinent points of the first part of Oncken's analysis. As Adam Smith would say, it is necessary to risk "tediousness in order to be perspicuous."

The origin of the formula, said Oncken, is French without question; but as to the time and place where it was first used, opinions differ. Its casual use has no significance in history, he continued. It is of no importance whatsoever, except when it becomes the conscious maxim of the political economy of a country.[2]

Most histories of political economy of our day designate the co-founder of the Physiocratic system, Gournay, as its originator. Although not a theoretical writer, he pronounced this maxim, and made it the nucleus which lived on in his pupils. "This is only a tradition, however; nothing definite is reported." If this tradition is followed up, another name makes its appearance: that

[1] August Oncken, *Die Maxime laissez faire et laissez passer, ihr Ursprung, ihr Werden. Ein Beitrag zur Geschichte der Freihandelslehre,* Bern, 1886. Development of two lectures delivered before the Historical Society of Bern.
[2] *Ibid.,* p. 4.

of a certain Legendre. Thus, the foundation of the usual view begins to totter.[3]

Oncken quoted Garnier as having said that Turgot in his Gournay *Eulogy* stated, " 'One knows the words of M. Legendre to M. Colbert: Laissez-nous faire.' " Nevertheless, that the statement should be attributed to Gournay is the leading view in France. Oncken accounted for this by the fact that most of the sources of "French assumptions, good or bad, right or wrong," go back to J. B. Say. "Such was his prestige that his statements were taken as those of an oracle." Say's source was Turgot's *Eulogy* also. Oncken thus went to the *Eulogy,* and found that Garnier, and not Say, had quoted correctly. How did Say come to make the mistake? He was misled by Du Pont's introduction to the *Eulogy,* in which the latter, "unconcerned about the statement in the *Eulogy,*" attributed the origin of the maxim to Gournay.[4]

The two conflicting views, said Oncken, can be harmonized. The formula is composed of two parts, related but not having the same meaning. "Laissez faire" means freedom of production; "laissez passer," however, means freedom of trade. Turgot speaks only of laissez faire. "Laissez passer" is not found prior to the Physiocrats. Gournay was responsible for the completion, not for the origin, of the slogan. Furthermore, Oncken continued, a distinction must be made between the incident giving life to the maxim and its appearance as a theoretical principle.[5]

After much search Oncken found the earliest use of the expression "laissez-nous faire" by an anonymous writer in *Journal œconomique* for the year 1751. It is on account of this "article," he thought, that the expression is attributed to Legendre.[6] The remark is ascribed therein, Oncken stated, to " 'the most sensible and plainest spoken' " of the merchants whom Colbert had called together to seek their advice. The name of the merchant was not given in the article. However, when Turgot quoted the ex-

[3] *Ibid.,* pp. 4–5. German writers and *Handbücher* prior to Kellner, states Oncken, uniformly attribute the expression to Gournay.

[4] *Ibid.,* pp. 8–10.

[5] *Ibid.,* pp. 10–11.

[6] This article, or letter, rather, which Oncken correctly, I think, attributes to D'Argenson, was translated into English in *Select Essays on Commerce, Agriculture, Mines, Factories and Other Useful Subjects,* London, 1754.

pression in the Gournay *Eulogy,* he imputed it to Legendre. Both agreed, Oncken continued, that the reply was given in an assembly of merchants called together by Colbert.[7]

After having examined the literature of the period of Louis XIV carefully, Oncken found that none of the contemporary writers mentioned the incident. Nor did those who have written on Colbert. Yet he thought there was no reason to regard the occurrence as a myth. Councils on commerce were held by Colbert from time to time. Referring to the one reported by Amylot de la Houssaye, Oncken said one might be tempted to assume that this incident is the source of the tradition, the facts of which might have become transformed. This theory, however, Oncken did not accept, because "it is contradicted by the fact that it is attributed to Legendre, and the slogan was supposed to have been used which would scarcely have been added later." By a process of elimination Oncken placed the incident itself around the year 1680.[8]

Who was Legendre? Oncken attempted to find out. Turgot gave no other name. He was known, however, to have been a merchant. One François Legendre wrote *L'Arithmétique en sa perfection mise en pratique selon l'usage des financiers, banquiers, et marchands avec un traité de géométrie pratique apliquée à l'arpentage et au toisé, et un abrégé d'algèbre,* the first edition of which, said Oncken, appeared in 1657.[9] He also wrote other works, Oncken said, but in none of them was the Colbert incident mentioned. Was Legendre an active merchant? Oncken asked. Today, he thought, when theory and practice are seldom combined, the assumption would be against it. It was different then, and it may be assumed that he was one. In any event, he was dead before 1687.[10]

Oncken next tried to determine where the incident occurred. One might assume, he thought, that it occurred at Paris or Versailles. He considered it unlikely, however, as in that case it

[7] *Die Maxime,* pp. 12–14.
[8] *Ibid.,* pp. 14–29.
[9] As a matter of fact, and indeed a fact of considerable importance at this point, the first edition appeared in 1646, according to E. Castelot.
[10] *Die Maxime,* pp. 29–34. The permit to print the ninth edition was given to his widow in 1687.

probably would have been recorded. He quoted Gozenbach [11] as believing it occurred in Lyons. Gozenbach spoke of a society of merchants in Lyons, and told of Colbert receiving a deputation of merchants who went to see the king. According to Gozenbach, on being asked what could be done for them, the provost of the merchants replied, " 'Laissez faire, laissez aller.' " Gozenbach had heard this as a tradition, mentioned by a chief customs inspector in 1834. Oncken had the list of provosts in Lyons searched. No provost or outstanding merchant by the name of Legendre was found.[12]

As to this legendary part of the history, Oncken thought there was a possibility that François Legendre was identical with the great merchant Legendre to whom tradition attributes the expression. This point could not be completely cleared up. The place Lyons, and the date 1680, are only proverbial. In any event, he again repeated, the slogan does not originate the science. It becomes significant only when it becomes the nucleus of a theory.[13]

We now turn to Oncken's account of Boisguilbert's part in the use of the expression. "Laissez faire," said Oncken, was the slogan of the third estate in the economic field. In the political arena it took the more aggressive formulation, liberty, equality, fraternity. The third and fourth estates, he continued, were not differentiated [14] prior to the Revolution. The third estate was composed of capitalists and the wealthy farmers. They had shifted the taxes to the fourth estate, from whom the complaints came.[15]

Two authors, in the time of Louis XIV, as spokesmen for the lower estates, had the courage to point out the necessity for political reforms for them. These authors were Boisguilbert and Vauban. "There is no greater critic of the argument of governmental omniscience in things economic than the Rouen magistrate." [16]

[11] *Einige Gedanken über die Aufstellung eines schweizerischen Schutszollsystemes.* Zurich, 1840.

[12] *Die Maxime,* pp. 34–36. [13] *Ibid.,* pp. 38–39.

[14] Oncken referred, presumably, to lack of legal differentiation.

[15] *Ibid.,* p. 41.

[16] *Ibid.,* p. 42. This, said Oncken, quoting the full title of *Factum,* did not prevent him from thinking that he himself was omniscient. This title, he said,

All the study and researches of Boisguilbert, Oncken quoted Horn as having said, lead to "laissez faire, laissez passer." The same opinion was expressed still more strongly if possible by Felix Cadet. "This view has been opposed by Dühring, Cohn, and Skarzinski, with the objection that this liberty of trade could not be thought of as an absolute one." This was Oncken's view. "One must ask what he means by liberty of trade." Although "liberty of trade, especially of grains, forms the fulcrum (*Angelpunkt*) of his theory," nevertheless, this "does not mean too much, if one considers that even in the *Memoirs* of Colbert there is found the demand that commerce be free, even 'extremely free.'" [17]

First of all, Boisguilbert had in mind proposals exactly opposite to the goal of modern free-trade theory. Not low grain prices as are sought, but high ones, *as high as possible (möglichst hohe),* were the aims of Boisguilbert, as well as of his successors, the Physiocrats, and free trade should bring this about. Not only the interests of the industrialists, but also that of the farmers, especially the small farmers, were the beginning and the end. *Industry was looked upon with envious eyes.* If the peasant has high-priced grain, then he enjoys a large amount of money and is able to buy more manufactured goods; if the prices are low, the farmer is losing income and with that, purchasing power; moreover, the value of his property is falling with the decline in the rentability of the soil, and because of that the foundation of the State becomes undermined. Therefore the slogan formulated later by Quesnay, which, however, already dominated all the reasoning of Boisguilbert: *Pauvre paysan, pauvre royaume; pauvre royaume, pauvre roi. . . .*[18]

How does it occur that free trade is to be recommended as a means of raising the price of grain? The explanation gives proof of the relativity of all economic measures, and of the necessity for testing the meaning of the term "free trade" everywhere it is encountered.

Boisguilbert in no case understands by "liberty in the commerce

---

shows that political economy had its period of alchemy. Boisguilbert thought he had found the philosopher's stone. This, Cncken added, is one of the reasons why the Manchester school, which claims omniscience, claims Boisguilbert as the ancestor of its theory.

[17] *Ibid.*, pp. 43–44. To clear up the paradox of one who expressed the ideal of liberty, yet whose name has become synonymous with *restriction,* Oncken should have explained that Colbert, along with his apparent love for liberty, had also a love for *order* that amounted to little less than a mania.

[18] *Ibid.*, p. 44. My italics.

of grain" the liberty of grain imports, which forms the focal point of the modern free-trade theory, but only and exclusively liberty of exportation. . . . The standing reproach which he directs against Colbert is that the latter had prohibited the exportation of grain in order to keep the grain in the country at a low price and at the farmer's expense, so that the urban industries could have cheap bread and thereby low wages. *The postulate that our modern free-trade theory takes as its goal is branded by the so-called ancestor of the theory as the darkest evil of injustice.*

That the free import of grain lowers prices Boisguilbert knows very well, and this is the very reason why he declares himself explicitly *against it everywhere it is referred to.* In Chapter XI of *Factum,* in which he discusses the authorized importation of Barbary wheat into Provence he wants the import prohibited. However, through this prohibition the price of grain would be raised as if it were through an impost. Nevertheless he thinks: *"Les bleds de Barbarie exclus de la Provence, redonneront au Languedoc six fois cette hausse d'impôt, et à la Provence même."* Only in times of sterility should this import be permitted and only as a necessary evil. . . . This commerce only serves the interest of the middlemen, who are only looking out for private gain, but not for the interest of the king and the nation. The latter runs contrary to the interest of capital, and therefore parallel with the value of the soil, because *l'augmentation du prix des denrées fait celui des terres, qui seules font vivre tous les États.*

In order to prevent grain prices from the destructive sinking, Boisguilbert even makes at another place, namely, in his famous special treatise *Traité de la nature, culture, commerce et intérêt des grains,* the *proposition to follow the example of the English in fixing exportation bounties on grain.* Nor has he in another place anything to criticize in the procedure of the Dutch, who destroy a part of their grain, so that the remainder will bring higher prices.

Let us add further, that the old advocate of free trade also recommends for the internal trade governmental fixed prices (*Preistaxen*), in order to prohibit *"par une autorité puissante" "qu'une marchandise ne devienne la proie et la victime de l'avidité d'un commerçant,"* [19] and one receives an ample judgment concerning the correctness with which the modern free traders call him their ancestor, as he could rather be designated the progenitor of modern agrarianism.

In the previously mentioned passage in the book of I. E. Horn

[19] Presumably Oncken was having such a difficult time to determine the thought of this paragraph that he is to be excused for giving the reference as *Traité des grains,* Pt. I, chapter ii, whereas it is in chapter i.

one could conclude that our formula occurs already in the works of Boisguilbert. That this is not the case, at least not in the sense in which it is later used, we have just now seen. That is not to say that the slogan has not been used at least in form. . . .[20]

In embryo we already notice in Boisguilbert the principle of the harmony of interests which was later connected with the formula. However one must read this everywhere with a grain of salt. This is the point at which Dühring and Skarzinski, and to a certain degree Cohn, have driven the wedge in to oppose the pretenses of the Manchester school; however, as it seems to me especially, not here with very much luck.

The *Factum* gives in Chapter IV at first an explanation of the harmony of interest of economic life under free trade, and immediately following the striking remark, that *"par une corruption de cœur effroyable"* this harmony of interest is constantly disturbed because each individual thinks only from morning to evening how to hit his neighbor over the ear; only at the point of the sword can justice be upheld in social life. Dühring concludes from this contradiction that "if anywhere a thought has been born in two contrasting halves it has occurred here." However, the supposed contradiction resolves itself immediately if one reads the respective sentences more carefully. In one case he talks of professional barter; in the other case he speaks of the warding off of cheating and robbery through the public law. In the latter sense he has stated it thus: *"Ce n'est qu'à la pointe de l'épée que la justice* (sic)[21] *se maintien dans ces rencontres."* The harmony of interests, however, applies as such only to commerce. Because he quotes as follows: *"Ainsi dans le commerce* (sic) *de la vie, elle (la nature et la providence) a mis un tel ordre, que pourvu qu'on laisse faire la nature, il n'est point au pouvoir du plus puissant, en achetant la denrée d'un misérable, d'empêcher que cette vente ne lui procure sa subsistence; ce qui maintien également l'opulence, à laquelle l'un ou l'autre sont redevables de leur subsistence proportionée à leur état."* [22]

Never was there a protagonist of laissez faire and of the postulate of the harmony of interest who wanted to extend these principles to the judicial system. And if Skarzinski thinks that through the introduction of the word "justice" in the explanation in the *Factum* beside the word "commerce" the ideas are unnecessarily lacking clarity, and have created "a real nest of all kinds of contradictions and given material for fathomless controversies, wrong conclusions, and unnecessary hypotheses, so, on the contrary, I am of the opinion that

[20] *Die Maxime*, pp. 45–47. My italics.
[21] Oncken's insertion, also that below after "commerce."
[22] See above, pp. 250–251, for translation.

the ideas of Boisguilbert only become clarified when he draws exactly the boundary wherein those harmonies prevail and wherein they do not exist.

All in all we will have to admit that laissez faire vaguely (*in Anklängen*) exists in Boisguilbert, but in no wise in the sense and with the same connotation as that of the newer free-trade theorists, who, furthermore, try to reach a practical goal opposed to the one he pursues.[23]

If Oncken denied the first theoretically significant use of the term "laissez faire" to Boisguilbert, to whom did he credit such usage? This honor he bestowed upon René-Louis de Voyer, Marquis d'Argenson.[24] Liberty, D'Argenson declared, is the mother of all good things if it is allied with justice. The decline of manufactures he attributed to over-protection, and famines to lack of liberty. Free trade would eliminate them.

Laissez libre, tout ira bien.
Eh morbleu, laissez faire.

The more this maxim is followed, D'Argenson declared, the more prosperity there will be. Here in D'Argenson, said Oncken, laissez faire is "erected for the first time into a theoretical principle and formulated as a slogan." [25]

Oncken himself thus summarized his findings:

The slogan "laissez faire, laissez passer," consists of two parts, one of which is about eighty years older than the other. The root occurs in a meeting of merchants whom Colbert had assembled to discuss the means to restore trade. The answer on the part of one member of the assembly named Legendre which soon became proverbial, was: "Laissez-nous faire." Probably the one who replied is identical with the author of a commercial arithmetic book with a wide circulation in those days. According to a Swiss tradition that meeting took place in Lyons. The time, we have been led to assume from external reasons, was about 1680.

In written form or in literature, the slogan does not appear in Boisguilbert, as has sometimes been assumed, or in Vauban, but for the first time in the manuscript of the Marquis d'Argenson about the

[23] *Die Maxime*, pp. 47–49.
[24] *Mémoires et journal inédit du marquis d'Argenson, ministre des affaires étrangères sous Louis XV*. Paris, 1857. D'Argenson's writings circulated in the eighteenth century in manuscript form, according to Oncken.
[25] *Die Maxime*, pp. 55–61.

year 1736; and it was printed in an anonymous treatise in the *Journal œconomique* in the year 1751, of which, according to our investigation, D'Argenson is the author.[26] From D'Argenson also comes the well known slogan *Pour gouverner mieux, il faut gouverner moins,* which later became known in its abridged form: *Pas trop gouverner.*[27]

Criticism of Oncken's View

Let us examine the points made by Oncken. First there is his definition of the term "laissez faire," which he declared to mean freedom of production. So, literally, would it appear to do when contrasted with the latter half of the maxim. Nevertheless, in no place where found in the early writers did it have exclusively, or even primarily, this connotation. Such a limitation of its meaning is in conflict with Oncken's own belief that "laissez-nous faire" was the demand of merchants. They were less concerned with production than with the right to buy and sell freely. Indeed as used by Boisguilbert and by D'Argenson, the addition of "laissez passer" to the expression was completely redundant, and its redundancy is indicated by the fact that it has gradually been sloughed off.

Oncken rejected the assumption that Amylot de la Houssaye might be the source of the tradition, the facts of which might have become transformed. In doing so he seemed to be unduly credulous, first, in assuming that no changes or additions would creep into a repeated story, and, secondly, in assuming that D'Argenson and Turgot were infallible. We know that such was the character and the power of Colbert that his inferiors did not speak to him freely and frankly, or in a manner to imply criticism. When such an event occurred it would in truth be news. Yet the only record of such rashness is that left by De la Houssaye. It may be assumed that it was the uniqueness of the event which led him to take notice of it.

It is worth while to look at the complete story as he related it:

> M. Colbert having called together the most notable merchants of Paris and other neighboring cities to confer on the means to restore

[26] I quite agree with Oncken that D'Argenson is the author of this anonymous *letter*, which is scarcely to be termed a "treatise."

[27] *Die Maxime*, p. 120. As Boisguilbert reiterated: "It is not necessary for the government to act, but to cease to act."

trade, they assembled on the day named. But no one dared speak, everyone waiting for another to begin. "Gentlemen," said the minister, "are you mute?" "No, my Lord," said an Orléannois named Hazon, who was very intelligent (*qui avoit beaucoup d'esprit*), "but we all equally fear to offend your Grandeur, in case some word should escape us which displeases you (*lui*)." "Speak freely," replied the minister. "That one who will speak with the most frankness will be the best servant of the King, and my best friend." Thereupon Hazon began to speak: "My Lord, since you command us to do so, and as you promise to approve that which we shall have the honor to set forth, I shall say to you frankly that when you came to the ministry you found the chariot upset, and since you have been there, you have raised it only to tip it over on the other side." At this shaft of wasp-like liberty, M. Colbert's face burned, and he said with feeling: "How you speak, my friend!" "My Lord," Hazon replied, "I very humbly demand your Grandeur's pardon for my stupidity in relying on your (*sa*) promise. I shall say nothing further." Then the minister commanded the others to speak, but no one would open his mouth. So the conference ended. That is how the Great are made. They wish to learn, but they do not wish to listen. This has been related to me by an able Master of Requests, who was present at this assembly along with the late M. Pussort, uncle of M. Colbert.[28]

Two points must be considered. One was that the memoirs of Amylot de la Houssaye were widely read after their publication. The other is that documentation or absolute accuracy in factual detail is not always to be found, or perhaps even to be expected, in early authors.

D'Argenson was an exceedingly wide reader as his *Mémoires et journal* show. That he had read a work such as Amylot's is to be assumed. Furthermore, he was intrigued with the expression and the concept "laissez faire." The Colbert story was one which would not be forgotten in its general outline. Assuming, as Oncken correctly did, that D'Argenson wrote the letter published in the *Journal œconomique* in 1751, it does not place too great a strain upon credulity to assume that the latter, recalling the essence of the Colbert story ten or fifteen years after he had read

[28] Amylot de la Houssaie, *Mémoires historiques, politiques, critiques et littéraires*, Amsterdam, 1737, Vol. II, pp. 364–366. Amylot died in 1706. The date of the writing of the above is unknown, except that it occurred prior to 1706, and therefore before the expression "laisser faire" had been used by Boisguilbert in print.

it, should have supplied some of the details, and among others, put his favorite expression into the mouth of the outspoken merchant. Certainly there is more than a hint of a resemblance between Amylot de la Houssaye's outspoken merchant *qui avoit beaucoup d'esprit* and D'Argenson's "most sensible and plainest-spoken one."

But where did Turgot get the name of Legendre which he added to the story when he told it five years later in the Gournay *Eulogy?* He was relating the incident otherwise as it appeared in the *Journal.* Turgot, student of literature and history, must also have read the De la Houssaye *Memoires.* Recalling the original story without necessarily recalling its source, or its details, he at least remembered that a merchant was named in it. But why use the name Legendre? [29] For the simple reason that he was the most obvious merchant for the student of history to name. Turgot had also read *État de la France.* Casting about in his mind for the names of merchants of the period of Louis XIV, Legendre would be the first to come to mind. His wealth and importance as the greatest merchant in France in his day would have made his name something of a household expression for merchants. He was by far the richest merchant in Rouen, the most important commercial city of the time in France. The intendant of Rouen in 1697 thus reported on the merchants of the city: "The Sieur le Gendre has correspondents in all the places where one can have them, and is believed worth four or five millions. The Sieurs Guenet, Asselin, Le Menages and others, are worth seven to eight hundred thousand livres. But of these [merchants] the first is dead and his son has taken charge." [30] Those merchants having fortunes in the hundreds of thousands were of sufficient importance to be named, but Legendre's fortune was six or seven times as great as the next wealthiest.[31]

The essence of the Legendre myth is that Oncken accepted as fact, on the authority of a casual and unimportant statement of

[29] By Turgot, as by Boisguilbert and by Boulainvilliers, the name was spelled "Le Gendre."

[30] *État de la France,* Vol. IV, p. 31.

[31] Boisguilbert, it will be recalled, speaks of "*even* the Sieur le Gendre" having been financially embarrassed. See above, p. 216.

Turgot, an addition to a retold tale. He accepted as fact a retold tale which D'Argenson had adapted to suit the need of the moment. It must be added that there would have been nothing extraordinary in what may have been essentially an ordinary French idiom being used by merchants who suffered under the Colbert restraints and regulations. The fact remains that there is no record of such use until three-quarters of a century later in a story related by one who liked to use the expression "laissez faire."

Had a man named Legendre spoken so frankly to Colbert, the facts are quite against the possibility, which Oncken tended to accept, that it would have been François, author of the applied arithmetic and geometry, and summary of algebra. The first edition of his book appeared in 1646, and not in 1657, as Oncken stated. It may be taken for granted that he would scarcely have gained sufficient experience to write this book before he was, say, thirty-five years of age at least. The dates of his birth and death are unknown, but this would place the former around 1610. He would then have been seventy years of age in 1680, at the time the incident is assumed to have occurred, and probably not an active merchant, especially considering the fact that he had, as Oncken shows, artistic and literary tastes, which his wealth would have given him an opportunity to retire to indulge. If one must have a Legendre acting as spokesman it would seem more plausible to assume that it was Thomas, the great merchant of Rouen, friend of Boisguilbert, who was still active in 1694, and died between that year and 1698, when the intendant was writing.[32]

As to the Swiss tradition which localized the incident in Lyons, what more is to be expected than that the Swiss, retelling orally the Turgot version of the story, should have placed it in Lyons, the chief center of commercial contact between the Swiss and the French, or that the Lyons merchants themselves should have had it occur in their city.

It is only when one comes to Oncken's treatment of Boisguilbert in relation to laissez faire that excellent evidence is obtained

[32] In his letter of July 4, 1704, Boisguilbert spoke of Le Gendre having been hard pressed for funds *ten years before*.

to sustain Boislisle's statement as to the difficulty of reading Boisguilbert. Yet he is not unreadable. It is simply that his meaning cannot be obtained on a single reading no matter how painstaking. He must be read and reread. Often the different parts of his works must be collated and compared before his meaning can be determined, not only as to terms, but as to context. He does not lend himself to a casual review of his ideas, or to casual criticism. Yet that is what Oncken displayed as far as Boisguilbert is concerned. If it were not amazing, it would be amusing to see how Dühring and Skarzinski made a mountain out of what ought to have been a molehill, and to see how Oncken settled the point in question with a greater absurdity and misinterpretation than the others. Oncken had too little understanding of the spirit of the man, and made gross errors in reading the text. At the same time he gave an air of finality to the history of laissez faire which is unjustified either by the complexity of the material, or by the extent of his analysis.

Let us take up his errors in reading or interpretation. First, he stated that Boisguilbert wished the highest possible prices. This has been answered elsewhere.[33] Boisguilbert was not talking of an "excessive price of grain which always causes an infinite number of wretched beings to perish." He was not referring to an exorbitant price, he said, because all extremes are defective. Elsewhere he was more specific. To be proportional to the change in the prices of other things after 1650, he declared, wheat should have been at twenty-two livres (the Paris setier), but he did not ask this. He thought the price should have been what it was forty years before, which was approximately eighteen livres the Paris setier, or ten or eleven in the provinces. It was *"le bon prix,"* as he called it, which he thought to be socially desirable.[34]

"Industry was looked upon with envious eyes," said Oncken. Whatever Oncken implied by this, there is no place where such a statement can be verified. The most that Boisguilbert ever said was that "it is not necessary that one part should overbalance

[33] See above, p. 135.

[34] *Traité des grains*, pp. 356, 363, 385–386. *Mémoire sur les blés* (1707 ed.), pp. 159–160.

(*passe*) the other." [35] His entire thesis was that it is not only unnecessary and unwise to crush agriculture, but ultimately impossible to do so without a repercussion on industry.

"The postulate [i.e., low-priced grain] that our modern free-trade theory takes as its goal is branded by the so-called ancestor of the theory as the darkest evil of injustice." That Oncken did not distinguish low prices from prices which were below the cost of production in a great wheat-growing country which he himself stated had been an exporting country, indicates that either he did not understand what Boisguilbert was talking about, or else woefully misrepresented it. Certainly it was never the postulate of free trade that one group should profit through restrictions upon another group, which is what Boisguilbert protested against. France sought to sell manufactured goods abroad; she prohibited the exportation of grain, of which she had always had an exportable surplus. As a consequence, the domestic price of one class of goods was artifically raised; that of the other, artificially lowered. The purchasing power of one class was destroyed, to the eventual detriment, as Boisguilbert thought, rather than to the advantage, of the favored group. What Boisguilbert saw was that producers and consumers are not two different classes in society, but the same individuals acting first in one capacity and then in another. Although he demanded justice for an oppressed group, he would not injure another group to bring about this justice. A day laborer, he said, is not wretched because he pays (as consumer) five or six deniers or even a sol more for his bread, but because he (as producer) cannot get work, which results from the low price of grain.[36] One cannot accuse Boisguilbert of having had the special interests of one class at heart when he rigidly adhered to a theory, correct or incorrect, which dealt with the prosperity of all groups in society. Such was his theory of solidarity and of proportional prices.

Boisguilbert clearly indicated that he understood that a new and rich source of supply will cause the decline of an industry in a country which has its foundation in an inferior source. Ex-

[35] *Traité des grains*, p. 355.
[36] *Mémoire sur les blés*, p. 159.

cept for Russia and Hungary, the French lands were among the richest in Europe. Furthermore, he implied that French agriculture was not suffering from the competition of American wheat, as were German silver mines from the mines of the new world.[37]

"This commerce [with Barbary] serves only the interest of the middlemen who are only looking for private gain, but not the interest of the king and the nation. The latter runs contrary to the interest of capital." Boisguilbert was talking about army purveyors, who were monopolists, incidentally, and tax farmers, who conspired with the purveyors. Boisguilbert did not regard the interest of capital as opposed to that of the nation. Even in the case of the monopolist he thought that he would eventually obtain all wealth only to be worse off than the most wretched beggar. But there are times when he is misleading, as when, in this passage, for instance, he referred to tax farmers as "entrepreneurs." He specifically said that there were only three hundred persons in France whose interests were opposed to the interests of the people.

Oncken stated that Boisguilbert "even makes at another place . . . the proposition to follow the example of the English, to fix exportation bounties on grain." The reference is to *Traité des grains,* Part II, chapter i. This reads as follows:

> However frightful and however horrible the picture of the [effect of the] abasement [of the price] of grain may have appeared, so that there is much more of it than is essential to make out a case [against such prices], there is indeed another piece which renders them still more criminal, and which ought indeed to promote [their] condemnation, in spite of the vulgar who canonize them in France, in contrast to what is practiced in England, where the people decide the fate of their subsistence.

[37] See above, note, p. 233. That Boisguilbert was correct in this is shown by an early American report:

1715—Good trade with Lisbon during the last war when provisions were scarce in France.

1734—Wheat cannot profitably be shipped to Europe to compete with English wheat. Market news travels too slowly. The market is supplied by the time a ship reaches the European market. War time freight rates 2s. 6d.; peace time, 18d. Wheat molds on voyage.—"Papers Relating to the Trade and Manufactures of the Province of New York. 1705–1757." *London Documents,* No. XVI. pp. 713, 723.

Now, here is no mention of bounty. It is not the bounty, here or elsewhere, which is praised, but English institutions, and the English people whom he regarded as wiser in their price policy than the French in theirs. Not at any point did Boisguilbert recommend that France pay a bounty for the exportation of grain. Boisguilbert was not stupid. It was not a question of positive encouragement to export grain that he could hope for, but a reluctant permission.

But, continued Oncken: "Let us add further, that the old advocate of free trade also recommends fixed prices (*Preistaxen*) for the domestic trade, in order to prohibit "*par une autorité puissante*" "*qu'une marchandise ne devienne la proie et la victime de l'avidité d'un commerçant*" and one receives an ample judgment concerning the correctness with which the modern free traders call him their ancestor." Let us see what Boisguilbert said:

Through all this reasoning it is easy to see that, while every private individual may work for his own particular well-being, he must not lose sight of equity and the general welfare, because it is from the latter that he must secure his subsistence. And in destroying them for a moment with regard to a dealer with whom he trades, although, on account of a common error, and on account of the corruption of the heart, he believes he has gained everything, he must on the contrary expect, if this conduct becomes general, as sometimes happens, to pay dearly for his folly by his own destruction, which he brings about as a consequence, as is going to be shown. Nevertheless, all the work of men, from morning to night, is to practice just the contrary. And, so much does [self-]interest blind men, that there is no one who would not be happy, in buying merchandise from another, to obtain it not only at a loss on the part of the seller, but even [to take] all his property beyond the sale. Thus if a *superior and general authority* did not intervene to stop this avidity with regard to absolutely necessary products, as grains, determining their quantity (*en y mettant le taux*), there are men quite inhuman enough to wish to save the lives of their fellow creatures on pressing occasions, only at the price of all their property. And as this regulation (*police*) cannot be just in the detail, it must be supplemented in an indirect manner by a *powerful authority,* to prevent a product from becoming the prey and the victim of the avidity of a dealer who would be happy, if this were his disposition, to sacrifice everything to his individual interest, without regard for religion or for humanity, which are banished from all operations of sale and purchase, because one has believed that he satisfied God and man in not using fraud and deceit, and in profiting solely by the necessities of the occasion.[88]

Surely Oncken was right in his interpretation. Here is *taux* used, and here is the *autorité puissante*." Admittedly this is a difficult paragraph, and one that yields its thought only after much care has been bestowed upon it.

It will be noted that there are two authorities spoken of in the paragraph, and it is the first one, a "superior and general authority" which places the *taux* upon grain. Now *taux* in the sense of "fixed prices," as interpreted by Oncken, obviously does not express Boisguilbert's meaning. It appears that the writer on taxation was using it more in the sense of "total," and such is the meaning which has been given to the term here. Elsewhere the term was used in this sense: for instance, speaking of grains, Boisguilbert said that "it is their price (*prix*) alone which seeds the lands . . . [and] the harvest . . . receives [its] quantity (*taux*) or its orders from this same price (*prix*)."[89] How is this *taux* to be brought about by "a superior and general authority"? And who is the latter? It is nature. It is nature, the superior authority, who has provided that everyone must obtain a livelihood from his "shop" or that he must give it up and provide himself another one. It is famine, nature's penalty, exacted where her design has been defeated, which will act to fix or to raise the price. But, continued Boisguilbert, the "police" of the "superior and general authority" "cannot be just in the detail." In other words, nature acts only in long swings, as it were. She must be supplemented at any time by an *autorité puissante* acting in an indirect manner. This "powerful authority" is the government. What must it do to supplement the actions of nature who acts only in the long run?

No wonder Oncken did not know. Others have been confused by Boisguilbert's reference to "MM. the Ministers being the absolute masters of the fate of grains," which Oncken ought also

[88] *Traité des grains*, pp. 355–356. My italics.

[89] *Ibid.*, p. 374. I have deliberately shown the use of *prix* to distinguish it from *taux* used here very figuratively in the sense of an "assessment" or an order on land, or its harvest, to yield,—price being, as it were, the assessor of the quantity of grain to be expected.

to have quoted. Why was Boisguilbert so mysterious about the means to be used? Because "it is in the interest of this step that it be not absolutely public. It is like the secret, which loses its life as soon as it sees the day." [40] Only in his letters did Boisguilbert reveal all his meaning. It rested upon the fact that he regarded the extreme rise and fall in the price of grain to be partly the result of psychological factors. The report of the coming of a shipload of wheat prevented a shortage of grain from attaining famine proportions because it was thought others would follow. The shortage, he thought, was almost never sufficient to cause famine. This occurred only because grain was held back from the market in the hope of a still higher price. Likewise when the crop was large, the limited numbers of grain dealers, "organized as a body (*métier*) through the orders of the Council," knowing that they had no foreign buyers as competitors, compelled the farmers, hounded by landlords and tax collectors for money, to take what was offered. So did Boisguilbert think that, with complete freedom to export, it would never be possible to export more than one-twentieth of the supply, because, on account of the "delicacy" of grain, that is, its delicate response to actual or presumed changes in supply, "the least rumor of exportation created a furor and a raising of price which [made] it impossible for foreigners to buy"; yet the increase in the price encouraged production. Thus he wrote to the controller general "that the exportation of wheat, true or *pretended* (*feinte*), that you can practice at all times with regard to this last product will serve to increase a hundredfold that which is harvested . . . all because the price will support the expense." [41]

Such was the manner in which the *autorité puissante* was to aid nature in controlling the price and the production of grain through making use of the "panicky terror" of the people. Not price fixing in the sense that Oncken thought, but a rather innocent method of equalizing its swings by having noised about reports of intended or pretented importation or exportation. The paragraph which gave Oncken so much difficulty is simply Bois-

[40] *Factum*, p. 326.
[41] Letter of July 15, 1704. My italics.

guilbert's preliminary statement which he developed in the subsequented chapters.

We now reach the ultimate in absurdity. Yet so simple is the passage in *Factum* which gave rise to the situation [42] that there was no reason for Dühring, Skarzinski, or Oncken to make anything difficult or mysterious out of it. Their difficulty hinged wholly upon the sense in which the words "harmony" and "justice" are used. Because Boisguilbert was an exponent of harmony of interests all have jumped to the conclusion that that is what he was referring to in this passage when he used the word "harmony." As a matter of fact Boisguilbert did not use the phrase. He used the term "solidaire," or simply an illustration. "Harmony" as used above [43] referred to the balance or proportion among prices, whereby everybody could cover his cost of production and obtain a livelihood, thereby creating prosperity. "Justice" as first used [44] referred to the same proportional prices which permit all men to deal upon a basis of equality, that is, the one was prevented from taking advantage of the other. The second use of "justice" [45] which stirred up the hornet's nest, simply meant the necessity to divide the profits, which constituted economic justice in Boisguilbert's eyes, and which he regarded as the determining factor in the maintenance of the economic structure. Yet Oncken spoke of Boisguilbert's reference to the "warding off of cheating and robbery through the public law!" He mentioned the "judicial system" (*Rechtspflege*)! Had his commentators studied Boisguilbert's terminology carefully, and as a whole, rather than in isolated sentences, they could not possibly have made such errors. The two words were much used by him, and were used almost synonymously. At the same time the reference is usually sufficiently clear as to seem obvious. Had they carefully studied the *Dissertation sur la nature des richesses,* they would have saved themselves much perplexity. Here the same idea is expressed, and the same words used:

It is necessary then for this commerce to continue without inter-

[42] See above, pp. 250–251, for the complete paragraph and Mirabeau's comment on it.
[43] *Loc. cit.*, p. 250, lines 7 and 23 of quotation.
[44] *Loc. cit.*, line 9. [45] *Loc. cit.*, line 28.

ruption, and at a price which is obligatory, although this be unrecognized as such, namely, a price which prevents the merchant from losing, so that he may be able to continue his trade with profit. If this is not done it is as if he did not sell at all; and with his destruction it will be like the case of those grappling vessels, in which one touches the powder off which causes both to blow up.

Nevertheless, due to a frightful blindness, there is no trader of any kind who does not work with all his power to disconcert this *harmony*. It is only at the point of the sword, either in selling or buying, that it is maintained; and public prosperity, which furnishes a livelihood for all the people, subsists only because of a superior Providence.[46]

Then there is the use of the word "justice":

It never occurs to the buyer that every seller is only an agent for the buyer, and that he must keep an exact account with him, as a factor with a merchant, allowing him all his just expenses disbursed, and paying him for his own work. Unless this rule is observed no more work will be done, and as a consequence there will be no more profit for the master.

This *justice* which, being the natural law, must be observed in every exchange of the least important product unless each is to destroy the other, is an indispensable obligation in the trade of grains with all other products.[47]

Economic justice, in other words, requires that every man obtain his livelihood from his trade; harmony of interest results from the necessity for people to deal with one another in order to obtain a livelihood; harmony among prices, i.e., proportional prices, make the continuation of such dealings possible.

Whatever one's conclusion as to the relation of Boisguilbert to the theory of laissez faire, it cannot correctly be based upon Oncken's study, which is one-sided and incomplete. His conclusion, it much be confessed, rests upon a defective knowledge of the works of the author, a misinterpretation of terms, and a careless and erroneous interpretation of the facts presented.

In crediting D'Argenson with the first scientific use of the expression "laissez faire," Oncken said that in him is not to be found the mercantilist distinction between active and passive trade; that nowhere is there a discussion as to what trade is advanta-

[46] *Dissertation sur les richesses*, p. 404. My italics.
[47] *Ibid.*, p. 410. My italics.

geous and what is not; that trade is seen as advantageous to both parties. He saw that national well-being lies in good agriculture, in the industry of the inhabitants, and in a sound and healthy domestic commerce. Unfortunately mankind is so made that it prefers gains made through damaging others to the righteous or just behavior in which all could profit. " 'Detestable principle, that of wishing our grandeur only through the abasement of our neighbors! Only the wickedness and malignity of the heart is gratified by this principle, and [self-]interest is opposed to it. Laissez faire, morbleu! laissez faire!!' " "One sees," said Oncken, "that our formula cannot be used more expressively than by D'Argenson." "One sees," he continued, "that the formula is used in such a manner as to indicate that it has been picked up from outside." [48] True! The inexplicable thing is that Oncken did not realize he could well have been summarizing the principles of Boisguilbert; that he did not recognize that every thought in the above summary is found in the paragraph in Boisguilbert which he presumably had dissected, that that entire paragraph is a protest against the "abasement of our neighbors" which D'Argenson repeated.

Had Oncken been as familiar with the ideas of Boisguilbert as he should have been to justify his categorical statements with regard to them, he could not have failed to see that D'Argenson's rather limited economic opinions are, for the most part, a restatement of those of Boisguilbert. To be sure D'Argenson did not mention the latter; it was the Abbé de Saint-Pierre whom he acknowledged to be his master. But his maxims, whether obtained directly from Boisguilbert, or indirectly through Saint-Pierre, are based upon the philosophy of the former:

> All our political maxims ought to be reduced to the strictest laws of morality and generosity: to relieve the weak, to abase the wicked, to do good, to prevent evil, to do unto others as we would have them do unto us; finally, to reign in the civilized world only through justice and good deeds. It seemed obvious to him that by such conduct France would attain a grandeur and an abundance of which there had been few examples in the universe.[49]

[48] *Die Maxime*, pp. 62, 65–66.

[49] *Mémoires et journal inédit*, Vol. II, p. 306. This part is written under the name of one of his secretaries.

D'Argenson, although not mentioning Boisguilbert by name, nevertheless crudely and indirectly documented his source when he wrote: "I have read a book of financial plans. There was a chapter to prove that what one calls *great financiers* was the true cause of the destruction of finance in France." [50] This must be regarded as a reference either to chapters vii and viii of *Factum*, or to *Traité du mérite et des lumières de ceux que l'on appelle gens habiles dans la finance, ou grands financiers*, included in the complete works.

D'Argenson belongs to political science rather than to economics. But he is of peculiar interest to both fields of thought, because it would be difficult to find a better example of the ultimate connection between the economic doctrine of laissez faire, and philosophical anarchism in the political field. He was one of the great political radicals of his day. The carrying over of Boisguilbert's guiding principles of liberty, justice and reason from the economic to the political field, and thus to the French Revolution, is yet to be written. When this is done the descent will be traced through Saint-Pierre, D'Argenson, Diderot, Rousseau, and Voltaire.

Had Oncken sought fairness and exactness of thought rather than to uncover a new claimant for the honor of introducing the concept of laissez faire to the world, he could not have denied Boisguilbert a place in the development of the theory from the standpoint of his influence on D'Argenson if for no other reason. Though Boisguilbert used the term; though his theory is essentially incomplete without the inclusion of the concept to which it leads logically; nevertheless, the most that Oncken could say is that, "as a concrete formula . . . as a slogan, 'laissez faire' is never mentioned [by Boisguilbert], although it seems as if it had been ringing in the ears of the writer constantly." [51]

[50] *Ibid.*, Vol. V, p. 200. Aside from the term "laisser faire," D'Argenson used two rather unusual expressions found in Boisguilbert. With regard to the tax system, both said that France "is treated like an enemy country," while grain was referred to as a *denrée délicate*. Boisguilbert referred to its fluctuating value, whereas D'Argenson, showing no knowledge of value, used *délicate* merely as a descriptive adjective.

[51] *Die Maxime*, p. 47.

BIBLIOGRAPHY

BIBLIOGRAPHY

All the commerce I have in this with the world, is, that I borrow the instruments of their writing, as more speedy, and more easie: in requitall whereof I may peradventure hinder the melting of some piece of butter in the market, or a Grocer from selling an ounce of pepper.—MONTAIGNE.

WRITINGS BY BOISGUILBERT IN THE ORDER IN WHICH THEY APPEAR IN THE EDITIONS OF 1707[1]

Le Détail de la France. La Cause de la diminution de ses biens, et la facilité du remede, en fournissant en un mois tout l'argent dont le roi a besoin, et enrichissant tout le monde.

Traité du merite et des lumieres de ceux que l'on apelle gens habiles dans la finance, ou grands financiers.

Traité de la nature, culture, commerce et intérest des grains, tant par report au public, qu'à toutes les conditions d'un État. Divisé en deux parties. Dont la premiere fait voir que plus les grains sont à vil prix, plus les pauvres, sur tout les ouvriers, sont misérables. Et la seconde, que plus il sort de bleds d'un roiaume, et plus il se garantit des funestes effets d'une extréme disette.

Factum de la France, ou Moyens très-faciles de faire recevoir au roy quatre-vingt milions par dessus la capitation, practicables par deux heures de travail de messieurs les ministres, et un mois d'execution de la part des peuples, sans congédier aucun fermier général ni particulier, ni autres mouvemens que de rétablir quatre ou cinq fois davantage de revenu à la France, c'est à dire, plus de cinq cens milions sur plus de mille cinq cens aneantis depuis 1661. parce qu'on fait voir clairement en même-tems, que l'on ne peut faire d'objection contre cette proposition, soit par raport au tems et à la conjuncture, comme n'étant pas propre à aucun changement, soit au prétendu péril, risque, ou quelques autres causes que ce puisse être, sans renoncer à la raison et au sens commun, en sort que l'on maintient qu'il n'y a point d'homme sur la terre, qui ose mettre sur le papier une pareille contradiction, et la souscrire de

[1] The spelling, punctuation, and accent marks are those of the original text of the 1707 edition of *Le Détail de la France.*

son nom, sans le perdre d'honneur: et l'on montre à même tems l'impossibilité de sortir autrement de la conjuncture presente.

Memoire, Qui fait en abregé, que plus les bleds sont à vil prix, plus les pauvres sont miserables, ainsi que les riches, qui seuls les font subsister; et que plus il sort de grains du royaume, et plus on se garantit d'une cherté extraordinaire.

Sentence du Chatelet de Paris, qui fixe le prix du pain. Du sixiéme May 1649. De par le roy. Et Monsieur le Prevost de Paris, ou son lieutenant civil. In Testament politique de M. de Vauban.

Causes de la rareté de l'argent, et éclaircissement de mauvais raisonnemens du public à cét égard.

Dissertation de la nature des richesses, de l'argent et des tributs, où L'On découvre la fausse idée qui régne dans le monde à l'égard de ces trois articles.

Supplement du Détail de la France.[2]

Letters to the controllers general, including short memoirs. In Correspondance des contrôleurs généraux des finances avec les intendants des provinces, Vol. II, Appendix xii; Vol. III, Appendix v. Collection des documents inédits sur l'histoire de France.

The Life of Mary Stewart, Queen of Scotland and France. [1674.] Translated into English by James Freebairn. Edinburgh, 1725.

Works on Boisguilbert Crowned by L'Académie des Sciences Morales et Politiques at the Annual Public Session, July 14, 1866

Cadet, Félix, Pierre de Boisguilbert, précurseur des économistes, 1646–1714; sa vie—ses travaux—son influence. Paris, 1870.

Horn, Ignace Einhorn, L'Économie politique avant les Physiocrates. Paris, 1867.

Theses

Durand, René, Essai sur les théories monétaires de Pierre de Boisguilbert (1646–1714). Poitiers, 1922.

Frotier de la Messalière, Boisguilbert et la liberté du commerce des grains. Paris, 1903.

Skarzyński, Witold von, Pierre de Boisguillebert und seine Beziehungen zur neueren Volkswirthschaftslehre. Berlin, 1873.

Talbot, Albert, Les Théories de Boisguilbert et leur place dans l'histoire des doctrines économiques. Paris, 1903.

[2] Le Détail de la France, Factum de la France, Traité des grains, Dissertation sur la nature des richesses, and Supplément au Détail de la France are included by E. Daire in his Économistes financiers du 18e siècle. Paris, 1843. All references to these works are to this edition.

Other Studies on Boisguilbert

Boislisle, Arthur M. de, "Boisguilbert et les contrôleurs généraux." In Mémoires de Saint-Simon. Paris, 1879–1928. Vol. XIV, Appendix xii.

——— "La Proscription du projet de dime royale et la mort de Vauban." In *Comte rendu de l'Académie des sciences morales et politiques*, 1875, Deuxième semestre, pp. 229–247, 522–551. Supplements the above study.

Cohn, Gustave, "Boisguillebert. Ein Beitrag zur Geschichte der Volkswirtschaftslehre." In [Tübingen] *Zeitschrift für die gesammte Staatswissenschaft*, Jahrgang 1869, Vol. XXV, pp. 360–407.

Daire, Eugène, "Notice historique sur la vie et les travaux de Boisguillebert." In Économistes financiers du 18e siècle. Paris, 1843. Pages 157–170.

Dühring, Eugen, Kritische Geschichte der Nationalökonomie und des Sozialismus. Leipzig, 1879. Erster Abschnitt, Drittes Capitel, secs. 10–14.

Harsin, Paul, Les Doctrines monétaires et financières en France du XVIe au XVIIIe siècle. Paris, 1928. Pages 104–114.

Marx-Engels, Gesamtausgabe. Berlin, 1932. Erste Abteilung, Band 3, pp. 563–583.

Mirabeau, Victor Riquetti, marquis de, "Notes inédites sur Boisguillebert par le Marquis de Mirabeau (publiées par G. Weulersse)." In *Revue d'histoire des doctrines économiques*, 1910, pp. 113–151.

General

Amelot de la Houssaie, Mémoires historiques, politiques, critiques et littéraires. Amsterdam, 1737. Vol. II.

Ami de la paix, L', Amsterdam, 1761. Attributed to Rivière.

Argenson, [René-Louis de Voyer,] marquis d', Ministre des affaires étrangères sous Louis XV, Mémoires et journal inédit. Paris, 1857–1858.

——— "A Letter to the Author of the *Journal* [*œconomique*], concerning the Dissertation upon Commerce by the Marquis Belloni." In Select Essays on Commerce, Agriculture, Mines and Fisheries and Other Useful Subjects. London, 1754. (Translation into English of Articles from the *Journal œconomique*.) Published anonymously.

Babeau, Albert Arsène, La Ville sous l'ancien régime. 2d ed., Paris, 1884.

——— Le Village sous l'ancien régime. 4th ed., Paris, 1891.

Bailly, Antoine, Histoire financière de la France, depuis l'origine de la monarchie jusqu'à la fin de 1786, avec un tableau général des anciennes impositions et un état des recettes et des dépenses du trésor royal à la même époque. Paris, 1830.

Bonar, James, A Catalogue of the Library of Adam Smith, Author of the "Moral Sentiments" and "The Wealth of Nations," with an introduction by James Bonar. London and New York, 1894.

Boulainvilliers, Henri, comte de, L'Estat de la France, dans lequel on voit tout ce qui regarde le gouvernement ecclésiastique, le militaire, la justice, les finances, le commerce, les manufactures, le nombre des habitans, et en général tout ce qui peut faire connoître à fond cette monarchie: extrait des mémoires dressez par les intendants du royaume, par ordre du roi Louis XIV, à la sollicitation de mgr. le duc de Bourgogne, père de Louis XV, à present régnant. Avec des mémoires de l'ancien gouvernement de cette monarchie jusqu'à Hugues Capet. 2d ed., London, 1737.

Cantillon, Richard, Essai sur la nature du commerce en général [1737]. Edited and with an introduction by Henry Higgs. London, 1931.

Clément, Pierre, Histoire de la vie et de l'administration de Colbert, contrôleur général des finances, ministre secrétaire d'état de la marine, des manufactures et du commerce, surintendant des bâtiments; précédée d'une étude historique sur Nicolas Fouquet, surintendant des finances; suivi de pièces justificatives, lettres et documents inédits. Paris, 1846.

——— Le Gouvernement de Louis XIV; ou La Cour, l'administration, les finances et le commerce de 1683 à 1689; études historiques accompagnées de pièces justificatives, lettres et documents inédits, par M. Pierre Clément faisant suite à l'histoire de la vie et de l'administration de Colbert du même auteur. Paris, 1848.

Condillac, Étienne Bonnot, abbé de, Le Commerce et le gouvernement, considérés relativement l'un à l'autre. Amsterdam, 1776.

Condorcet, Marie Caritat, marquis de, Réflexions sur le commerce des blés [1776]. In his Oeuvres. Paris, 1847–1849. Vol. XI.

Correspondance des contrôleurs généraux des finances avec les intendants des provinces, publiée par ordre du ministre des finances d'après les documents conservés aux Archives nationales, par A. M. de Boislisle, sous-chef au ministère des finances. Imprimerie nationale, Paris, 1874–1897. Collection des documents inédits sur l'histoire de France.

Cossa, Luigi, An Introduction to the Study of Political Economy (English translation). London and New York, 1893.

Depping, Georges Bernard, editor, Correspondance administrative sous le règne de Louis XIV. Imprimerie nationale, Paris, 1850–1854. In the Collection des documents inédits sur l'histoire de France.

Desmarets, Nicolas, Mémoires sur l'administration des finances, depuis le vingt fe'vrier de l'année 1708, jusqu'au premier septembre, 1715. Paris, 1715.

Dupont de Nemours, Pierre Samuel, "Notice abrégée des différents écrits modernes qui ont concouru en France à former la science de l'économie politique." In *Éphemérides du citoyen, ou Bibliothèque raisonnée des sciences morales et politiques,* janvier-septembre, 1769.

Esmonin, Edmund, La Taille en Normandie au temps de Colbert (1661–1683). Paris, 1913.

Fénelon, François de Salignac de la Mothe, Les Aventures de Télémaque [1697].

Ferguson, Adam, An Essay on the History of Civil Society. 2d ed., London, 1768.

Forbonnais, François Véron de, Recherches et considérations sur les finances de France, depuis 1595 jusqu'en 1721. Liège, 1758.

Funck-Brentano, Franz, The Old Régime in France (English translation by Herbert Wilson). London and New York, 1929.

Harsin, Paul, Crédit public et banque d'état en France du XVIe au XVIIIe siècle. Paris, 1933.

Hearnshaw, F. J. C., editor, The Social and Political Ideas of Some Great French Thinkers of the Age of Reason; a series of lectures delivered at King's College, University of London, during the session 1928–29. London [1930].

Isambert, François André, Annales politiques et diplomatiques; ou Manuel du publiciste et de l'homme d'état, contenant les chartes et lois fondamentales, les traités, conventions et notes diplomatiques, les proclamations, actes publics, et autres documens officiels, relatifs à la Constitution politique et aux intérêts généraux des états de l'ancien et nouveau-monde, avec tables chronologique et alphabétique des matières, précédées d'une dissertation sur le droit public et des gens au XIXe siècle. Paris, 1823–1824.

Joubleau, Félix, Études sur Colbert, ou Exposition du système d'économie politique suivi en France de 1661 à 1683. Paris, 1856.

La Bruyère, Jean de, "Les Caractères, ou Les Moeurs de ce siècle [1688]." In his Oeuvres. Paris, 1865. Vol. II.

Lavisse, Ernest, editor, Histoire de France depuis les origines jusqu'à la révolution. Paris, 1900–1911. Vols. VI-VIII.

Mémoires des intendants sur l'état des généralités. Imprimerie nationale, Paris, 1881. Vol. I. A. M. de Boislisle, editor. Collection des documents inédits sur l'histoire de France.

Mémoires et documents pour servir à l'histoire du industrie en France. Publiés sous la direction de Julien Hayem. Paris, 1911–1929. Séries 4, 7, 9, 10, 11.

Mirabeau, Victor Riquetti, marquis, de, Théorie de l'impôt. n.p., 1761.

Oncken, August, Die Maxime laissez faire et laissez passer, ihr Ursprung, ihr Werden. Ein Beitrag zur Geschichte der Freihandelslehre. Bern, 1886.

Perkins, James Breck, France under the Regency with a Review of the Administration of Louis XIV. Boston and New York, 1892.

Petty, Sir William, The Economic Writings of. Hull ed., Cambridge, 1899.

Piganiol de la Force, Jean Aymar, Nouvelle description de la France; dans laquelle on voit le gouvernement général de ce royaume, celui de chaque province en particulier, et la description des villes, maisons royales, châteaux (et) monumens les plus remarquables [1716]. Paris, 1753–1754.

Quesnay, François, Tableau économique avec ses explications. n.p., 1760.

Rae, John, Life of Adam Smith. London, 1895.

Rivière, Hippolyte Ferréal, Précis historique et critique de la législation française sur le commerce des céreals et des mesures d'administration prises dans les temps de cherté. Paris, 1859.

Saint-Pierre, Charles Irenée Castel, abbé de, Mémoire pour l'établissement de la taille proportionnelle, n.p., 1717.

——— Oeuvres de politique. Paris and Amsterdam, 1729–1741.

Saint-Simon, Louis de Rouvroy, duc de, Mémoires. A. M. de Boislisle, editor. Paris, 1879–1928.

Sée, Henri Eugène, Esquisse d'une histoire économique et sociale de la France depuis les origines jusqu'à la guerre mondiale. Paris, 1929.

——— L'Évolution commerciale et industrielle de la France sous l'ancien régime. Paris, 1925.

Smith, Adam, Essays, Philosophical and Literary. Ward, Lock and Co., London, n.d.

——— An Inquiry into the Nature and Causes of the Wealth of Nations, with introduction and notes by Edwin Cannan. London, 1925.

——— Lectures on Justice, Police, Revenue and Arms, delivered in the University of Glasgow. Reported by a student in 1763, and edited with an introduction by Edwin Cannan. Oxford, 1896.

[Souligné, de,] The Desolation of France Demonstrated. London, 1697.

Stewart, Dugald, "Account of Life and Writings of Dr. Smith." In Essays on Philosophical Subjects by Adam Smith. Dublin, 1795.

Turgot, Anne Robert Jacques, baron de l'Aulne, "Éloge de Gournay." In his Oeuvres. Paris, 1808–1811. Vol. III.

Vasson, Michel [?], Soupirs de la France esclave qui aspire après la liberté. [Amsterdam], 1689.

Vauban, Sebastien le Prestre, maréchal de, "Projet de capitation sur le pied du denier quinze." In Correspondance des contrôleurs généraux des finances, Vol. I, Appendix ix.

——— Projet d'une dime royale [1707]. In Économistes financiers du 18e siècle, E. Daire, editor. Paris, 1843.

Voltaire, François Marie Arouet de, Siècle de Louis XIV. In his Oeuvres complètes. Impr. de la Société littéraire-typographique, n.p., 1785–1789. Vols. XX–XXI.

Weulersse, Georges, Les Physiocrates. Paris, 1931.

INDEX

INDEX

W

VITA

Hazel Van Dyke Roberts was born at Elizabeth, West Virginia, on December 8, 1891. She is the daughter of George W. and Anne Moody Thorn Roberts. She was educated in the public schools of West Virginia, at West Virginia Wesleyan Academy and Normal School, and at West Virginia University. She received the degrees of A.B., A.M. (Phi Beta Kappa) from West Virginia University and the degree of Ph.D. from Columbia University.

Bei Fragen zur Produktsicherheit wenden Sie sich bitte an:
If you have any questions regarding product safety,
please contact:

Walter de Gruyter GmbH
Genthiner Straße 13
10785 Berlin
productsafety@degruyterbrill.com